SPECTACULAR POLITICS

Spectacular Politics

THEATRICAL POWER AND
MASS CULTURE IN EARLY
MODERN ENGLAND

PAULA R. BACKSCHEIDER

THE JOHNS HOPKINS UNIVERSITY PRESS
BALTIMORE AND LONDON

© 1993 The Johns Hopkins University Press
All rights reserved
Printed in the United States of America on acid-free paper

The Johns Hopkins University Press
2715 North Charles Street
Baltimore, Maryland 21218–4319
The Johns Hopkins Press Ltd., London

LIBRARY OF CONGRESS CATALOGING-IN-PUBLICATION DATA

Backscheider, Paula R.
Spectacular politics : theatrical power and mass culture in early modern England /
Paula R. Backscheider.
   p.   cm.
   Includes bibliographical references (p.) and index.
   ISBN 0-8018-4568-8 (acid-free paper)
   1. English drama—Restoration, 1660–1700—History and criticism. 2. Politics
and literature—Great Britain—History—17th century. 3. Politics and literature—
Great Britain—History—18th century. 4. English drama—18th century—History
and criticism. 5. Popular literature—England—History and criticism. 6. Politi-
cal plays, English—History and criticism. 7. Gothic revival (Literature—Great
Britain. 8. Power (Social sciences) in literature. 9. Popular opinion—England—
History. 10. England—Popular culture—History. I. Title.
PR698.P65B33 1993
822'.409358—dc20   92-40746

A catalog record for this book is available from the British Library.

CONTENTS

LIST OF ILLUSTRATIONS

ACKNOWLEDGMENTS

THE WRITING OF THIS BOOK WAS SUPPORTED BY A JOHN SIMON
Guggenheim Memorial Fellowship generously augmented by the University of Rochester and by the British Council Prize. With affection, I
offer thanks for support, encouragement, and helpful comments to Margaret Anne Doody, Robert D. Hume, John Michael, Ronald Paulson,
John Richetti, James Thompson, Richard Wendorf, and James Winn. I
owe a special debt of gratitude to a remarkable group of graduate students who filled my seminars and office, engaged the issues I cared
about, and challenged and stimulated my work day by day: Nandini
Bhattacharya, Troy Boone, Michelle Brandwein, Catherine Craft, Cathy
Decker, Kathy Ivey, Ed Katz, Kathy Leicht, and John Roberts. As in the
past, the librarians and archivists of the Rush Rhees Library of the
University of Rochester, the Harvard Theatre Collection, the Guildhall
Library, City of London Record Office, Public Record Office, and City
Livery Companies showed patience and ingenuity in helping me. As
always, my greatest debt is to my husband, Nick, who contributes gener-
ously and with engagement to every part of my work.

This book is dedicated to my son, who shared his music and his space
with me during my Guggenheim leave, and to my daughter, who shares
the special joys and challenges of a research life.

Finally, a few remarks on presentation are in order. Notes give author, short title, and page references, and readers should consult the Bibliography for full citations. Manuscript citations are given in full in the Notes alone. Unless specifically stated, dates are to first stage production rather than to first printing. Until 1752 England retained the Julian, or Old Style, calendar, and I have retained the Old Style dates but taken the year to begin on 1 January. As is standard modern practice, the Johns Hopkins University Press seldom uses ellipsis points at the beginning or end of quoted passages and alters initial letters of quotations according to the syntax of the sentences in which they appear.

INTRODUCTION

THE SUBJECT OF THIS BOOK IS LITERATURE AS PLEASING EX-
perience, civic discourse, and hegemonic apparatus. I began by identifying times in which writers sought to participate actively in their culture,
in which notably, remarkably popular works were produced, and in
which serious social turmoil boiled up and then cooled. The Restoration
and eighteenth century is known as a period when writers and readers
were highly conscious of genre; they had strong expectations and yet
they delighted in experimentation. Writers brought the heroic couplet,
the ode, formal verse satire, the philosophical verse essay, and many
traditional forms to new heights and created a range of mock-pieces that
are among the finest literary works in English.

We know that new forms and even genres were born then, and I
discovered that in those moments I had chosen to study exceptionally
original literature was produced, some of it of major, lasting significance.
At issue for me is how literature is created and then takes on a life and
meaning of its own in a free society. Within that inquiry, I am primarily
concerned with what characteristics and factors open the possibility for a
work to become popular and with analyzing the relationship between
popularity and progression to mass culture and, most important of
all, hegemonic apparatus. The significance, then, of the technical innovation and achievement that I found is as often in the realm of litera-

ture's participation in civil life as in its aesthetic influence.

I deliberately selected three unrelated "cases" that met two conditions: all included phenomenally popular texts and all appeared at pivotal moments in early modern English history. Each is different enough from the others to reveal different things about literature, its participation in cultural processes, and its power to absorb and enchant its audience. It happened that the most significant examples seemed to me to be three denigrated and neglected groups of texts. I shall analyze them in detail and argue that they provide rich access to greater understanding of the functions literature performs in modern societies, especially as agencies of knowledge, power, and pleasure; as ways of changing human desires and thereby of dreaming a better world into reality; and as means of containing personal and social anxieties. One of my major concerns is to begin to define how a text or a class of texts becomes an effective or even important hegemonic apparatus, what kinds of literature can function effectively in hegemonic processes, and what characteristics those that function most powerfully have.

The history of a nation seems to be composed of times when there is a dominant ideology and of times when that ideology breaks down and no longer functions as an organic, relational whole that seems both "valid" and "natural." In essence, it fails to describe "the way the world is"— both lived experience and metaphysical "truth." The result is a society in crisis, one experiencing turmoil that may result in permanent change. This stress is reflected in all of the discourses available for use in negotiating and reshaping consent to what will become, at least temporarily, a dominant and stable ideology. During these periods of renegotiation, many components of society and most discourses necessarily become hegemonic apparatuses.[1] Medical texts, sermons, legal decisions, school curricula, and even etiquette books become mechanisms in the process and, like literature, become crucially important and unusually visible signs of the process under way. Yet modern literature occupies a special realm, for it is freer than any other civil discourse. First, it is a creative act, the production of an individual imagination. Second, in the Western tradition, it often sets itself up to be timeless as well as timely and unabashedly takes human emotion and human existence as subjects. Third, even a state-regulated artistic venue such as the Restoration and eighteenth-century theater is freer than, for instance, the commercial press or the medical profession. It is less subject to restriction because there is no "faculty of advocates" and no set of subjects and methods— there are no boundaries.

In Part 1, I argue that Charles II attempted to use theater in its broadest sense to help establish his conception of the monarchy and its prerogatives, but that this effort was met by the corrective tropes and themes of writers who had spent the Commonwealth period in England and held a different idea of the monarchy and, more significantly, of the future. In Part 2, which is centered on the 1695–96 theater season, the season during which four women had a total of six plays performed, I take up another but very different struggle for control of representation and for means of access to the public. In that same season Aphra Behn's posthumously performed *Younger Brother* premiered, and Thomas Southerne helped "save" the season with an adaptation of Behn's *Oroonoko*—thus, one-third of all of the new plays on the London stage were by women. In this section I argue that the time was crucial to the beginning of the renegotiation of "woman," "woman writer," "ideal man," "successful courtship," and "good marriage," topics that have received much recent attention and have been located as occurring later in books such as Nancy Armstrong's *Desire and Domestic Fiction*. I also explore the ways that writers attempted to find new, more effective channels of access to the public; and in Chapter 4 I analyze the way Aphra Behn drew upon a number of now largely forgotten literary kinds to create a new form of political propaganda and inadvertently actualized important elements of the emerging modern English novel. In this section I propose a master text for the English novel.

In Part 3, the final section, I apply my theory of literature and society to gothic drama, with primary emphasis on that produced between the Regency Crisis of 1788–89 and Nelson's victory at Aboukir in 1798. During this decade, the British had to overcome fractures in society made obvious by events as serious as the Gordon Riots in order to fight one of the most threatening wars in their history, one fought under the leadership of a king who had nearly been judged "hopelessly mad." Events abroad penetrated in especially threatening ways; for instance, within two weeks in 1793, the British people learned of France's declaration of war against England and King Louis XVI's beheading, "his body flung into a deep grave without any coffin,"[2] an event that must have recalled the execution of Charles II and the exhuming of Cromwell's body. Perhaps the first indisputable example of what we call "mass culture," an artistic configuration that becomes formulaic and gratifies a large cross-section of the population of a nation, gothic drama offers a third kind of hegemonic apparatus, one that both expresses and contains the deepest anxieties of a nation in crisis.

It seems obvious that those works that reach the existing and, if different, emerging power groups and those that become mass culture have the greatest opportunities to participate in the reconfiguring of social order and value structures. For this reason, I am concerned with communal popular literature more than with limited circulation elite art. Parts of this book, then, are unapologetically descriptive in that they are the first modern, detailed reconstructions of such relatively unfamiliar and inaccessible popular forms as London street pageants and gothic Christmas pantomimes. In fact, some of my arguments are based on aspects of them that are not accessible by reading printed texts. Because dramatic works were received both as political statements and as high art, I have used that genre almost exclusively to illustrate my method. This choice means that I am as concerned with what has been called the "spectator text" as with the printed text and have made determined efforts to bring together eyewitness accounts and even set designers' notes.

Although I fully recognize the impossibility of reconstructing a past event (performance), of determining what appealed to a long-dead audience (what needs and desires were met, what specifically triggered strong responses), and of articulating the complex relationship between social life and works of art, a wealth of evidence survives that permits new discoveries about how they were experienced and provides a commentary on the conditions of existence of the problem of interpretation itself. Martin Esslin has said that "in ritual as in drama the aim is an enhanced level of consciousness, a memorable insight into the nature of existence."[3] Because I work with dramatic texts, identifying what activates a text becomes more challenging, and the fact that any performance is composed of a shifting hierarchy of what Marco de Marinis calls "all its partial texts—the spoken text, the gestural text, the scenery, music, sound effects, etc."—must be taken into account in a variety of ways.[4] Just as social life is mediated and transformed by a writer, who is at least in large part a constructed personality, the work is interpreted and transformed by the reader, whose responses are never wholly free from horizons of expectation and social conditioning. Therefore, the work of literature is always a process—not an object, but a living force—and each successive group of spectators can reaccentuate it.

Although mine is not a historical study and these cases are not closely related historically, a number of themes and motifs are developed that trace historical change. Among the necessary concerns are the rise and formation of the concept of public opinion and the political public sphere. As J.A.W. Gunn says, historians have generally agreed that it was the latter part of the eighteenth and the early nineteenth century in which changes "signalled the *arrival* of public opinion as a significant force" (emphasis mine).[5] My book offers evidence that can be used to push back the date by which an evaluative, critical, political public was recognized to exist in England and discusses some of the effects of the apprehension of the nature, significance, and usefulness of public opinion. In the representation of the public political sphere in these texts and in the interplays between texts and society, Gramsci's more subtle and flexible model of the integral state allows us to see the wide diffusion of power and the full play of the "ensemble of organisms" that is civil society (235–98). He insists, moreover, that those in power must have both the intellectual and the moral consent of the governed, and my study will also look at the ways literature serves as arena for the working out of satisfying communal fictions even as it relates these fictions to monarchs and other historical manifestations of power.

Habermas's insistence upon the necessity of a literary public sphere as a condition for the development of a political public sphere has been a somewhat neglected, or at least too uncritically accepted, part of his argument.[6] It is clearly possible to contest the primacy of the literary public sphere. Literary critics and historians have probably overestimated the part that printed texts and literacy played—and play—in the formation of public opinion and of a politically involved public.[7] This fact as well as the establishment of public opinion intensifies the need to understand the rise of what we call modern popular and especially mass culture, both of which I believe appear in the eighteenth century. By popular art I shall mean a cultural form accessible and appealing to almost all levels of society that, in Ronald Paulson's words, was "read or seen by almost everybody; [was] part of the consciousness of the learned and educated as well as of the uneducated."[8] This definition demands that its reception be considered but perhaps devalues such considerations as mode of address or records of the author's intentions (or the patron's or employer's intentions). Inherent, too, is the demand for the recognition of the spectrum of opinions and aspirations held within each social class and of the impossibility of using any simply binary or even tripartite conception of social class.[9]

Literature of all kinds almost invariably contributes to the circulation and confirmation of the dominant ideology, but literature touches responsive chords in its audience and simultaneously joins other discourses in contesting, subverting, or transforming it. Especially when set beside nonliterary texts and other civic discourses, the participation of literature in a national endeavor reveals itself. Literature is more than a civic discourse, and human beings are both individual selves ("natural objects," in Leopold Damrosch's words) and constructed personalities ("cultural products").[10] Thus, regardless of how mass produced, propagandistic, or "commercial" the art form is, it must bear something that speaks meaningfully and movingly to its audience. Fredric Jameson has said that the effectively ideological must have a utopian dimension, and he has set the importance of the glimpse of "the treasure" beside the power of "the Censor."[11] Because, as he says, the Censor is more easily discerned, I shall try to bring out the utopian elements, the "collective folk dream" that charged the experience the audience had with the work of art and that unleashed its potential for expressing "the spirit of a nation," for conveying deep human longings, and for explaining "the way the world is." Such works of art become unified experiences that, upon analysis, we see substitute a feeling of completeness for the "feeling of meaning" (Jameson, 12). Thus, spectacle assumes considerable importance, and popular works that apparently lack resolution and, indeed, have persistently resisted interpretation take on new centrality in my theory of art in society.

The Restoration and eighteenth century was a time in which people—including the writers themselves and those in authority—believed in the power of literature and optimistically created new forms in energetic efforts to expand the influence and functions of literature in society. In the times that Gramsci describes as "delicate and dangerous, because the field is open for violent solutions, for the activities of unknown forces," highly original literature is produced, and new forms and even genres may be born. Jameson equates the content of a work of art with "lived experience" and the form with "the very possibilities of Experience itself" (17); therefore, it is to be expected that unrest and traumatic events as well as the dawning awareness of new possibilities, of the implications of change, will generate innovative and challenging texts.

Long before the Restoration, City pageants and public ceremonies had traditionally been part of street politics and had participated interactively in the formation of national consensus. They quickly moved beyond being vehicles for the restoration of the Stuart monarchy to expressing the revolutionary aspirations of the people who had spent the Commonwealth years in England. Soon the royal theaters and their courtier-playwrights produced plays so rich in political content that they could be reaccentuated for propagandistic statement for over a hundred years. The technical innovations of the Restoration water pageants are common to popular and to revisionary literature, and the fictions of the women writers of the turn of the century and the special effects of the gothic theater also became highly effective pleasure and "fantasy machines"[12] as well as means of access to public discussion and debate.

At every moment, this study is concerned with cultural imagery and its interpretations. A number of themes, including a central concern with how sex and gender are constituted and used as political categories, grow naturally out of this emphasis. During this time period, structures of order and authority of all kinds were being studied, reconceived, and renegotiated, and woman, that sign for something else, figures prominently. Since at least the fifteenth century woman had been used extensively as such on the English stage, primarily as moral rhetorical or socio-rhetorical constructs. To us as twentieth-century readers, they provide discernible contrasts to the individualized representations associated most often with the rise of the novel. In the first texts discussed in this book, groups of women are often tropes for unauthorized forms of power. In the middle section, in texts largely written by women at a time when the theater was a major forum for the discussion of relationships between the sexes, womankind's nature, position, value, and aspirations are at issue. In the final section, women are emblems of a seductive philosophy. In every case, sex and gender are inseparable from roles, cultural needs, and value judgments, and spellbinding roles for women were created. Each section analyzes representations of transgressive women: Elizabeth Cromwell, a group of heroines including Behn's Angellica Bianca and Manley's Belira, and finally Sarah Siddons.

Together these cases illustrate the fact that the public sphere became increasingly gendered and was described in terms that contributed to establishing sex and gender as binary oppositional vocabulary that could be powerfully deployed by writers such as Edmund Burke in times of crisis. In a variety of ways, they develop how social relationships, no matter how private, are always power relationships that impact on the public sphere. By the end of the eighteenth century, as is true for our own time, on many levels sex and gender were political.

At all times, this study is designed to show struggles for the control of representation. How people imagined themselves and their "stories" was at issue in each case. In these examples, we can see how writing can be both a civil discourse and a mode of imaginative exploration and radical discovery—rapid, creative "modeling" of problems and solutions. Among the most significant literary insights is the importance of closure, or at least a strong sense of it. Over and over, satisfactory resolutions to texts are seen to depend on the representation of moral order. In the first case, closure is initially imposed and then breaks down in texts such as Robert Howard's *The Committee*. In the second, in a group of works often criticized today for their improbability and lack of resolution,[13] indeterminacy lays bare the lack of satisfactory solutions to human problems in the culture at large; in the final case, a kind of communal conspiracy to "dream" a satisfying order leads to formula art.

Because this book moves through new interpretations of three neglected periods of Restoration and eighteenth-century drama, it might be perceived as directed at a highly specific audience. In order to understand the cultural world in which we live, however, we must go back to that moment when the modern uses of literature were being formed, when the concept of public opinion was firmly established as an important social force, and when the number of writers and the economics of printing allowed rapid experimentation and innovation with literary form. Moreover, the method can be applied as effectively to medieval drama and to U.S. movies about the Vietnam War. For example, we can readily see our nation negotiating an acceptance of the complexity of the Vietnam experience and of a patriotic interpretation of it by comparing such films as *The Green Berets* (1968), *Apocalypse Now* (1979), *Rambo: First Blood* (1983), *Platoon* (1986), and *Born on the Fourth of July* (1990). From the use of John Wayne and the attempt to superimpose World War II on Vietnam through the confusion of mixed messages in *Apocalypse Now* and the rewriting of myths in the *Rambo* films to the unsettling ambivalence of the films of the 1990s, the attempts to preserve an idealized self-image and to contain things about ourselves, the Other, and our nation are writ large.

My own examples of times when an art form became a powerfully hegemonic apparatus have been selected in part for their differences and, therefore, their usefulness in exploring the applications and potential of the method. The application of this methodology reveals new things about literature and its social contexts, about how writers' new orchestrations of literary languages can create radically original and culturally important texts, and about how literature functions in a free society. We can see how it influences culture, thereby going beyond the ways it reflects society to how it creates our social world and even our reality. We can even begin to see some of the necessary conditions for the transformation of a literary kind into mass culture and hegemonic apparatus.

PART ONE

Charles II's London as National Theater

 ISTORIANS DESCRIBE ENGLAND AS HAVING BEEN in a state of virtual anarchy during the last months of 1659 and under King Charles II's firm control by the beginning of 1661. In this interval, no aspect of public life was left untouched by the Restoration, and study of many of them reveals the kinds of effort inherent in the movement from anarchy to strongly regulated order. Among other things, and perhaps of prime significance, was the establishment of a dominant ideology of monarchy. When Charles was invited to assume the English throne, he brought with him the Stuart conception colored by years in court circles in absolutist France. Many of his subjects, however, conceived the nature of the monarchy and the right of the monarch in a different way. Official communication and declarations at the time of the invitation had made it clear that *both* monarchy and Parliament with their interdependent powers and privileges were at issue. The House of Commons of the Convention Parliament behaved as a partner in power, not like a group summoned at pleasure to endorse or facilitate a sovereign's policies and plans.[1] And some citizens were deeply ambivalent or even opposed to the restoration.

In this time before mass literacy and a well-developed press and propaganda network, the best means of mass communication available was public spectacle.[2] Traditional royal ceremonies, existing civic events, and even public displays of the operations of government (such as street pavings and hangings) were available as hegemonic apparatuses.

The first chapter of this section demonstrates how Charles II made London a national theater and used it in a variety of ways to help secure his throne and establish his interpretation of the monarchy. As E. H. Gombrich said, successful propaganda is "the art of imposing a pattern on reality, and to impose it so successfully, that the victim can no longer conceive it in different terms"; I show Charles attempting this act.[3] The second chapter evaluates Charles's success, identifies competing visions, concrete hopes, and currents of resistance inscribed in these same events, and suggests briefly how the public theater mirrors the course of the hegemonic process discernible in the larger society. I consider theatrical events produced between 1659 and the 1662–63 season, concluding with Robert Howard's *The Committee,* which began production shortly before the City's Court of Aldermen failed to raise the £200,000 loan that the king had requested.[4]

I

THE CONSOLIDATION OF POWER

CHARLES HAD BEEN NINETEEN WHEN HIS FATHER WAS EXE-
cuted and thirty when he took the throne, and he had had plenty of
opportunities to see the political potential of dramatic spectacle. In the
duke of Newcastle's *Letter of Instructions to Prince Charles for his Studies, Conduct, and Behaviour* (1638), William Cavendish, himself a dramatist, had asked rhetorically, "What preserves you Kings more than Ceremony" and continued, "In all triumphs whatsoever or publick shewing
your self, you cannot put upon you too much King."[1] The numbers and
uses of public ceremonial spectacles on the Continent were traditionally
greater than in England, and Louis XIV, whose own coronation had been
in 1653, certainly knew how to evoke the power of the monarchy.[2] Indeed, Louis had staged a spectacular *joyeuse entrée* with his new queen in
1660, an event Charles would have wanted his coronation to surpass.[3]
   Moreover, Charles was descended from a long line of monarchs who
had self-consciously used symbolism and representation effectively—
and from a father who had not. For instance, Queen Elizabeth had once
told a deputation of M.P.'s, "We princes are set on stages in the sight and
view of all the world."[4] Still very much alive in the minds and hearts of
Charles II's subjects, she had been willing and able to sustain herself as
an emblem of chastity, wisdom, virtue, and prosperous peace. Her coronation had been a spectacular event; magnificently dressed, she rode in

an open litter, accompanied by a thousand horsemen, and "as she moved, a vast didactic pageant unfolded, stage by stage, before her, settling her into the moral landscape of the resilient capital." Richard Mulcaster, a witness to her progress, wrote that "he could not better tearme the citie of London . . . than a stage wherein was shewed the wonderfull spectacle, of a noble hearted princesse toward her most loving people."[5] James I's *Basilikon Doron* makes clear that he conceived of himself as an actor almost invariably on stage. He wrote, "A King is as one set on a stage whose smallest actions and gestures, all the people gazingly doe behold."[6]

Between 1617 and the Civil War, however, there had been no street pageants directly associated with a reigning monarch, and Charles I's neglect of such events has been offered as one of the causes of his downfall. Peter Heylin made a telling comparison:

> [Queen Elizabeth] did very seldom end any of her summer progresses but she would wheel about to some end of London, to make her passage . . . through . . . the City. . . . By means whereof she did not only preserve that Majesty which did belong to a queen of England, but kept the Citizens (and consequently all the subjects) in a reverent estimation of her. . . . But these being laid aside by King James . . . and not resumed by King Charles . . . there followed first a neglect of their persons, which Majesty would have made more sacred, and afterwards a mislike of their government.[7]

Telling phrases, "did . . . preserve that Majesty" and "kept . . . a reverent estimation of her," emphasized the way a monarch preserves and even produces power. Elizabeth often spoke of herself as she did in her speech to the people as they prepared for the Spanish Armada: "I know I have the body of a weak and feeble woman, but I have the *Heart* and *Stomach* of a *King*—and a King of England, too, and think it foul scorn, that any shall dare to invade the borders of my realm."[8] The physical or moral body is subsumed and transcended by the regal body, and even her sex becomes inconsequential beside her position and her role as unifier of her people. Charles II had seen street demonstrations against his father instead of street pageants that acclaimed him, and there is some truth to the opinion that "it is scarcely an exaggeration to say that Charles needed to raise an army in the spring of 1642 because, during the previous months, he had become the first English monarch since the Middle Ages to lose even the passive loyalty of his own capital."[9]

Charles II intended public spectacles to perform a number of functions. Above all, he wanted to reinscribe the monarchy on his country,[10] the country that the prologue for the first play at the Cock-pit had described thusly: "This spacious Land their Theatre became."[11] During the month of April, portraits of Charles adorned with royal symbols were mass produced and displayed in large numbers of houses and shops or in their windows.[12] In an act that leaves no room to doubt the deliberate, contrived nature of his actions, Charles sent Edward Hyde to study past royal ceremonial events; he stated specifically that he wanted "the novelties and new inventions, with which the kingdom had been so much intoxicated for so many years together . . . discountenanced and discredited in the eyes of the people, for the folly and want of state thereof." According to Hyde, he wanted "all forms accustomed [to] be used, that might add lustre and splendor to the solemnity." When it was discovered that most of the royal symbols and regalia had been sold or lost during the Commonwealth, a committee appointed by the king met "divers times" "not only to direct the remakeing such Royall Ornaments & Regalia, but even to setle the form & fashion of each particular."[13]

Awarded £70,000 for his coronation, Charles felt the sum inadequate.[14] He participated in the commissioning of some of the men most responsible for the coronation spectacles, Edward Walker, John Ogilby, and John Tatham. Edward Walker, Garter King at Arms since 1645, had been with Charles I throughout the Civil War, had often served as emissary then and during the exile, had been secretary of the Privy Council, and at the Restoration became one of the three clerks of the council. According to contemporary records, "The whole Ceremonie and proceedings were principally drawn up and ordered" by him.[15] John Ogilby, the former dancing master who had recently published his translation of the *Iliad*,[16] had been commissioned to help with the triumphal arches for which the City would pay, and he and John Tatham, a dramatist and the City Poet from 1657 to 1664, were chosen and paid to provide the spoken texts for the pageants.[17]

The arches and pageants were actually designed and built in collaboration with Peter Mills, one of the Surveyors of the City of London.[18] A Committee of Common Council had been appointed for the "managing and carrying on of the tryumph intended to be made in the Cittie of London," which would take place the day before the coronation. This group, experienced from years of Lord Mayor's Day shows, functioned smoothly and included such lord mayors (or mayors-to-be) as Thomas

Allen, John Robinson, and John Lawrence. Records show that they were familiar with Livery Company holdings and drew upon already-built pieces. From the Clothworkers, for instance, they received two griffins and several lambs.[19] It was common for the Surveyors to be fully involved in the designing of the essay that the pageants would be for Lord Mayor's Day, and it could be expected that they would contribute extensively to the designing of these pageants and arches.[20] They engaged extremely experienced City carpenters, and it appears that they put each one in charge of an arch. Such distinguished craftsmen as the painters William Lightfoot and Andrew Dacres and the carver Richard Cleer were also commissioned by the City.

The king himself would take the unusual step of inspecting and approving the pageants for Tatham's evening show, *Neptune's Address*.[21] He also inspected and approved Walker's and Ogilby's detailed plans and Tatham's barges, and he would insist upon control of their published descriptions as well. A declaration by the Garter King at Arms at the beginning of John Ogilby's description of the coronation serves as its license:

> I Have perused a brief Narrative of His MAJESTIES Solemn CORONA-
> TION, printed by Mr. OGILBY, together with his Description of His
> MAJESTIES Entertainment passing through the City of LONDON to His
> Coronation, &c. and, in pursuance of His MAJESTIES Order unto me
> directed, have examined, and do approve thereof; so as the said Mr.
> OGILBY may freely publish the same.

Among the changes made from the manuscript, which survives in the London Public Record Office, were the deletion of a description of an altercation between the king's footmen and the barons of the Cinque Ports[22] and, more significantly, of at least one figure from the procession. The duke of York had been granted permission to have his master-of-horse follow him with a riderless horse, as General Monk, now the king's master-of-horse, conformed to tradition and so followed the king. Edward Hyde and others were offended; Hyde writes, "It issued from a fountain, from whence many bitter waters were like to flow, the customs of the court of France, whereof the king and the duke had too much the image in their heads, and than which there could not be a copy more universally ingrateful and odious to the English nation" (1:457). The illustration of the procession would omit this riderless horse.

The acts of "discountenancing and discrediting" that the king had mentioned to Hyde were carefully separated from those designed for splendid solemnity, but they were staged nearly simultaneously. For example, Charles's first entry into London was arranged to coincide with his birthday on 29 May. On the twenty-third, Charles had changed the names of all the ships in the fleet that might be associated with the Commonwealth,[23] and on the twenty-fourth, the day General Monk arrived in Dover to meet Charles, and again on the twenty-ninth, effigies of Cromwell, his wife, and the arms of the Commonwealth were burned in huge bonfires in Westminster. On 24 June, an effigy of Cromwell was hung by its neck in the court of the palace; because of a long tradition of "politically sponsored demonstrations," the people knew its purpose. They "thronged to see it" and "spared no act of contempt and ignominy."[24]

Later in the year, the trials and executions of the regicides and especially the desecration of Cromwell's body became hideous but magnificent theater. Charing Cross rather than Tyburn was chosen as the execution site for the regicides, and English people would be reminded not only of its destruction during the Commonwealth, allegedly at the final instigation of Hugh Peters, one of the men on trial,[25] but of its ancient meaning. It was at this great crossroad, "ever regarded as the gateway to the city of London,"[26] that Edward I had erected the most elaborate of the twelve crosses for his queen, Eleanor of Castile. Proclamations were routinely read and distributed there. In 1554, royal forces defeated a group of rebels at that spot. Later, Charles II chose it for the equestrian statue of Charles I that a brazier had bought, had pretended to melt down, but had kept hidden during the Commonwealth. An inspired spot to use to mark the city his, Charles recognized in Charing Cross what Samuel Johnson described: "I think the full tide of human existence is at Charing Cross."[27] When the regicide Harrison's heart and head were held up for the crowd's viewing, "there were great shouts of joy."[28]

On 30 January, the exhumed bodies of Cromwell, Bradshaw, and Ireton were dragged to Tyburn, dismembered, and the body parts exposed to the people's view for months. Played out in public places, including that most ignominious, most public place, Tyburn, the spectacle went on interminably as the severed heads and body parts rotted on pikes and on the gates of the city. In these violent acts perpetrated upon human bodies at this symbolic spot, Charles gave the people the kind of "predominance of public life, the intensity of festivals" that Foucault has described as giving a society "new vigour" and forming it "for a moment

[into] a single great body."[29] This spectacle went beyond showing people their "folly" to aiming at an ultimate discrediting. As Foucault observed, "The extreme point of penal justice . . . was the infinite segmentation of the body of the regicide: a manifestation of the strongest power over the body of the greatest criminal, whose total destruction made the crime explode into its truth."[30]

One of the regicides, John Cook, had said the king "must die, and monarchy with him."[31] Now Charles was determined to mark the nation as his and to reinscribe the monarchy. The king's procession from Rochester to Whitehall took seven hours, and on some of the viewers it had the desired effect. The diarist John Evelyn described his reaction to the planned spectacle that fed on itself, and his emotions must have been shared by many:

> I stood in the strand, & beheld it, & blessed God: And all this without one drop of bloud, & by that very army, which rebell'd against him: but was the Lords doing, *et mirabile in oculis nostris:* for such a Restauration was never seene in the mention of any history, antient or modern, since the returne of the *Babylonian* Captivity, nor so joyfull a day, & so bright, ever seene in this nation: this hapning when to expect or effect it, was past all humane policy. (Evelyn, *Diary,* 3:246)

The Restoration was history, and Charles made his entrance into London an unforgettable moment, one that, even in the eyes of a well-read man, dwarfed all but the portentous return of the captive Israelites to build the temple at Jerusalem. Charles had begun the effort to impress his subjects with his magnificence, confidence, popularity, and even absolute authority.[32]

Every surviving document reveals attention to detail. Livery Companies, for example, were ordered to select as riders in the procession with the king on his entrance into the City "the most Gracefull Tall and comely personages," who were "to be well horsed and in their best array of furniture of velvett and plush or satin" and to wear chains of gold.[33] For the coronation, Charles would have the Privy Council ask the City to put gravel on the streets and rails on both sides.[34] Evelyn described the scene: Charles entered the City with "above 20000 horse & foote brandishing their swords and shouting with unexpressable joy: The wayes straw'd with flowers, the bells ringing, the streetes hung with Tapissry. . . . The Mayor, Aldermen, all the Companies in their liveries, Chaines of Gold, banners; Lords & nobles, Cloth of Silver, gold and vellvet every body clad in." Thomas Rugge wrote that there was "such shouting as the oldest man alive never heard the like" (90).

The English have carefully developed and maintained public shows of power, such as the wigs that judges still wear, that are reinforced by ancient, carefully repeated symbols. In the first two years of his reign, Charles exploited every opportunity for public display as successfully as he had at his entry into the city. In carefully designed ways, he, Sir Edward Walker, and a small group of powerful royalist supporters orchestrated events that seemed to *claim* the city—and by extension, the nation—for Charles by his physical presence. Thus he propagated the rightness of the restoration and the impression of the return of prosperity and happiness. As Clifford Geertz has observed:

> At the political center of any complexly organized society . . . there is both a governing elite and a set of symbolic forms expressing the fact that it is in truth governing. No matter how democratically the members of the elite are chosen . . . , they justify their existence and order their actions in terms of a collection of stories, ceremonies, insignia, formalities, and appurtenances that they have either inherited or, in more revolutionary situations, invented. It is these—crowns and coronations, limousines and conferences—that mark the center as center and give what goes on there its aura of being not merely important but in some odd fashion connected with the way the world is built.[35]

As Edward Walker wrote, Charles made "*his* Royall entry into *his* Capitall City of London upon the 29th day of May 1660, the day of his Nativity" (emphasis mine, 27). In November Charles staged another entry into London, ostensibly to bring the court back to Whitehall. In April 1661 he made his consecration and crowning a two-day celebration that an observer described as "exceptional and memorable for ages to come."[36] Walker described the coronation banquet as far superior to any held in Westminster Hall "since the Coronation of Queen Elizabeth 102 yeares past" (131).

From the beginning, these events deliberately reached toward all levels of society and carefully included frivolous amusements. In the days immediately before Charles entered London in May, huge bonfires, some as tall as buildings and one constructed out of a towering ship's mast, were erected and made ready for lighting for the celebrations to follow his entry into the city.[37] Such things happened by official agreements that were invisible to the ordinary citizen and probably forgotten even by the knowledgeable participants, and when necessary they were supported with public money or, more usually, with contributions made by those hoping for royal reward. For instance, the towering maypole erected in the Strand the week before the coronation was paid for by the adjacent parishes and raised and secured by order of Prince James, then Lord High Admiral, who sent seamen with their cables, pulleys, anchors, and other equipment.[38] Because each bonfire, picture, or maypole inspired people to build more bonfires, by some accounts almost one to each home, and encouraged revelry and dancing to music played by strollers or neighbors, they fostered an illusion of spontaneous celebration and of universal joy at the restoration. As Rugge said, "Every privat house laid in some provision or other to express their Joy" (97).

Tatham included two "drolls," farcical or parodic compositions, the second with a famous fairground entertainer named Pretty and tumblers in the City's July entertainment, and dancing woodmen and a tumbler in the October event. An earlier city poet, Thomas Heywood, explained the common opinion about the elements that "meerly consisteth of anticke gesticulations, dances, and other mimicke postures, devised only for the vulgar, who are better delighted with what pleaseth the eye, than contenteth the ear, in which we imitate custome, which always carrieth with it excuse."[39] More self-consciously, Louis XIV wrote, "Les peuples . . . se plaisent au spectacle, où au fond on a toujours pour but de leur plaire; et tous nos sujets, en général, sont ravis de voir que nous aimons ce qu'ils aiment. . . . Par là nous tenons leur esprit et leur coeur, quelque fois plus fortement peut-être, que par les récompenses et les bien faits."[40] The fact that most modern scholars have concluded that eyewitnesses failed to comprehend the historical and literary symbolism suggests that celebration and spectacle reaped the greatest benefits.[41]

As might be expected, the royal processions assured that every window and balcony and the streets were jammed with people eager to see the richly dressed dignitaries and to join in the festive mood. Adding to the impression of the king's great popularity that processions and street crowds gave were numerous entertainments arranged for the king by various groups such as the Livery Companies and his acceptance of invitations to events such as the lavish banquet with special entertainment held by the City in his honor in July at Guildhall and to the annual dinner held by the Middle Temple on 2 November where he saw Beaumont and Fletcher's *Wit without Money.*

The establishment of power is but part of the message new monarchs need to deliver. Charles had to make a symbolic statement about Law, demonstrating if possible that it would be authoritatively and rightfully administered and would combine the divine attributes of justice and mercy with the wisdom of their king's "great original," God. Charles had hoped to deliver the Act of Indemnity and Oblivion rapidly, but it was not until early September that it passed the seals.[42] In the meantime, Charles's entertainment by the City promised a kind of oblivion and a new start. The City of London had reason to be concerned about its relations with Charles II, who might well remember that the City's Common Council had raised large sums of money for Parliament at the time that it had granted his father's requests reluctantly or not at all. It had also marshaled one hundred thousand people, including one thousand oyster wives from Billingsgate to enclose the City with ramparts and trenches during the Civil War, and had sent the trained bands to Gloucester and Newbury, where they were, in Edward Hyde's words, "the preservation of that army that day. For they stood as a bulwark and rampire."[43] The published principal speeches from this entertainment, *London's Glory Represented,* carefully followed the precedent of the parliamentary proclamation of 8 May by dating the beginning of Charles's reign to the year of his father's execution and appeared by the Lord Mayor's decree with "the order and management of the whole day's business."

Above all, Charles needed to inscribe his authority. Not only would that establish his own position, but, more essentially, the ancient authority of the monarchy, the Right of Kings and the rightness of his family's reign. His instructions to Hyde demonstrate his intention to use forms and symbols in this interest. He began, of course, by choosing to enter the city on his birthday, and the organization of the progress was deeply symbolic. Of medieval origin, the formal entry was a grand pageant symbolizing unity, cooperation, and the relationship among kinds of authority. Those who participated represented what the French would call an estate (although those groups in England are not exactly the same estates as found in France), and they were coming together to accept Charles as a unifying emblem. At Blackheath, General Monk presented the army massed in formation and introduced each of the chief officers, who kissed the king's hand. It was the army that had brought the Commonwealth to an end, and General Monk who had met the king upon his first stepping on English soil.

Next Charles met the Lord Mayor of London, sheriffs, aldermen, and the entire City militia. This second military body and the nation's most powerful corporation swore allegiance here. The Lord Mayor presented the key to the City to Charles, and Charles returned it. This ancient ceremony served to remind the king of the City's Charter privileges and liberties and underscored the ideal represented by the progress. Charles knighted the City officers, including the aldermen and the militia's officers, and they joined his entourage. Walker noted that Charles "(to gratify the City), permitted the Lord Mayor to carry the Sword before him, which had not been done in any other publique Entry."[44] The City streets were lined with the liveried Companies in carefully prescribed order. At Whitehall, the speakers of both houses and the members of Lords and Commons presented themselves to him and promised their loyalty. That Charles came to each of these groups but that they moved to meet him represented the hope of the Restoration, a restoration that most English people saw as one of king, Parliament, and constitution. Thus, the participants expressed hope for a constitutional union of powerful social and political groups with the king at the center.

By the time of the coronation, Charles's conception of his monarchy had taken shape, and his firm control of the two-day ceremony argues that he directed this very different celebration of kingship. Unlike the entry, which drew upon traditional constitutional rituals, the coronation progress emphasized dynastic right and sovereign authority. Upon consideration, he selected St. George's Day, a traditional English holiday on which people celebrated their nation's patron saint with "ridings," elaborate parades that included figures of St. George and the Dragon.[45] A few days before the coronation, two pamphlets, *The History of that most famous Saint and Soldier St. George* and *A Perfect Catalogue of all the Knights of the Garter,* were published and distributed widely. The number of Knights of the Garter created by Charles upon his landing and in the subsequent months became another sign of Charles's authority and the establishment of the monarchical order. Later Sir Robert Vyner reworked a famous equestrian statue into a St. George-like representation of Charles II with Cromwell's face on the trampled dragon.[46] Walker and Ogilby, the men commissioned to arrange much of the public spectacle, drew upon Jean Gaspard Gevaerts's *Pompa Introitus Honori Serenissimi Principis Ferdinandi Austriaci Hispaniarum Infantis* (Antwerp, 1641), upon the description of the spectacular entry designed by Rubens for Ferdinand's entry into Antwerp in 1635, and upon their and others' knowledge of the entry of Louis XIV on 26 August 1660.[47] For Charles's coronation entry on the day before the coronation, representative groups including the Lord Mayor of London went to the Tower to process to Whitehall with the king.

The ordered ranks of this procession marked not only the restoration of his family's monarchy but also of the monarchy's status code, of the nobility, of the House of Lords, and of long-banished individuals. Samuel Pepys noticed that the bishops came after the barons and speculated "that the next parliament they will be called to the House of Lords."[48] Many people, including John Evelyn, thought the order important enough to record it in great detail in their diaries. The Livery Companies lining the streets were in centuries-old order, uniformly dressed, and silently inscribing their contrasts to the nobility and to the crowds of people behind them and watching from windows. As J. R. Jones argued, "The return of the old order meant that once again there was a place for everything, and now everything should be in its proper, legal place."[49] Men selected to ride took great care with their own and their liveried servants' dress; the duke of Buckingham allegedly spent £30,000 on his outfit and the earl of Wharton £8,000 on his horse's trappings, which were set with diamonds, pearls, and other ornaments.[50] Pepys commented that embroidery and diamonds were "ordinary among them" and, in the brilliant sunshine of the day, "So glorious was the show with gold and silver, that we were not able to look at it" (2:82, 83).

Throughout Europe, royal progresses included speeches, music, commemorative structures, and pageants. Charles's coronation included all of these, and their elaborate symbolism is far from subtle. Ogilby traces the history of building arches to Rome,[51] and the pageants, like the royal entrance, have medieval English origins. Around the end of the fourteenth century, the guilds began to organize the pageants for royal entries as welcoming tributes to the monarch. Thornbury notes the royal passage of King Henry III and Eleanor of Provence through the City to Westminster in 1236 but locates the first pageants in the reign of Edward I and water pageants in 1444 (1:317). Pageants retained much of their medieval character into the eighteenth century, including the dominance of allegorical, typological, and emblematic elements and the use of decorated, temporary arches. Although the ornaments seem derivative and conventional, they are actually personalized, often highly coherent, and reveal an ideological unity. In fact, the plan of the best of them has been called an "original and complex essay."[52]

Originally, "pageant" referred to the scaffolding, the stage, or the float, but the word came to signify the text of the drama and the *"ensemble* of the *fête"* as well.[53] The original pageants had looked like medieval manuscript illuminations or paintings staged on wagons or temporary stages. Once the monarch and his party had had a chance to admire the tableau, a speech or short play would be performed by the people mixed among the painted emblematic human figures on the pageant. By 1550, royal entry pageants had become narrative; for instance, Rouen presented Henry II with allegorical pageants tracing the complete Roman imperial triumph.[54] Thus, the streets became a grand stage on which a didactic play unfolded. Not only could large numbers of people participate, but pageants could be set up at symbolic locations in the City, thereby gaining enhanced emblematic richness.

Ogilby incorporated the arches into his pageants, and the pageants, music, and speeches made the streets a theater with each arch at center stage for one act of a national epic.[55] At the first arch, for example, thirty trumpet players and eighteen drummers entertained the crowd with the marches of several nations until the king arrived. At that moment, they sounded a charge, and the emblematic figure of Rebellion on the arch came alive and made a speech to the king. Then Monarchy and Loyalty "unveiled" themselves on the arch and frightened Rebellion. Monarchy addressed the king:

> May You, and Yours, in a Perpetual Calm
> Be Crown'd with *Laurel,* and Triumphant *Palm,*
> And all Confess, whilst they in You are Blest,
> I, MONARCHY, of Governments am Best. (42)

Then "a lofty English March" was played as the king moved on. Such dramatic confrontations and instructive speeches occurred at each arch.

These entertainments presented Charles as a deified ruler rather than as symbol of an ideal order. They drew upon classical and biblical allusions, upon representations associated with Charles's immediate ancestors, and upon images that had emerged during Charles's nearly eleven months in England. These images were woven through the day's entertainments so that they were repeatedly reinforced in the people's minds and so that a narrative of divinely ordained history unfolded. Among the most important figures used were the Platonic phoenix year, the Roman conqueror, the Tower of London, Neptune, the sun, and the oak.[56]

Many of these symbols were highly traditional and could be identified in most of the spectacles staged in Europe over the preceding century. Although analysis of any group of them could be used to demonstrate the unusual propagandistic unity of purpose in Charles's entertainments, three were deliberately personalized and, therefore, command unusual interest as they took their place in social discourse. The most traditional of these was the sun. Associated with God, light, life, and spring, it took on additional significance as a symbol of order and control in a post-Galilean world. Endlessly given the sun's powers, monarchs sometimes played the part of the sun in court masques, and Louis XIV had long been referred to as the Sun King. The interpretation of its symbolic suggestiveness in Louis XIV's *Mémoires* might have been made by any number of astute contemporaries: "On choisit pour corps le soleil qui, dans les règles de cet art, est le plus noble de tous, et qui par la qualité d'unique . . . par le bien qu'il fait en tous lieux, produisant sans cesse de tous cotés la vie, la joie, et l'action; . . . par cette course constante et invariable . . . est assurément la plus vive et la plus belle image d'un grand monarch."[57] From the time of his birth, Charles II had been associated with the sun because a noonday star had appeared on that day; references to the sun were ubiquitous in the panegyrics of the first two years of the Restoration. Robert Wild's *Iter Boreale* (April 1660) celebrated General Monk's part in the Restoration and includes the lines, " 'Twas at his rising that our day begun; / Be he the morning star to Charles our sun."[58] In *Astraea Redux,* John Dryden wrote,

> How shall I speak of that triumphant Day
> When you renew'd the expiring Pomp of *May!*
> . . . .
> The Star that at your Birth shone out so bright
> It stain'd the duller Suns Meridian light,
> Did once again its potent Fires renew
> Guiding our eyes to find and worship you. (lines 284–85, 288–91)

The first arch included a rising sun, the third a bright star; at the fourth, Plenty, the central allegorical figure of that arch, greeted the king, "Great Sir, the Star, which at Your Happy Birth / Joy'd with his Beams (at Noon) the wond'ring Earth, / Did with an auspicious lustre, then, presage / The glitt'ring Plenty of this Golden Age" (165). At the first arch, Monarchy had greeted the king, "Enter our *Sun,* our *Comfort,* and our Life" (42). Later, Concord, Love, and Truth sang, "Comes not here the King of Peace, / Who, the Stars so long fore-told, / From all Woes should us release, / Converting Iron-times to Gold?" Here Ogilby cleverly invokes both the Christian savior, "the Prince of Peace," whose coming was marked by the Christmas star, and the Platonic phoenix year, which would usher in the Golden Age.

The second symbol, Neptune, god of the sea, held a special place in English hearts. As fishermen and explorers, the sea was their special destiny, and future commercial and military superiority rested on their mastery of it. Because of their aspirations and the fact that Charles had come across the sea for the restoration, the association had particular contemporary appeal. Ogilby quoted Themistocles, "Whosoever desires a secure Dominion by Land, must first get the Dominion of the Sea" (37). Symbol of control and power over the elements, Neptune in English iconography usually appeared as the rider of a powerful beast. In Inigo Jones and Ben Jonson's 1625 masque *Neptune's Triumph for the Return of Albion,* James I is represented as Neptune, "chief in the art of riding." Stephen Orgel points out that bringing "the destructive energies of nature under control, both within and without, was the end of Renaissance education and science."[59] A water show arranged by the City in 1610 to honor Prince Henry featured a scene in which a "huge" whale and a dolphin leaped out of the Thames; Neptune subdued them and "seated two of his choycest Trytons on them, altring their deformed Sea-Shapes."[60] In Tatham's entertainment, titled, significantly, *Neptune's Address,* Neptune rides a whale and welcomes the king home. He explains that the whales, present on the second and this fourth barge, are the foes of God, "yourself," and the country: "Who to maintain their Monstrous Bulk, persue / Not the Barque only, but the Traffick too; / By which *Trade* perish'd, all *Commerce* was barr'd" (7). The second arch included two representations of Neptune, one driving a chariot-like seashell pulled by sea horses, and the other inscribed, NEPTUNO REDUCI (53). Here Thames greeted Charles:

> Hail, Mighty *Monarch!* whose Imperial Hand
> Quiets the Ocean, and secures the Land;
> . . . .
> You are our *Neptune,* every Port, and Bay
> Your Chambers: the whole Sea is Your High-way.
> Though sev'ral Nations boast their Strength on Land,
> Yet You alone the Wat'ry World command. (104)

Then a group of seamen sang a song beginning, "*King* Charles, *King* Charles, *great* Neptune of the Main!" The central shield for this arch read, "Neptuno Britannico, Carolo II, Cujus Arbitrio Mare Vel Liberum, Vel Clausum" ("To the British Neptune, Charles II, at whose will the sea is either open or closed"). Panegyrics written for the occasion often subjugated Neptune to the king or to the powers that brought about the Restoration. Wild wrote, "[Monk] shall command Neptune himself to bring / His trident and present it to our King" (*Iter Boreale,* lines 396–97).

The third symbol was the oak, and the designers chose it as background to the featured figure of Charles II on the first arch. On this stunning, eighty-foot arch, Charles wore the robes of state.[61] For the common people, the oak immortalized Charles's escape after the battle at Worcester, when he hid in a large oak at Boscobel House. This tree had great sentimental value for the English, and Charles himself grew oaks from acorns he personally brought from the tree. Other trees grown from its saplings were carefully nurtured in places like the Physic Garden, Chelsea.[62] Instead of acorns the arch's oak bore crowns and scepters, the promise of dynastic glory for Charles Stuart's line. Dryden used the same image in his "To His Sacred Majesty, A Panegyrick on His Coronation" (1661):

> Two Kingdomes wait your doom, and as you choose,
> This must receive a Crown, or that must loose.
> Thus from your Royal Oke, like *Jove*'s of old,
> Are answers sought, and destinies fore-told:
> Propitious Oracles are beg'd with vows,
> And Crowns that grow upon the sacred boughs. (lines 127–32)

With the restoration of Charles, the oak became the visible sign of the failure of the parliamentary forces. Like the noonday star, the oak seemed a miraculous sign of Charles's divinely ordained destiny, and the trees grown from its acorns and saplings partook of the representation of Charles as a strong, life-giving, regenerative force.

Ogilby also associates the oak with England's naval might, "those Floating Garrisons made of Oak" (37). In discussing the third arch, Ogilby deepened the significance of the oak by pointing out that the Romans crowned those who rescued citizens with wreaths of oak leaves; figures of Julius Caesar, for instance, often wore the "Crown of Oak, as dedicated to the Saviour of his Country" (129). Ogilby mentions the classical associations to Julius Caesar, to Dio of Augustus, to Jupiter and Juno, and, most significantly and also noted by Dryden, to Jove.[63] John Tatham used the oak as the central symbol for the opening of his enter-

For his coronation, Westminster Cathedral became a theater, complete with a raised stage for the coronation. (Illustration from Ogilby's *Entertainment of Charles II.*)

tainment, *Neptune's Address*. The procession of barges on the Thames began with the positioning of "A Gallant Large Fabrick, made in the likenesse of the *Tower* of *London,*" which Tatham said represented "the Emblem of Your Peoples Love, / From whose united Strength Your Actions move." The next barges moved around the Tower. On the second, three whales, representing the enemies of Charles, the country, and God, circled a large rock out of which the Royal Oak "springs, decorated with Crowns and Scepters." At the end, the whales are blown up by the gunner on one of the king's ships.

In a wonderfully symbolic gesture, Charles had a stage built in Westminster Abbey for his coronation. Every mention of the setting for his crowning uses that word: "stage." So mundane a document as the directions to the carpenter insists upon "stage," and the Privy Council even determined the dimensions.[64] Samuel Pepys and others appreciated the gesture and admired the sheer theatricality of the setting: "And a pleasure it was to see the Abbey raised in the middle, all covered with red and a throne (that is a chaire) and footstoole on the top of it. And all the officers of all kinds, so much as the very fidlers, in red vests." Pepys called the procession "a most magnificent sight," and Elias Ashmole noted how it passed through the choir, "went up the Stairs toward the *great Theatre;* and as they came to the top thereof" were divided into seats in two galleries.[65] From that stage the bishop of London presented the king four times, and each successive part of the audience shouted its allegiance. The king stood by the throne and turned to face each side of the stage as the bishop spoke.

At this point, theater as a mode of power reached its fullest potential. The unsheathing and display of the naked Sword of State, carried erect as the sign of royal sovereignty, thereby emphasizing its phallic primacy, visually dominated the other symbols of the king's authority. During the dinner that followed, the King's Champion, Sir Edward Dymock, rode in on a huge white horse. He paused dramatically, then advanced, stopped again, and delivered the ritual challenge:

> If any Person of what degree soever, high or low, shall deny, or gainsay Our Sovereign Lord King Charles the Second . . . to be right Heir to the Imperial Crown of this Realm of England . . . here is His Champion, who saith, that he lyeth, and is a false Traytor, being ready in person to Combate with him, and in this Quarrel will adventure his Life against him, on what day soever he shall be appointed. (Ogilby, 189)

He threw down his gauntlet. After a few minutes of silence, it was handed back, and the Champion advanced again, stopped, and repeated the challenge. In this ritual as old as King Arthur's court and resonant with heroic and chivalric echoes as found in *Sir Gawain and the Green Knight,* the court exerted its claim through rites and images that emanated both might and dynastic right. Three times, finally at the foot of the steps to the throne, he repeated the ceremony. A toast followed, and only then did the kings at arms and heralds proclaim the king.

The spectacles of the coronation year gradually rewrote the nation's history and became increasingly aggressive in the presentation of Charles's restoration as dynastic apotheosis. The evolution from Charles's ceremo-

Illustrations of Charles II often incorporated the central
symbols he had chosen for himself; here the artist has
created a resemblance to the lion of Great Britain.
(Illustration from *Roxburghe Ballads.*)

nial entry from Rochester to his exultant coronation procession is the
movement from respectful observation of ritual to the creative display of
the monarch that the Caroline masques inscribed. The symbolic presentations of Bibles and keys, the ritualistic greetings and responses,
brought to mind the king's duties and pledges; the coronation celebrations and ceremonies consisted of the rituals and mysteries of king wor-
ship.[66] Ludwig von Feuerbach once said that "the highest degree of
illusion comes to be the highest degree of sacredness"; the royal plan,
stated early according to Hyde, had been to substitute the "Forms" that

would give "Lustre and Splendor to the Solemnity" for the "Inventions" of the Cromwell era. These words are startlingly like Geertz's: "they justify their existence . . . in terms of a collection of stories, ceremonies, insignia, formalities, and appurtenances that they have either inherited or, in more revolutionary situations, invented" (quoted in Debord, *Society of the Spectacle,* n.p.).

Charles as well as Cromwell was in a revolutionary situation. Although he could draw upon many inherited symbols, he had to obscure some and, more crucially, invent new stories, ceremonies, and insignia in order to restore the monarchy's sacred distance and authority. His father had been tried and executed, he had hidden in a tree, he had been invited to the throne by Parliament; as Geertz reminds us, " 'A woman is not a duchess a hundred yards from her carriage,' and chiefs are changed to rajahs by the aesthetics of their rule."[67] The awesome impression of invulnerability, of holy taboo, had to be reimprinted. The spectacle, "enormously positive, indisputable, and inaccessible," became the deified king, demanding, in Guy Debord's words, "passive acceptance which in fact it already obtained by its manner of appearing without reply."[68] The sun, Neptune, and the oak, all made distinctively contemporary and all with unusual personal associations, drew upon the essential signs of the monarch with indisputable right to rule: the elements and the acclaimed Roman conqueror's dedication to political economy. Yet each partook of the miraculous and the ordained. Thus, Charles transformed the ignominy of cowering in a diseased tree into a providential deliverance. He wrote a new plot for the story and fixed it with insignia shown on medals, arches, and a new honorary order. He symbolically reclaimed each historically significant place, treating each as a cultural object to be inscribed with new, renewed, or revised meaning. Collectively, then, the places that served as public stages during the coronation year became a new history and a legible icon of the ideology of the temporarily created community.[69] He connected himself with "the way the world is built."

As he obliterated the fear, dishonor, and defeat of the early 1640s, he wrote the Interregnum out of the nation's history. The triumphal arches endlessly depicted James I and Charles I with figures of Charles II placed before or above them. Charles's coronation year was officially the twelfth year of his reign; Cromwell's body was not only expunged from Westminster Abbey but an attempt was made to assure that every remnant of it would be eaten by birds or rot away and become dust in the wind.[70] For the moment, the English people were overwhelmed by the size, sweep, and magnificence of the spectacle, overwhelmed into feeling a part of it, and, therefore, reintegrated into the monarchy. That is what Charles II intended.

In times of revolutionary change, a nation feels a strong need to justify actions and to unify opinion. In the case of the Restoration, expressions of this need tended at first to consolidate support for the king and to establish the monarchy on his terms. Most ordinary people do not have a unified philosophy of life; therefore, signs, symbols, ceremonies, and myths construct reality for them. As Kenneth Burke once said, human beings live in "a fog of symbols," for they "must erect a vast symbolic synthesis, a rationale of imaginative and conceptual imagery that 'locates' the various aspects of experience. This symbolism guides social purpose."[71] City festivals and entertainments incorporated the symbols and stories of the coronation year, and, regardless of the degree to which their designers understood or shared Charles's conception of the kingship, they helped propagate it. For instance, the welcoming pageant arranged by the City of London, *London's Glory Represented Time, Truth, and Fame, at the Magnificent Triumphs and Entertainment of His Most Sacred Majesty Charles II . . . At Guildhall, on Thursday, being the 5th day of July 1660, and in the 12th year of his Majesty's most happy reign,* employed the metaphors of the sun and spring. At Fleet Street Conduit, "a person representing Time in a very glorious pageant . . . addresseth himself to his Majesty" used an extended metaphor comparing the king's influence to the sun's effect:

> Such is the vertual fervour of your beams,
> That not obliquely but directly streams
> Upon your subjects; so the glorious sun
> Gives growth to th' infant plants he smiles upon.[72]

Here, too, Time compared the misery of the Interregnum to the present, a theme introduced in highly similar words in Charles's declaration from Breda.[73] In St. Paul's Churchyard, the procession saw "another pageant, very much amplified and adorned." Here Truth took up the themes introduced in the first speech and added a brief portrait of a merciful king.

"Fame" concluded the serious part of the work at the Great Conduit in Cheapside. This speech offered what was becoming the standard interpretation of recent history. "Fortune's utmost hate" had been at work in the time of trouble; "Heav'n, that orders all things as it list" consented and finally restored "golden times." In addition to casting opprobrium on Cromwell's supporters and removing human beings from responsibility for historical events, this pageant is especially rich in portentous emblems and allusions. For instance, the poet, John Tatham, implies that the Cromwell years were like the years the Israelites spent in Egypt, years of divinely ordained and miraculously concluded suffering. Tatham represents Charles as the visual sign of an abstract truth, of "a history." The conclusion of this speech bears significant similarities to the prologue that William Davenant would write for the November performance of *Epicoene* that General Monk arranged in the king's honor:

Tatham: Fame now shall spread his wing,
              And of your after glories further sing;
              Since in your self you are a history,
              A volume bound up for eternity.

Davenant: But this Great Theme must serve another Age,
              To fill our Story, and adorne our Stage.

Like John Evelyn and many others, they felt themselves watching history being made, and they knew their part—to record and celebrate. Struck by the scene and instinctively moved to compare it to great scenes in the history books he had read, Evelyn colored the day with light and found God's miraculous love in it (*Diary* 3:246). Like the playwrights who were self-consciously writing the history—description and interpretation—of the moment, Evelyn felt himself in a great scene.

At this early stage, the establishment of a hierarchy of ideological symbols was a joint enterprise and flowed from the king down and from the people up. For example, one of the key symbols of the coronation, the royal oak, had been featured and popularized in a street pageant six months earlier. On 29 October, Lord Mayor's Day, the Merchant Taylors, the livery company that had contributed eight thousand men to build the London fortifications in 1642, slanted the traditional entertainment to honor the new Lord Mayor decidedly toward the king by financing Tatham's pageant, *The Royal Oake*.[74] Presented on land and on the Thames, this entertainment featured Charles's escape at Boscobel. The central tableau featuring the royal oak was set up at Cheapside Cross.

Prefaced by songs and dances by woodmen, forest nymphs, and others who spoke and sang rude, familiar lines in dialect at Cheapside Key, the oak episode featured a troop of tumblers including the lower orders' favorite, Mr. Dyamond. "Sylvanus," dressed as huntsman, then gave a long speech praising the oak, its leaves, and the oak in the ship that brought the king to England; he concluded, "Bout the Oke write *Hony soit qui maly Pence*" [*sic*].[75] This performance contrasted strikingly with the portentous descriptions of the oak given elsewhere in this text and in other places on the event. The complete title of *The Several Speeches Made to the Honorable Sir Richard Brown* includes the line "Representing the *Royal Oak*, and its Pendant Leaves, that preserv'd and enshadow'd our Gracious Lord and Sovereign King Charles, from the hands of his Bloodthirsty Enemies." Another pamphlet compares the Roman "Corona Civica," "Corona Ovalis," "the one of Oake, the other of Mirtle," to the "Corona Aurea" and praises the oak and myrtle wreaths as infinitely superior.[76]

In this and other entertainments, Tatham and others cast Charles as light, the head, the sun, God's vicegerent, and endlessly as reborn, as regenerative force, and as harbinger of a new, prosperous time. The City spent £7,888.2.6 for the July entertainment, which included a huge, elaborate Guildhall dinner with vocal and instrumental music.[77] Thomas Jordan, who would be Tatham's successor as City Poet, wrote a welcoming poem for the king that brought many of these images together even as it drew upon Renaissance conceptions of art's power to communicate higher reality: "Mirrour of Majesty, bright Rising Sun, / The virtues of all Kings compriz'd in one."[78] These events inscribed a meaning on the people who participated in or watched these spectacles; and, in a variety of ways, including the selection of which speeches to print, their creators attempted to assure the transmission of more serious messages. For instance, Time's speech from *The Royal Oake* is carefully transcribed in a pamphlet, and it comes at a significant moment. The Act of Indemnity and Oblivion had not received the seal until September; the trials of the regicides had been held off until 9 October, and the executions had begun on 13 October. Time's speech, significantly given on 29 October, is largely devoted to the benefits of retributive justice:

> Treason may flourish for a little space,
> But Time at length writes villane in its face.
> Whil'st Julius Caesar's death revengeless past,

Rome nere was free from sword, fire, plague, and waste.
Till Time reveal'd the murderers, and then
Their better genius did return agen
. . . .
That monstrous murder that outfac'd the sun,
Appears to me as yesterday but done;
So home hath justice follow'd them, their heels
Are now tript up, each his own horror feels. (104)

Just as the rowdy had pelted, spat upon, and burned effigies of
Cromwell and the leaders of his government, so writers joined in the
defamation and discrediting in their own ways. For instance, one of John
Tatham's plays aims little higher than satire of the fallen leaders. In fact,
Charles II may have seen Tatham's first Restoration effort, *The Rump; or,
The Mirrour of the Late Times,* which had played successfully at Dorset
Court since at least June 1659.[79] In it Cromwell's brother-in-law John
Desborough, the loyal soldier who had opposed kingship or a hereditary
Protectorate for Cromwell, is depicted as a total fool whose major concern is his shopping; he must "bespeak . . . a pair of cards for my
thrasher, a scythe for my mower, . . . a skreen for my lady wife" (235). In
an especially ugly scene, Wareston, Whitelocke, Fleetwood, Lambert,
and Huson assign lucrative positions or large monetary gifts to themselves and their friends. Bulstrode Whitelocke, the most cynical of the
lot, demands to know where his money will come from and is happy to
hear his will come from so secure a source as the customs (236–40). In a
line sure to enrage the London audience against the Committee of Safety,
John Lambert says, "The city's big with riches, and neer her time, I hope,
to be delivered" (240).

Cromwell's family comes in for ridicule, and Oliver's wife, Elizabeth,
is used to condemn him and ridicule their children; she acknowledges an
affair between Oliver and Lady Lambert and chides her daughter,
"Hang honesty! 'tis mere foolery, Thy father had more wit then to be
thought one of that needy crue" (255). Edward Howard's *The Usurper*
(1664) included enough parallels to Oliver Cromwell's life to assure that
the audience would identify Damocles, the usurper, with him. For instance, the Senate asks Damocles to "exchange the Title of our General / And take from us the offer of a Kingdom." Like Tatham's Cromwell,
Damocles is lascivious. Strong hints suggest that he lusts after a page,
whom he thinks is a boy, and he kills his son in a jealous frenzy over the

African queen Timanda. Like Cromwell, he dies during a storm. Abel
Day, the Richard Cromwell figure in Robert Howard's *The Committee*
(1662), is consummately stupid. He cannot remember simple lines, repeats "forsooth," behaves obsequiously, and innocently exposes his parents. For instance, he hesitates over telling the girl he is courting that he is
busy with state affairs: "I am afraid my mother will be angry, for she takes
all the state matters upon herself" (17).

In Tatham's play, clever lines designed to reveal Cromwell's hypocrisy, lack of discrimination, and inept aping of kingly actions probably
made the audience roar with laughter: "[He] made brewers, draymen,
coblers, tinkers, or anybody, lords. Such was his power; no prince e'er
did the like." The play ends with a cacophony of street cries, a parody of
the songs and dances that usually concluded plays. The characters, reduced to their common origins, are now orange wenches, cobblers, and
worse. Tatham, always intimately aware of the City, included celebratory
cheers for the king and a song for General Monk, and he staged such
actual events as the bonfires and public roasts of mutton and beef rumps.
Thus his play, like the diaries of John Evelyn and Samuel Pepys, records
the reactions of ordinary people to the restoration in its earliest stages.

To read the drama performed in the first two years is to be struck by
the reiteration of the base motives of characters easily identified with
members of the Committee of Safety, of the condemnation of their destructive jealousies and crass ambitions, and of the deliberate portrayal
of them as without intelligence, depth, vision, and concern for the people. Edward Howard's *The Usurper* included bonfires to celebrate the
establishment of a free senate, a transparent reference to the joy at
the restoration of Parliament, and could even be read as approval of the
mutilation of Cromwell's body. Cleander says of Damocles, the Cromwell figure, "[He] left his name behind; A Glorious Villain: / His Head
shall be advanc'd upon the Castle, / But let his Body crow'd for Burial, /
I' the Common Execution place" (70). Abraham Cowley says that his
play, *Cutter of Coleman-Street* (1661), derides "the Hypocrisie of those
men whose skuls are not yet bare upon the Gates since the publique and
just punishment" of their crimes (emphasis mine).[80]

Many of these plays worked in subtle ways toward the same ends as
the poems, prologues, masques, pageants, and plays that presented a
sovereign monarch as the instrument of divine order and human happiness. For instance, the misogyny that abounds in *The Rump* is common
and frequently used for this purpose. Tatham used the women characters

to expose the crudest desires of the men; what Lambert was too politic to say, his wife would. Long before Lambert's power is established, she makes her servant Pris call her "highness." Mrs. Day, the character reminiscent of Elizabeth Cromwell in Howard's *The Committee,* is a crude, loquacious, peremptory, self-important autocrat. Characters who knew her when she was a kitchen maid can hardly get out the "your honour's" and "your ladyship's" that she demands without laughing. In Tatham's play, she and the other women meet in a mock committee and compose new laws that obviously serve their pleasures and vices rather than the good of society. From that time on they agree, for example, that women can walk or talk with anyone. Lady Lambert, Lady Fleetwood, and Mrs. Cromwell are presented as influencing their husbands inappropriately and, therefore, moving outside their natural sphere. In Howard's play, Mrs. Day insists upon managing business before the men's committee herself.

Similarly, Ben Jonson's *Epicoene,* which was one of the most popular plays performed in the first years after the Restoration and was chosen to entertain the king in the Cockpit-in-Court theater, satirized a group of women called the Collegiates. Truewit describes them as "an order between courtiers and country madams, that live from their husbands and give entertainment to all the wits and braveries [well-dressed fops] of the time, as they call them; cry down, or up, what they like or dislike in a brain or a fashion, with most masculine, or rather, hermaphroditical authority" (1.1.72–76). When they assemble to meet Epicoene, their leader, Lady Haughty, demands the scarves and gloves usually given special guests at a wedding and chides Morose for failing to exploit the opportunity to receive gifts. They instruct Epicoene to "manage" Morose from the beginning and to demand a coach and four and a host of servants, including four grooms. Jonson goes on to show them to be as lascivious and pleasure loving as they are greedy. They promise Epicoene cards, trips to the places they enjoy most (Bedlam, the Exchange, and china shops, the last already a cant word for a place to pick up men), and recipes for preventing pregnancy. Just as the women in *The Rump* expose the true feelings of the men, Mrs. Otter, the lower-class bear garden captain's wife, exposes their affectations and motives through her attempts to imitate the collegiates.

A contemporary complained that "Lady Cromwell" surrounded herself with "twenty proud women," and Lady Haughty recruits women whom she expects to be impervious and self-seeking. Although *The*

Rump shows Lady Lambert with the coterie, the play does not fail to remind the audience that Elizabeth Cromwell could behave as her single surviving letter to Oliver suggests. In that letter, she tells Oliver that it would be politic for him to write letters to powerful men (whom she lists), and in the play rages at her impotence.[81] Howard's Mrs. Day forges a letter from the king for her husband's use. As has often been true in Western literature, these playwrights let women represent unsanctioned, unofficial kinds of government, inappropriate kinds of influence, and illusionary forms of power. Their meetings are cabals, and they have no interest in the welfare of the state, which is the true purpose of ethical government and the responsibility of legitimate authority.

Playwrights could count on the audience's familiarity with such prose works as *Newes from the New Exchange, or the Commonwealth of Ladies* (1650) and *The Parliament of Women. With the merrie Lawes by them newly Enacted. To live in more Ease, Pompe, Pride, and wantonnesse: but especially that they might have superiority and domineere over their husbands* (1645; other editions in 1656 and 1684). William Cartwright's *The Lady Errant,* produced between 1637 and 1643 but first printed in 1651, also used the device of women plotting to take over the state. Some of these pieces, such as *Newes,* printed real people's names and identified their illicit liaisons: "Peters with Mistris *Ireton,* she with *Bradshaw,* he with Madam *Castlehaven,* as *Cromwell* with Mrs. *Lambert*" (10). Others indicted their victims through allusions, especially to class and occupation. *The Parliament of Ladies* (second edition, 1647) concluded with the appearance of a woman who insists she is "as good a member as any there, most of them knew she had alwaies stood stiffe in the businesse"; she promises to show herself to aldermen's wives alone. Uniformly presented as discontented, sexually insatiable, and intent upon dominating men, members of these women's clubs frequently wrote laws such as "Item, it is concluded and fully agreed upon, that all women shall have their husbands Tenants at will; and that they shall do them Knights service, and have their homage paid before Sun-rising, or at every weekes end." Often ignorant, like the She Senate in John Wilson's perhaps unproduced *The Projectors* (1665), who say "oil and garlic" for "oligarchy," their groups inevitably end, as Wilson's does, in chaos, contention, and cacophony. The women in these plays are self-satisfied pretenders to wisdom and insight whose end is the most devastating of all: irrelevance. Performance could certainly have increased the association in the audience's mind of the women's circles with the inner circle of the Protectorate, and both a statement dismissing the recent past and satire of unsanctioned authority resulted.

Epicoene had a lot to offer the Restoration playgoer. The fine plot with its variety of strongly drawn characters is the best of the many appearance-reality comedies selected for revival in the first two seasons after the Restoration. Edward Kynaston, one of the king's favorite actors, played Epicoene brilliantly, and many who went to the play would have especially anticipated his performance. Thus, they would have been quite conscious of his sex. When he appeared first as a modest city woman and then in the dress of a fine lady, they would have wanted to see and admire his ability to carry off the illusion in either costume—Pepys noted that he "was clearly the prettiest woman in the whole house."[82] Finally, Epicoene is revealed to be a man, just what the audience knows him to be. Then seventeen years old, Kynaston had light hair, large blue eyes, and delicate features, yet he was not a slight man and appears to have needed to shave carefully before performances in which he acted women's parts.[83]

These appearance-reality comedies seem especially appropriate to a nation surely intrigued by artifice, illusion, and complicity. After all, many Englishmen had felt Cromwell to be a usurper; he had worn poor man's clothes and then the trappings of nobility. The restoration of Charles seemed to reveal what they had always known—or feared—Cromwell and his government to be. Jonson's play makes clear the audience's complicity in the illusion of Epicoene's deception, and they seem to have felt great pleasure in the restoration of Kynaston's true sex. Pepys noted that Kynaston was "likewise" "the handsomest man in the house." The committee in Howard's play knows Day for what he is and recognizes his maneuvers and motives, yet its members keep silent, collaborate, and profit. At the end, however, everyone—characters and audience alike—feels relief at his fall.

Epicoene multiplies images of sexual confusion and develops them into a dissertation on natural order. The collegiates live separate from their husbands and often threaten physical violence; La Foole and Daw are tricked into confessing adultery with Epicoene; Morose pleads that he "is no man." Yet the sex of each is clear, as are their motives for acting as they do. Truewit's caustic comments and ensnaring questions keep what ought to be, what was "natural," in the audience's minds. One of the most popular plays was the revival of Beaumont and Fletcher's *Scorn-*

ful Lady. Here, too, a man disguised as a woman with the audience's full knowledge brings about a satisfying conclusion. Welford, disguised as a soft-spoken, submissive woman and pretending to be the Elder Loveless's fiancée, accompanies him to chastize the proud and persecuting Lady.

In *The Rump* and *The Committee*, Tatham and Howard drew upon familiar jokes about Elizabeth Cromwell and depicted her as a crude, rustic, frumpish woman—which she appears to have been. Contemporaries recorded her keeping cows in St. James Park and a dairy at Whitehall, exclaimed at her blunders in dress, and noticed that she served small beer, bread, and butter to the highest-ranking army politicians and ate marrow pudding for breakfast. "Commonly called Protectresse Joan . . . even at the height of her Husbands power," her critics had given her the generic title of an ill-mannered, disheveled, unclean, rustic woman or scullery maid.[84] The conclusion of *The Rump* shows her in the streets, crying, "What kitchen stuffe have you, maids?" The allusive possibilities are rich. Since the female street hawkers were known for their volubility, loud voices, and powers of crude repartée, to choose this fate reinforced the unpleasant aspects of her personality as depicted in the play. The audience would have imagined Elizabeth as a grease dealer, the woman who bought grease ("kitchen stuffe") from scullery maids and resold it at "a tiny profit" to tallow chandlers. These hawkers scraped each household's grease into their tubs with a knife lodged in the hoop of it.[85] This identity might also remind the audience of the frugal Elizabeth serving leftovers, selling them as hog slop as the street women did, or giving them to the poor of St. Margaret's or St. Martin's-in-the-Fields as she had the scraps of Protectoral dinners during her "reign." After the Restoration, Elizabeth was accused of selling the royal jewels and pictures at a fruiterer's warehouse.[86] Since shops that bought kitchen stuff also commonly received stolen goods,[87] the contemporary audience might have read in this charge against her.

At the same time that Charles made London the stage for a giant, protracted public masque, these plays were contributing to the establishment of Charles and his authority. Notably, these disparate genres—crude satire, comedy, and tragedy—united to celebrate the king's return as the reestablishment of natural order and the harbinger of personal and national well-being. These plays present the monarch characters as ideally virtuous and as somewhat abstract and unemotional figures. They rewrite history by recasting a number of the chief actors in the restoration of Charles, as the author of *Cromwell's Conspiracy* (1660) does when he represents General Monk as a firm and heroic Royalist. In contrast, the usurpers and Commonwealth characters are lusty, avaricious, jealous, and passionate. They eat, drink, quarrel, and make love. This contrast celebrates the displacing of the humble origins, unpolished manners, and crude ambitions of the "low" Commonwealthmen. More significantly, it represents the republicans as the embodiment of private self-interest while the rightful monarchs stand for public virtue and disinterested service.

2

EN, WOMEN, AND RESISTANCE

THOSE WRITERS WHO PORTRAYED CHARLES II WITH HIS CHO-
sen allusions and symbols and Cromwell and his circle with such malice
were part of other traditions and of a community coming to terms with
the Restoration. As carefully (and perhaps wholeheartedly) ideological
as Ogilby's *Entertainment of Charles II* was, it began with the expression
of a widely held definition of the event: "the glorious Restauration of our
Sovereign to His Throne, and of us His Subjects to our Laws, Liberties,
and Religion" (1). "Our" laws, liberties, and religion, Ogilby wrote, and
official communications and declarations made it clear that *both* monarchy and Parliament with their interdependent powers and privileges
were to be restored. Charles's carefully worded declaration from Breda
stated, "Nor do we desire more to enjoy what is ours [by right], than that
all our subjects may enjoy what by law is theirs . . . in the Restoration
both of king, peers, and people to their just, antient, and fundamental
rights." He went on to promise "a free Parliament, by which, upon the
word of a king, we will be advised."[1] The House of Commons of the
Convention Parliament did indeed behave as a partner in power.

In this revolutionary moment, the nation stood poised between the
desire to reclaim its history (to go back) and a will to direct and shape its
future (to change).[2] The civic pageants and even the national public
theater captured this state of being and simultaneously represented the

residual and emergent structures of feeling so strongly present in the larger culture. During the Interregnum, the commercial classes had grown, had experienced considerable autonomy, and had had time to reflect upon the political and economic power that they had exercised during the Revolution and its aftermath. Forced to choose between Parliament and the king, they had experienced personal, individual responsibility and the power that ordinary people could exert. Lucy Hutchinson described how her husband assiduously read "all the publick papers" and "private treatises" in an attempt to understand "the things then in dispute."[3] The multitude of petitions that characterized the Civil War era are signs of the sense of responsibility and empowerment that even women and groups of tradesmen felt.

At this pivotal moment, both an individual sense of selfhood and the concept of public opinion began to form. People began to see themselves as Colley Cibber described himself at a similar moment in English history: "And it is a solid Comfort to me to consider that how insignificant soever my Life was at the Revolution, it had still the good Fortune to make one, among the many, who brought it about."[4] He states that he is "one," an individual, and *he* had decided to act, and yet he was "among the many [part of a community], who brought it about." In the same passage he refers to "the common people" and "the People of *England*" who had discussed King James's actions and had finally given "real Being" to their "ancient Liberties." A generation before Cibber, Defoe had written about "the Dawn of Politicks among the Common People," and he and others remarked on avid readers among, for instance, the chairmen near Whitehall, lower-class men gathered "in the streets," coffeehouse patrons, and servant maids. In 1687, yet a generation earlier, the author of *An Address of Thanks* complained that Elinor James's "tracts had 'edified' the Tripe-Women and Convinced the Porters' of her view of the Church of England."[5] Before the Restoration, a royalist complained that "the rude multitude says more in a petition than armed men in battle." Peter Burke has concluded that political demonstrations were "something of a London specialty in the period 1640–80."[6]

From that point on, the concept of "the people" began to attract analysis and comment. "It were to be wish'd / This beast, the people, either never knew / Their strength, or always knew to use it right," John Wilson wrote in *Andronicus Comnenius* (1663). Richard Atkyns in his treatises on the press referred frequently to "the Common People," and his rhetoric makes clear that he felt no explanation necessary of whom he meant or why they needed to be kept in mind. In one typical allusion, he writes, Parliament "so totally possest the Press that the King could not be heard: By this means the *Common People* became not only *Statists,* but *Parties* in the *Parliaments* Cause."[7] Within a hundred years, Lord Egmont reminded Commons, "a general popular opinion . . . ought never to be neglected by those in authority; and a wise magistrate will never persist in a measure if not absolutely necessary, which he finds to be against the general bent of the people."[8] In addition, because of the drastic political changes and the rise of economic expansionism, the class system not only had lost some of its rigidity but appeared more open to English citizens. As Ian Watt has pointed out, each person felt responsible for determining his or her own economic, social, political, and religious roles.[9]

Although both the City and the court were attempting to close the cultural gap between what was suddenly "the state" and society, the mind of a Stuart king brought to full maturity in an absolutist kingdom and that of a Protestant, commercial people with distant memories of a monarchy (and for many, few of them happy) were products of irreconcilable societies. Later Edward Hyde would recall the king's apparently enormous initial popularity, record its decline, and conclude that "there must be some wonderful miscarriage in the state, or some unheard defect of understanding in those who were trusted by the king in the administration of his affairs; that there could be in so short a time a new revolution in the general affections of the people."[10] Clarendon was correct: there was a "defect of understanding." Quite simply, the collection of stories, ceremonies, formalities, and symbols offered to the people did not conform adequately to their experiences and aspirations. Already evident were important revolutionary hopes that Charles had not recognized and divisions in structures of feeling.

Charles's primary efforts were concentrated upon reclaiming English history, not toward directing a breakaway future. But as he and his immediate circle attempted the former, the foundation of imperial England was already being laid, and their lack of appreciation and respect for the changes and ambitions that had shaped the minds of many subjects led to conflict and resentment that began to break out in communities throughout the nation and that colored many contemporary plays. Significantly, historians note the imperial ambitions implicit in the fact that "blue water" assumptions and strategy can confidently be dated from the Commonwealth and Protectorate and can be identified in the nation at large as well as among ministers.[11] Documents in the Public Record Office include numerous references to unrest throughout the nation. A typical example appears in a letter to one of the clerks of the Privy Council asking for more effective orders for the militia: "You maie perceive the condition of this Country and how pregnant the ill humor that lately disturbed this Kingdom doe still abound amongst us." Other reports described refusals to pay taxes, riots in Somersetshire, Salisbury, Lancashire, Taunton, and other places, and "general disturbances" threatened for July 1662, near the time of the new queen's entry into England. Especially alarming to the government were descriptions of "meetings and much riding in the night of Disaffected persons."[12]

A major reason for social turmoil and the numerous expressions of disquiet was this lack of a dominant ideology or even of an established hegemony. As Gramsci noted, ruling bodies almost universally depend upon consent to their "intellectual and moral leadership." When this consent is received and as long as it is maintained, a nation usually experiences both internal peace and peace of mind, for the people feel that they are in harmony with "the way the world is." Even a tyrant can foster this state for a while if the people believe his rule and their suffering to be divinely ordained and likely to be rewarded. As Gramsci recognized, the values and behaviors of the power group must be widely shared before its culture attains hegemony. Very quickly after the Restoration, the lack of a "hegemonic we" came to be felt.[13]

It is the rhetoric of a culture reinforced in all social discourses that provides the means for the negotiation, establishment, and maintenance of the hegemony. Both Clifford Geertz and Raymond Williams have demonstrated that symbolic representations that are not truly indigenous and confirmed by a people's lived experience will fail to communicate or will be rejected outright, regardless of how skillfully they are transmitted.[14] Even those rather close to the Restoration events recognized this phenomenon. A contemporary historian wrote, "Tho' outside Shew serves to dazzle those who regard Outside only, it will not convince those who carry their enquiries to the Heart."[15]

Inherent in the civic entertainments, then, were other traditions, other structures of feeling, and other ambitions than the king's. An oppositional conception of the sovereign emerged within the very pageants conceived as part of Charles's "tryumph," and by 1662 the signs of a definitive rejection of absolutist monarchy were unmistakable in them and even in the productions in the royal theaters. Moreover, some of the people's divergent desires are evident almost from the moment of Charles's arrival in England.

The traditional *laudando praecipere* of the civic pageants provided a well-developed means of giving advice. Beginning with the royal entrée of Queen Elizabeth, the city pageants had presented specific desires as well as praise and conventional expressions of hope for the sovereign's benevolence toward her people.[16] It has been said that, in sharp contrast to Americans, "every European poet . . . in his heart of hearts [knows that] the audience he desires and expects are those who govern the country."[17] Queen Elizabeth had delighted the crowds at her 1559 progress by insisting upon hearing the speakers, inquiring the meanings of the pageants, and answering each with pledges such as "for the safetie and quietnes of you all, I will not spare, if nede be to spend my blood."[18] Thus, dramatists in the early 1660s were working within a long tradition of addressing, even instructing, their sovereign. They could hope for an attentive hearing, and they took advantage of the opportunities the coronation year offered to make their hopes known.

The City's greatest concern was trade, and the performances the king saw made its hopes clear. Even before he arrived in England, the theme was clearly formulated. For example, after a lavish dinner for General Monk at the Clothworkers' Hall, a dramatic dialogue between Countryman and Souldier included the phrase, "Our truth, our trade, our peace, our wealth, our freedom."[19] One of the many petitions "declaring" for a free Parliament, demanding tax reform, and suggesting government reform asks that government "be mindfull for the quickning of Trade."[20] In June the king could have seen John Tatham's satirical *The Rump,* which included such acknowledgments of City ambitions as promises that "your cellars will become warehouses, your shops exchanges, and your mistresses persons of honor."[21] *London's Glory Represented,* the tribute arranged by the City for 5 July, mingled the sun and spring imagery with the same economic idea: Fame lamented that "they have not known / A sommer since your father left his throne" but now know that "you do their golden time revive."

Had Charles, Clarendon, or Walker been attentive, they might have prevented some of the consequences of their "defect in understanding." Every part of this event was planned, reviewed, and carried out by the City and drew upon the Lord Mayors' shows rather than the royal rituals. In fact, its title allied it with the name given to the Lord Mayors' shows immediately before and after it. *London's Glory Represented* suggested that it would present what the October shows took for granted in their productions of the successive versions of *London's Triumph Celebrated.* The 1661 show drew upon the 5 July and usual Lord Mayors' show titles with *London's Triumph Presented.*

The Lord Mayors' shows were major events in the people's lives, and their emotional significance was recognized even then. In 1659, during a time of rampant public disorder, the Grocers' Company wrote and met with the Court of Aldermen regarding the wisdom of mounting pageants and shows for their newly elected Lord Mayor. They feared that the large crowds might get out of control.[22] The Court responded with objections to any reduction of "the usual Showes" and concluded, "It is concerned the minds of the Citizens will be troubled at such a disappointment."[23] The Minute Book records Thomas Allen's denial of any feeling of intimidation and the decision to proceed (27 October).

As Steven Mullaney has said, London was already "a vast memory system, an extensive memory theatre."[24] Thomas Rugge wrote that there were twelve pageants set up in the streets between Temple Bar and the Guildhall.[25] Descriptions, and those quite sketchy, of only four and of one droll seem to have survived. Three of the pageants featured the emblematic speakers Time, Truth, and Fame. The fourth was of Industry and a group of carders and spinners. The Clothworkers' Company presented this tableau vivant, and each of the emblematic pageants also had a Livery Company sponsor (Skinners: Time; Clothworkers: Truth; Grocers: Fame). From these facts, it seems certain that the other eight pageants were also the productions of individual Companies and probably of the other eight "great" Companies. John Tatham's text matches the emblematic pageants, and the Merchant Taylors was set up at St. Paul's Chain near the Churchyard where Truth spoke and was classified as one of the two drolls, essential parts of the official "essay." These four Companies were allowed fifty-two riders, while the others had only twenty-four in the procession.[26]

The Grocers, who had invited the king to join their Company and whose Thomas Allen was the present Lord Mayor, sponsored the pageant at Cheapside, always the center of the London shows.[27] In addition to the speaking tableau with Fame, the second droll with the popular "Pretty and the tumblers" was there. The dedication to Thomas Allen in Tatham's *London's Glory Represented* notes that he had "served" Allen at his Lord Mayor's celebration. Rugge says that the procession lingered at Cheapside "som littl space" and that the king "beheld a famous pagien" there (163–64). Rugge's language suggests that the Cheapside tableau largely reproduced the Grocers' signature pageant, which represented the "four parts of the world" from which the grocers' commodities came. Even if the 1660 pageant was not a real reproduction, the fact that the Companies always included an emblematic representation of their crest and reused the expensive, carefully crafted figures, banners, and badges[28] would have made the pageants appear highly similar, especially to the ordinary observer whose memory would have been none too precise. In the same entertainment, the Clothworkers' pageant seems to have been a genuine repeat of the major pageant from their 1658 Lord Mayor's show. In both, Industry appeared with a ram (representing their crest), and the spinners and carders paused from miming their work to sing and dance.[29] Known for a bounteous cornucopia effect, lavish costumes, and skilled performances by professional actors hired for each occasion, the Grocers identified themselves with Commerce.[30] For those who had seen the pageant the October before in the same location, the equation of Fame with Commerce would be easy. The 1661 *Triumph,* although far more literary and unified, also includes a Cheapside scene with Europe and America "figured and habited in the fashion or manner of several Nations [whose] Trade . . . relates to *Europe*."[31] For this privilege the Grocers paid £270 to Common Council, the highest amount contributed by any Company for the entertainment.[32]

The most important artist for the entertainment was not Tatham, the writer and "City Poet," but Edward Jermyn (or Jerman, Jarman, or German), one of the City Surveyors. Succeeding committees for Lord Mayors' shows and other City entertainments met with him in the initial planning,[33] and he was the acknowledged historian and master of the inventory. He knew his job to be the expression of the City's traditions, symbols, and stories-in-progress. After the Great Fire, the Drapers and Fishmongers hired him to design and oversee the construction of their new halls. When Christopher Wren's and John Evelyn's plans for rebuilding the Royal Exchange proved impractical, Jermyn took over. His design, which included dozens of symbolic representations, was approved by the king and the City and then built under his supervision at a cost of about £70,000.[34] Queen Elizabeth, always linked with the nation's trade and prosperity in the minds and hearts of the City, occupied a commanding position in the tower and was given an equal place with Britannia in another place. Huge griffins bearing the City's arms in the manner of those on City badges and barges and a statue of Charles II at the center of the arcade linked past and present. Other emblems of the City and its Companies and statues that included Sir John Barnard, a living merchant, showed Jermyn's historical imagination.

A number of documents record payments to him for "ordering and composing the pageants," and the minute books show that the standard practice was for him to present designs and give progress reports.[35] For this major event, the Lord Mayor directed many of the Companies to make their entire inventory available to Jermyn, and he would often choose such pieces as the Clothworkers' lambs and griffins. He would disburse £400–500 even for Lord Mayors' shows, and his pay was always more than double Tatham's. The Haberdashers, for instance, paid him £30 "for his rare paines and oversight" in 1664 and "the Poett" (who was not even named) £12; the Clothworkers had paid him £65 and the Grocers £100.[36] Occasionally brief allusions to discussions over the number and choice of tableaux appear in the minutes, and, on at least one occasion, a newly elected Lord Mayor added an entire pageant without the committee's approval.[37]

The *praecipere* became more prominent and increasingly explicit. From the time of Elizabeth, Tatham and others held hopes of similar attention from their monarch and also sent them printed copies of the speeches. *The Royal Oake,* performed on 29 October, opened with a speech by Oceanus that invoked King James's name and observed, " 'Tis peace that barbs the billows, scumbs [*sic*] the foam, / Inviteth trade abroad, and brings it home" (98). The final speech, by Peace, promised, "Ceres shall cram your barns, and Bacchus crown / Your boles [*sic*], no more of penury be known / Trade, long since dead, reviv'd shall be again, / By th' vertual influence of your soveraign" (105–6). In the coronation pageant, *Neptune's Address,* Charles routs the whales that "persue / Not the Barque only, but the Traffick too; / By which *Trade* perish'd, all *Commerce* was barr'd." Similarly, Ogilby's *Entertainment* included a speech by Thames that described the river as "Exporting Yours, importing Foreign Goods" and rejoiced: "Now with full Joy she welcomes Your Return; / Your blest Return! by which she is restor'd / To all the Wealth remotest Lands afford" (104).

In the early months of his restoration, Charles made a number of visible and highly politic gestures toward the City. In the summer of 1660, for instance, he issued declarations to encourage the fishing trade and to build ships to employ the poor.[38] The Lords of Council wrote the Lord Mayor and Court of Aldermen:

[The king] haveing this day, taken into his Princely consideration, how necessary it is for the good of this Kingdome, that Trade and Commerce with foreyne parts, bee with all due care encouraged and maintained, And for the better Settling thereof, declared his gracious Intention to appoint a Committee of understanding able persons to take into their particular consideration all things conducible there-unto.

They asked for names from which the king could select a committee that "by their prudent and faithful Counsell and advice his Majesty may . . . insert into the Severall Treaties, such Articles & Clauses as may render this Nation more prosperous & flourishing."[39] In December it was duly appointed. Even the king's marriage showed concern for his interest. Catherine of Braganza's dowry included free trade with Brazil and the East Indies, a "treasure trove" for British merchants.[40]

In 1662, the existence of several variations of two compelling ideologies became painfully apparent. The processes of negotiation, which are quickly characterized by strife and turmoil but eventually result in a reestablished or adapted ideology, became highly visible in art as well as in social actions and institutions. Indeed, such highly unstable times produce notably original works of art, art that carries heightened interest because of its participation in the formation of what we now call public opinion. At this point I would like to examine in some detail three such dramatic compositions: Tatham's *Aqua Triumphalis,* the anonymous *London's Triumph: Presented in severall Delightfull Scenes,* and Robert Howard's *The Committee.*

In midsummer 1662, the City was ordered to stage a royal entrée for the new queen, Catherine of Braganza. In a series of directives, the Companies were ordered to be ready at half a day's notice; to prepare their barges with "banners, streamers, and other graceful ornaments"; to have their dress, regalia, and banners in splendid condition; and to "have attending on them by water something of Padgeantry relating to the mistery or such other signification as they shall think meete on the Day of Tryumph."[41] This demand—and it was a demand, as the Clothworkers' attempt to refuse demonstrates—meant that Companies had to hire or build a second barge, either for themselves or for their tableau.[42]

The City, urged by the court, designed an entertainment that would cost £1,202.4.11; the additional cost for the individual Company barges was paid by each Company. In addition, the Lord Mayor on the City's behalf presented the queen with a £1,000 gift, carefully converted into 20s. gold pieces in an embroidered purse of crimson velvet. When the purse and coin conversion were figured into the cost, the City's total was £1,100. The watermen, bargemaster, and food added another £144.10.2.[43]

This entertainment existed in a sea of resentment and resistance. A power struggle between the City and the king was in progress and evident. The king had been furious at the results of the first election of London M.P.'s in March 1661, and his efforts to influence future results in London and elsewhere were unconcealed.[44] At issue all over England were the rights and privileges vested in people by the City charters, many of which had been granted or enhanced during the Interregnum, and London's was no exception. In October 1661 the king informed the City that he would renew the Charter, but he had not done so, and officials knew that he intended to displace several of the aldermen.[45] Money was a major point of contention. In the spring of 1662, concrete evidence that the people were tired of lending the king large sums of money surfaced. He had asked for £200,000 in February, but by 15 April only £100,000 had been subscribed. The annoyed king demanded that the Court of Aldermen call a Common Council and work harder to raise it. The directive went on to order the Lord Mayor and City Chamberlain to appear in person "to certify" to the king their "farther endeavour to raise the remaynder."[46] The Excise and Hearth taxes were extremely unpopular in London, and both had been major disappointments to the king. In the wrangling over their inadequate revenues, the king accused the City of allowing citizens to report themselves dead.[47] On 17 August 1662, only six days before the queen's entry, the Nonconformist preachers were silenced.

The most conflicted feelings about the entrée, however, probably involved the woman to be celebrated. Ironically, the last queen to enter the City accompanied by barges and water pageants had been Anne Boleyn, and she had been greeted by stubbornly silent crowds.[48] Catherine of Braganza was Catholic, and many citizens suspected Charles of Roman Catholic leanings. Burnet wrote, "It was soon observed, that he was resolved not to marry a protestant" (1:283). One of the first acts of the Parliament had been to make calling him a Catholic a crime. Whether this was a "reward for his apparent fidelity to the Anglican Church during exile"[49] or a warning to him, such an act could only be imagined in a time of suspicion and fear. This foreign Catholic woman who spoke little English elicited a measure of sympathy, however, because Charles was forcing his favorite mistress on her. Not only had Lady Castlemaine taken up residence in Richmond near the honeymooning couple but she arranged a public christening for her second child by Charles, a son named Charles. When the king installed her as one of Catherine's Ladies of the Bedchamber, the new queen balked, and it became public knowledge that she and the king were already divided. Uncomplimentary ballads about Castlemaine, some assigning her part of the blame for the need for the Hearth Tax, already circulated, and now new ones made the rounds. Broadsheets with titles such as "Song to a Charming Fair One" protested the king's extravagance toward her. In mid-July, Charles's mother arrived with his son by Lucy Walker, the woman some believed Charles had married. As Ronald Hutton notes, this was "a nation which a scant twelve years before had made death the penalty" for adultery (189).

Thus, this entrée posed special difficulties for the City and illustrates the truth of Gramsci's insistence that ruling bodies depend upon public consent to their *moral* leadership. Physical complications comically glossed the deeper problems. For obvious reasons, the king was very slow in announcing the date of the progress. Moreover, the queen's progress would be down the Thames from Hampton Court to Whitehall, but the usual stationary pageants and lines of ceremonially dressed dignitaries and citizens were demanded.

The event finally took place on 23 August. The Company barges with their pageants in front of them moved slowly into position as crowds watched from the banks;[50] by noon, they were at Chelsea, positioned in a line forty to fifty yards from shore. Anchored at the prow and stern, they were viewed on their left by a steady stream of people in boats, while the right was reserved for the passage of the royalty and the official procession. The Company barges were sixty to eighty feet long with nine oars to a side. The bargemaster stood in the stern; banners and the seal decorated the prow, and there was a well for musicians at the front.[51]

Those who saw the barges reacted with delight. Some pageants mimed the trades: "the pageans that belonged to such a hall as the gold smiths [had] men at work to the life and that of the vinteners men draying of wine, a bar boy and bell at the bar and the motions used in that way." Others were emblematic: "that of the mercers, very curiously trimmed with virgins . . . the fishmongers was most noble—gilded and a great sea horse and the show of fishes to the life."[52] The Drapers featured a "grave" Roman magistrate accompanied by Loyalty ("a Grave Citizen, plain and decent"), Truth, Fame, and Honour. He carried the banners of England and Portugal in one hand and a sword to defend their rights in the other. The Merchant Taylors constructed an entire wilderness with camels, Indians, Moors, Faith, Hope, Charity, and a Pilgrim beside a gold lamb (the latter "alluding" to their patron, St. John). Each figure carried shields or banners with symbolic figures. For instance, Faith wore the colors of the sun and carried a shield decorated with the figure of a young man "endeavouring to fathom the Sea with a Staff, with this Motto, Nil Profundius."[53] Many of the barges carried some representation of a queen in state.

The three pageants that constituted Tatham's *Aqua Triumphalis* were at Chelsea, Lambeth, and Whitehall, respectively. Peter Mills, the Surveyor who had been responsible for the coronation structures, and the two experienced, official City Painters, Andrew Dacres and William Lightfoot, worked with Tatham and a committee appointed by the Lord Mayor and the Court of Aldermen. In spite of the demand that the Companies produce emblematic displays, they had permission to examine all of the Companies' existing pageants and figures and "to make choice of and fitt and trim upp with all expedition" those they found appropriate.[54] These pageants, then, were filled with familiar badges, banners, animals, and emblems of the City.

In this, his most elaborate and unified effort, Tatham joined pointed statements about trade with tributes to the queen. The increasingly obvious theme of trade in the City pageants and the shift in concentration of imagery from national industriousness and the symbols of Charles's restoration to the insistent image of the sea as a necessary part of Charles's kingdom and as the key to prosperity paralleled the growing strain between the king and some of his subjects. The first and third pageants featured sea chariots, the first carrying Isis and the latter Thetis. Isis, the principal goddess of Egypt and often identified with Aphrodite, Ceres, Venus, and the Phoenician Ashtoreth, had been worshiped in three ancient empires as the goddess of fertility. The part of the Thames River at Oxford was commonly called "Isis"; in the pageant she was identified as the wife of Tham, and she carried a cornucopia scepter. Thetis, chief of the Nereids, wore a triple crown representing her three roles, in Tatham's words, as mother of the gods, goddess of the sea, and empress of all rivers. In the visual art of the time, her wedding and representations of her bringing arms to Achilles from Hephaestus were popular subjects, and both were pertinent to the royal marriage. That she

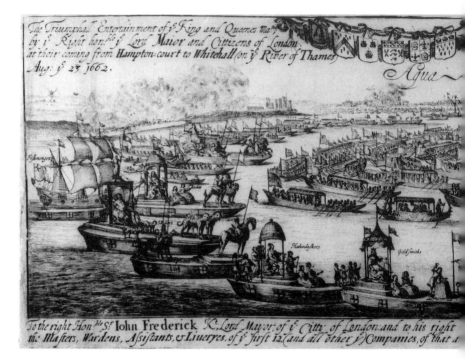

The Companies' decorated barges lined the Thames in honor of the new queen. The king's barge can be seen immediately behind the Merchant Taylors' barge. (Courtesy of Guildhall Library, City of London.)

was fated to bear a son mightier than his father expressed the nation's hopes for an heir to the throne but was not entirely complimentary to Charles. Gray-haired to show "the Antiquity of Navigation," Thetis expanded and concluded the themes introduced by Isis, who had prophesied, among other things, *"Plenty* in each house with freedom seen."[55]

The narrative moved from the narrow beginning of the Thames to the opening out to the vast oceans. The central pageant was built to represent a floating island decorated with a lion and a unicorn, a Scot and an Englishman, and the arms of England. Tatham's description of Tham emphasized its symbolism: he holds a trident in his right hand because he is viceroy to Thetis and is king of rivers, and his left hand holds a pitcher because he is son to Achelous, father of rivers, and grandchild to Oceanus. He is surrounded by nymphs—one wearing Greenwich Castle, the other Windsor Castle on her head (8).

Throughout this progress and in its two drolls, Tatham relentlessly

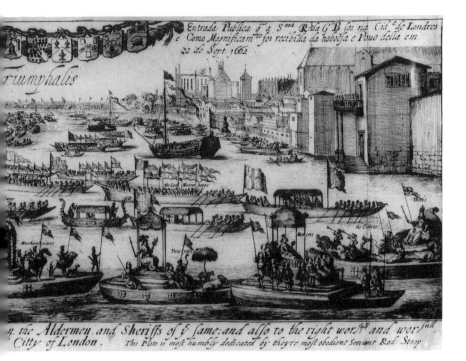

identified mastery of the seas with trade, which united the rich produce carried by all Britain's rivers to cosmopolitan London with its international trade. Sixty years later, Defoe would articulate a detailed vision of London as such a hub. Books such as *A Plan for the English Commerce* and *A Tour thro' the Whole Island of Great Britain* enumerated and praised the bounty pouring in from all over the nation and balanced that with catalogues of imported luxuries. Many cities, he wrote, "can send Ships Loaden out, but few can bring them Loaden home."[56] In Tatham's pageant, even the songs in the drolls advanced the idea. For example, the Watermen sang, "The King and Queen draw nigh . . . Like Hailstones from the Skie, / The Town to fill / And fears to kill / The Tradesmen had of breaking / Who scarce a pennie / Would spare to any" (4). These pageants make obvious structures of feeling extant in all of the Restoration entertainments. The coronation entertainment had used the Athenian bee, symbol of community and industry, and, at the second arch, the arms of the Merchant Adventurers and the Turkey and East India Companies. In places, even that *Entertainment* had approached the didactic as it presented elements of the commercial community's agenda for Charles. Gerard Reedy is surely correct to read a conditional into part of Thames's speech at the second arch:

> *King* Charles, *King* Charles, *great* Neptune of the Main!
> Thy Royal Navy rig,
> And we'll not care a Fig
> *For* France, *for* France, *the* Netherlands, *nor* Spain.

If Charles were to improve and deploy the Royal Navy, then England could become an economic power to be reckoned with.[57]

Shortly after the entry of Queen Catherine, the Clothworkers staged the Lord Mayor's show. The pageant for it, *London's Triumph: Presented in several Delightfull Scenes; both upon the Water and Land,* is both more original and more intricate than any other Restoration Lord Mayor's entertainment, and the signs of the strain of competing ideologies are unmistakable. On the one hand, the pageant insists upon the union of City and court; and, on the other, it pushes the *praecipere* to a new level of pragmatic advice. Highly unified and incrementally instructive, it departs from the usual form by bringing all of the pageants together after dinner in a scene in which they announce that they will give the meaning of each individual scene, and then do so.

The author, probably not John Tatham,[58] made much of the fact that Robinson was also the king's Lieutenant of the Tower of London:

> So faithful a *Lieutenant* of the *Tower,*
> You're now *Vicegerent* of the Civil Power.
> . . . .
>   in you
> This *City* meets Trade, Wealth, and Power too.
> And may with Reason bless this happy houre
> When *Mint* and *Magazine* are in your Power. (6)

These opening speeches take place at a representation "of Fortification, like the Tower of *London*" with warders, soldiers, and money-coiners miming their work and speaking. Insisting upon the mutual concerns and interests of the City and the court here, the pageant returns repeatedly to the theme. At the first pageant after the dinner, the poem to the king includes the lines, "Whil'st we employ our *Magazines* for you, /

And you to us have *yours* committed too! / Whil'st one do's rule the *City* and the *Tower,* / Plac't in your seat of *Justice* and of *Power*" (18).

The first speaker had been dressed as a soldier, and the pageant continues to break with the tradition that the speakers be personifications of virtues. The third speaker represents an Asian merchant and the fourth "a civilian," but it is the second that is most startling. For this pageant, which was at Cheapside and predictably presents the usual tableau of the working clothworkers, the central figure was Jack of Newbury, the man who allegedly introduced the making of broadcloth into Berkshire. As "the most considerable clothier (without fancy and fiction) England ever beheld,"[59] Jack was something of a "natural" choice for a Clothworkers' show. Since Jack was the subject of a popular novel by Thomas Deloney, of folk literature including a chapbook *The History of the Famous Clothier of England, called Jack of Newbury,* and in 1662 of an entry in Fuller's *Worthies of England,* the author could count on the audience's having some knowledge of him.[60] Aspects of his life could be used to reinforce the themes of "magazines" and of the mutual exchange of benefits. Like the City's "magazine," its store of money and capital, Jack's wealth could quickly be converted for the king's needs, as it had been when he had responded with 150 fully outfitted fighting men when asked for a quota of six. The king's "magazine," his military and his arms, defended Jack and his countrymen, and Jack was ready to respond. Also, according to Thomas Deloney's account of Jack's life, King Henry and Queen Katharine had given him and his workers valuable and useful gifts, and he had given his king a golden beehive.

Coincidental parallels between 1662 and the time of Jack offered the author opportunities for addressing the monarch. For instance, restrictions put on trade because of foreign wars were driving Jack and English clothworkers into poverty and unemployment; similarly, hostilities with Europe were adversely affecting Restoration trade. King Henry's proclamation that merchants "should freely traffic" on the Continent and in England returns Jack and the clothworkers to great prosperity, and the story offers Charles II an example.

The author of this pageant seems to have known Deloney's text as well as Thomas Fuller's retelling of the life in his *History of the Worthies of England* (1662), and the more the viewer or reader knows about Jack of Newbury the more subversive the message may seem. Jack, after all, instigated a census of clothworkers, and with 112 other leading clothiers accosted King Henry in St. James's Park with a petition asking for trade

relief. Struggling for its trade and the return of its charter, Newbury in
1662 was in the same "decayed" state as London and other major towns
and in a situation that might have sent Jack back to St. James's Park with a
petition.

The Jack of the pageant is carefully dressed in his russet coat, the sign
of his refusal to be knighted,[61] and he wears a dagger and purse, both
common to tradesmen. His clothing, however, gives mixed citizen-
cavalier-rustic signals, for he has a high-crowned hat with a rich jewel and
feathers, wears a sword, and has a ruff. Moreover, the author describes
him as in "Antick habit" and places him on the Clothworkers' ram,
"playing a bag-pipe and making sport" (7). This picture of a chapbook
Jack could remind auditors that Jack was known in his time for liberality
and keeping good company, but that he was also identified with fiscal
discretion; these were qualities in the king about which the City had
expressed concern and that it openly hoped would come to be balanced.[62] Again Deloney's text offers a startling gloss. Jack intrigues his
king by sending him a message that he is the Prince of Ants, who defends
the kingdom against "the force of the idle Butterflies" in their "golden
apparell" (27–28). Jack refuses to go to the king, pleading that it would
be dereliction of duty. Like the highest City officials, who awaited their
king upon his restoration, Jack imposes a hierarchy of values and an
ancient vision of the duties and prerogatives of "subjects." In Deloney's
story, Wolsey, who is always represented as richly dressed, resents Jack's
fable, is the enemy of trade, and is identified with the butterflies.[63]

King Henry's queen, Katharine of Aragon, was displaced by one of
her maids of honor, Anne Boleyn, whose royal entrée had also been by
water. *Aqua Triumphalis* had made much of Catherine of Braganza's
Christian name, the Haberdashers had reverted to earlier traditions to
feature St. Catherine in their pageant, and there were strikingly large
numbers of virgins and symbols of integrity and purity in the show. This
patroness of the Haberdashers had spoken eloquently and ineffectually
to the Alexandrine elders, but the broken wheel and ax on the float
reminded everyone of the superiority of her triumph. An especially rich
tradition of admonitory speeches surrounded St. Catherine, one developed during the time Thomas Heywood was City poet. In both 1631 and
1632, her character had made the speech giving moral and political
instruction to the Lord Mayor. Enumerating the virtues that the Lord
Mayor should strive to develop and embody, she carried the burden of
the moral theme in the public celebration.[64] These pageant elements may

have been covert commentary on the king's continued, public affair with Lady Castlemaine. The scandal of Lady Castlemaine's baby Charles, her desertion of her husband (known not to be the baby's father), and her move to Richmond near the king during his honeymoon unfortunately coincided with the unpopular Hearth Tax and the St. Bartholomew's Day ejection of Nonconformist clergymen.

After this show, St. Catherine became a common character in City shows. In 1664, for instance, a living St. Catherine dominated the Cheapside pageant. Although she carried the banner of St. George, she occupied the center of a scene described as "an Imperial Crown Garnished with *Festoons* and *Flowers*." Tatham titled his scene with St. Catherine "Hyroglyphick of Integrity," and the speech reminded the king that he was "both our *Triumph* and *Spectator*."⁶⁵

Additional evidence of the religious and moral concerns of the City is in the most unusual aspect of *London's Triumph,* the fourth pageant. Among the information that Fuller's *Worthies* gives about Jack is that he was responsible for the construction of part of St. Nicholas Church in Newbury.⁶⁶ This assertion provides a link to that stop. The Clothworkers' "Orders of Courts 1649–1665" for 9 December 1662 includes the following somewhat testy and, as far as I know, unique entry:

> Whereas at the Tryumph of Sr John Robinson Lord Mayor of this Cittie there was a Padgeant erected representing and alludeing to St Paules Church by order of the sd Sr John Robinson without any consent of this Company. Yet notwithstanding out of the respect the Company owes to the said Sir John The Court have this day ordered that the expense and charge of the said Padgent shall be borne . . . by Mr. Warden Edwards out of money in his hands.

The Quarter and Renter Warden accounts show £365.19.10, an unremarkable sum, transferred to Edwards "for shews and tryumphs due him for Robinson's Ld Mayors Show" and a number of smaller expenses, including £20 for Jermyn "for his paynes and care" "in ordering & composing" the pageants and show and £8.13.4 to the ordinance in the Tower.⁶⁷ There were signs of Company ambivalence; the minutes show that a number of men refused to contribute to the triumph or to be in the procession, and a dispute over payment to the chief painters dragged along for months and in March had to be referred to the Painter Stainers Company for arbitration (16 March 16 $\frac{62}{63}$). An entry in the Calendar of State Papers, Domestic, for the previous March notes that "at the City election, the other candidates, viz. the Recorder, Sir John Robinson, Sir Rich Ford . . . had almost none to speak for them. . . . The taking away of purveance and the Court of Wards, and laying the tax on the excise are much disliked in the City, but none of their members opened their mouths against them."[68]

This controversial addition to the plans approved by the Clothworkers' original committee features several speakers who give the history of St. Paul's Cathedral and insistently ask the king to repair it. St. Paul's, originally dedicated by King Ethelbert in 604 for Mellitus, one of St. Augustine's missionaries, had been rebuilt as a gothic cathedral of Caenstone during the time of William the Conqueror and his son. Larger than the present St. Paul's, it had the tallest spire "ever to have been built."[69] During a thunderstorm on 3 June 1561, the steeple burned and its lead roof "poured down like lava." The roof had been repaired, but the steeple was not rebuilt. By 1628, extensive repairs under the direction of William Laud, bishop of London, and Inigo Jones, the King's Surveyor, were under way; King Charles I personally paid for the portico. During the Commonwealth, Parliament seized the £17,000 fund and used it to pay their troops; Cromwell used the cathedral as cavalry barracks, rented the Jones portico for shops, and sold the silver vessels to buy artillery.

Placed at the west end of Cheapside, the site from which the king ordinarily watched the show, the first speech addresses Robinson: "My Lord. This *Church* we justly in your *Triumph* shew, / Since none can see it without shame, but you." The speech continues, recounting that when kings and the nation "forsook" it, his uncle repaired it; the second speech recites the history of the cathedral and repeats the request for repairs. The final speeches, performed by the "Genius loci," were intended to be spoken to the king. These speeches compare the time when "my tow'ring Height, and loftier spire / Mated the Stars" with its present "ravaged" state and, by implication, Charles II to Ethelbert. Charles is told that *"London* is now your Chamber, and your fort, / And you are here but in a larger Court" (17–18).

The request is the most concrete and immediate of any surviving *praecipere,* and it offers a way for the king to make a highly visible gesture of love toward the Anglican Church at a highly propitious moment. The history of St. Paul's can be woven into the Jack of Newbury story in a variety of ways and with suggestive results. In Deloney's account of Jack, Wolsey accuses Jack of being tainted with Luther's ideas. The Newbury of 1662 was still torn by "disturbances," many suspected to be caused by the Nonconformist element; very recently, Benjamin Woodbridge, a Presbyterian, had been displaced as the moderator of Westminster Assembly. During Wolsey's struggle with Henry over the divorce of Queen Katharine, St. Paul's had fallen into severe disrepair; but, after the resulting Reformation, it had been repaired and had become England's national cathedral, the symbol of the union of Church and Protestant state. Thus, the pasts of Jack and the Cathedral work to associate the restoration of St. Paul's with a Protestant cause, one shaded by conflict with Wolsey and modern fears of Catholicism.

It was traditional for the king to receive the text of the speeches and some description of the scenes before Lord Mayor's Day; sometimes the printed edition was already available. The king's unexplained and unexpected absence may be attributable to the content of this pageant. Not only was Robinson his Lieutenant of the Tower, a public servant he cared enough about to have christening gifts sent to his children, but the house and refreshments were prepared and waiting for the king.[70] Had the king been present, concrete expectations might have been raised and also damaging comparisons would have been invited. His physical presence would have made the "triumph" and "spectator" tangible. Indeed, Jack of Newbury's monarch, Henry VIII, might call to mind both kings' many adulteries.

Yet Robinson and the other proponents of the repair of St. Paul's seem to have had some limited success. In 1663, a large Commission, headed by Robinson and composed of most of the major Court and City officials, was given responsibility for the restoration of the church. Charles's financial pledge was the arrears of rents and the profits of all impropriations and ecclesiastical livings not pardoned by the Act of Indemnity.[71] Not only were there few left unpardoned after the Act, no provisions for collection were built in. In another symbolic gesture, he urged judges of the prerogative courts and others to "take especial Care, out of such Moneys as shall from time to time fall into their power . . . to remember that some *convenient* proportion thereof be assigned" for St. Paul's (emphasis mine, 14). The pageant, however, made a startling gesture within an original framework aimed at providing Charles with a powerful propaganda strategy.

In spite of this intrusion, the 1662 pageant celebrates trade more insistently than the other early Restoration Lord Mayors' shows and, like the prose lives of Jack of Newbury, hammers home the value the cloth-working industry has for the nation as a whole. In both, English prosperity is tied to this trade. Jack is characterized as having "set continually five hundred poor people at work," both actions having great contemporary resonance. Deloney's prose fiction, like the pageant, trumpets unity: "This sore of necessity can no way be cured but by concord; for like as the flame consumes the candle, so men in discord waste themselves." The third pageant, a rigged and manned ship, surrounded and loaded with symbols of trade, extends these themes to the wider trading world. One of the Asians leading a camel says, "May Trade encrease, all things propitious be, / And this year prove a year of Jubile" (13). After the Guildhall dinner, two more pageants perform; then all of the pageants gather at Clothworkers' Hall and the chief actors in a quite unusual finale speak to one another. Here Jack of Newbury is further identified as loyal and prudent but liberal, the exemplar of "an Heroick mind," and each speaker recites virtues and skills that will together make England prosperous and great.

The finale begins with stage directions that will make Robinson the visible representation of the virtues and desires that the emblematic speakers and their words are bringing together: "His Lordship riseth up between them, but being come to the center of the Pageants, is entertained by the four speakers" (19). Appropriately, Jack of Newbury, the most illustrative of the special civic duties of the City's merchant element, begins. Celebrating loyalty, liberality, and charity, Jack, employer of hundreds, champion of the clothworkers' trade, and, according to Deloney, one who could forgive a debt, set the debtor up in business, and reap a profit, states didactically: "Whatever we present, in you are met" (20). The soldier contributes fortitude, prudence, temperance, patience, and vigilance; the church, religion; and the Asian, "knowledge that no Magistrate should miss," specifically arithmetic, fortification, and "bold Astronomy." These speeches are more dense and more allusive than ordinary Lord Mayors' entertainment speeches. "Ours the Maritime part, which though it treat / Of Trade, doth give to Navigation heat," the Asian says. Here concisely captured is the sense of the size and importance of trade's association with navigation as well as of the relationship between merchants and those who build, finance, and sail ships and those who protect the commercial fleet. Once more the City, the hub of English trade, becomes the life force that animates and supports yet another necessary element of English prosperity. As Tatham's and Ogilby's oak conceits had, these lines could suggest the intimate and mutually dependent relationship between the merchant and the military fleets.

Although addressed to Robinson, who actually stood in the traditional position of the person to be both blessed and charged in numerous English religious-civic ceremonies, the pageant finale offered instruction about the City and, by extension, about the ideal virtues of magistrates, Charles being the supreme magistrate. At this time, as John Reresby says, the king "did not soe much trouble himselfe with business,"[72] and the unusual detail in the pageant's citing of practical knowledge and of concrete, timely actions to take are signs of the demands that educated, successful people were beginning to make upon their king. In the passage Reresby comments, "The kingdom at this time was very rich." Compared to France perhaps it was, and for the king and courtiers who had struggled for money and even resorted to humiliating appeals for financial help, the change was dazzling. Restoration men of the City, however, were experiencing and describing conceptions of prosperity, autonomy, and possibility that, joined to the clamors of towns and representatives of trade, challenged the smooth, glittering surface of Charles's spectacle of kingship.

Charles's Christmas message, which reaffirmed his intentions to support religious toleration even of Catholics, increased the doubts intensified by his marriage regarding the sincerity of his Anglicanism.[73] By the next autumn, the Parliament of 1663 had made tensions between the king and his people painful. Disputes over whether the Act of Uniformity had rendered void the Declaration of Breda, over money, and over the Triennial Act, as well as the introduction of a bill to prevent the sale of offices, had put Charles in a defensive and even supplicating position.[74]

In 1663, the Cheapside pageant provocatively featured Albion surrounded by representations of London, York, Bristol, Leeds, and other chartered cities. This pageant might have reminded spectators that this was no new idea. Mildmay Fane's *Candy Restored* (1641) had celebrated mixed government in a somewhat similar way. Three ailing women, Albinia, Ibernia, and Caledonia, represented England, Ireland, and Scotland. Cured by Dr. Psunodarke, a figure representing Parliament, they declared themselves "monopolye and project free," issues then being addressed in the recently convened Long Parliament. Rather than celebrating the monarch, Albion in the Cheapside pageant hailed the return of "Religion, Liberty, and Laws."[75] This pageant juxtaposed reminders of recent events and what has been called the Norman Yoke myth. In his struggle for control of his country, Charles had skirmished with many of the corporations. He had, for example, begun *quo warranto* proceedings against Bristol and forced an entirely new council on Leeds. The Corporation Act set up commissions with the power to remove town councilors at will; shortly before this Lord Mayor's show, the provision that office holders had to take Anglican communion as well as the oaths went into effect.[76]

Notable in this and in much of the City pageant rhetoric from the earliest days of the Restoration are references to "liberty," which is inseparably linked to religion and to law. In his analysis of the Revolution, Cibber asserts, "though [James] might be too hard for our Laws, he would never be able to get the better of our Nature; and that to drive all *England* into Popery and Slavery he would find would be teaching an old Lion to dance." He goes on to say that "the People of *England*" "had many successful Contests with their Sovereigns for their *ancient Right* and *Claim* to it," but "I doubt it will be difficult to fix the period of their having . . . full Possession of what, 'till then, we never had more than a perpetually contested Right to."[77] Cibber's faith in "our nature" is part of the Norman Yoke theory. There is a strain in English literature and history that consistently holds that some group often designated metaphorically as the English yeoman bears good sense and will assert itself in time of great national danger. Eighteenth-century thinkers offered various explanations, but the faith in what John Locke called the "law of opinion" and Edmund Burke "real public wisdom" continued to be seen as the bulwark of the ancient (and largely mythical) constitution, of laws, morality, and religion, and it could assert itself in group actions ranging from petitions to riots. As E. P. Thompson said, "It is possible to detect in almost every eighteenth-century crowd action some legitimizing notion. . . . The men and women in the crowd [believed] that they were defending traditional rights or customs; and, in general, that they were supported by the wider consensus of the community."[78]

No better statement of this myth of the people and the Norman Yoke can be found than in Richard Steele's *Englishman*. According to Steele's history, which was given in a series of December 1713 essays, the Norman invasion aroused the people to "assert their ancient just Rights," and he counts among these "Freedom in Religion" and "in Property, in being subject to no Laws to which we have not ourselves assented."[79] Edmund Burke would subscribe to this concept, locate it in the ancient Saxon culture, and say that "customs" operate "better than laws, because they become a sort of Nature both to the governors and governed" and that authority could never be "stretched to despotism; because any despotic act would have shocked the only principle by which that authority was supported, by the general good opinion."[80] John Locke had said that he did not know what would "hinder" the people from asserting their rights, and Steele uses charged, gendered language to caution them: in England, he says, the "Manly Government" common to the northern European tribes survives, but "if hereafter this Nation should so far lose its Virtue . . . there will not be wanting evil Ministers" to enslave them (no. 28). This was, as Christopher Hill says, both a patriotic and a class theory.[81] It actually lodged good sense (not common sense, to use Gramsci's distinction) in the people, in the honest English yeoman who throughout history had never forgotten their Anglo-Saxon rights, had maintained determined vigilance, and whenever necessary had fought for their return. Belief in these rights, because shared by all the people regardless of social position, probably undergirds the kind of nearly ritualized political crowd behavior described in the work of Tim Harris, Nicholas Rogers, E. P. Thompson, and Roger Shoemaker. All find evidence that the people believed that they were defending legitimate rights in legitimated ways. Shoemaker, for instance, points out how men and women rushed to a disturbance, "investigated it," and, if they sympathized, joined it.[82] Shoemaker calls the Lord Mayor's show "politically sponsored demonstration," and the celebration of "civic pride and merchant grandeur" served to remind the people and the court of the power and rights vested in the people.[83] This pageant's prominent celebration of "Liberty" was a code word with rich associations and a covert call for resistance to arbitrary government, arbitrary taxation, and encroachments on conscience.

By 1664, the framing pageants of the Lord Mayor's show featured tradesmen and merchants and militant speeches that eclipsed those of the 1662 entertainment, startling as it had been. At St. Paul's, the central figure dressed as "a grave Citizen" warned, "Birth may advance, or may not, but We see / *Labour* and *Art* raise Men to *Dignitie*" (6); at Bow Church, a merchant said that "Examples of publique *good* . . . claim a greater Privilege than Blood," and "in a word / A *vertuous Man* sounds better than *my Lord*" (14). As Steven Mullaney has reminded us, places are endowed with meaning and power, and, as open as they are to new and even antithetical associations, they are the possessions of memory, which is tenacious and inseparably linked to lived and felt experiences.[84]

In 1660, 1661, and 1664, the king watched the Lord Mayor's procession from a house overlooking the Cheapside pageant site.[85] By 1663 he could have recognized that, although Whitehall and even Charing Cross were his, Cheapside had reverted to the City. Cheapside would never be the king's.

Even though Charles had given two courtiers a monopoly of the London royal theaters, opposition ideologies began to emerge there as well as in the City entertainments. Robert Howard's *The Committee* is a third play of 1662 that captures the ambivalences and complexities of the moment. Ironies abound when its composition is considered. Its author happened to be a member of the seven-person royal Commission for Concealed Lands charged with "recovering" the king's lands,[86] and *The Committee* dramatizes the hardships and injustices perpetrated by Cromwell's Committee of Sequestration. The play shows the pain of troubled consciences faced with the requirement to subscribe to the Solemn League and Covenant at the moment when thousands of ministers and others were losing their livelihoods over the oaths of allegiance and supremacy and the Act of Uniformity. He had been knighted at Newbury and imprisoned in Windsor Castle but had negotiated successfully with the Commonwealth government for the return of his father's lease of the Post Fines (1657). Howard was from a distinguished family that included William Cecil, Lord Burghley, and was a courtier whom Pepys credited with gaining £20,000 from the king. Yet he would write a play that Pepys interpreted as so critical of the king's adulteries as to warrant interruption,[87] would support the Glorious Revolution, and would become one of King William's Commissioners of the Fleet. The play is a well-constructed city comedy, and, although it includes some commonplace elements of the Royalist plays, it also effects a utopian dream—a blending of people, an end to hostility.

The relationship of *The Committee* to *The Rump, Cutter of Coleman-Street,* and other Restoration satires of the Cromwellians is obvious. Howard levels the same accusations of avarice and hypocrisy and to a great extent uses the same characters in the same ways.[88] His satire of them is certainly as virulent and unpleasant. His sympathetic treatment of the Cavaliers is of a piece with these plays, but there are major differences. Howard, a more skillful dramatist and by 1662 part of a group of playwrights who collaborated formally and informally, created somewhat deeper characters with the potential for expressing more of the experiences and emotions of the Cavaliers. Blunt rises to real poignancy in lines that capture mingled anger, outrage, and grief when he says, "Then farewell acres, may the dirt choak them." Howard makes the Cavaliers seem to be exiles in their own country. Faced with demands, oaths, rules, and codes of conduct as foreign to their own past as those of an alien nation, confronted by kitchen maids turned ladies, and arrested without warrants, they consider real exile; at one point in the negotiations, Careless exclaims, "Why then hoist sails for a new world." Occasionally their lines are direct expressions of this experience in Cromwell's world; Careless says to Mr. Day, "This is strange, and differs from your own principles" (71).

Howard cleverly uses Teague to develop this aspect of the play. It is he, not the Cavaliers, who are the exiles abroad; and, as an Irishman, a lower-class person, and a Royalist, his position is triply estranged. Like the Roundhead women in Restoration plays, he says and does what they are too initiated, polite, or circumspect to do. He laughs at Mrs. Day's pretensions and pronounces to her, "You are a foolish, brabble-bribble woman, that you are" (79) and wishes "your ladyship" and "kitchenship" to the devil (80). As the naive outsider, he can express wonder at the hypocrisy he encounters, can take literally what is said, and therefore can expose the distance between words and meaning, words and actions. His statements about his dead master might be felt by a person of higher station about Charles II. Like the Cavaliers, with the loss of his master he has no occupation and is seeking a new economic and social place. As both Hume and Scouten point out, the Cavaliers had been forced into economic and social competition with "this new Gentry," the rising and increasing merchant class that would continue to be associated with Nonconformist religion and Whig conceptions of the monarchy.[89]

The Cavaliers are, as Susan Staves and others have said, idealized: they "take oaths seriously, reject material considerations for the pursuit of their ideals, and are finally rewarded with both money and women."[90] They take the stance that no matter what happens, they will remain essentially the same and will continue to resist; Careless asks Ruth, "D'ye think a prison takes away blood and fight?" (107) Yet there are jokes that may be signs of a critique of the myth of the gallant Royalist. For example, the given name of the Cavalier character called "Careless" is Charles.

In any event, this Cavalier myth is preserved by an even more inspired structural element than Teague: the character of Ruth. She functions as a bridge between the Days and the Cavaliers, and it is her energy and ingenuity—and willingness to coerce and blackmail—that rescue the Cavaliers and bring about the happy ending. She also bears the weight of a major theme: that it is hard to identify and classify people in repressive times. She is a wonderful mimic and actress; once she acts Blunt to perfection (77) and in a virtuoso episode coaches Abel in a mock-courtship scene (60–61, 65–66). The Days, who have appropriated more than adopted her, think her obedient and enlist her in such causes as tutoring Abel in the art of lovers' language; Careless, who loves her, cannot believe that she is not the Days' daughter. In one of the most complex scenes in the play, he asks her, "Do but swear then, that thou art not the issue of Mr. Day; and tho' I know 'tis a lie, I'll be content to be cozened, and believe" (89); and again, "do but swear me into a pretence" (108). He asks her to do for love what he cannot do for property. She does, and he responds, "Poor kind perjured pretty one, I am beholden to thee; wouldst damn thyself for me?"

By housing the unwillingness to swear in the man, by having Careless willing to accept *her* love of him as worth damnation, Howard uses gendered categories to illustrate additional contradictions inherent in oath taking. By that time, however, the audience and Ruth know that she is the daughter of a Royalist, and her oath is honest. Things are not what they seem to Careless, and Careless calls himself, rightly, a compounder. Like *Epicoene* and *The Scornful Lady, The Committee* through Ruth gives the audience the pleasure of knowing that things are as they ought to be. Like Epicoene and Welford, who can move successfully in both the male and female worlds, Ruth can move in both the Puritan and the Cavalier societies. That she must steal documents and use threats in the Days' world has usually been described as making her look clever and practical, but there is no denying the fact that Careless and Blunt, not Ruth, survive as the idealistic people of uncompromising honor.

The contrast between the Royalist men and women is suggestive of social change, including the reassessment of the position of women and the formation of clearly defined public and private—or, in Gramsci's terms, political and civil—spheres. As they had in earlier plays and pamphlets, female characters represent unauthorized behaviors and structures of feeling. The earlier women were objects of ridicule because they aspired to influence in the public sphere; Ruth and Arbella are almost wholly concerned with the private, domestic sphere. Their goals are not power, wealth, or the welfare of the state but happy marriages and economic security. They have a strong sense of property and of justice, but at the end, their power and property belong to Blunt and Careless. They are, in short, in no danger of making honor an idol, as Day accuses the Cavaliers of doing (71). The conclusion returns them to the position that is "right," to the way the world ought to be, both in the public sense of property and in the private sense of marriage. Tellingly, the closing lines of the play are the male character's pronouncements and commands.

Ruth represents yet another contrast to the Royalist men: while the men have been away with the army or even across the channel, the women have had to live and, therefore, make compromises with the victors at home. As Margaret George demonstrates, they coped "with ingenuity, intelligence, and courage" (38–39). The way the Days have appropriated Ruth and her property and that Arbella must petition for hers would have been familiar to the audience. Lieutenant Story's praise of his wife gives a glimpse of the life of such women: "A most violent cavalier," she has traded food and tobacco for news of the army.[91] In order to survive, Ruth and women like her wait their chances, and the code that emerges is that the Days commit active evil, actually introducing evil into the human community, while she and her friends merely take advantage of others' evil. By committing adultery and forgery, the Days become vulnerable, the objects of the kinds of "biter bit" jokes popular in English folklore.

Ruth's character serves to bring out the uncompromising rigidity of the Cromwellians and the Cavaliers. Both groups seem to be hypnotized by the past and adhere stubbornly to prejudices and positions.[92] Unlike the men on both sides who act out the moods of those who have known oppression, injustice, and defeat, Ruth is one of the first of a group of characters that would be part of the construction of the myth of the Cavalier woman. Left alone to face hardship and even, perhaps, an army, this clever woman shared the men's loyalty and flair and enjoyed "playing the man." The Cavalier has been described as that "merry, fearless, improvident good fellow," "that perennial gallant, wearing with an air his tattered finery, and cracking broad jests with his penniless comrades."[93] Merry, fearless, and even gallant, the Cavalier woman would be far from improvident. John Lilburne praised his wife's Civil War efforts for the "gallant and true masculine spirit" that she displayed.[94] They can stand firm, but they prefer to fight with persuasion and, if necessary, flanking maneuvers rather than direct confrontation. Arbella says, "I have no need to compound for what's my own," but she recognizes that the Days are "marriage-jobbers" and joins Ruth's scheme (54, 65).

In language and gesture, the Cavalier woman, like her male counterpart, could soar above the wealthy cits, and characters like Ruth often appear to have the allegedly feminine ability to reconcile others. In Howard's play, however, a crucial element in reconciliation is missing: the Days do not love Ruth. Just as Mirabell in *The Way of the World* ends Fainall's threat with coercive power, so does Ruth end the Days' menace. In the Restoration dramatic world as much hate and hostility exist as love, and Mirabell cannot rekindle what, if any, affectionate or friendly feelings the Fainalls held for each other. Ruth may release Abel and offer the Days £500, but absent is the good nature of later plays that end with characters saying and accepting, "Come, forgive . . ."

Pepys had commented on Castlemaine's behavior at the queen's entrée: "her Lord and her upon the same place, walking up and down without taking notice one of another; only, at first entry, he put off his hat and she made him a very civil salute"; her running down, alone "of all the great ladies," to see if a child had been hurt in the street, "which methought was so noble"; "one there, booted and spurred, that she talked long with. And . . . being in her haire, she put on his hat . . . it became her mightily" (3:175–76). The gestures of this woman being watched watching her rival's grand celebration and knowing she is watched were bold and theatrical. Later, Aphra Behn would have one of her many unconventional women characters say that she was "pleased with the cavalier in herself."[95] Ruth, whose metaphors come from war more often than from the home, has felt the Cavalier in herself before her identity is confirmed.

Throughout history, women have played different roles during wars and have emerged envisioning themselves differently, and the dramatists of the Restoration found the myth of the Cavalier woman attractive, useful, and the stuff of good theater. Etherege's women, for instance, seek adventure, have wit and independent spirits, and considerable flair. All of these heroines are distinguished as much by their alertness to trickery and to opportunity as by their more recognized dashing, witty personalities. Etherege's Gatty and Ariana are never the victims of the forged letters; Wycherley's Hippolita admonishes herself, "Courage, Hippolita, make use of the only opportunity thou canst have to enfranchize thy self . . . shift for thy self." Within a short time, this heroine was a firmly established type, and the clear association with the Cavalier mind and experience lingered. Gatty and Ariana were surely in Behn's mind when she created Florinda and Hellena, and Thomas Durfey's Phillipa, not the hero, is the one who has the needed money to send to Charles II (*The Royalist,* 1682).

A brief comparison between Howard's play and Cowley's *The Cutter of Coleman-Street* indicates the superior degree to which Howard was in touch with his audience's sentiments and also something of the distance they had traveled. *Cutter* had opened about thirteen months before *The Committee* and had been, according to Dennis, "barbarously treated" the first night; in the printed edition, Cowley had felt it necessary to deny that it satirized the "King's party."[96] Cowley, unlike Howard, lets Colonel Jolly marry Widow Barfebottle ("a pretended Saint") to get back his estate and Cutter her daughter in order to get the rest. Moreover, Cutter and Worm are *pretending* to have been officers in the royal army, and Cutter has escaped Worcester in disguise. It had been, as Downes says, "not a little injurious to the Cavalier Indigent Officers" (57). Two years later, John Wilson could write of his similar characters that they were "no wise strange to any man that knew this town between the years '46 and '50." Burnet would write cynically, "The herd of the cavalier party" is "now very fierce, and full of courage over their cups, though they had been very discreet managers of it in the field, and in time of action. But now every one of them boasted that he had killed his thousands."[97] In 1661, however, the audience wanted an idealized, even somewhat sentimental Cavalier who would not go so far as to marry the enemy.

Howard's prologue insisted that he had tried "to show some newer-fashioned stuff" (50). In this play, the audience found a wealth of lived experience, but also saw the utopian image emerging. The Royalist characters are genuinely cooperative and caring; for instance, several converge on the prison to rescue Careless, and the soldiers within help. The resolution of the play goes beyond what could be dismissed as part of the sympathetic portrait of the Cavaliers to deliver a glimpse of a dreamlike ending: a blending of people, an end to hostility, a harmonious dance for the king. Everyone dances and the cavaliers insist repeatedly, "we are all friends."[98] Fredric Jameson has said that the effectively ideological must have a utopian dimension and that it rouses and then harnesses authentic desires in the people. He has also pointed out, however, how powerfully the Censor acts.[99] It is not surprising, then, that Howard's rendering of experience is more accessible to modern readers than the hint of harmony. Throughout the play, characters have said that their positions are irreconcilable; at the end, Mrs. Day says to her husband, "that they may *perceive* we are friends, dance" (emphasis mine, 117). Obadiah, who has been led in wearing a hangman's rope and must dance the woman's part with Teague, says nothing at all.

Both the burden and the hope of reconciliation are housed, then, in the Royalists, and yet there is no king. No character comes in to announce the coming of General Monk or the restoration of the king. The very fact that the king, even one distant in space or time, does not serve as *deus ex machina* suggests the crumbling of the Stuart conception of the power of the sovereign. This play goes beyond questioning the king as the supreme power and symbol of the nation to finding dubious his power to unite and mediate. Perhaps Howard saw that in a play whose characters are all gentry or below, such intervention would be jarring; perhaps the Howard who in that very year as the king's Serjeant Painter was paid such sums as £84.4s. for "guilding and paynting colouring and mending" a small boat was having enough contact with ordinary citizens to sense the powerlessness of the kingship to heal the deep divisions between people.[100] Many Restoration and eighteenth-century plays took up problems not yet resolved in the culture, and many elided the lack of true resolution with a dance.[101] In doing so, the playwright could give his audience a glimpse of a utopian hope, even as the representation of lived experience dominates and ideology appears intact. This play is no exception.

Perhaps at no time in English history have the court and the theater been so close, and few men have been so sure of the king as audience as the court dramatists of 1660–62. Charles attended regularly, suggested plays he wanted translated or adapted, and took a personal interest in the managers, players, and playwrights. Just as City pageants conceived of Charles as "Triumph and Spectator," therefore both spectacle and student, so the patent theater constructed him and other powerful men. Dryden spoke for all of them: "Poets, while they imitate, instruct. The feign'd Heroe inflames the true: and the dead vertue animates the living. . . . that kind of Poesy which excites to vertue the greatest men, is of greatest use to humane kind."[102]

So small and close-knit were the professionals and the audience that plays abounded with in-jokes. References so slight as to Howard's playing trap-ball at school or impersonations of, for instance, Sir Charles Sedley could be effective.[103] The king, the duke of York, and the earl of Oxford let Betterton, Harris, and Price wear their coronation suits in Davenant's *Love and Honour*. Years later, Dryden captured one example of the reciprocal relationship between court and dramatic content in his epilogue to *The Pilgrim* (1700): "Perhaps the Parson [Collier] stretch'd a point too far, / When . . . He tells you, That this very Moral Age / Receiv'd the first Infection from the Stage. But sure, a banisht Court, with Lewdness fraught, / The Seeds of open Vice returning brought." The earl of Chesterfield selected this period as the perfect example of the result of a stage "made subservient to the politics and the schemes of the court only," where "whatever man, whatever party, opposes the court in any of their most destructive schemes, will, upon the stage, be represented in the most ridiculous light the hirelings of a court can contrive." Chesterfield uses the portrayal of Cavaliers, dissenters, and City "knaves," "usurers," and "cuckolds into the bargain" as a concrete example. He makes clear the transfer of attitudes and taste from court to playwright.[104]

Yet in the royal theaters, too—and even after a difficult near-hiatus of eighteen years—traditions and an indigenous core of people existed and assured that the structures of feeling in the larger culture would be expressed within the plays produced. Modern critics have generally underestimated the potential of Howard's play for the repeated release of its political content.[105] As late as 1797 it was adapted as *The Honest Thieves* by Thomas Knight. William Morrice describes a performance in Oxford in July 1686 in which the reason Teague might hang Obadiah was that "he has changed his religion." The audience received this modification in the text with "a great Stamp, and a universal acclamation continuing for a great while." Morrice says he was told that the play was interpreted as a reflection upon Obadiah Walker, master of University College, Oxford, who had "turned Papist." Morrice remarks, "It seems the Players have done a great deale for their Religion but what has the University done. Publicans and Sinners are more concerned to keepe Popery out than they."[106] Morrice's entry speculates that the players chose that play at least partly for its political thrust. Such an interpretation, which requires translating the Puritans into Catholics, is, in fact, not far from Richard Steele's characterization of the play. Sir Roger de Coverley calls it "a good Church of *England* Comedy."[107]

Although the play immediately became a repertory piece, it enjoyed an especially large number of revivals between the 1717–18 and 1720–21 seasons, the years of the Bangorian controversy and of the heated debate over the repeal of the Occasional Conformity and Schism acts. Giles Jacob wrote, "The *Committee* has lately been forbid to be acted, the Audience turning some Scenes of it, by Party Interpretations, to Times they never were intended to represent."[108] At the time Jacob wrote, evidence abounds that the audience came to plays ready to find political meanings;[109] the 1718–19 season had seen riots over both *The Nonjuror* and *Cato*. Hans Robert Jauss emphasizes the importance of the "specific disposition" of the audience, what it brings to the performance that helps shape the interpretive reception.[110] That they expected political comment predetermined their reaction to plays, especially when the authors were courtiers of Charles II, the future poet laureate, or a secretary of state. These 1718–19 plays, however, like *The Committee, Hudibras,* and other 1662 works, exhibit the signs of texts produced at moments when a culture is renegotiating ideology and, therefore, tend toward becoming Marco de Marinis's "open texts," or at least toward including ambiguous and unresolved elements.[111] The popularity and reaccentuation of Howard's play serves as a crude gauge of the longevity of the religious and social divisions born in the mid-seventeenth century.

The public performances of 1662—street pageants, processions, royal theater productions—articulate the pattern of the negotiation of a stabilizing ideology that is common to all traumatized societies. Almost from the moment of the first true Restoration performances, the processes of refinement, competition, and selection and rejection of symbols and myths are visible. Although unarticulated, humankind's most essential questions are at stake: What is both "right" and "natural"? What is "the way the world is"? and, What determines the legitimacy of authority?[112] From these questions spring a series of crucial subpoints, such as, Is authority "naturally" vested in the people or in the monarch? and, Is the monarch the state?

Clifford Geertz has argued that politics is one of the "principal arenas" in which the structures that give meaning and shape to experience are constructed—therefore, negotiated.[113] The drama of the Restoration illustrates the transformation of the people's conception of their duty as citizens from acting with "public spirit" (a "political task" aimed at common goods such as contributing to war efforts) to being "public opinion," that is, adding responsibility for participating in an evaluative process (a "civic task" characterized by debate).[114] Thus, in these early performances we can find evidence of the beginning of the conception of Habermas's public sphere. In the first months of the Restoration, the intensity of Charles's spectacles and the people's hopes and psychological needs worked to reconcile their dreams and ambitions with the representation of the Stuart concept of the monarch. Almost immediately, however, it is clear that this representation was being evaluated and monitored by the people who quickly rejected and adapted the part that did not contain their hopes and confirm the indigenous Zeitgeist.

In *Attitudes toward History,* Kenneth Burke wrote, "One must erect a vast symbolic synthesis, a rationale of imaginative and conceptual imagery that 'locates' the various aspects of experience. This symbolism guides social purpose: it provides one with 'cues' as to what he should try to get, how he should try to get it, and how he should 'resign himself' to a renunciation of the things he can't get."[115] That symbolic synthesis, however, became less a matter of consent to received, repeated certainties about "natural" order than a process of resistance, limitation, transformation, and incorporation of propagated ideology. With the revolution in the dissemination of information and the increase in literacy, literature became the primary place where such "modeling" was done.[116]

Habermas insists that the existence of a literary public sphere was a necessary precondition for the development of a public sphere that functioned in the political realm. He calls it "the training ground for a critical public reflection still preoccupied with itself."[117] To some extent, theatrical production always asks for and even requires its audience to legitimate its characterizations and resolutions. In the early Restoration, when the theater was identified so closely with the court and when the theater openly accepted its function as a site of distribution and interpretation of news, the theater was a hegemonic apparatus that was being used to influence a critical public in order to legitimate an ideology. After all, the royal theaters carried a long history of royal patronage and direct involvement. The fact of the existence of the royal box made the monarch no less triumph and spectator than the City processions.[118]

The Restoration theater tells the story of how wide and deep political processes are and of how power is never localized. City pageants and public ceremonies had long traditions of being street politics and of participating interactively in political processes, and the theater had been an active site for political commentary before the Civil War.[119] Estimates are that between eighteen thousand and twenty-four thousand Londoners attended the theater every week in the early 1600s. Just before the Commonwealth, they saw such plays as Robert Davenport's *King John and Matilda,* an entire play on Magna Carta; *A Projector Lately Dead,* which satirized Charles I's attorney general and his economic projects; and Richard Brome's *Court Beggar,* which has been described as "a great festive, Saturnalisan . . . [celebration] of anti-court feeling."[120] Political plays never died; Tatham's *The Distracted State* was published in 1651 and depicts the unrest in a nation unfortunate enough to be governed by a usurper. Twelve characters die violently, eight of them on stage. Agathocles says, "People dispos'd for change / Survey the vices of their Prince through optics / That rather multiply than lessen them." His friend speculates on the justice of the usurper's fall: "Was it not / His own insinuating tenet to / The people, 'gainst his brother, that the virtue / And the justice of the Prince were th' only bonds / That bound the people to him, and when he / Should violate either they were tied no longer?"[121] Both courtiers go on to discuss the limits of royal power, accept the contract theory, and become competitors for the throne.

Pamphlet controversies, published accounts of trials, and public executions, book burnings, and monument razings had put rival cases before them and asked their consent and even participation.[122] Records of 320 periodicals published between November 1641 and October 1655 survive, and George Thomason, a London bookseller, collected over twenty-three thousand books and pamphlets between 1641 and 1660.[123] Locke's "Law of Opinion" had been born. Geertz has pointed out that when a ruler's chosen insignia are not indigenous, disbelief and disorder arise.[124] In the first years after the Restoration, drastic consequences were unimaginable, but already evident were important revolutionary hopes that Charles had not recognized and a deep ideological chasm that would fuel the Glorious Revolution, the Sacheverell turmoil, and the riots of 1715, and would not be laid to rest until after the Jacobite rebellion of 1745. The theater lays bare the multiplicity of motives and aspirations behind the enthusiasm for the Restoration and the divisions in structures of feeling that would account for phenomena as diverse as the rise of the novel, the bitter factionalism of Queen Anne's reign, and the commodification of culture.

PART TWO

Negotiating the Text

LETCHER OF SALTOUN, ONE OF THE SCOTS WHO
fought the Union between England and Scotland treaty
clause by treaty clause, once said, "Let me make the ballads
of a nation, and I care not who makes the laws." At the end
of that same century, a woman writer, Letitia Barbauld,
quoted him and posed a revision: "Let me make the novels of a country,
and let who will make the systems."[1] Fletcher, a man on the losing side,
and Barbauld, a woman, knew that access to and control of representation is power.

In the twentieth century, Virginia Woolf rephrased their insight yet
again: "Toward the end of the eighteenth century a change came about
which, if I were rewriting history, I should describe more fully and think
of greater importance than the Crusades or the Wars of the Roses. The
middle-class woman began to write."[2] Woolf goes on to note the crucial
importance of authorship moving beyond "the lonely aristocrat shut up
in her country house among her folios and her flatterers." Thus she
insisted upon the importance of class as well as sex and remarked upon
the need for writing to be part of public discourse. For the twentieth-
century reader the forceful linking of ballads, novels, and writing by
women—all nonprestige literature—with ideological state apparatuses,
including the law and "systems," is tantalizing.

In Part Two, I present a second case of struggle for control of representation and illustrate in different ways how the control of representation is control of history, identity, and morality. The starting point is the 1695–96 London theatrical season, the year in Anglo-American history during which the highest percentage of produced plays were by women. At that time, as Barbauld says, "theatrical productions and poetry made a far greater part of polite reading than novels," but the dawn of the novel's triumph as moral propaganda and major "channel of access" to the public sensibility could be detected. At that time, too, women and "woman" seem to have been something of a collective obsession, and the "feminist controversy" was at its height. As an outgrowth of the amount and kinds of discussions of women's nature and position, women writers came to be in the position described by Weimann in which "the givenness of cultural materials, literary conventions and traditions" finally produces a pressing "need to appropriate . . . the means and forms of literary production; . . . to make them their own precisely because they confront the conditions and means of literary production and reception as something alien, as produced by others, as something which they cannot unquestionably consider as part of the existence of their own social and self-fashioned intellectual selves."[3]

That women became writers in significant numbers during this period is now well established, and their struggle to make professional writing an acceptable occupation for those who wanted to remain deeply respectable was beginning in earnest around 1695.[4] At that moment in history, who might write and on what subjects and who might have access to print and in what circumstances was being contested by men of different social classes and educational backgrounds as well as by women; and the unstable, rapidly evolving world in which they lived would be gone by the middle of the eighteenth century. Because we stand on the other side of the flowering and condescending approval of the domestic novel, it is often forgotten how insistent the earliest professional women writers were about their stake in what has come to be called the public sphere. Barbauld's "systems" is but one small sign. Neatly framing the period in which middle-class women established an acceptable identity for the woman writer, a stance from which to write, and ways of articulating their engagement with "public" issues are two very similar observations:

> History can only serve us [women] for Amusement and a Subject of
> Discourse. It cannot help our Conduct or excite in us a generous

Emulation . . . and the Men being the Historians, they seldom con-
descend to record the great and good Actions of Women; and when
they take notice of them, 'tis with this wise Remark, That such Wom-
en *acted above their Sex.* By which one must suppose they would have
their Readers understand, That they were not Women who did those
Great Actions, but that they were Men in Petticoats. (Mary Astell,
The Christian Religion, 1715)

I do not think I ever opened a book in my life which had not something to say upon woman's inconstancy. . . . But perhaps you will say,
these were all written by men.
    Yes . . . if you please, no reference to examples in books. Men
have had every advantage of us in telling their own story. Education
has been theirs in so much higher a degree; the pen has been in their
hands. I will not allow books to prove anything. (Jane Austen, *Persuasion,* 1818)

These statements recognize the significance of control of representation
and of the writing of history. They even understand that writers intend
for "their Readers to understand" the world and experience as they
present and interpret it.

Even as they negotiated their place in society and in the literary
marketplace, women writers were struggling to create new means of
representation. As Susan Staves has demonstrated, surviving texts confront us with how "much female feeling, so much female bitterness, was
not only unexpressed but almost inexpressible."[5] In spite of being constrained by the means of access to publication and production, by the
demands of literary forms and genre expectations, by long-established
semiotic codes, and by conceptions of sex and gender, the earliest professional women writers, those women from the "middle station," challenged the hegemony on a number of crucial fronts.

This section argues that literature in these early women's hands became a hegemonic apparatus. As they wrote on subjects of crucial importance to women, they transformed them, represented them differently,
and contributed to significant changes in the way the culture saw women,
courtship, marriage, and family relations. They gave impetus to the
bringing of questions of women's nature, circumstances, perspective,
and access to the modes of production into public debate and negotiation. As they sought ways to take part in public discourse that affected
them, they created new literary strategies; as they sought ways to write

and publish about subjects and actions invisible or of little interest to men, they created new codes, new conventions, and new forms. Their greatest contribution, however, may be in the way they brought their reading and their experiences to the creation of new kinds of literature that proved to be ideally suited to participation in hegemonic processes under way in the public political sphere. Their texts deconstructed conventions of social symbols and of reading and demanded new interpretative strategies and, by doing so, forced new insights on readers.

In Chapter 3, I analyze some of the ways that the earliest professional women writers inserted their revisions into literary discourse. I argue that they began the process of creating a space in which women could, in Hélène Cixous's words, begin to "write themselves." I briefly consider two of the writers, Katherine Philips and Aphra Behn, as a prominent part of the context for the women writers of 1695 and treat them primarily as "author functions," ideologically constructed identities often differing markedly from contemporary historical and biographical descriptions,[6] before moving to a discussion of the way Behn inserted herself in hegemonic processes already under way. In Chapter 4, I extend my analysis of Behn's participation in hegemonic processes to her prose fictions in order to demonstrate how she created a new kind of propaganda and contributed to the development of the form we call novel with its special availability as a space in which women could write themselves. She and her generation of nonaristocratic—male and female—writers were actively and self-consciously experimenting with ways to enter and influence public discourse on the great national questions as well as on pressing domestic concerns. I conclude with an explication of a set of devices and strategies deployed by women writers to give them influence and to make their experiences and opinions not only comprehensible but persuasive to men.

3

REPRESENTATION AND POWER

In 1696, Delarivière Manley's cruel satire of Katherine Philips, "the Matchless Orinda," played on the boards of Drury Lane as part of her short-lived *The Lost Lover*. What was especially remarkable about this event was that in the same year, her poem "To the Author of Agnes de Castro" praised another woman writer, Catherine Trotter. Trotter was part of the triumvirate of women who were openly supportive of each other and, like Manley, one of the women who made the 1695–96 theatrical season unique—absolutely unique—in British history. Manley, the best known today, had two plays produced in that season, which included Trotter's *Agnes de Castro* and Mary Pix's *Ibrahim* and *The Spanish Wives*. To open that same season, the Lincoln's Inn Fields company chose a comedy, *She Ventures, and He Wins*, "by a Young Lady" who called herself Ariadne. Trotter's *Agnes de Castro* was deliberately pitted against Congreve's *Love for Love*. In that same magic season, Behn's own *The Younger Brother* posthumously premiered, and Thomas Southerne's adaptation of her prose fiction *Oroonoko* was one of the two plays that "saved" the season for Christopher Rich and Thomas Skipwith's theater.[1] Over one-third of all the new plays that season were by women or adapted from women's work.

These women benefited from a number of circumstances that helped open access to production to them. For the first time in thirteen seasons, there were two commercial theaters in competition, for the Actors' Rebellion had culminated in a license being granted to the company they formed on 25 March 1695.[2] Even before the split, as Robert D. Hume says, "no kind of drama was really flourishing," and the theater was in a precarious state. In 1695, both companies desperately needed new plays and broader audiences.[3] The prologue to Ariadne's comedy suggests the climate of tense competition between the companies:

> . . . Our Author hopes indeed,
> You will not think, though charming *Aphra's* dead,
> All Wit with her, and with *Orinda's* fled.
> We promis'd boldly we wou'd do her Right,
> Not like the other House, who, out of spite,
> Trump'd up a Play upon us in a Night.
> . . . .
> These Champions bragg'd they first appear'd in Field,
> Then bid us tamely article and yield. . . .[4]

Her comedy included a City subplot featuring a vintner's family, and the new Actors' Company may have hoped that it would appeal to a broad audience. Similarly, the epilogue to Manley's *Lost Lover* begins, "Kind hearted City Wives, if any here . . ."

The five years before this season were characterized by nearly unprecedented debate and discussion about the nature and place of women. Not only were they written about but they were writing, and evidence abounds that middle- and higher-class women were beginning to display what Ernesto Laclau calls "mobilization," the "process whereby formerly passive groups acquire *deliberative* behavior."[5] Interest in women had never been greater, and they had become an increasingly significant group of "culture consumers." Their contemporaries saw them as an important part of the theater audience and believed that they had begun to have considerable influence. By that time, "she-tragedies" and plays by men who allegedly catered to the female audience held secure places in every season's repertoire and were even said to have "overrun the Nation."[6] It was a heady time; the prologue to the production of *The Younger Brother* included the lines, "The Ladies too are always welcome here, / Let 'em in Writing or in Box appear."

The women whose first plays were produced that season were openly supportive of each other. In a tribute to Manley that year Pix wrote,

As when some mighty Hero first appears,
And in each act excells his wanting years

. . . .

So you the unequal'd wonder of the Age,
Pride of our Sex, and Glory of the Stage;
Have charm'd our hearts with your immortal lays

. . . .

Your infant strokes have such Herculean force,
Your self must strive to keep the rapid course;
Like *Sappho* Charming, like *Afra* Eloquent
Like Chast *Orinda* sweetly Innocent. . . .[7]

Two years later, Trotter would contribute an epilogue to Pix's *Queen Catharine*. Poems by Pix and Trotter would appear in Manley's *The Nine Muses* (1700), a collection of poems published on the occasion of John Dryden's death. They were also willing to call attention to themselves, each other, and earlier women writers. Only Philips, however, became a character in one of their plays.

"Orinda" adds little to Manley's Restoration sex comedy,[8] thereby making Manley's attack appear even more striking. Orinda functions briefly in fairly widely separated episodes as another woman with whom Wildman can flirt rakishly and as contrast to Marina and Belira. Since none of the other characters, male or female, has aspirations to be a writer, the slander appears unmotivated and becomes more personal than artistic. The Orinda of Manley's play is a hypocritical, crude, affected, shallow woman. Nearly a quarter of her lines are silly, ignorant observations about fashion. Her idiomatic speeches usually include the countrified and profane expletive, "O Gud." Refusing to publish, she gives manuscript copies of her poems to everyone, even slight acquaintances.

Manley's major satiric thrust, however, is at the subject of Philips's verse, which the heroine Marina identifies as Orinda herself.[9] Orinda seems to live to record only her feelings, not her experiences. She says she longs to leave town in order to "entertain my Muse alone with the reflections of what she has left behind," describes her most recent poems as "upon the different addresses I have had made to me of late" (13), and finally exits to record her reaction to the end of a single dance. Her words, "O I can't hold my Muse!" (25) have sexual overtones and imply that her "writing to the moment" is either a self-important, affected posture or an operation of the body that she has no desire to control. Manley's introduction and her two leading female characters valorize wit, "Nature's best Gift," and Manley complains bitterly in her preface that tender "billets" and short "songs of Phillis" are the kinds of writing allowed women, writing that would "confine" "my Sense." She had already been brought to say ruefully that politics—and the theater— were "no way proper for a Woman." She had seen the "better half" of her *Lost Lover* cut, making it, as she says, far "too rapid."[10] Already feeling beaten away from the public arena, Manley describes the constraints of a gendered literary world.

Although Philips has the distinction of being a character in a play, the presence of another deceased woman writer is nearly ubiquitous. The inspiration for Manley's Wilmore and Belira in *The Lost Lover* had been Aphra Behn's two *Rover* plays, and the source for Trotter's first play was Behn's short prose fiction of the same title.[11] All four of the female playwrights of 1695–96 mention Behn as an important precursor, and Ariadne may have chosen her nom de plume as a reference to Behn's Ariadne, the virtuous heroine in *Rover II*. Pix's *Spanish Wives* is the kind of intrigue comedy that brought Behn her most consistent success. Both Philips and Behn were part of the context for the work of the 1695–96 playwrights, and I would like to begin this chapter with a brief look at the author function Philips had become before moving to an extended discussion of the importance in hegemonic processes of Aphra Behn's career. As Foucault observed, a transformation takes place in which the name is no longer designation but description; then it becomes a type, a means of "classification," and is "regulated" by the culture. This process with Philips's and Behn's names affected women writers and print culture into the twentieth century.

Katherine Philips is known today almost exclusively as a poet, and critics often play with the idea that she is one of the two best of all the many Restoration and eighteenth-century women poets.[12] By 1696, Philips was firmly established as what men wanted in a woman writer.[13] Allegedly she had denied any literary ambition and had reacted to the unauthorized publication of her poems with a "sharp fit of sickness." She complained in a letter to her friend Charles Cotterell:

> I . . . am that unfortunate person that cannot so much as think in private, that must have my imaginations rifled and exposed to play the mountebanks, and dance upon the ropes to entertain all the rabble;

to undergo all the raillery of the Wits, and all the severity of the Wise; and to be the sport of some that can, and some that cannot read a verse.[14]

Urged to do what most writers of the time did, which was immediately to set about publishing a genuine edition, she wrote that she would agree "with the same reluctancy as I would cut off a limb to save my life" (491). This letter was published with the posthumous edition, which was titled in part *Poems By the most deservedly Admired Mrs. Katherine Philips, The matchless Orinda.* In addition to the heavy-handed "most deservedly," the title conferred the identity that in Cotterell's day was ordinary précieuse practice but would soon be repeated with condescension and ridicule to the present day.[15]

The poems of tribute that prefaced Philips's poems contributed to the "matchless" theme. Abraham Cowley, for instance, was sure Apollo would choose her as "Woman-Laureat" (502); each poet inseparably linked her literary achievement to her virtue. As Cowley wrote, "But Wit's like a luxuriant vine, / Unless to Virtue's prop it join, / Firm and erect towards Heaven bound, / Though it with beauteous leaves and pleasant fruit be crown'd, / It lies deform'd, and rotting on the ground" (503).[16] In a particularly macabre tribute, Thomas Flatman urged women to use her crypt as a mirror and concluded, "With envy think, when to the grave you go, / How very little must be said of you, / Since all that can be said of virtuous / Woman was her due" (502). As Roger Lund concludes, for the seventeenth century, "Orinda was all but synonymous with virtue."[17] Even women writers came to show a particular affinity for the adjective "chaste." Trotter had used it; "Philomela's" prefatory poem for Elizabeth Singer Rowe's *Poems on Several Occasions* included the line, "In thee we see the Chast Orinda live." Married to a much older man from whom she was often absent, and perhaps sexually oriented toward women,[18] Philips represented a sociosexual option for writing women that would hold an appeal for some women throughout the century. Philips was able to evoke a very early picture of the "counter-universe" of female friendship, which analysts such as Simone de Beauvoir describe as attractive for its intimacy, its "affirmation of the universe they have in common," and the "sensual sweetness" they find in each other's bodies.[19] Not only could it be argued that chastity had strong scriptural approval, but as woman came to be conceived of as intrinsically modest and even asexual, celibacy became more "natural" and, therefore, acceptable for women.[20] By the second half of the eighteenth century, poems by women in the Orinda tradition praised female friendship as "The brightest passion of the human breast" and a consoling refuge from the discovery of love's "delusive joy, or killing pain."[21]

Within these poems and those that invoked Orinda's name in the next two decades are the signs of the construction of the ideal woman writer.[22] Not only is virtue necessary, but even the appropriate subjects for women are beginning to be defined. The earl of Orrery, for instance, had declared himself untroubled and unsurprised by Philips's success, for "Since every Poet this great truth does prove, / Nothing so much inspires a Muse as Love; / Thence has your sex the best poetic fires" (493). However, in encouraging her translation and production of *Pompey,* he may have seen himself as going little beyond the long tradition of courtly encouragement of wives' and sisters' translations. The effort put into the public production and the number of prestigious men who contributed, however, mark an important moment in the history of women's writing.[23]

The real Katherine Fowler Philips differed significantly from the "author function" she had become to Manley thirty-three years later, and a decade-by-decade analysis makes evident the signs of this construction in the published writings of women as well as men. Born the daughter of a cloth merchant and a Presbyterian on New Year's Day 1632, Philips had been educated at Mrs. Salmon's school, one of the excellent Nonconformist academies in Hackney, near the area that would develop into an enclave of well-to-do Dissenters.[24] She married Colonel James Philips, a relative of her Welsh stepfather, when she was sixteen. By 1651 she had published at least one poem in a visible, prestigious place. In 1663 she became one of the first, if not the first, English women to have a play produced on the British stage. Her translation of Corneille's *Pompée* was performed in Dublin in February 1663 and in London in January 1664.

Cotterell's edition of her poems with its insistence on her reluctance to publish obscured the truth about her time in Ireland and her personality, for she worked diligently and competitively to best the translation of *Pompée* by Waller, Sedley, and their collaborators, and she did so as a dramatist intent not only on publication but on production. Her posthumously published *Letters from Orinda to Poliarchus* (1705) contradicts the 1667 edition's letter expressing distress and reluctance to publish an authentic edition of her poetry. She makes it clear that she is ready to follow Cotterell's advice if he still thinks it "proper" for her to prepare an authorized edition of the poems and that the letter he would later print was written to show to "any body that suspects my Ignorance and Innocence" (219–21).

These letters also record her careful work on her translation of *Pompey;* her involvement in its production; and her race to complete, polish, and present her *Pompey* before the collaborators could theirs, as well as her intense curiosity about their progress and version. She shows no reluctance to publish and openly courts public recognition. As Maureen Mulvihill has pointed out, Philips was well connected and carefully cultivated and maintained court and literary relationships.[25] Once "the Confederate" translators' edition of *Pompey* was available, she wrote a long, negative critique expressing surprise at their bad rhymes and the "liberties" they took with the text. These letters also reveal a woman willing to carry on a clandestine correspondence with a man,[26] to scheme and nag to leave her home and husband in Wales for the opportunities of London,[27] and to quibble, fret, and then hold firm over individual words in her manuscript.[28]

One modern scholar has called the " 'Orinda' myth" "a remarkable literary campaign conceived and promoted by Philips herself, her relatives, and some of the literary bosses of the Restoration old boys' network."[29] Although this statement goes too far in blending elements of the later construction of the chaste songbird with Philips's attempts to construct herself as a literary artist, it rightly notes her ambition. Contemporaries, too, recognized the importance of her *Pompey* and her assertive, competitive spirit:

> A woman translate *Pompey!* which the famed
> Corneille with such art and labour framed!
> To whose close version the wits club their sense,
> . . . .
> Yes, that bold work a woman dares translate
>
> . . . .
> That sex, which heretofore was not allowed
> To understand more than a beast, or crowd;
> . . . .
> And all the painful labours of their brain,
> Was only how to dress and entertain:

. . . .

From these thy more than masculine pen hath reared
Our sex; first to be praised, next to be feared. . . .[30]

Rather than being concerned about appearing ambitious to publish her poems, she said that she was worried about "exposing all my Follies"— her private emotions and strong feelings about her women friends that may seem "very ridiculous and extravagant"—and about the reactions of those whose names are "exposed" without their permission (231, 236). She was surely sensitive to the fact that her poems differed considerably from those of the précieuse and of married women such as the duchess of Newcastle. Notably, the arrangement of her poems in the Cotterell edition works against the cumulative impact of, for instance, her Rosania and Lucasia poems.

Cotterell and others in her circle would have known that poems of hers had been published before, and in such visible places as the preface to a posthumous edition of William Cartwright's plays (1651) and in the *Second Book of Ayres* (1655).[31] Philips was also by then an experienced translator. Writing at the peak of the transition from aristocratic manuscript circulation as the form of publication to the printed publication of work through booksellers, Philips may have been expressing class anxiety as well as gender confusion.[32] It was not uncommon for manuscripts to have very wide circulation, and recent scholarly work suggests that there were not as many differences between the behavior of men and of women as we have thought. Margaret Ezell, for instance, argues that including manuscript circulation in our picture of women's writing "bring[s] into question the current theory that women writers lacked sufficient numbers to form 'an alternative literary society'" and may be a sign that women writers were conservative (as many men, especially aristocrats were) rather than "modest" or excluded from the means of production.[33]

The basis for Manley's satire could easily have been Philips's letter to Cotterell, which prefaces his edition of her poems; in it she confesses to having given away copies of her work and losing even the originals. There is a pattern of advance–retreat/deny to much that Philips does and says. At the moment she was repeating Orrery's compliments and feeling competitive toward the Confederate translators, she was fearing that her play "will not be deem'd worthy to breathe in a place where so many of the greatest Wits have so long clubb'd for another of the same Play"

(180). As she was asking Cotterell to present her play to the duchess of York and the king and to help her brother negotiate with two London publishers, she wrote that she could not bear to have her name affixed to it (but, of course, her authorship was already known); at the end of her critique of the rival *Pompey,* she wrote, "I really think the worst of their Lines equal to the best in my Translation."[34] At work on a new play, she continued to deny ambition. Perhaps able to see translation as less assertive and original than independent composition and, in a time when the theater was patronized and attended largely by a group of people who knew each other, the writing of plays as more private than publication, Philips lived out the contradictions that would intensify before lessening for women writers. Philips's ambition and willingness to take risks, however, cannot be denied, and it seems likely that, had she lived a little longer, she would have seen *Horace* performed[35] and would have done an authorized edition of her poetry.

The contradictions between the historical woman and the author function can be multiplied. Described as "of a middle stature, pretty fat, and ruddy complexioned" and one who "Ow'd not her glory to a beauteous face" by women in her own time,[36] this historical reality jars with a typical tribute that begins, "We allow'd you beauty, and we did submit / To all the tyrannies of it."[37] This latter, by her friend the poet Abraham Cowley, is typical of the writing that put in motion the construction of the beautiful, charming, graceful lyricist. Another typical poem, "An Elegie, upon the death of the most incomparable, Mrs. Katharine Philips, *the glory of her sex"* (emphasis mine), asserts, "She, who in Tragique buskins drest the Stage, / Taught Honour, Love, and Friendship to this Age . . ." [London, 1664]. James Granger observed tartly that her poems "are more to be admired for propriety and beauty of thought, than for harmony of versification, in which [she] was generally deficient," but his approval and even admiration for her are greater than for other women writers.[38] George Ballard summarizes the character that has come down to us: "Her remarkable humility, good nature and agreeable conversation greatly endeared her to all her acquaintances, and her ingenious and elegant writings procured her the friendship and correspondence of many . . . persons of the first rank in England."[39]

Embedded in Ballard's description may be acknowledgment of another significant and often obscured fact about Philips, one that was surely another source of her personal anxiety about publication: she was middle class. Ballard's description suggests that she knew her place.

Good-natured, humble, careful to make agreeable conversation—these are the phrases Jane Austen applies with such force to dependent female characters. Like many women of the Commonwealth and early Restoration, she did nothing special when she had to apply her "good sense and excellent way of negotiating" and use her contacts in an attempt to protect and improve her moderate Cromwellian husband's estate.[40] The performances of her plays at court, the platonic names she used in her poems, and the fact that Cotterell, later the Master of Ceremonies to the king, edited and published her poems obscured these aspects of her life and background, but she may have been uncomfortable about the reactions of her friends and acquaintances from Mrs. Salmon's Hackney school and among her gentry-class Welsh neighbors. She writes to Cotterell, "Let me know what they say of me at Court and every where else, upon this last Accident, and whether the exposing all my Follies in this dreadful Shape has not frighted the whole World out of all their Esteem for me" (224–25).

Undoubtedly, however, Philips's virtuous married life, her lyrical, lovely verse, and her romantic early death at age thirty-three made her a difficult and even undesirable act to follow, and her literary career left women a troublesome legacy. The deeply political plays of her last years or the unpublished essays "on several subjects"[41] might have meant a great deal to Aphra Behn and the woman Delarivière Manley would become, but in 1696 they were confronted by the idealized image of Philips and the kind of woman writer Cotterell and others had constructed. When a woman such as Delarivière Manley tried to use this author function as a model, she felt pressure on every aspect of her art and personality.

Like Philips, Behn was already a larger-than-life figure, but whereas Philips had been glorified by men, Behn would soon become the object of vilification and would be so systematically discredited that by 1723 Jane Barker would write that her name ought not to be mentioned with Orinda's.[42] Just as "chaste" redounds throughout the descriptions of Philips, "loose" came to resound through those of Behn.

This woman, dead since 1689, who could still carry a share of a theatrical season on her shoulders, meant a number of things to women writers. First, she was an unapologetic professional writer; as Virginia Woolf said more than two hundred years later, she "earned [women] the right to speak their minds . . . [and] makes it not quite fantastic for me to say to you tonight: Earn five hundred a year by your wits." Although women had been writing since the beginning of recorded English history, with few exceptions they were not what we would call "professional writers" in the modern sense; that is, people who write seriously for money. The category simply did not exist—and before it was established, women writers were forced into one of two classes: the new position of the shameless, crass, fallen woman jostling with men and willing to live by her illicitly gained sexual knowledge, a place in stark contrast to the other, which was the long-accepted practice of the aristocrat writing for herself and her circle and tastefully circulating manuscripts.

Of course, the images of the prostitute and the prostituted pen are hardly less restricting than the constraints of elevated gentility that imposed deliberate silences and a constricted range of subjects. These roles are constructed, of course, and we often forget how recently the first entered social discourse. Even more recently did the third category, the respectable, unapologetic professional, become established. In 1769, nearly one hundred years after Behn's career, Clara Reeve wrote, "I see many female writers favourably received, admitted into the rank of authors, and amply rewarded by the public; I have been encouraged by their success, to offer myself as a candidate for the same advantages." Reeve mentions that she has seen "daily examples" of women who have overcome the "prejudices" against women's literary merit.[43] For her and other aspiring women, female models' lives testify to the fact that others have felt and wanted what Behn, Manley, Ariadne, Trotter, and Pix wanted. They give silent permission to try, because their lives show they did not think they were wrong or unnatural or freakish. "A Lady" wrote that Behn's "Harmonious Lire / Did me, the meanest of thy sex, inspire. / And that thy own inimitable lays / Are cause alone that I attempt thy praise."[44] Thus, Behn helps give others the confidence to write and publish, and their cumulative successes encourage others and add authority to the female voice.

The quality of Behn's literary work, unlike Philips's, has never seriously been disputed. Judith Drake called her "incomparable" in *An Essay in Defence of the Female Sex* (1696). Gerard Langbaine concluded his sketch of her in *An Account of the English Dramatic Poets* (Oxford, 1691) with this judgment: "I doubt not but she will be allowed equal with several of our poets, her contemporaries." Pix's tribute to Manley called Behn "Eloquent" and Orinda merely "Chaste." Defoe listed her with Cowley, Rochester, and Waller in *The Pacificator* (1700). *Poems by Emi-*

nent Ladies (1755) printed a large selection of her poems, including the 128-page *A Voyage to the Isle of Love.* In his "Prologue for the Opening of Drury Lane," Samuel Johnson wrote, "Perhaps if skill could distant times explore, / New Behns, new D'Urfeys, yet remain in store," and Clara Reeve insisted that "there are strong marks of Genius in all this lady's works."[45] Genest concluded, "Mrs. Centlivre, Mrs. Cowley, Mrs. Inchbald and other females have distinguished themselves by their plays, but no female is to be put in competition with Mrs. Behn" (3:79). As George Woodcock has said, her prose fictions "are . . . superior to anything else that was being written at the time in the way of fiction" (168).

When Manley saw her first play produced, she was already the defrauded, impoverished victim of a bigamous marriage and the dismissed former employee of the scandalous duchess of Cleveland, Barbara Villiers.[46] She and her contemporaries knew that Behn had carved out for herself a marginally acceptable, independent position in society.[47] Many of Behn's personal and critical remarks are bracing, as her forthright challenge in the preface to *The Dutch Lover* was:

> Plays have no great room for that which is men's great advantage over women, that is learning; we all well know that the immortal Shakespeare's plays (who was not guilty of much more of this than often falls to women's share) have better pleased the world than Jonson's works, though by the way 'tis said that Benjamin was no such rabbi neither, for I am informed that his learning was but grammar high.

In one stroke, she made writing for the stage seem within woman's range. Most crucial, she demonstrated that women could make a good living by writing, and she said without apology that she had to "write for Bread and [was] not ashamed to owne it" and "ought to write to please."[48] In a society in which employment for women was a great problem, Behn stood like a shining signpost.

Unlike Philips, Behn left a substantial body of published texts in which she explicitly and implicitly asserted her equal right to contest representation, to participate in public and even political debate, and to have access to the language and modes of production in which it was carried on. Because of her sex and isolated historical position,[49] because her success ranks with that of the four or five most successful male writers of the Restoration, and because she gained and held a very wide audience, her texts have major, special significance. In this section, I shall look at some of the ways that Behn committed the revolutionary act that Hélène Cixous has identified and demanded: "Woman must write her self: must write about women and bring women to writing, from which they have been driven away as violently as from their bodies—for the same reasons. . . . Woman must put herself into the text—as into the world and into history—by her own movement."[50]

Virginia Woolf said that "of greater importance than the Crusades or the Wars of the Roses [was that] the middle-class woman began to write."[51] Although Woolf does not develop this observation, the hegemonic implications are clear, for whoever controls representation controls identity, history, and morality. When Behn and other women writers began to modify representation, they were participating in a hegemonic process. Specifically, they were re-negotiating elements of the patriarchal ideology such as "woman" and woman's "place" as well as things of crucial importance for women's lives such as "satisfactory courtship," "good marriage," and options for single women. Whenever these negotiations occur, "man," man's "role," and "perfect husband" are re-negotiated as well, because of the relations between the sexes and of the nature of power. After all, as Foucault says, power is "relations, a more-or-less organised, hierarchical, co-ordinated cluster of relations."[52] Women were seeking to wrest away man's power to define women's nature, needs, aspirations, and acceptable conditions of existence.

Behn had to work within the same kinds of forms and conventions that gave aspiring male authors access to publication and production. Thus, she had useful models of successful work and effective conventions. However, she, like the female producers of private manuscripts, had to struggle to invent appropriate language and forms to express profoundly different experiences and a pronounced sense of dissimilarity. Behn came to write often about the reception productions of her plays received, and in the preface to *The Lucky Chance* (1686)[53] she writes at length for the first time about what would become the most vexing issue for women writers. This problem was language, and it is always a problem for women writers and is intensified when they contest representations at the heart of a dominant ideology. Whether one subscribes to the theory that many of their experiences are simply inexpressible because they must use a masculine medium or to the idea that social prohibitions limit and even disable women writers,[54] it cannot be denied that many of women's most crucial concerns had not been presented from their perspective and some were not even part of social discourse. How, for instance, could the experience of being bartered through marriage to a stranger be made acceptable and accessible—that is, comprehensible—to men?[55] How could middle and old age, so vastly different for women and men in that society, be made interesting and accessible?

The literary codes, conventions, and myths that already existed in the public literary arena were both help and hindrance. Like all writers, she could use them for efficient, reliable expression, but subjects that could be treated in "private" circulation could become quite problematic when offered to the general public in print. It has become a modern commonplace to recognize the greater scrutiny that diction in women's works received, and Behn occasionally seems to be responding to criticism of a woman "writing bawdy," as she did in the preface to *The Lucky Chance:*

> I make a Challenge to any Person of common Sense and Reason . . .
> to read any of my Comedys and compare 'em with others of this Age,
> and if they find one Word that can offend the chastest Ear, I will sub-
> mit to all their peevish Cavills; but Right or Wrong they must be
> Criminal because a Woman's. . . . Had I a Day or two's time . . . I
> would sum up all your Beloved Plays, and all the Things in them that
> are past with such Silence by; because written by Men: such Mas-
> culine Strokes in me, must not be allow'd.
>
> And I must want common Sense, and all the Degrees of good
> Manners, renouncing my Fame, all Modesty and Interest for a silly
> Sawcy fruitless Jest, to make Fools laugh, and Women blush, and wise
> Men asham'd. . . . Is this likely, is this reasonable . . . ? All I ask, is
> the Priviledge for my Masculine Part the Poet in me . . . to tread in
> those successful Paths my Predecessors have so long thriv'd in, to take
> those Measures that both the Ancient and Modern Writers have set
> me, and by which they have pleas'd the World so well: If I must not,
> because of my Sex . . . I lay down my Quill. (3:185–87)

In "To the Reader" prefacing *Sir Patient Fancy,* Behn complained that a "bawdy" play from a woman was seen as "unnaturall" (4:7). In fact, male playwrights as well as Behn were attacked for their "immoral" subjects and themes and for bawdy language, and scholars have amassed substantive evidence that political factions used criticisms of language in attempts to limit the size and breadth of audiences. These were two of

Behn's most political plays, and what she was experiencing was a relatively minor way in which the established, hegemonic, gendered language system could be used against her.

The most serious problem that Behn had with language was one shared by all who would revise representation and interpretation, and it was intensified because of her lonely position as a woman writer. In every revisionary statement she made, she ran the risk of having Other plot lines, Other statements taken to be hers, thereby reducing her work to conventional ideas and familiar morals. As Bakhtin remarked, "A language [male or female] is revealed in all its distinctiveness only when it is brought into relationship with other languages, entering with them into one single heteroglot unity of societal becoming."[56] The tendency of the dominant culture, however, is to deny the distinctiveness, often by appropriating it. Revisionary acts always require deliberate devices that frustrate readers' natural tendencies to see familiar plot patterns or archetypes.[57] Yet these revisions must be carried out within economically viable literary forms.

When Behn began to write, she faced a limited number of roles, plot lines, interpretations, and resolutions for women's lives and experiences. These limitations came not only from the conventions, expectations, and beliefs of the culture and its literature but also from the tendency consumers have to impose meaning on a text or a production, sometimes in spite of explicit events and statements in the work itself. The seventeenth century saw the opening up of access to publication[58] and was characterized by unprecedented faith in the power of the printed word. Women writers, like all oppressed or subordinate groups of writers, have always taken up the pen in order to say, "Not that way, *this* way." For economic, personal, and philosophical reasons, then, women writers became in large numbers part of the generation who said with Andrew Marvell that the lead in type is more deadly than the lead in bullets. Numerous critics have argued that "literary and cultural models tend to shape the way in which people regard themselves"; others would go even further: "We live our lives through texts. Whatever their form or medium, these stories are what have formed us all."[59] They might have gone on to say that these models also tend to shape the possibilities and institutions open to human beings at a given moment in history and how those possibilities and opportunities are regarded. To change these things is to change the hegemony, and Behn created a series of transgressive women characters and provocative plot lines.

When a text that violates expectations and challenges comfortable ideological position appears and gains popularity, writers, who incidentally represent a category of culture consumers, often respond in ways that dramatize the kinds of hegemonic movement and negotiation described by Gramsci. One group of consumers when encountering a text that challenges established ideological positions attempts to protect and propagate these elements, for they represent desires and needs they recognize and wish to keep in circulation. A second group attempts to appropriate the text and reproduce it in ways that support the hegemony. Thus, they seek to control, transform, or at least incorporate oppositional ideologies. Feminists have demonstrated how Behn took the commonplaces of marriage comedies—the marriage market, the valorizing of the libertine lifestyle, and the forced marriage—and exposed women's experience of being exploited and oppressed and the drama's dependence upon the fetishizing of women.[60] To me, the most original aspect of Behn's work is that she opens a new discourse of sexuality, admitting not only woman's experience of love but also their knowledge of sexual difference. These aspects of her work and her transgressive characters can be set beside texts that follow hers to demonstrate the importance for hegemonic processes of the tendencies either to protect or to appropriate.

The plays by women produced in the 1695–96 season illustrate efforts to protect and legitimate many of the revisionary elements in Behn's plays.[61] Most striking in these plays are these depictions of women's utopian dreams of married love and of their fears of loneliness, insult, and rape. Behn and the others often give familiar lines to unexpected characters in order to foreground women's common lot. For instance, Behn houses sentiment and romantic dreams in her prostitute Angellica Bianca and makes her virtuous character, Hellena, hold the hard-headed opinion: "What shall I get? A Cradle full of noise and mischief" (122). Trotter's Constantia first discovers from what she lacks that the prince does not love her (*Agnes de Castro*), and Selima laments that she could not make her husband feel love and passion for her (*The Royal Mischief*).

In later plays, Behn intensifies her efforts to make strange common statements by putting her heroines' sentiments into the speeches of male characters. Gayman, for instance, sells his sexual favors for survival, and there is no question but that he does it for subsistence and hates it. When he expresses the sentiments of the trade, they can be received with amusement or sympathy even as they convey the shocking necessities:

"She pays, and I'll endeavour to be civil." He fears the embraces of an old, ugly woman, just as wives like Julia regret that they "languish in a loathed embrace" with an aged husband. Both Gayman and Bellmour's reputations have been damaged and are, therefore, more dependent on the women's initiative than most heroes.[62] Ariadne's comedy is a true woman's fantasy. The heroine, Charlot, takes to the streets dressed as a man in hope of meeting "the Man I can find in my heart to take for better or worse." Her disguise will allow her, she says, the liberty she needs to move through the city safely. Moreover, she says, "Should I meet with the Man whose outside pleases me, 'twill be impossible by any other means to discover his Humour; for they are so used to flatter and deceive our Sex, that there's nothing but the Angel appears, tho' the Devil lies lurking within, and never so much as shews his Paw till he has got his Prey fast in his Clutches" (1). She meets this perfect man, who turns out to be an impoverished younger brother, tests him, and with what must have struck the audience as an unconventional if not downright improbable touch marries him with her brother's approval. In fact, the brother says, "She has a plentiful Fortune, enough to make any Man happy; she's free and absolute, and has as much Right to dispose of her self and Fortune as I of mine" (13). Songs praise Charlot for her mind and wit as well as for her appearance, and the concluding scenes mingle generosity, seriousness, and mutual physical attraction.

Openly depicting female sexuality, these plays have good women as well as bad describe woman's passion. Constantia longs for "a transport of Fierce Love." In lines similar to those that she will write in her autobiographical *Rivella*, Manley describes Homais's first sexual experience: "at your new found Joys / An Unbeliever till you prov'd the wonder, / And felt the mighty Ecstasy approach." Homais insists that true pleasure includes the "warmth of kind desire [and] joy" (240–41). Woman's discovery of and opening herself to love is an important theme in Behn's works, and her texts offer an early example of what Julia Kristeva has called "traversal" in texts, places where writing confronts and inscribes the process of the discovery of sexual difference.[63] Many of Behn's texts include what was fast becoming an expected part of fictions about young women: the discovery of what adult love is.

In another groundbreaking, revisionary text, Madame de Lafayette's Princess de Clèves becomes an extremely discriminating expert. At first, "All these shades of sentiment [about love were] above her head," but she soon "saw only too clearly that her feelings for [de Nemours] were exactly those which the Prince de Clèves had so often besought her to have for him."[64] Finally, she concludes that she cannot be happy in a situation in which she will "feel the difference between" the two men's love for her (191). Such detail and such development of the process of rational judgment is unusual, but the plot line is not. Behn's *Love-Letters between a Nobleman and His Sister* (1683) begins with the assertion that Sylvia did not know what love was and traces her discovery of "My new desires, my unknown shameful flame," what "those sighs and pressings meant" (60, 62), and dramatizes the moods of love. This awakening in women's texts is initiation not only into lovers' addictive physical pleasures and female sexuality but also into a previously unimagined intimacy. Katterina and Isabella in Behn's *The History of the Nun* describe the process, and in this intimate sharing of recognition scenes both women mention conversation with the lover as prominently as "trembling at his touches."

In Behn's texts, the discovery of love moves from an awakening of physical desire to a conception of intellectual, temperamental, moral, and sexual affinity, and, in many cases, to an awareness of woman's ability to control herself and the expression of her desire. As sexual feeling is portrayed in distinctively feminine ways in *La Princesse de Clèves,* so it is in many of Behn's texts, inscribing not a phallic body but one that "experiences [sexual] pleasure almost everywhere," not fetish but "body-sex organ."[65] Sylvia writes in detail of her sexual emotions: "I have wishes, new, unwonted wishes, at every thought of thee I find a strange disorder in my blood, that pants and burns in every vein, and makes me blush, and sigh, and grow impatient, ashamed and angry." (63). Thus, they open a new discourse of sexuality, admitting not only woman's experience of love but also their knowledge of sexual difference. Earlier critics have struggled to describe Behn's contribution. George Woodcock quotes Allardyce Nicoll: "Love, with her, is something more than simple sensual passion, and mere cuckolding does not suffice for her lovers" (121).

Women critics, however, have found it less indescribable. Marilyn Williamson remarks that Behn's work does not "deny the pain, the social penalty, or personal risk of aroused female sexuality, but it asserts that sexuality and describes how it feels." Natascha Würzbach says that Behn "describes with some subtlety and persuasiveness the phenomenon of sensuality."[66] Her *jouissance* and experimentation are similarly apparent in her dramatizations of affinity. Where Angellica Bianca's sentimental idealism fails, both Hellena and La Nuche match Willmore's commitment to personal autonomy. In *The Lucky Chance,* Behn juxtaposes two love scenes and makes genres interact. In order to test Gayman's constancy, Julia arranges a masquelike seduction experience for him, complete with romantic songs and pastoral characters. In a subsequent scene, she confronts Gayman as a virtuous wife whose venal and avaricious husband has gambled away a night with her for £300. Both unacceptable extremes, the scenes lay bare Julia's hopes and their context, devastatingly presenting a masculine world in which Julia's true love can say to her husband that she will "be never the worse for my wearing." The fanciful beauty of the first, with its poignant revelation of the utopian hope and the mercenary and dissolute transaction that has brought Julia to call herself "a foul adult'ress," makes this text approach true dialogism. Similarly, Behn contructs *Oroonoko* as a thwarted romance in Africa and a grim, polemical novel in Surinam.[67]

Irving Howe has written that the "political novel," which Behn's certainly are, is always "in a state of internal warfare," for "it exposes the impersonal claims of ideology to the pressures of private emotion."[68] Howe goes on to say that this kind of novel is "always on the verge of becoming something other than itself." On the surface, Behn's characters and their situations are more conventionally the stuff of the comedy of her time; neither hero in *The Lucky Chance* is the original that the Rover is, and the resolution lacks the novelty of the two *Rover*s, yet using deliberate parallels and juxtapositions, explicit speeches, and some of the best poetic lines in seventeenth-century drama, she displays here remarkable ability to present both male and female perspectives, even as she often implants within the male perspective additional insights into womankind's experiences and position. By managing to make the orchestrated voices of the texts dialogic, she puts ideology in contact with the individual. This achievement is political in a different sense and of a different order from conflict between individual and community, for the interests of the hegemony may not be those of community any more than they are the interests of the individual.

In ideal love, women find sex the final step in mutual communication, the state that Constantia and Agnes in succeeding scenes describe as liberty and "Heaven." Amurat's and Morena's ideal love reaches its pinnacle in the scene in which he denies all meaning to her rape by Ibrahim; he insists on marrying her and asks, "Shall I forsake the Christal Fountain, / Because a Rough-hewn Satyr there / Has quencht his Thirst?"

Morena responds, "Talk on, methinks I taste of Heaven / To hear thee!" (40). Surely the most powerful scenes in Manley's *Lost Lover* are the ones in which the seduced and abandoned Belira confronts Wilmore.[69] She asks, "How often hast thou told, thou could'st for ever Love me?" He responds, "I told you that I cou'd, not that I wou'd." Her insight is devastating: "Poor Caviller, those who can jest with Oaths, can play with Words." Her last words to him are a curse: "yet think on me and sigh for such a Friend—But may no Friend be found." He comes to recognize that she would never have been unhappy if she had not known him. Behn's Willmore recognizes the beauty of Angellica Bianca's hope of love: "By heaven, thou'rt brave, and I admire thee strangely, / I wish I were that dull, that constant thing / Which thou wouldst have" (116). Her Cloris in *The Amorous Prince* goes out to find the prince who has "ruined" her, wins him, and he says that he will "still" receive her as "a gift from Heaven."

Such fantasies of redemption for "fallen women," for the love and understanding of men with whom they could communicate and who would understand their deepest desires, however, usually end even in these plays with culturally acceptable solutions: the death of the raped woman, the marriage of the rake to the virtuous woman. In these plays, however, the "fallen woman" is not what she is in plays by men: proof of the hero's superiority and of his deserving a better woman. Just as they would be in Burney's novels, the rakes are more brutal in plays by Behn and Trotter than in the plays by men. These playwrights, like Burney, could create the feeling of being taunted, trapped, and reminded of physical inferiority. Florinda, for instance, in Behn's *The Rover* meets the angry Blunt intent on raping her for revenge and then finds herself surrounded and facing what we have learned to recognize as a potential gang rape as male bonding ritual. Jacqueline Pearson rightly points out that this is a "realistic" portrayal of rape, since it is motivated by anger rather than "lust." She calls it "in some respects the most realistic attempted rape in the drama of the period,"[70] but other women playwrights, including Pix, make it clear that rage and desire to dominate, not overwhelming sexual attraction, are the causes of rape.

Many of Behn's transgressive women have violated comfortable conceptions of women's sexuality and their attitudes toward men, and the 1695–96 playwrights not only attempted to preserve and develop her work but suffered, and still suffer, for the effort. Behn never denied women's sexual desires and that they would act upon them. Jane Miller argues in *Women Writing about Men* that women writers often represent men in startling ways, and she shows that men may reject women's heroes as unheroic, especially when these "heroes" appear empathetic, playful, or vulnerable. Rejection, then, of the entire literary work becomes, in their opinion, justifiable. For example, Maximillian E. Novak suggests that the failure of *She Ventures and He Wins* "may have been due to its feminist reversal of sexual roles. Not only does Charlot pursue Lovewell in a man's disguise, she also humiliates him to an uncomfortable degree." He goes on to compare Valentine in Congreve's *Love for Love,* who "loses some dignity" to Ariadne's Lovewell, who "has suffered a complete humiliation."[71] This masculine reaction, especially notable because it is so many centuries removed from the play, suggests the barriers that transgressive women's writing must overcome to be approved or canonized. Ariadne locates women's perceptions and desires in these characters; a tallying up of the words that define the object of desire in men's and in women's writing of the last decades of the seventeenth century reinforces her work.

Behn's best-known transgressive women are female characters often called libertines. Angellica Bianca, La Nuche, and others have come to be synonymous with the plays and their creator, but they have been misnamed and underestimated, and the women playwrights of the 1690s knew it. Both Angellica Bianca and La Nuche do sell sex. They are crass about it and, more startling yet, put high prices on themselves. In these plays, Behn is doing what many writers of the Restoration and eighteenth century did: drawing parallel after parallel between the fashionable, polite world and the underworld, between socially approved practices and the conduct of the "immoral." In the first *Rover,* Florinda's speeches can be set beside Angellica's; the similarity between, on the one side, jointure and settlements and, on the other, fees for the prostitute's services is obvious. Hellena tells her brother that Florinda's marriage to Don Vincentio "would be worse than adultery." Willmore tells Angellica, "Poor as I am I would not sell myself," but she counters: "When a lady is proposed to you for a wife, you never ask how fair, discreet, or virtuous she is, but what's her fortune" (45). The idealistic Willmore wins Angellica's "virgin heart" by answering, "It is a barbarous custom, which I will scorn to defend in our sex, and do despise in yours."

The two sisters in *The Rover,* one to be forced into the distasteful marriage and the other into a convent, are virtuous, although Hellena is more of a true libertine than Angellica, and they are as outspoken as the

prostitutes. Behn's plays are full of virtuous women and of women waver-
ing between virtue and moments of happiness. Frequently (and with
varying degrees of fancifulness) invoking *divorce a vinculo,* Behn rescues
even married women from the forced marriages she sees as male guard-
ians' prostitution of their female "property." In *The Lucky Chance,* Julia,
already Lady Fulbank, is reunited with Gayman and given a fortune at
the end of the play.[72] Invoking canon and common law spousal *de prae-
senti* contract enforcements, which led to annulments, Behn reinforced
the concept that the engagement freely pledged makes the later ceremony, especially since Julia believed Gayman dead, nonbinding. Before the
happy ending, however, Julia has participated in the juxtaposed scenes.
She rails at Gayman, "Could nothing but my fame reward your passion?"
Not only has he been indiscreet, made Julia's adultery known, but he, no
less than her husband, has gambled with her as the stakes. Her own
romantic, idealized scene contrasts sharply with the merchant's chest,
jokingly described as holding smuggled goods brought in to cheat customs and, thereby, the king's coffers, and the crude exchange of the
woman called "a bauble" and "a small parcel of ware." That Julia is a
transgressive woman is clear, not only by her taking initiative in actions
such as arranging the first scene and by stealing her husband's money in
order to rescue Gayman, but also in the way that her husband laments
that she is "a wit." Julia notes that she is incapable of simpering and
looking demure.

Just as Behn's Angellica can be found in Manley's Belira, her Julia can
be found in Manley's Olivia. Both women are sympathetic to their elderly
husbands; Julia, for instance, is sorry Sir Fulbank was frightened, and
Olivia is angry that Smyrna was knocked unconscious. In spite of temptation and inclinations Julia intended to remain faithful to her husband,
and Olivia is to Smyrna. She says to Wildman, "You know I am honest;
neither my Husband nor you can make me otherwise." What Manley and
other women preserved was the explicit expression of a range of emotions: outrage at being assessed, bartered, and sold; despair and repug-
nance when married without love; pride in their virtue and integrity.
They also preserved the hope of free love—love freely chosen and given
and constant because free. Most important of all, they insisted upon the
possibility of female self-control and self-possession.

In these plays by women in 1695–96, courtship is a travesty, for
wooing ranges from inarticulate ineffectiveness to violent rape; all of the
marriages except one short, secret one are arranged, and none is happy.

These plays, like the women's novels that followed them, showed court-ship and marriage in troubling terms. They added elements and perspec-tives largely absent from the host of plays that attacked the marriage market and introduced criticisms of courtship that would become com-mon in novels by women. Men play upon women's sympathies or plan to take advantage of what they believe to be the sex's characteristic weak-nesses. For instance, the king promises Alvaro that Agnes's pride will "draw her to the Hook, / Which I will hang with such a glittering Bait, / She can no more resist the gay Temptation, / Than Streams can stop" (11).

The best men have made women toys; Elvira's resentment has been kindled because of the prince's behavior toward her. "Was I a Trifle to be plaid with, / Fit but to entertain his leisure hours," she asks. Even Agnes says, "I heard indeed / He had a while *amus'd* himself with her" (2, 5, emphasis mine). The worst men consider rape acceptable wooing. Hom-ais is pursued and Agnes persecuted by undesirable suitors; Agnes's is determined to rape her if necessary (in Behn's text, the king gives Don Alvaro permission to do so); Morena is raped and then expected to return to Ibrahim with "a more complying Nature."[73]

Another and larger group of playwrights produced plays that appro-priated oppositional and alternative elements.[74] Thomas Southerne's very popular *Oroonoko* is an example of how the dominant culture, even a relatively sympathetic bearer of it, naturalized or even eradicated Behn's transgressive woman. From its publication, Behn's *Oroonoko* was recognized for what it is—an original and provocative masterpiece.[75] In "A Tryal of the Poets for the Bays," the author allowed Behn to compete with Dryden, Etherege, Wycherley, Lee, and others, and called *Oroo-noko* "her black Ace."[76] Not seen as an "abolitionist piece," as some twentieth-century critics have labeled it, but as a well-told, moving tale and part of her Tory *oeuvre,* it was praised as evidence of her "great Strength of Mind" and for its literary style. In recent years, the complex-ity of the work and the originality and significance of the narrative point of view have received extended, sophisticated comment. The narrator of the story is often interpreted as a construction of Behn herself, and statements within and outside the text insist upon the identification of Behn with her narrator. An advertisement appended to "Two Congrat-ulatory Poems to their Most Sacred Majesties . . . By Mrs. A. BEHN" (2d ed., 1688) described the book as "the most Ingenious, and long Ex-pected History of *Oroonoko*." According to several contemporaries,

Behn had frequently told Oroonoko's story, and always "more feelingly, than she writ it."[77]

Among the self-referential statements in the text itself is one very much in consonance with the confident, self-assertive writer she had become and of the ways that she was inserting herself into the text and into the world: "I hope the reputation of my pen is considerable enough to make his glorious name to survive to all ages, with that of the brave, the beautiful, and the constant Imoinda."[78] In Behn's text, she, the narrator, rivals Oroonoko for central place. In addition to the fact that the story is told from her perspective, her perceptions, reactions, and assessments of *her* position and power are steadily asserted and analyzed and are not simply frame but clearly part of the subject of the text. The daughter of the man who died en route to assume his appointment as lieutenant general of thirty-six islands as well as "the continent of Surinam," the narrator is housed in "the best house" and amuses herself with visits and sightseeing.

In insulting contradiction to his praise and acknowledgment of Behn's novel, Southerne opens his play with Charlotte and Lucy Welldon admitting that they are in Surinam to find husbands and confessing that they had become "shopworn" in London.[79] They are pretending to be the relatives of a newly dead rich planter and joke crassly that he "left us the credit of his relation to trade on." Part of a farcical subplot, they are nearly oblivious to the ethical and historical pageant that is Oroonoko's life. Thus, Southerne has written out not only the kind of woman and human being Behn represented but, perhaps, suggested that her description of her father and her Surinam trip was a pretentious lie. He also omits the thematic part she wrote for herself. As witness and historian and as well-wisher of the good characters (Oroonoko, Imoinda, Trefry, and Martin), the narrator brings news that England needs. She offers an insight into England's distant colonies and a demand that English conduct and native people be judged by the codes—religious and juridical—her countrymen profess.

The narrator is also in a position somewhat similar to Oroonoko's. Without her father's *position,* she is entertainment as much as entertained, spectacle as well as spectator, captive on the island until another passenger ship departs, and, like Oroonoko, housed comparatively well and occupied with visits. She is appropriated into a circle of men and used to keep Oroonoko busy and to find out his thoughts—in short, to spy on him.[80] Just as he cannot protect his people and must finally sacrifice Imoinda, she cannot free or protect Oroonoko and must finally report his torture and death. The respect shown her and the power she has assumed are proved as illusory as that shown him and as his charisma.

In Behn's text, however, women's actions still sometimes partake of the heroic; for instance, it is a woman who demands attention to this story that is so critical of Englishmen as authority figures, gentlemen, and Christians, and it is Imoinda who shoots the governor. Southerne appropriates their initiatives. His Blandford makes a powerful speech reminding the governor that Oroonoko surrendered on "Your Word! which honest Men will think should be / The last resort of Truth and trust on Earth" (2:165). He enhances Oroonoko's heroism by saving him from the responsibility of killing Imoinda and by allowing him to kill the governor and himself. The final scene is the men's, and Blandford closes the play. In contrast, Behn's *Oroonoko* closes with Oroonoko's stoic death, her mother and sister "by him all the while," and with the narrator's pronouncements about his life and her art.

The final words of Behn's text, as well as the African part of the novel, are an acknowledgment that her text is also the story of Imoinda. Imoinda is "the brave, the beautiful, and the constant" in Southerne's play, too, but she is white, and the other women "hate her, / From an instinct of natural jealousie" (2:129). In Behn's plays and novels such as *Oroonoko* and *Agnes de Castro,* all but the worst women appreciate the good and make loyal friends to other women. Thus, many of the transgressive characters have virtues usually ascribed to men, virtues that women writers would like recognized in their own sex.[81] Both Behn's novel and Trotter's play base friendship on intellectual as well as temperamental congeniality and fully admit, were the prince not enamored with Agnes, a happy marriage for one woman. Unlike the competitive jealousy found in many plays by men, including Southerne's *Oroonoko* or in figurations of the friendship cult of the poetry of Philips, neither Behn's nor Trotter's conception of female friendship is expressed in the language of the précieuse or of platonic romantic drama nor do they include the emotionally overwrought dependencies Philips describes.[82] Moreover, Behn is well aware of Imoinda's position in slavery: her captors lock her up in order to protect her unborn child, "not in kindness to her, but for fear . . . they should lose a young Slave" (67). Southerne makes the governor an attempted rapist.[83] Behn shows lust as a motive for evil in Africa, but her white men are motivated by greed and desire for power, both characteristics associated with capitalists and imperialists.

As Helene Keyssar and others have demonstrated, women's texts, even undeniably feminist ones, are seldom primarily assaults on men. Instead, they move women, their perspectives, and their experiences into the center of the text. The best of these plays, Trotter's *Agnes de Castro,* features three strong female parts. The Princess Constantia and Agnes, unwillingly forced into a love triangle, are the model of trusting, devoted friendship, and Elvira, the villainess, is disappointed lover, jealous friend, violent murderess, and frightening lunatic. No less extreme in their perfection and evil are Pix's Morena and Shaker Para and Manley's Bassima and Homais.

In drama, female characters—or their perspectives—often open and close the plays, and women's situations and emotional discomforts must be resolved. Frequently they reveal the complexities of women's choices and circumstances and correct images of their daily existence and their relationships with women as well as with men.[84] Agnes fears the loss of the companionship of her friend more than the loss of her life. Often treated as though stupid, the women protest as Selima does when she says to Osman, "In this thou wrong'st my wit as well as love." He answers, "One of your woman's fits, I'll leave you to them" (246). Manley's Wilmore pleads with his abandoned mistress to help him, to "be Noble, like the Love you promised." She lashes out, "What Generosity canst thou hope to find, where only injuries are given? what suffering, tame, deluded Monster doest thou think me?" (*Lost Lover,* 36). Alvaro taunts Elvira, "You scorn, because that's all you have in Pow'r: / Cou'd you enjoy by Force the Man you love'd, / You'd think that best Revenge" (19). Beside these fantasies of perfect love and glimpses of impossible happiness are fantasies of female power. These writers explore its nature and its limits in such contrasting modes as in the commanding dignity of Agnes de Castro and Bassima that comes from virtue and "constancy of mind" or in Homais's raw sexuality that has a succession of men confess: "Thou, goddess, who hast taught me best to love" (see 213, 227, 238, 240–41, 243).

Many of them do expose women's actual situation and the ways even "good" male characters maintain the hegemony. The representation of the narrator and Imoinda as admired and respected for their beauty, intelligence, and character and yet of the powerlessness of Behn's narrator and the securing of Imoinda as breeding-woman are examples of the complexities and contradictions of women's situation that such texts inscribe. In fact, Behn often thematized the irrational position of women as well as the breakdown of categories within language systems. One familiar example comes from existing women's discourses: pointed comparisons between women and slaves.[85] *Oroonoko* can be read as a detailed, horrifying development of that analogy. Oroonoko, deprived of the male right to choose and possess his love object, then enslaved, is progressively feminized and then physically emasculated. Like a woman, he is asked to trust and remain passive in the face of evidence that such behavior leads to exploitation and pain.[86]

Other adaptations of Behn's works show similar acts of appropriation and naturalization. In Southerne's adaptation of *The History of the Nun*, Isabella responds to pressures rather than makes choices (*The Fatal Marriage*, 1694). She calls herself "Bankrupt every way" (1.3.1). Behn's text begins with the depiction of Isabella making a series of decisions, thereby being established as a thinking, responsible individual. When Henault returns, Isabella contemplates suicide, but her decision is quite different from that made by Southerne's character: "she resolv'd upon the murder of Henault, as the only means of removing all obstacles to her future happiness" (199). The character who is egoistic and accepting of the consequences of her actions becomes in Southerne's text a deranged suicide. Both Southerne and Garrick (who adapted Southerne's play as *Isabella: or, the Fatal Marriage*, 1757) give Isabella a child, a revision that puts additional limitations on her actions and also inscribes her sex in yet another way.

These plays are very much the story of competing men; in Garrick's, Biron, Carlos, and Villeroy are or have been rivals for Isabella's love. The conclusions restore the patriarchal line of eldest sons; the child comes to fear the mad Isabella and runs to the grandfather, and the repentant, reformed man promises, "There's not a Vein but shall run Milk for Thee." The final speeches refer to Isabella and Biron as nameless "offending Children" best left to Heaven and direct attention firmly toward the child and the grandfather. Both playwrights create the "constant woman," reduce Isabella to object by making her the male characters' means to revenge, and write scenes that turn her into spectacle. Behn's Isabella is also a sexual being and an economic unit; she says she likes her second husband's "person" very well, and she takes jewels and money from the nunnery. Behn's Isabella redeems herself with charitable acts, confession, and repentance. In contrast, Southerne's and Garrick's heroines are totally disempowered by madness and are early examples of the male construction of female hysteria. Manley complained of Southerne's play as "wrought up with all the natural Artifice of a good Poet" and has Hernando use it to argue the benefits of "double marriages," especially polygamy (*New Atalantis* 1:218–20).

Farquhar's *The Constant Couple* (1699) adapts major parts of *The Rover*. Although most of the changes can be attributed to the standards for acceptable comedy in the early eighteenth century, signs of Farquhar's appropriation of the threatening Angellica and the revisionary themes are still evident. In his play, Angelica is merely mistaken for a prostitute by Sir Harry Wildair, the brave rake just back from the Continent. In spite of the similarity in names, Farquhar's Lady Lurewell is more like Behn's Angellica than his Angelica. Jilted, she believes, by an unprincipled seducer, she has determined to take revenge on any man unlucky enough to fall within her sphere. Like Behn's Angellica, she believes all men inconstant and her heart invulnerable, yet the play reveals that her love for her seducer has never cooled. Angelica's betrayed, ringing speeches in Farquhar's text are divided: part are addressed to the wrong man and part are wrongly directed at Standard, for Wildair has not betrayed her and Standard has never ceased to love her.

In contrast to Willmore, neither Wildair nor Standard has broken his vows. Lurewell and Standard are revealed to be devoted, virtuous, and constant lovers. Angelica, who has few scenes and no depth, and Wildair are united by social class more than anything else. One of Wildair's speeches chastises Lurewell when he warns Standard, " 'tis unpardonable to charge the failings of a single woman upon the whole sex." In the last act, a chastened Lurewell pronounces, "Then men are still most generous and brave." Farquhar foregrounds the men's problems and their disappointments and hopes rather than the women's. None of the women has the spirit and initiative of Hellena, Florinda, or Angellica, and the themes of forced marriage and distinctions among kinds and expressions of love and constancy are entirely eliminated. Action and all kinds of authority are given to the men. Wildair, not Angelica, sets the unusually high price on her body, and, unlike Angellica who has willingly and quixotically given Willmore money only to see him "set himself out for other lovers," Lurewell is Smuggler's victim, faced with "bussing" for her own guineas.

A more complete appropriation is John Philip Kemble's *Love in Many Masks* (1790).[87] Three of the four major kinds of changes he made can largely be explained by reference to dates of production. For instance, shorter plays were in fashion in the 1790s, and some of the

Cavalier allusions would have sounded quite dated.[88] Scanning a list of cut speeches makes starkly obvious how much freer the language of the dramatists of Behn's generation was than that of Kemble's. Among lines cut are "[I could] kiss the bed the bush grew in." Behn writes, "A beauty passable? A vigor desirable? Well shaped? Clean limbed?" and Kemble emends, "a beauty passable—a tolerable shape."

Kemble's fourth set of changes, however, edits out some of the strongest revisionary and oppositional elements in Behn's play. She is intent upon emphasizing the similarities between socially accepted behavior and criminal (or sinful) conduct, upon exposing the double standard, and upon demonstrating that women, regardless of class, share many of the same conditions of existence. Lines that do this work are often omitted by Kemble, and neither Angellica nor Hellena is as developed in Kemble's play. Some of their most important speeches are omitted or collapsed, as Hellena's proviso lines are (5:407–29) and Angellica's soliloquy when Willmore leaves her (4:397–415). Some of Hellena's more earthy conceits are excised or changed, and she becomes less the Cavalier; the omissions of selected speeches by Angellica reduce audience access to her suffering and her softer side.

Behn's text is most powerful when it brings the contradictory aspects of Angellica's character to the fore. The woman who can be lyrical about her first love and persuasive about having a "virgin heart" also brings the most extreme statements of capitalism and the marketplace onto the stage: "This is a trade, sir, that cannot live by credit" (2:120). Kemble eliminates almost all references to her trade and consistently substitutes words or even scenes for Behn's frank discussions. In one notable case, he cuts Moretta's description of the fate of whores and substitutes a love scene filled with birth and breeding images. By grinding down both the most romantic and the most mercenary aspects of Angellica, Kemble produces a female character who competes less with Hellena and who is easily experienced as part of a patriarchal plot pattern.

An important part of Hélène Cixous's formulation of what women need to do to insert themselves in hegemonic processes is to "write her self . . . put her self into the text—as into the world and into history—by her own movement." Surely Behn's most revolutionary act is the way she put herself into her texts and into the world and even into history. Frequently reminding her readers of her sex and of her ambitions for her writing, she extends her use of her life, experiences, and aspirations to contest the nature, roles, and life resolutions assigned to women. By doing so, she allows us to see that her position within and without a text is often analogous. In a sense, she offers her self as hegemonic apparatus and accelerated and even initiated processes that will continue until women writers and women's experiences are fully integrated into our culture.

Surely among her most transgressive acts are her presentations of herself as playwright and as one who would take "any subject the vast World affords." She aggressively laid claim to the political world and to private personality. In a perceptive move, she insisted that the masculine "Method, and Rule" was out of fashion and that personality, manners, and human relations were what theater audiences wanted:

> That we have nobler Souls than you, we prove,
> By how much more we're sensible of Love;
> Quickest in finding all the subtlest ways
> To make your Joys, why not to make you Plays?
> We best can find your Foibles, know our own,
> And Jilts and Cuckolds now best please the Town;
> Your way of Writing's out of fashion grown.
> . . . .
> We'll let you see, whate'er besides we do,
> How artfully we copy some of you:
> And if you're drawn to th' Life, pray tell me then,
> Why Women should not write as well as Men.
>   (Epilogue to *Sir Patient Fancy,* 4:116)

Repeatedly, as in her introduction to *The Lucky Chance,* she demanded fair play and insisted on her own good judgment and responsible conduct, and she did not mind reminding her readers that she had produced "as many good Comedies, as any one man that has writ in our Age" (4:186). Unselfconscious about her influence, she felt free to write, "I gave [the actor Angel] the part, because . . ." (preface, *Dutch Lover*).

By necessity and by design, Behn wrote herself and woman's perspective into the text and into the world. In the epilogue to *Sir Patient Fancy* she asks, "What has poor Woman done, that she must be / Debar'd from Sense, and sacred Poetry?" (4:115) She was also raising the question of what women had done to be judged primarily by their sexual choices and to be debarred from making decisions about their lives. Largely in her prefaces, prologues, and epilogues but also in carefully integrated statements in her works, Behn described the frustrations, obstacles, and satisfactions, including the active help of male friends, that she experienced. By inserting herself, she both offered another example of the conditions of existence for women and entered the public world where these conditions are scrutinized and contested. For example, by telling Oroonoko and Imoinda's story, she recorded her own complicitness and the limits of her influence on men with authority, but she also left a moving, permanent record of the perfidy of Englishmen allegedly bound by their government's and their religion's codes. Increasingly she came to use first person narrators in her fiction, often giving them experiences or opinions known by contemporaries to be hers or claimed by her, and she more consistently published analyses of her own work as a woman writer.[89] From her, women could learn that prejudice against women's work would be a far from negligible handicap, that it would be painful and infuriating,[90] but that it could be overcome. They could learn that success bred success and credibility.

Behn was constructing herself as a professional woman writer even as she introduced the concept of such a writer into the ideology of womanhood.[91] Concomitantly she was carving out a place in which women could find a writing space and gradually claim that space as a tradition, and tradition gives both identity and permission. In a 1679 poem titled "To Madam Behn," "Ephelia" wrote

When first your strenuous polite lines I read,
At once it wonder and amazement bred,
To see such things flow from a woman's pen,
As might be envied by the wittiest men.

Although references to herself and her experiences abound, Behn deployed them within assertions about the work at hand and about the seriousness of her practice of her profession and her choice of subject matter. Unlike most women writers of the early modern period, she never denied that she studied, crafted, and deliberately shaped her work, that it was "labour" and "Industry," and that she expected to earn money by it.[92] She represented herself as qualified and confident, and she effortlessly drew upon serious knowledge of past and contemporary plays, of stagecraft, and of the contribution and position of players.

Behn was also important because she accepted her creativity as well as her vocation as a writer. For many writers of both sexes, creativity is a fascinating and frightening force, a troublesome gift often associated with madness or at least with periods of obsession. For many women of Behn's time, the desire to write was associated as well with masculine traits, both natural and gendered. Among these were the desire for fame, which was often identified with the desire for public admiration, for power, and even for competition. As is true of Behn's writing many times over, she stated more succinctly and powerfully these common sentiments and accepted them calmly as parts of her personality that deserved expression. Rather than internalizing the conflict and expressing the desire to suppress this part of her personality, she wrote of conflict with external pressures and opinions. Let me, she asked repeatedly, express "the Poet in me."[93] In contrast to her, Elizabeth Polwhele, a playwright working at the same time as Behn, described herself as "an unfortunate younge woman haunted by poetick divills."[94] Katherine Philips had described her "incorrigible Inclination to the Vanity of Rhyming" (*Letters,* 234). In 1696, both Ariadne and Pix confessed that they had had the "inclination" to write since childhood; Ariadne had not been able to "conquer" it, and Pix, who was the most successful female playwright between Behn and Susannah Centlivre, used her dedications to ask that it be indulged.[95]

These women used "inclination," the word commonly used in seventeenth-century literature for an inexplicable, even fated and inexorable, preference for a member of the opposite sex. The number of women who associated writing with powerful physical drives and the heightened, often wondering, tone of these passages suggest that none of the existing ways of expressing the desire to write was adequate, but that it was associated for them with strong natural feelings and with urges that needed to be controlled because they could lead to transgressive, and therefore punishable, behavior. Frances Burney describes her compulsion to write as "an inclination at which I blushed . . . [and] had always kept secret" (Epstein, 25). In "The Laugh of the Medusa," Cixous compared women's feelings about writing to their opinions about masturbation; both, she says, women allow themselves just enough "to attenuate the tension a bit, just enough to take the edge off. And then as soon as we come, we go and make ourselves feel guilty" (246–47). Rather than dwelling on the apparently inexorable nature of the urge to write or its cultural status as taboo, however, Behn familiarized the act. She matter-of-factly mentioned her motives for writing, her sources, her failures, and her successes, and she reacted with pleasure, resignation, wit, outrage— in short, with a range of honest human emotions that invariably were expressed in confident tones.

In her most extended reflection on her playwriting and its purposes, Behn engages both questions of woman's nature and measures of her art and success. Although *The Lucky Chance* is not as overtly political as plays such as *The Roundheads*,[96] Behn describes herself in the dedication as serving the Royal Cause with her "Heart and Pen"[97] and as working for the most noble, public purposes of the theater. That she conflates the experience of writing nearly allegorical political plays such as *The Roundheads* with producing plays about marriage such as *The Lucky Chance* suggests that Behn saw herself as constantly engaged in hegemonic discourses and as consistently and competitively contesting representations in both the public and private spheres.

In the best dedications of the period, the author often goes beyond citing the virtues (and wealth) of the dedicatee to pointing out the appropriateness of the choice, thereby conflating the world of the text with the world in which the honoree acts. The material Behn added for published editions of her plays took advantage of this existing convention to write herself into the world, and the dedication to James, duke of York, in the second part of *The Rover* (1681) is a good example. Like many dedications, hers draws attention to her acquaintance with the great: "The incouragement Your Royal Highness was pleas'd to give the Rover at his first appearance, and the concern You were pleas'd to have for his second, makes me presume to lay him at Your feet; he is a wanderer too, distrest; belov'd, the unfortunate, and ever constant to Loyalty" (1:113–14). Behn's Rover, an exiled Cavalier, she says, shares the experience of Charles and James during the Interregnum but is now doubly appropriate because James was forced abroad during the Exclusion crisis.[98] Already on the path that would lead to her arrest for criticism of the duke of Monmouth and Shaftesbury, Behn aligns herself with the Tory playwrights engaged in party polemics, and she places herself, in the text of the play and in the prefatory matter, with the loyal, self-sacrificing friends of the king.[99] As she will do in *Oroonoko,* she witnesses, judges, and aligns herself with the good people.

Behn's situation in the theater as playwright and as woman was similar to her position in the narrative of *Oroonoko.* During the turmoil of 1681–82, Behn was one of several Tory playwrights vigorously putting their views before the public and turning the stage into a dynamic vehicle for propaganda. The dedication to *The Roundheads* (1682) admits disappointments in the outside world; Behn quotes Whig gloating after the recent City election, which she identifies with carrying on "the Good Old Cause": "Tho' the Tories have got the better of us at the Play, we carried it in the City by many Voices" (1:337). As in *Oroonoko,* Behn pushes herself into the larger issues. She compares those who would have damned her play "for its Loyalty" to the factious rebels who "wou'd be at the *Old Game* their fore-Fathers play'd" and to the City jury that acquitted Shaftesbury (1:338). She and her play, thus, join the group of plays to which the Whigs concede defeat, yet she takes note of outside events and the fact that the Tory victory is not yet decisive.[100]

The most neglected part of Behn's career is what may have been most central to it: this refusal to be shut out of the public political sphere. She knew well the part art played in sustaining an ideology. In the epilogue to *The Emperor of the Moon* (1687), one of her last plays, she wrote that poets in Roman times "were useful in a City held, / As formidable Armies in the Field. / They but a Conquest over Men pursu'd, / While these by gentle force the Soul subdu'd" (3:463). Her contemporaries consistently saw her work as political. A typical tribute published in 1685 reads, *"England* has a nobler task for you, / Not to tame Beasts but the brute Whigs subdue, / A thing which yet the Pulpit cou'd not do." Another reads, "Long may she scourge this mad rebellious Age, / And stem the torrent of Fanatick rage."[101] Indeed, recently amassed evidence suggests that a political faction, not "modest ladies," was behind the objections to *The Lucky Chance.*[102] In this play's preface, she repeats an opinion Charles II's reign displayed: "Plays and publick Diversions [are] . . . one of the most essential Parts of good Government."

4

WOMEN, MEN, AND THE INEXPRESSIBLE ROLE

BEHN'S FIRST MAJOR PROSE FICTION, *LOVE-LETTERS BE-tween a Nobleman and His Sister,* was licensed on 20 October 1683, eighteen months after the production of *The City Heiress.* A year after the performance of *The Emperor of the Moon* (the last of her plays produced during her lifetime), she published in rapid succession *The Fair Jilt, Oroonoko,* and *Agnes de Castro;* in the year of her death, *The History of the Nun* and *The Lucky Mistake* appeared. It has become a commonplace to note that the circumstances were similar in both cases: lean years for the London playhouses and an inhospitable political environment for Behn. In fact, however, the plays produced immediately before these fictions had been successful, and there were a number of more profitable publishing ventures available to Behn than prose fiction—and she took advantage of many of them.[1] Moreover, Behn's fiction is daringly original and outspoken, and these qualities are not often characteristic of the work of a writer wishing to be safer, less conspicuous, and quickly solvent. In form, subject matter, and language, her last writings seem to be those of a person grappling with a new national order, of one seeking new modes of political expression and influence, and of a woman conscious of her past achievements and perhaps her approaching death now desiring to write herself into history and into the world.

By the early 1680s, the stage was still a site worth contesting by political parties, but it no longer offered the best forum for political propaganda. Behn compared the theater to the City of London in 1682, and noted that the Tories' hold on both seemed threatened and tenuous. The ironic dedication to *The Roundheads* admitted disappointments in the outside world: "Tho' the Tories have got the better of us at the Play, we carried it in the City by many Voices" (1:337). Aware of the factions now always present at the theater, she compared those who would have damned her play "for its Loyalty" to the factious rebels who "wou'd be at the *Old Game* their fore-Fathers play'd" and to the City jury that acquitted Shaftesbury by an *ignoramus* verdict (1:338). Sixty Dissenters had been elected to the Court of Common Council in 1681, and the king faced a City government in which seven of nine aldermen, three of four London M.P.'s, and an average of nearly two-thirds of empaneled jurists were not only Whigs but Dissenters.[2] The nation was moving toward "the most elaborate propaganda campaign" yet waged in Europe, and any writer could see the shift to print as opposed to performance.[3]

That and the narrow, factious, and declining audience was sending the entire group of dedicated party writers in search of new means of reaching the public even before the union of companies in 1682. Dryden, for instance, was publishing a series of poems that included *Absalom and Achitophel* and *The Medall: A Satire Against Sedition,* and Durfey issued a pindaric poem, *The Progress of Honesty, or a View of Court and City* and a continuation of *Hudibras, Butler's Ghost,* in which Hudibras was a Whig and Shaftesbury a pygmy. Plays, like these poems, were forms of news, actually more similar to editorials that both mentioned events and interpreted them. One prologue read, "The Stage, like old Rump Pulpits, is become / The scene of News, a furious Party's drum."[4] The theater commented on almost every political event, if not in the plays themselves then in the prologues, epilogues, or printed dedications, and playwrights found themselves increasingly subject to arrest or censorship. A series of exchanges over John Crowne's *City Politiques* shows that its license was recalled in June 1682 by the Lord Chamberlain, the earl of Arlington; in July, he ordered that Lee and Dryden's *Duke of Guise* not be acted.[5] Behn was called to account for her epilogue to the anonymous *Romulus and Hersilia* in August 1682,[6] and although a better poet than Durfey chose to try to reach the public with prose.[7]

Marxists have theorized that new genres are born when old ones are no longer adequate to express a nation's experiences and aspirations;

many of the poems, plays, and fictions of the 1680s are richly experimental and original. Bakhtin has argued in "Discourses in the Novel," in *The Dialogic Imagination,* that the inevitable decay "of the religious, political and ideological authority connected with [a particular literary] language" opens texts to the "social heteroglossia of national languages" (370), and Marx called the novel a "simple abstraction," an apparently and deceptively monolithic category that encloses a complex historical process. More pessimistically, Michael McKeon has said that "the birth of genres results from a momentary negation of the present so intense that it attains the positive status of a new tradition."[8] It seems clear that Behn produced work representative of such times, yet the "negation" not only laid bare some of the utopian treasures alive in her culture but brought current experience, the present, into art in a new way.

Love-Letters between a Nobleman and His Sister is news and, in fact, says many of the things that Behn had put in the prologue and epilogue to *Romulus and Hersilia.* In the prologue, she had written, "How we shall please ye now I cannot say; / But Sirs, 'Faith here is *News from Rome* to day." This reference to a title used now and then throughout the seventeenth and eighteenth centuries would have associated the play with propagandistic interpretations of current events; these tracts and periodicals usually claimed to be Jacobite self-incriminations, but Behn turns the title around to reflect on the Whigs. The prologue attacks the *ignoramus* decision, Whig plots and "cabals," and, as Dryden had in the suppressed prologue to *The Duke of Guise,* "the Sham Sheriffs Party." The epilogue, the part Behn and the actress were brought in to discuss, reads:

LOVE! like *Ambition,* makes us Rebels too:
And of all Treasons, mine was most accurst;
Rebelling 'gainst a KING and FATHER first.
. . . .
Some of the Sparks too, that infect the *Pit,*
(Whose Honesty is equal to their Wit,
And think *Rebellion* but a petty Crime,
Can turn to all sides Int'rest does incline,)
May cry, *"Igad I think the Wench is wise;*
Had it prov'd Lucky, 'twas the way to rise.
She had a Roman *Spirit that disdains*
Dull Loyalty, and the Yoke of Sovereigns.

A Pox of Fathers, and Reproach to Come;
She was the first and Noblest Whig of Rome."

The epilogue also calls the rebels ungrateful and treacherous.[9]

What readers encountered in *Love-Letters between a Nobleman and His Sister* was a deceptively packaged, sophisticated political satire. Obviously allying it with the fashionably popular French romances and with Continental, amorous epistolary fiction, Behn had based it upon a sensational news event and drawn as well upon available, more openly political forms. Thus, she brought the novel into the "zone of maximally close contact between the represented object and contemporary reality"[10] and also released the form's potential for participation in the immediate life of a civic society. So good is her work that the satire accrues and finally establishes the character and nature of her object rather than striking the reader as satire per se. Bakhtin has said that the more sophisticated a new form is, the more visible are its "orchestrated languages" and the more significant the process or re-accentuation (418–21). In writing this piece of propaganda, Behn not only created a new form of political propaganda, but she actualized some of the potential as hegemonic apparatus inherent in the form that would be called novel and that would be recognized by the end of the eighteenth century as a "well-worn channel of access to the public."[11] In fact, her text may also pose an answer to a question that comes to all critics of the novel: where is "the original example of a work to be held up as *the* dangerous, [indecent], and misleading" example of the novel form?[12]

The news event that Behn exploited was the scandalous relationship between Ford Grey, later earl of Tankerville, and his sister-in-law, Lady Henrietta (Harriet) Berkeley. The 22–25 August *London Mercury* reported, "We have News from *Epsom,* That a daughter of the Lord *Berkley* was stollen away in the Night; and since 'tis discovered that she is married to a Gentleman who was a former Suitor to her, her Father being averse thereto." Shortly afterwards, other papers announced that she was married to "one *Forester*" and, depending on the day, that he was a man of "considerable Estate; so that 'tis hoped she may the more easily be reconciled to her Parents" or that this event "causeth great grief in that Honourable Family."[13] Soon news followed that she was not married, not found, and that reports in the *Domestick Intelligence* that she had advised her father of the marriage were false.[14] Called "the most notorious case of seduction in a profligate age,"[15] their romance became a King's Bench trial before Lord Chief Justice Francis Pemberton and was tried again by the partisan periodical press.[16] It also happened that Grey was so trusted a friend and adviser of the duke of Monmouth as to be styled his "Elector-General" and was part of the Exclusion agitation most closely associated with Anthony Ashley Cooper, first earl of Shaftesbury. In the years after the first part of Behn's fiction appeared, Monmouth led a rebellion and was executed before a huge crowd that dipped their handkerchiefs in his blood for souvenirs.

Since 1680, Behn had been working on the side loyal to the succession of James to the throne. She had effectively used a variety of ways to link the Whig opponents of James with the rebels of the 1640s and 50s. For instance, her play *The Roundheads* (1682) was based on Tatham's *The Rump,* a fact that would strengthen the parallels between the two decades' Royalist playwrights and between their representations of the allegedly capricious, self-aggrandizing, ambitious rebels. The Grey scandal was perfect for her purposes. Grey was Presbyterian, and his maternal uncle was General Henry Ireton. He also had distinguished Cavalier forebears, but Behn could play on the rebel blood. She gave Monmouth the name of Cesario and, as in her story, he had been romantically associated with Grey's wife Mary Berkeley both before and after her marriage.[17] As early as 1678, Grey was part of a cabal of Whig extremists. He even joined in supporting the charge that Queen Catherine could be implicated in the Popish Plot,[18] and he was one of eight Whigs who tried to have James indicted as a popish recusant.

By 1683, when Behn was writing *Love-Letters,* Grey had already been before the Privy Council to explain a cache of weapons stored in his Charterhouse Yard home and had been fined 1,000 marks for his part in inciting Midsummer's Day rioting.[19] On 26 June he had been arrested as a conspirator in the Rye House Plot but had escaped at the door of the Tower. Behn's book concludes with a letter from Philander (Grey) to Sylvia (Harriet): "Haste [to me]; bring what news you can learn of *Cesario;* I would not have him die poorly after all his mighty hopes, nor be conducted to a scaffold with shouts of joys [*sic*], by that uncertain beast the rabble, who used to stop his chariot-wheels with fickle adorations whenever he looked abroad."[20] "Cesario" did not die that year, although the trial and exection of Lord William Russell had led many to believe that Monmouth could not be spared. Indeed, the attorney general had issued warrants with £500 rewards for Monmouth and others.[21]

Behn, cautious about political statements and something of a cynic about plots,[22] locates her fiction in France and casts Cesario and Philander and their largely nameless associates in a series of vague meetings, travels about the country, and amorphous plans. She captures, therefore, the actual indecisiveness and disorganization of Monmouth and the Whigs better than those of her contemporaries who believed in firm leadership, organized plans, or even isolated plots with drastic objectives. By 1683, too, Grey had been convicted by a London jury on the *de homine replegiando* writ, the complaint of his father-in-law, Lord Berkeley. The sensational trial had featured the appearance of Lady Harriet, who insisted not only that she had left home on her own initiative but also that she was married to William Turner, son of Sir William, a prominent London merchant and Nonconformist; the younger Turner would fight with Monmouth. William Morrice commented that at the trial "a great many things were laid open by the parties concerned, that it had been much for the honour of them all to have . . . buried in perpetual oblivion." Turner and Lady Harriet spent three days in King's Bench prison while the court verified the legitimacy of their marriage.[23] Before sentencing, however, Pemberton had recorded a *Noli Prosequi,* and after Grey's escape at the Tower the lovers had gone to Holland. Behn focused her book on the love life of Grey and the Berkeley sisters and depended primarily on details from the trial and from published accounts, both satiric and journalistic.[24] By doing so, she avoided dangerous reflections on Monmouth and other powerful men, yet she could vilify the type working against the succession of James.

Thus, Behn offered a new kind of propaganda at an opportune moment. The Whigs were in some disarray, and it was a good time to further discredit the tarnished Monmouth and his proponents. Since at least the 1640s English readers had been bombarded with political tracts, but Behn created a pleasure vehicle to carry her propaganda.[25]

Depending on the reader, the most familiar relative of Behn's *Love-Letters* would probably have been either the amorous epistolary novel or the political memoir, and she could count on recent, sensationally popular publications to attract readers to her own. One of these was *Lettres portugaises traduites en français* (1669), and Behn could take advantage of its even wider readership after its recent translation into the English *Five Love Letters from a Nun to a Cavalier* (1678, second edition 1680).[26] By this time, too, a sequel as well as pretended answers from the Cavalier had appeared. English epistolary fiction was quite rare at the time,[27] but a few texts had been published with political aims. *Coll: Henry Marten's Familiar Letters* began with a spurious letter "in justification of the Murther of the Late King Charles" and concluded with a "letter" attacking it.[28] The personal letters, probably genuine, are full of easily ridiculed Puritan sentiments and arrangements for supplying Mary Ward with such things as soap and food. The last letters by Marten, who was confined in the Tower as a regicide, complain of infrequent visits and are followed by several fictional letters from "Dick Pettingall," Mary's "Inamoretto." Whereas Marten's are simple and domestic, these letters are full of the rhetorical flourishes of seventeenth-century love discourses.

This book had enough appeal that a second edition was issued in 1663 and a third in 1685. Although it still probably had some anti-rebel propaganda value, the fact that its title had been changed to *The Familiar Epistles of Coll. Henry Marten* shows that its appeal might now be to those seeking amorous epistolary fictions.[29] *Lettres portugaises,* of course, was certainly known to more people than any of the political memoirs or epistolary satires, and it provided genre identity that assured sales and that obscured the deeply partisan nature of the text. Behn tapped into the form that seemed to promise readers people revealing themselves without intending to and emotions presented subjectively and "to the moment" without mediation. Just as Tatham and Behn had represented the minds, motives, and characters of Cromwell's inner circle in their plays, Behn presented herself as showing her readers the dangerous and socially irresponsible nature and temperament of Grey and his cohorts. Styling her text as epistolary romance and drawing upon the English traditions of using history to show the "tempers and principles of the chief actors" of public events[30] and of creating political propaganda that used exaggerated, fictionalized portraits and allegorical allusions to "explain" individuals and their actions, Behn produced a text seductive to many kinds of readers.

The English political memoir differed from the longer French ones by being limited to the "history" of a remarkable event rather than embedding the event in an extended, rather fabulous adventure narrative. Memoirs often had a fictional military or political attaché as narrator; this perspective created a knowledgeable observer and allowed the revelation of private behavior and of "secret springs" of actions affecting the public domain. The narrative point of view allowed interpretative commentary upon actual events with little or no risk of arrest and considerable freedom for propagandistic statements. The French expectation that amorous intrigues would be included had carried over into English memoirs to some extent.

Behn's readers might have thought of texts such as *The Memoirs of the Dutchess Mazarine* (1676), which related the life story of Hortense de Mancini up to the time she became part of Charles II's court.[31] The duchess, niece and heir to the famous cardinal, had spent years trying to avoid her husband and had finally fled to England. Sylvia's disguises, travels, and attempts to find refuges are somewhat similar to Hortense's; the women's restless spirits and ungoverned behavior could both be described by a modern historian's depiction of the duchess: she had "a powerful, reckless, passionate personality."[32] Charles had given her a home in St. James Palace, and it was known that he slipped through the park to spend his nights with her and had granted her £1,000. By the time the *Memoir* was licensed on 22 February 1677, Charles was no longer visiting her, but he was embroiled with Parliament over money, and the Exclusion Crisis was on the horizon. Although the narrative might justify Hortense's desertion of her husband, she was still a French Catholic and a notorious woman, and her conduct had been and was scandalous. As she said, "I know the chief Glory of a Woman ought to consist, in not making her self to be publickly talked of" (2). Whatever the translator's intentions, the text reflected upon the king and fed the reputation of the court as a place of license and licentiousness.[33] In such tracts, then, writers could use private lives and intimate details to influence public opinion.

Among the most visible of its "orchestrated languages" is that of the now often-mentioned but seldom-read multivolume French romance, and all of Behn's fictions bear traces of it.[34] This literary kind, like the memoir and amorous epistle, often claimed to be about actual people and public, political events. For instance, all of the important characters except the Princess of Clèves and her mother and many of the events and narratives in the text can be identified with actual people and events, and sixty-three people have been identified in *Clélie*.[35] For decades after the Restoration, compilers of lists of published books listed these French-style romances with histories.[36] This circumstantial evidence suggests that readers accepted authors' claims that their books taught their readers history and gave them the benefit of experience without the misfortunes of mistakes and unfortunate decisions.[37] The auditors of Madame la Dauphine in *La Princesse de Clèves* thank her for "teaching them so much about the English Court" and ask for additional information (96).

As the dedication prefaced to the English edition of the French romance *Artamenes; or, The Grand Cyrus* (English trans., 1653) explains:

> For the Intrigues and Miscarriages of War and Peace are better, many times, laid open and Satyriz'd in a *Romance,* than in a downright History, which being oblig'd to name the Persons, is often forc'd for several Reasons and Motives to be too partial and sparing; while such disguis'd Discourses as these, promiscuously personating every Man, and no Man, take their full liberty to speak the Truth.[38]

John Barclay's *Argenis* (1621) has been described as an instructive allegory because of its representation of historical events and people, and part of the subtitle of Richard Brathwait's *Panthalia* reads, "A Discourse Stored with infinite variety in relation to State-Government and Passages of matchless affection gracefully interveined [*sic*]."[39]

Behn exploited this potential in the romance form and recalled the power of the other forms to appear to be artless revelations of the hidden motives and baser natures of their subjects. Among other things, its authors claimed that the romance had earned "esteeme and Authority" from their representations of "images of life" and of "the passions and action of Men" and that their subject was "civil life," that is, the concerns of citizens self-consciously located within a social order.[40] Honoré D'Urfé, for instance, calls his *Astrea* "Academies for the *Lover,* Schools of War for the *Souldier,* and Cabinets for the *Statesman.*"[41] Although critical opinion today is that "no author demeaned himself to write them—or anything like them—except to relieve dire financial need,"[42] romances continued to be written and read, especially by the upper classes, at least through the middle of the eighteenth century. Delarivière Manley remarked that they had "for a long time been the diversion and amusement of the whole world . . . and all sorts of people have read these works with a most surprising greediness."[43] David Roberts cites evidence that shows that "romances, so widely read by women and so often plundered for stage plays . . . occasioned comment in the theatre about the shaping of scenes, the aptness of the dialogue, or the success of the casting" (42).

Among the most powerful strategies of these texts is their use of sex and gendering, and in Behn's work we can see the beginning of the use of sex as political category. Before the late seventeenth century, binary oppositions were habitually represented by differences in age, legitimacy (as in Edgar and Edmund in *King Lear*), or class; after that, the most

frequent representation of oppositions was in sex.[44] Philander can control neither his fears nor his emotions. Like so many thwarted women in
fiction, he "raves," "tears," curses himself (48), and tells his beloved of
his "thousand soft desires" (93). Both he and Sylvia cross-dress, but
where he experiences embarrassment, Sylvia rejoices in "the cavalier in
herself" and the "thousand little privileges, which otherwise would have
been denied to women" (117–18). He writes, "Those that love not like
me will be apt to blame me, and charge me with weakness" (38). At this
stage of their relationship, Sylvia evokes the ideology of the restored
Charles, who was

> born a king, and born your king; and holds his crown by right of
> nature, by right of law, by right of heaven itself; heaven who has
> preserved him, and confirmed him ours, by a thousand miraculous
> escapes and sufferings, . . . and endeared him to us by his wondrous
> care and conduct, by securing of peace, plenty, ease and luxurious
> happiness. . . . Would you destroy this wonderous gift of heaven?
> This god-like king, this real good we now possess, for a most uncer-
> tain one; and with it the repose of all the happy nation? (36)

Her arguments conclude with the reasoning of Dryden's *Absalom and
Achitophel*. Thus, one ideology is presented as rational and adult, and the
other as weak, childish, and selfish.

In the texts from which Behn drew her rhetorical strategies, cross-
dressing and gendered behavior often signaled the position and power of
characters. For some women, male attire emphasized what they did not
have. As Mrs. Verbruggen says archly in the epilogue to Trotter's *Agnes
de Castro,* "I fear these Breeches, Sword, and Manly shew / Ev'ry way
promise more than I can do." Hortense had traveled in men's clothes
but, in contrast to her very short maid, is never so "unfit to be Cloathed in
mens Apparel" that she routinely provokes laughter (68). These texts
could reveal that power is allocated not in accordance with biological sex
identity but with the perception of gendered, gender-assigned characteristics. Hortense is certainly "bold and hardy," while her husband is
reduced in her descriptions to the kinds of pettiness that make life
tedious. In England, her power is fascinating. Notably, Calista is tall and
"fashioned the most divinely for [masculine] dress of any of her sex"
(317). Cesario's "Hermione" is masculine in appearance, and she, too,
"weakens" him; he must be cajoled and shamed into resuming his public
role. Thomoso has found him a slave and "perfectly effeminated into soft

woman" (333). The "masculine" Laura can "pass for Man" in *The Feign'd Curtezans,* and Hippolita in *The Dutch Lover* says, "Methinks I am not what I was, / My Soul too is all Man" (1:293). D'Urfé's Celadon, disguised as Alexis, must wait the permission of Astrea to declare his love again; as Roland Barthes said, "This man who waits and who suffers from his waiting is miraculously feminized."[45] Marten is imprisoned, as is Aronces, and his beloved Clelia performs such heroic acts that a statue is erected in her honor in Rome. That Aronces repeatedly rescues his rival, Horatius, casts Horatius as something of a maiden in distress and disqualifies him from marriage to such an intrepid heroine. *Lettres portugaises* helped establish uncontrolled emotional outpourings as feminine, and when Behn departed from the "masculine" examples given in the French romances and even in Roger L'Estrange's *Five Love-Letters written by a Cavalier* (1683),[46] she effectively used cultural signals for propaganda purposes.

All of these forms could smoothly contain quite direct propaganda material, and the differences among the three parts of Behn's *Love-Letters,* especially when set beside her other late prose fictions, help illuminate some of the reasons why the novel became the most powerful form of moral propaganda yet devised and a favorite means of access to the public.[47] In the first part of *Love-Letters,* Behn concentrates her attack on the rebels and their cause. Indeed, the text includes a not insignificant number of absolutely direct statements.[48] Among the most effective is one in which Sylvia identifies the private with the public: "Your life and glory depend on the frail sacrifice of villains and rebels . . . ; if Sylvia could command, Philander should be loyal as he's noble; and what generous maid would not suspect his vows to a mistress, who breaks 'em with his prince and master!" (16)

Behn subtly keeps this idea before her readers and aggressively portrays Philander and the rebels as rash, passionate, and often ridiculous. This was, of course, a traditional representation of rebels, and she shows the justice of the portrayal by developing the character of Philander. For instance, Behn has Philander escape once from Sylvia's room in a woman's dress only to be accosted and lewdly propositioned. Prone to violence, they are often, however, powerless and sometimes even literally impotent. With Sylvia Philander is impotent after he has "passed all . . . the loose and silken counterscarps that fenced the sacred fort" (50). This long letter is filled with expressions intended to make Grey ridiculous. "Philander" writes, "What god. . . . Snatched my (till then) never failing power?" *"Philander* the young, the brisk and gay *Philander,* who never failed the woman he scarce wished for, never baulked the amorous conceited old, nor the ill-favoured young . . ." "Wholly abandoning my soul to joy, I rushed upon her, who, all fainting, lay beneath my useless weight, for . . . all my power was fled" (51–53). As Linda Kauffman says, the laughter is "a theoretical and political strategy; it demystifies the male. . . . the women imagine a man confronting his own mediocrity . . . the aim is a comical operation of dismemberment of the phallus as signifier" (297).

When Sylvia runs away, she discovers that Philander has wandered away, missed their rendezvous, and been wounded in a foolish duel. Later Brilliard doses himself with so much of an aphrodisiac that he becomes ill and cannot perform at all. Sylvia has substituted her willing maid for herself, and Brilliard is attempting to pass himself off as Octavia. His inept, crude letters combined with his sexual ineptitude make him the object of derisive laughter. Thus, both he and Philander are represented as being without adequate language and without the other sign of male power, phallic potency.[49]

Behn insists repeatedly that each rebel is really out for himself alone and that the group is without principles, even mistaken ones. Philander writes:

> The world knows *Cesario* renders himself the worst of criminals . . . , and has abandon'd an interest more glorious and easy than empire. . . . But let him hope on—and so will I, as do a thousand more, for ought I know; I set out as fair as they. . . . When every fool is aiming at a kingdom, what man of tolerable pride and ambition can be unconcerned, and not put himself into a posture of catching, when a diadem shall be thrown among the crowd? It were . . . stupid dullness, not to . . . make an effort to snatch it as it flies. (40–41)

By the time she published the third part, Monmouth had been executed and Charles was dead, and the volume is the rehearsal of a party line. Rather than propaganda it is a hegemonic apparatus participating in the establishment of an ideology. Behn retells a version of the story of the king's hope for reconciliation and of Monmouth's rebellion, and presents a craven, love-besotted end for him.[50] In places, she again uses direct statement, as she does in explaining Grey's conduct. Thought by his contemporaries and many modern historians to be either inept, cowardly, or disloyal as commander of Monmouth's horse,[51] Grey is portrayed as perfidious, weak, and inconstant in council and battle. In Behn's text, he has come to the conclusion that "he was weary of their actions, and foresaw nothing but ruin would attend them" (445), and "he had resolved to . . . prove false to a party, who had no justice and honour on their side, than to a King, whom all the laws of heaven and earth obliged him to serve" (446).

When Behn turned to fiction in 1687, she turned to it not only as political propaganda but also as a new means of expression. She grappled with a new political world order and challenged representations of men, women, and social relationships. Writing before the formation of the bourgeois public sphere, she could release the novel's potential to reveal ruptures and contradictions in the dominant ideology even as the fiction could operate as moral propaganda. In her texts she often produces the latter by aligning the individual conscience with the public conscience, thereby mediating the emergent capitalistic individualism and appropriating it in order to reinforce the old ideology of the individual's responsibility to sacrifice self for community interests. Simultaneously, she dramatizes individuals' harsh confrontation with their personal desires and their awareness of community.

In a text such as *Love-Letters,* echoes of Dryden's *All for Love* and other dramatic heroic romances work to demand that readers judge the lovers within a context of larger civic concerns.[52] Evoking "One day passed by, and nothing saw but love; / Another came, and still 'twas only love. / The suns were wearied out with looking on, / And I untired with loving" (2:285–87), Sylvia writes, "I saw the day come on, and cursed its busy light, and still you cried, one blessed minute more, before I part with all the joys of life! And hours were minutes then, and day grew old upon us unawares" (87). Philander, like Antony, has a wife, and his politico-social position with his estate and seat in Parliament, even exclusive of his involvement with Monmouth, makes his conduct a matter of national concern. Philander and Antony liken the world to toys and baubles (93 and 2:428–30, 442–45). Other references to well-known plays bring the consequences of irresponsibility and rebellion vividly to mind. "Who is it dares hurt the King?" Sylvia quotes from Thomas Otway's 1679 *Caius Marius* (34–35).

In life and in *Love-Letters,* after the decisive battle (Sedgmoor), Grey is imprisoned for a time but "was at last pardoned, kissed the King's hand, and came to Court, in as much splendour as ever" (461). In these concluding volumes, both principal characters become unfaithful and slaves to appetite and even whimsy; a transformed Sylvia becomes a discontented, mercenary, immoral person. With the cold clarity of the stage, Sylvia has stated in part 1 what is at stake for her: "I have lost my honour, fame and friends, my interest and my parents" (105). In the last section, she recognizes herself in Alonzo's description of "a whore—and how fine a one" (411).

The lovers' rambling adventures and the corruption of such basically sympathetic characters as Octavia and Calista show individual ruin and, simultaneously, the loss of potentially valuable citizens. Reared in a church tradition that used marriage metaphors to explain the relationship between God and his people and in a nation that used metaphors of the family to articulate relationships within the state and often saw the health and order of the family as a microcosm of the health and order of the state, English people could not avoid conceiving the sexes as binary political terms. Robert Filmer's *Patriarcha* (1680) and Jean Bodin's *Six Books of the Commonwealth* (Paris, 1576; trans. 1606) had politicized the family, and Behn's texts show her great awareness of the way the private and the public spheres were intertwined. Even Sylvia, a woman, has said, "I cannot forget I am the daughter to the great *Beralti,* and sister to *Myrtilla* . . . fit to produce a race of glorious heroes" (18).

But Philander is not lost to public service. With a stroke of bitter realism, Behn notes that he was "very well understood by all *good* men," pardoned, and returned to Court (emphasis mine).[53] *The Fair Jilt, Oroonoko,* and *The History of the Nun,* as well as other works written in the last two years of her life, are of a piece with this dark roman à clef. These texts tantalize with glimpses of the kinds of human evil waiting to be unleashed. Some is premeditated and Machiavellian, some commonplace and "the way of the world," some sudden and opportunistic, some inadvertent and regretted, some desperate and impetuous. Perpetrators may prosper, remain in power, fall into destitution and disgrace, or die on the scaffold. Nothing about these fictions is simple. Often about men and women who break solemn vows, they complicate vows and swearing in all the ways known to people who had had to cope with resolving their consciences to a series of oaths, including the Solemn League and Covenant (required of all men over eighteen in 1645) and the conflicting oaths of allegiance, supremacy, and nonresistance instituted by the Act of Uniformity in the early 1660s. Isabella can be seen as too young and inexperienced to be completely responsible for her nun's vows; Myrtilla's adultery might be seen as freeing Philander from his marriage vow.

With several of Behn's stage characters, she invokes the plea of mature choice and reason dictating a different vow.[54]

These works, like Otway's late plays, flirt with a vexed world in which "hero" and "villain" can seem indistinguishable,[55] and whimsical fate decides who will die and who will prosper. Sebastian, presented initially as a respected senior citizen and statesman, lectures his nephew:

> Cannot honest men's daughters . . . serve your turn, but you must crack a Commandment? Why, this is flat adultery; a little fornication in a civil way might have been allowed. . . . A little pleasure—a little recreation, I can allow: a layer of love, and a layer of business—But to neglect the nation for a wench, is flat treason against the State; and I wish there were a law against all such unreasonable whore-masters— that are statesmen—for the rest it is no great matter. (286)

Oroonoko is surely part of this vexed world. The problems of interpreting Oroonoko as seller of slaves and yet tortured sacrifice to dishonorable slaveholders is but one in the text.[56] Since Behn's authorship of both *Oroonoko* and *Love-Letters* was known, her readers would have probably come to the second text prepared for a political allegory and remembering that Cesario was Monmouth. Is "Caesar," Oroonoko's slave name, meant to identify Monmouth? Could any of Behn's readers not associate the two? As Laura Brown says, George Marten, brother to "the great Oliverian," "deplores the inhumanity" to Oroonoko. She also notes that Royalists are responsible for Oroonoko's death and are divided among themselves over what to do with him. The highest-ranking men, the king and the lord governor, are completely innocent of Oroonoko's death, and Trefry, who has compared Parham to Whitehall, a sanctuary exempt from Byam's "law," is lured away.[57] A story, her contemporaries testify, told so many times that it must have become formulaic to her, some of its parts nevertheless would have been re-accentuated by living experience. The glorification of Charles I and his son, kings she served actively, which so many readers of *Oroonoko* have recognized, is overlaid by awareness of Charles II's unsolvable, agonizing dilemma and by the painful recognition of a new world order signaled by the Glorious Revolution. Notably for comparisons with Behn's text, at a time when the king and many noblemen had struggled with policies toward Monmouth and after a rebellion, Monmouth's execution had been a botched and brutal affair. *The Fair Jilt* includes another horrendous execution scene, this one even more similar to Monmouth's.

Both *Love Letters* and *Oroonoko* depict the Caesar character as weak-

ened and besotted by love. Pressured by Imoinda's pregnancy, Oroonoko gives up his determination to wait for the lord governor and the
fulfillment of Trefry's promise, and he is captured lying beside Imoinda's
rotting body. Like Monmouth, impatient, suspicious, and in an unten-
able position, Oroonoko leads a doomed rebellion. About *Love-Letters* it
is easy to say that Behn was not impressed by Monmouth's refusal on the
scaffold to renounce his mistress Lady Henrietta Wentworth.[58] Sylvia,
caught in bed with another man by Brilliard, yet joins with him to
become a successful con artist. Philander recovers his immense wealth
and is "splendid" at court. Those in power remain so in *Oroonoko*.
Isabella is guillotined, but Calista and Miranda live to repent. When
Miranda in *The Fair Jilt* or Isabella in *The History of the Nun* act as
capitalists, they are increasingly alienated from their community. Secre-
tive and subject to unpleasant emotions, they feel the community's force.

   In her novels, Behn seems more seriously engaged with how public
opinion is constructed and how it participates in civic discourse than she
had showed in her plays. Here she achieves a representation of what
Gramsci described as the integral state by more fully mingling the private, or civil, sphere with the political. There is a sense of a coherent
community that judges Philander, Sylvia, and Lady Mary Berkeley and
even their families and might in earlier times have erupted in the "rough
music" of charivaris. Simultaneously, Philander's politics and the implications of his and others' actions are placed on the stage. As such they
challenge and arouse the coercive forces available in the political society
as they had the censoring and collaborative forces in the civil society.
Behn manages to produce a picture that was rare even in theoretical
discourse at this time of public opinion being contested; from above,
Monmouth and others staged events calculated to elicit impressions that
they could name, and, from below, the people gossiped, wrote, and
judged. Gunn points out that the English traditional opinion was that
public opinion was "largely the creation of the entire culture,"[59] and
here Behn gives us an example of a writer making meaning out of a highly
stratified community she depicts in the process of making meaning. Wary
as Behn is of those "common people" who might follow Monmouth, she
is aware of the people as a body, as Bakhtin's protean, fecund, grotesque
body, and that in them "a new, concrete, and realistic historic awareness
was [being born] and [taking] form: not abstract thought about the
future but the living sense that each man belongs to the immortal people
who create history."[60] Such awareness of herself as a political being

entitled and able to express herself and even to influence opinion and of some of the ways that literature can be a hegemonic force invests her novel at every level.

Like Dryden's Cleopatra, women in *Love-Letters* make men effeminate. While he lives with Sylvia, Octavio's countrymen "charge him with a thousand crimes of having given himself over to effeminacy; as indeed he grew too lazy in her arms; neglecting glory, arms, and power, for the more real joys of life; while she . . . grows so bold and hardy" (285). Unlike Cleopatra, who longs to be a "household dove," Sylvia grows "bold and hardy." The text here resists interpretation. Words such as "crime," the aggressive application of strongly gendered adjectives associated with the opposite sex, Sylvia's past and the socially transgressive relationship of the lovers jar with the descriptive terms chosen for those who condemn them: "sordid and slovenly men of quality," "stingy censorious nation," "busy impertinents."

The opposition of "glory, arms, and power" to "the more real joys of life" pits public against private but also recalls the strife and turmoil in the world. William Ray has pointed out that French literature, and especially prose fiction, persistently locates the individual in "an inexorable discursive economy that repeatedly takes [the individual's] story out of her hands." He sees that "for the French the various forms of authority confronting the individual are grounded primarily in the secular order of social practices."[61] Writers show characters like Celadon and Astrea, Aronces and Clélie, the Princess of Clevès, learning their places and choices as well as understanding and expressing their feelings and desires in terms of analogy and identification with public or archetypal figures. Clélie, for instance, exhorts her companions to join her in an escape across the Tyber River: "If we dye, we shall die with greater glory then [*sic*] *Lucretia,* since it will be in avoiding an unhappinesse, which she would not out-live" (5:144).

In Part 1 of *Love-Letters,* Sylvia and Philander would write a magic love story in which they are godlike, free from ordinary rules of marriage, and ideally enamored and constant. The impossible fiction is matched by that of the beautiful, beloved illegitimate son who would miraculously become the Protestant king. Their countrymen and -women may repeat and even express attraction to these stories, but the lovers and Cesario as well are repeatedly brought to confront the fact that their stories are taken out of their hands and placed firmly in the culture's "inexorable discursive economy." By Part 2 the lovers are sordid adulterers and banished traitors who are judged not so much by the Christian code of sin but by social mores that recognize threats to community and economic well-being. Similarly, Behn represents Angellica Bianca dreaming of stepping outside the systems that were economies of Restoration sexual relations; thus, Behn flirts with violating social codes. Thereby she releases the utopian potential and has Angellica and other heroines conjure up the image of ideal love so often found in later women's texts.

In these texts, and especially in Behn's, the French insistence upon the force of collective opinion on the definition of individual identity and the English conception of history as "philosophy teaching by example" came together to produce "moral" discourse. Behn's prose fictions lay bare the novel form's potential for political negotiation in both the public and private spheres. McKeon has said that the novel had "unrivaled power both to formulate and to explain a set of problems that are central to early modern experience" (20). It is significant that he does not say that the form has the power to resolve them. The novel became the major written form for disseminating, examining, and contesting ideology and the people's image of themselves. Because of its dialogic and open-ended nature, it could capture ambiguities and contradictions and construct a psychological realism that pleased people. "The power of a novel to move its audience depends on shared conceptual categories that constitute character and event. That storehouse of assumptions includes attitudes towards the family and towards social institutions, a definition of power and its relation to individual human feeling, notions of political and social equality, and above all, a set of religious beliefs that organize and sustain the rest."[62] These conceptual categories and assumptions are never free from contradiction. The same system that can deplore the cruelty to Oroonoko can endorse the punishment for his rebellion; it can admire Isabella and the institution that executes her.

More than most Restoration and eighteenth-century works, Behn's texts make private lives touch the public sphere. The women play a large part in dooming Oroonoko's rebellion with its utopian aim, and Imoinda's pregnancy has been its primary instigating cause. Women, both his first love and Miranda, affect Henrick's position and occupation in *The Fair Jilt*. Isabella's charitable work, social graces, and exemplary conduct make her a force in her community and influence the final interpretation of her life. In a plot line that conforms exceptionally well to that identified by Lincoln Faller in the published criminal lives of the period, Isabella commits an atrocious act that outrages community sensibility, confesses and claims repentance, is brought back into the community by her public speech, and transcends her punishment by a "glorious," public death.[63]

Behn's texts, like the printed forms that are their context, also show movement toward the modern recognition of the importance of controlling the formation of public opinion.[64] Characters in *Astrea,* for instance, ask such questions as "tell us how you heard it, that we may see how reports do jump" (56). At one point, Celadon asks how reports of his rumored death have been explained, and the shepherd answers, "it is variously reported . . . ; some speake as opinion leads them, others according to circumstances and appearance, and some, as others doe report: So it is divers wayes related" (196). He finds out that the most common report is that he fell asleep too close to the river and was swept away, a version that protects the reputations of a number of people. Celadon imagines that those with power "had prudently invented this report, to take away occasion of talking ill upon the accident." Through Celadon, D'Urfé points out how reputation, even *ethos,* is constructed and maintained.

Conversely, writers could do as Behn did and use the same strategies to discredit public figures. *Love-Letters* includes comments on the crowds that cheered Monmouth and on how that encouraged those of higher rank who hoped to see him king. At one point, Behn has Sylvia observe with heavy sarcasm that "those glorious chiefs of the faction" waited for the moment when "the dirty crowd" would "rise against their king." Opportunists rather than leaders, dependent on the mob, the rebels seem feminized. Indeed, upon his invasion, "men of substance" never join Monmouth, but "if the ladies could have composed an army, he would not have wanted one."[65] By the end of part 3, written after Monmouth's execution, the crowd is identified as primarily "peasants," "Reformed Religion" (Nonconformists), and voiceless.

In *Love-Letters,* the mob seems swayed by physical beauty and orchestrated shows of greatness. Writing nearer the time when Defoe noted "the Dawn of Politicks among the Common People" than Howard had, Behn describes previously ridiculed segments of the population with open-mindedness and, in fact, had earlier showed considerable insight into art as means of influence. In a dedication she wrote, "[Plays] are secret instructions to the people, in things that 'tis impossible to insinuate into them any other way. 'Tis example that prevails above reason or DIVINE PRECEPTS. . . . I have myself known a man, whom neither conscience nor religion cou'd perswade to loyalty, who with beholding in our theatre a modern politician set forth in all his colours, was converted . . . and quitted the party."[66] Her self-consciousness about the construction of public opinion is impressive in *Love-Letters:*

> [Cesario] understood all the useful arts of popularity, the gracious smile and bow, and all those cheap favours that so gain upon hearts; and without the expense of any thing but ceremony, has made the nation mad for his interest. . . . As the maiden queen I have read of in *England,* who made herself idolized by that sole piece of politic cunning, understanding well . . . the people; and gained more upon them by those little arts, than if she had parted with all the prerogatives of her Crown. (416)

Monmouth and his advisers staged miniature royal entrées, and townspeople responded. As Dryden said, in *Absalom and Achitophel,*

> This moving Court, that caught the peoples Eyes,
> And seem'd but Pomp, did other ends disguise:
> *Achitophel* had form'd it, with intent
> To sound . . . / The Peoples hearts;
> . . . .
> Thus, in a Pageant Show, a Plot is made. (lines 739–43, 751)

Yet when the rebellion begins, many of those formerly in sympathy with Monmouth's supporters hold back, "most" "disgusted" with his claiming the "title as king" (449). Behn here invokes the Norman Yoke myth—the good sense of the people will assert itself and their welfare be protected. A variant on the people's judgment of Monmouth is inscribed in *The Fair Jilt.* When Tarquin and Miranda marry, the people "despised" her for her former life and him for "espousing a woman so infamous." At the critical moment, the "magnificent" and "splendid" spectacle that they construct in their marriage ceremony and in their "great house" fails to dazzle: "though they admir'd, and gaz'd . . . they foresaw the ruin that attended it" (128). Thus Castlemaine, Mazarine, and Charles II.

Nowhere are the whims of fate, the mysteries of personality, and the influence of public opinion as obvious as they are when *The Fair Jilt* and *The History of the Nun* are compared. Miranda beneath the scaffold on which Van Brune died appears in sharp contrast to Isabella on the scaffold, but both are spectacles defined for the reader by public opinion.[67] At the end of *The History of the Nun,* Isabella is guillotined as a double murderess, guilty of a state crime—treason, in this case, since she has murdered husbands. Yet she dies a heroine, admired, even adulated. The final scene fixes her angelic beauty, pious charity, and preternatural purity. This move is, of course, irrational in the face of two murders and experienced as contradiction by the reader.[68]

In contrast to the easy interpretations of the somewhat comparable conclusion to *The Beggar's Opera,* Behn's text defies satisfactory artistic categorization. Yet her conclusion emphasizes the irrational status of women in society and art. Isabella's appearance cancels out her actions. A repentant vision is embraced. Feminine "virtue" is revealed to be different from real virtue. Her "virtues" are beauty, charity, and social graces, and they overshadow dishonesty, theft, and even murder. The narrator calls attention to this irrationality: "it was as amazing to hear her, as it was to behold her" (207). Again, juxtapositions of scenes are revealing. In order to become objects of admiration, Isabella becomes the beautiful, repentant spectacle and Prince Tarquin fights valiantly to escape apprehension as a criminal and, apparently, lies to the authorities about his future intentions. Tarquin's re-acceptance into the community is a cynical comment on masculine social codes, and Isabella's is a parody of the historical function Lincoln Faller has identified in the execution narratives of the period. Unlike feminist writers who tease out the subjectivity of their women characters, Behn forces Isabella back into object, into a one-dimensional representation of the object of our gaze. The more we resist and try to interpret or identify, the more she is a figure on a stage (scaffold). When Southerne rewrites Behn's text, he removes a special female fear: the failure of goodness and consequent loss of love.[69] Male playwrights consistently depict and express anxiety over the failure or even absence of power; women rarely do. Isabella's first thought in *The History of the Nun* is to enlist Villenoys as a helper; soon, however, she fears he will be "eternally" reproaching her, and she kills him. Behn, thus, inscribes desires for autonomy and happiness, while Southerne has Isabella go mad and commit suicide, the action Behn's character has rejected: "She was a thousand times about to end her Life, and, at one stroke, rid her self of the Infamy, that, she saw, must inevitably fall upon her . . . after a thousand convulsions, . . . she resolved upon the murder of Henault" (136).

Habermas has argued that as early as the last third of the seventeenth century, the press issued "pedagogical instructions and even criticism and reviews" as well as information.[70] Behn's *Love-Letters* was that kind of novel-news, and "reports" in her other texts often functioned similarly. As N. H. Keeble has observed, people came to seek "acquittal at the bar of public opinion," and the press was the vehicle for the presentation of cases.[71] Thus, both author and reader came to occupy a new place. This is another way that Behn contributed to the actualizing of the novel form's potential: she knew she could take advantage of the way some of the texts with which she allied hers were read.[72] They were intended to be read aloud, and then to be the subject of discussion and debate. D'Urfé observes, "They are the Correctives of *passion,* the restoratives of *conversation;* they are the entertainments of the *sound*" ("To the Reader," vol. 2). The mixed-sex inquiring, even ritualized discussions mirrored the ideal of the French grand salons in which the rich and talented mingled with the nobility and where intellect, refinement, and grace of expression determined superiority.[73] Just as the characters commented upon and championed positions, so readers could easily extend these discussions, and historical evidence survives that suggests the assumption of continuity between discourse in the text and about it.[74]

Deeply concerned with epistemological and even philosophical questions, these romances as well as the epistolary novels of the period often follow the formula of *Questions of Love,* and Linda Kauffman and others have demonstrated that they were often discussed as philosophy.[75] The open-endedness of these discussions and debates invites continuation in circles of readers, in salons and summerhouses, and in sequels and imitations. The significance of the constructed orality and dialogism can hardly be overemphasized, and the position and authority of the reader is startlingly, crucially different from that of the humanistic reader devoted to the identity, alleged intentions, and authority of a writer whose name, status, and even education are known. This latter reader's author is perceived patrilineally—his family, his place in the political order (which in drama at this time implied degree of familiarity with the courtiers), his friendships, and even his access to the modes of production (publishing with Herringman meant something quite different from publishing with Aylmar).

In Behn's texts and in the early English novel, what is so important are the positions of the author and reader. Both are dialogic players in an open, intertextual field. The *act* of the novel is to make the reader judge and to face the implications of judgments. Here Behn's experience as a dramatist was crucial. The performed drama of Behn's time wrote players, companies, and managers into texts that we recognize to perpetuate and sometimes modify literary and social conventions and systems, thereby functioning as vehicles for ideology. Former roles and what the audience believed about players often determined interpretation. Moreover, reactions of first-night audiences could determine revisions. In an age when the name of the playwright did not appear on playbills or in newspaper advertisements, the playwright literally lost control of the text as no other category of writer did.

The openness of the novel to multiple discourses, to the present, and to didactic purposes combined with the established habit of reading as if the text were to be extended into drawing room conversation or coffee-house debate; thus, it cast the reader as judge and interpreter as drama and other forms of literary discourse seldom had. Behn is a very early example of the English writers' appropriation of trial scenes and juridical discourse.[76] Sylvia, for instance, writes, "All that I dreaded, all that I feared is fallen upon me: I have been arraigned, and convicted, three judges . . . sat in condemnation on me, a father, a mother, and a sister; the fact, alas, was too clearly proved . . . a tender mother . . . an angry father, and a guilty conscience" (89). Henrietta Berkeley's stunning appearance in court during which she denied being raped or abducted, claimed her sham marriage, and, after a few nights in prison, went off to cohabit with Lord Grey is reenacted in the decisions and trials of several of Behn's heroines, and sexuality is often a prominent issue. It is significant that Behn's Sylvia is condemned and feels a guilty conscience, for the scene is one of the ways that Behn has Sylvia's (and Philander's) discourse tested against other discourses and ideologies. As Bakhtin says, "The idea of testing the hero, or testing his discourse, may very well be the most fundamental organizing idea in the novel" (388), and Behn's texts began to formalize this characteristic.

The Fair Jilt has several trial and punishment scenes and, significantly, large crowds witness and judge them. Tarquin's attempted murder of Alcidiana takes place in public. His desperate fight to escape draws a large crowd, which judges him gallant and brave and rejoices when his execution is botched. "With one accord, as if the whole crowd had been one body, and had had but one motion," the people carry the wounded Tarquin to sanctuary and refuse to return him to the officials (146–47). They insist, as Thompson describes English crowds doing, that "they now had a right to protect him." The crowd, thus, became the ultimate jury and acted as other execution witnesses did occasionally throughout the longer eighteenth century.[77] Behn saw that the attack on her political ideals and emergent social forces were threatening political stability, and her texts play out an optimistic scenario in which individual and community conscience coalesce again. Like the crowds that watched the executions, her readers were justices whose judgments emerged from a matrix of variable perceptions and values, but whose consciences were hoped to be identical with the ideals of community.[78]

Behn's writing after 1686 is full of self-assertion, of statements of her right to tell and interpret, to report her observations, and to judge. In the fictions, as she had not been before and could not be in drama, she was "present as source, guarantor, and organizer of the narrative, as analyst and commentator, as stylist (as 'writer')."[79] *The Fair Jilt,* for example, opens with an essay on love that would have reminded every seventeenth-century reader of the French romances and invited them to compare her performance to essays in the works of de Scudery and Calprenède. Part 3 of *Love-Letters* includes extended narrative sections that gradually invoke an eyewitness speaker. A thirty-two-page passage summarizes Monmouth's retreat to Lady Henrietta Wentworth, his brief reconciliation with his father, and the circumstances leading to the rebellion.[80] Here the perspective resembles that of many French memoirs in which a trusted subordinate (here Thomoso) is both witness and confidant; but here the perspective is clearly a double one, since the presence of a narrator behind the speaker is perceptible. The narrator of the interpolations is at ease in each country and a confident guide for the reader. From short, simple comments about, for instance, the amount of freedom women have, the narrator's part increases until it is as personal as the one in *Oroonoko:* "I myself went . . . having never been so curious" (396); "I never saw anything more rich in dress" (398). In this extended passage and in her late novels, especially in *Oroonoko,* her presence and her "will to style" contribute to the active work of her readers.

Finally, Behn begins to actualize the novel form as a space available to women writers. In appropriating an emergent form, she could create space for her subjects and find a place where it was easier to resist rigid interpretations of cultural signs and strong expectations about traditional lines of action. Behn is certainly part of the "mobilization" of women as a deliberative group, and her fictions can be identified with what Robert Weimann has called moments of "crisis in discursive appropriation," which are always accompanied by "crises in representativeness."[81] At such times, the concepts that had given the dominant ideology stability lose their "capacity for legitimation." Rather than appropriating the portrayals of "presupposed relations," writers begin to confront the dynamic contradictions between, on the one hand, their own lived experience and their social and self-fashioned intellectual selves and, on the other, accepted, conventional cultural materials. Weimann says that their texts' narratives widen "the gulf between the 'signs' of their reading and the symbols of their experience" (437). Writers who feel these contradictions often produce texts that resist readers' ordinary ludic and interpretative behaviors.

Behn's prose fictions make it clear that the tension created by literature's incorporation of lived experience and the utopian longing is heightened for women because of the fact of an established, hegemonic, gendered language system for literary discourse and even for each literary kind, which assures that women writers will often find the expression of their experiences and aspiration difficult.[82] Moreover, they confront on a heightened scale the reader's tendency to naturalize what is read, to appropriate and then interpret in ways that fit the text into the plot lines and messages of the dominant ideology. Behn's texts are especially interesting because they disrupt three of the most basic, shared reader experiences. These are expectations about identification, about a hegemonic, gendered language system, and about the lines and resolutions of plot.

Identification may be the most important *and* mysterious aspect of reading, and it is basic to both pleasure and interpretation. Ordinarily readers establish an affinity between themselves and a perspective (narrator, major character) in the text. In fact, many theorists believe that readers search the text for a character with which to identify, internalize an idea of that character, and even use that idea as an ideal on which to model or construct themselves, or at least to "formulate" things already in their consciousness but previously elusive. Reading is, therefore, one of several important ways that the self is created. As Wolfgang Iser says, identification is "a stratagem" by means of which the author conveys experience and stimulates attitudes in the reader.[83] When the "trance potential," the capacity to exercise dominion and superiority, is realized, readers feel as if they are participating, as if there were no distance between reader and read event.[84] Subject-object distinctions are then dissolved into the illusion of being actively involved in a process and a series of relationships.

Feminist critics argue that women readers oscillate between the reader positions available in the texts. They read both as men and as women, identifying with the desiring subject (usually male and the hero) and with the object of desire (usually a woman and an obstacle to fulfillment).[85] This movement can be regarded as schematizing Jameson's view of literature in the experience of the woman reader, for the desiring subject represents the utopian longing and the desired object lived experience.

Women readers, then, alternate between identification and moments of profound alienation from the subject with which they have joined their perspective. Highly skilled readers may even forget how to read as women.[86] Women writers, especially as early as Behn, must, then, problematize identification for both sexes. One way that Behn does this is by exploiting gender stereotypes and disputing them. Characters slide easily between male and female. Sylvia's conventionally feminine position and discourse give way to expressions of the "cavalier in her" and then veer toward familiar representations of the predatory villainess. Attracted to her as a beautiful youth, Octavio and Alonzo suspect her sex but waver uncertainly until she admits it. Behn writes, "which was yet more strange, she captivated the men no less than the women" when disguised as a man (119). Wellborn, like Alonzo, spends a night with a youth for whom he feels an attraction. Even her brother upon hearing her voice doubts her identity, and Wellborn later curses that "no Instinct, no sympathizing Pains or Pleasure" gave away her sex (384). Behn had expressed similar ideas in "To The Fair Clarinda, who Made love to Me, *imagin'd more than Woman*." This poem includes the lines,

> Thou beauteous Wonder of a different kind,
> Soft *Cloris* with the dear *Alexis* join'd;
> When e'er the Manly part of thee, wou'd plead
> Thou tempts us with the Image of the Maid,
> While we the noblest Passions do extend
> The love to *Hermes, Aphrodite* the Friend.

Here the speaker of the poem is attracted to Clarinda's "manly part" *and* to "the Image of the Maid." Earlier the speaker says, "Let me call thee, Lovely Charming Youth," thereby rebelling against biological sex categories. Clarinda becomes both Hermes and Aphrodite,[87] denying the possibility of Cloris joined with Alexis and actualizing the blatantly sexual possibilities of earlier lines:

> For sure no Crime with thee we can commit;
> Or if we should—thy Form excuses it.
> For who that gathers fairest Flowers believes
> A snake lies hid beneath the Fragrant Leaves.

In her *The False Count,* Francisco says, "I have known as much danger hid under a Petticoat, as a pair of Breeches," and Gulliam, in *The Amorous Prince,* when dressed as a woman, makes "the woundiest handsome Lass."[88] Fascinated with sex as categories and less certain than later generations that men and women were "fundamentally" different from each other,[89] Behn joins with many of her Royalist contemporaries and goes beyond many of them in admitting the attraction between those of the same sex.[90] Alonzo, for instance, finds the disguised Sylvia "so charming (and in his own way too)" (405). Philander's attraction to Calista is heightened when she is disguised as a man and resembles his "dear Octavio" (317). The affection and understanding between Constantia and Agnes is greater than that between the prince and either woman. In Trotter's play, the two women "mingle" kisses, and Agnes imagines their reunion in Heaven, where they "again will love."[91]

As McKeon has pointed out and reviewers have highlighted, in addition to comparisons between women and slaves, Behn used similarities between younger brothers and women to good effect. In her late plays, Behn puts many of her heroines' sentiments into the speeches of the male characters. Gayman, in *The Lucky Chance,* for instance, sells his sexual favors for survival, and there is no question but that he does it for subsistence and hates it. When he expresses the sentiments of the trade, they can be received with amusement or sympathy even as they convey the shocking necessities: "She pays, and I'll endeavour to be civil." He fears the embraces of an old, ugly woman, just as wives like Julia regret that they "languish in a loathed embrace" with an aged husband. Both Gayman's and Bellmour's reputations have been damaged; they are, therefore, more dependent on the women's initiative than most heroes. As early as her second play, *The Amorous Prince,* she had Curtius express the ideals of companionate marriage.

In her final fictions, she exploited analogies to yet another liminal social group, nuns. With this strategy she continues to develop ways to lay bare the fact that language is hegemonic and gendered, and the fact that it is gendered makes sex a political category and a vehicle for domination. The protagonists of many of Behn's late fictions are nuns, and they are more common in her fiction than in Restoration-era English fiction in general. The Spanish, French, and Italian novellas as well as *Lettres portugaises* and the Abelard and Heloise letters provided a context for her work and prepared the reader for women with sexual natures. Just as pointed comparisons between women and slaves and between women and younger brothers could effectively translate aspects of women's experiences and feelings for an unsensitized audience, so could stories told from the nun's perspective. As a modern feminist text asks, "What woman is not a nun, sacrificed, self-sacrificing, without a life of her own, sequestered from the world?"[92] Moreover, nuns were already eroticized; as L'Estrange said suggestively in the preface to his translation of *Five Love Letters,* "You will find . . . that a woman may be Flesh and Blood in a Cloyster, as well as in a Palace."[93]

Like all women, nuns were "cloistered," shut away. Moreover, they were carefully but narrowly and selectively educated and were disqualified from active, public life and from any hope of participating in many aspects of what we now consider ordinary life. Upper-class Englishwomen, like nuns, were forbidden choices for their lives. Neither was to fall in love without permission; their object of lifelong devotion was selected for them, and upper-class women's fathers' or husbands' houses could be prisons as surely as any convent.

The stories that Behn and her contemporaries knew usually included glimpses of the refined, even cultured, lives of the nuns. Isabella, in *The History of the Nun,* for instance, is made a pet, and the nuns

> cultivate her Mind . . . and whatever Excellency any one abounded
> in, she was sure to communicate it to the young *Isabella;* If one could
> Dance, another Sing, another play on this Instrument, another on
> that; if they spoke one Language, and that another; if she had
> Wit, and she Discretion, and a third the finest Fashion and Manners;
> all joyn'd to compleat the Mind and Body of this beautiful young
> Girl. (100)

Music, sketching or painting, languages, and conversation occupied their time just as these amusements filled that of gentlewomen. Visits with the nuns often sounded like the discourse of the salons, and the rank and social graces of the nuns' guests figure prominently. "All the men of wit and conversation meet at the apartments of these fair *filles dévotes,* where all manner of gallantries are perform'd, . . . there is no sort of female arts they are not practis'd in, no intrigue they are ignorant of," Behn writes in *The Fair Jilt* (105). These stories often highlighted the nobility, rank, and youth of the nuns—thereby calling into question their readiness to choose their vocation—or they featured a woman taking refuge in a convent. The duchess de Mazarine, for instance, recounts the pranks she played in a nunnery and compares the number of visits she could have in various convents (44–48, 92).

The convents and orders were, after all, powerful intellectual communities of women. They held well-known, fascinatingly powerful women, such as Peter the Great's wife and sister.[94] They did indeed serve as havens for abused wives and sanctuaries for many kinds of political and social refugees. Women could, as the duchess of Mazarine had, take shelter in convents, obtain a legal writ, and remain inviolably protected under canon law. As in the cases of slaves and younger brothers, gender categories break down.

Nuns, however, have the authority of men and govern themselves and others. Janet Todd remarks that Delarivière Manley's fictional separatist communities are "tinged with lesbianism and hedonism" (115), and this description could be applied to contemporary male fantasies about nunneries. Whenever communities of women exist without direct male domination, they become sites for male imaginings, and the literature exhibits fantasies of transgressive sexuality. A number of contemporary texts, and especially the epistolary ones, foregrounded the "feminine nature" of the nun and especially her sexuality. The letters of the Portuguese nun construct a suffering, abandoned victim,[95] but they include explicit (although in my opinion some distinctively male) descriptions of sexual experience and the intense memory of such moments: "Why may not I yet live to see you again within these Walls, and with all those Transports of Extacy, and Satisfaction?" "It should have been my Business even in the Nick of those Critical, and Blessed Minutes, to have Reason'd my self into the Moderation of . . . Excess."[96] Even more explicit are the letters of Heloise: "Even during the celebration of the Mass . . . lewd visions of those pleasures take such a hold upon my unhappy soul that my thoughts are on their wantonness instead of on prayers. Sometimes my thoughts are betrayed in a movement of my body" (133). Such texts made it possible to imagine the mind of the Princess de Clèves and for modern feminist critics to conclude that the princess leaves the court to preserve her passion.[97]

Behn's nuns perform like free radicals, and with them she commits the ultimate feminist writer's act: she makes her texts so alien that they cannot be appropriated and naturalized by the hegemony. She contests the culture's interpretative resolutions by tenaciously working against the tendency to define a woman's life by a single sexual moment. Miranda, for instance, who has been "possess'd by so many great men and strangers before" (128), marries a man who never ceases to love her, becomes part of a loving family, repents, and finds as much happiness "as this troublesome world can afford" (149). In fact, Behn's texts capture the patterns modern psychologists have identified for men's and women's lives. Her male characters' lives tend to be linear, as are male autobiographies; they trace a career or a movement toward an established personal life that is synonymous with a destined or discovered career. Her female characters' lives, like most women's autobiographies, revolve around relationships and do not progress so much as reveal what has been called a "discontinuous form."[98] Philander and Tarquin find their proper position; only a man like Hinnault, displaced from his patrimony, can duplicate the wandering, chaos, and open-endedness of the lives of Sylvia and Isabella.

These female characters resist easy interpretation. In 1990, a critic described Imoinda thusly:

> [She] is called to the bed of Oroonoko's king and grandfather. She dallies with him, allowing miscellaneous caresses, while retaining the virginity she saves for Oroonoko. One night Oroonoko steals to her, enjoys her, and escapes . . . , leaving Imoinda to protect herself as best she can—as she does by claiming that Oroonoko raped her. Her wit saves her life but gets her sold into slavery. Oroonoko, told that she was killed, stoically accepts that as appropriate, for in his culture women obey or die.[99]

Here the critic reads Imoinda as clever and scheming to protect her virginity rather than reading male impotence and has Imoinda act as Miranda actually does in making a false accusation of rape. Both of these readings could be interpreted to express male anxieties; their existence, as well as the feminist ones, illustrates the tendency to generate protective and enabling interpretations as well as the resistance to easy interpretation that Behn has built into the text.

Behn makes visible the fact that she has created a space in which to contest the authority of earlier representations: she reveals the dominant (male) culpability and the subordinate (female) power. She could extend these themes of irrational positions and blinding language systems into the public sphere and into relationships other than male-female. As Robert Chibka has pointed out, Behn manipulates pronouns so that the narrator places herself "half in and half out of the community of Europeans" and consistently exposes "the conceptual underpinnings of European modes of thought as examples not of truth but of ideological and political power." It has been pointed out that materialist feminist analysis of women's writing "reveals that women are not simply in opposition to men as writers, because the two sexes are not on sufficiently equal terms in society. . . . Rather they are to male writers as the most assimilated members of a colonized people are to the colonizers."[100]

Behn ruthlessly reveals the violence inherent in the act of colonizing and the possibility of a brutal, destructive result. Over and over in *Oroonoko,* but in *The Fair Jilt* and *The History of the Nun* as well, woman's irrational and unnameable position is made evident, but the irrationality is extended to male characters, especially as they act in and are integrated in the public, political sphere. Tarquin, for instance, is cheered by the people for his fighting ability and is called "heroic" by them, although he is fighting in an attempt to escape from the scene where, as the lovesick tool of an evil woman, he has attempted to murder a virtuous, innocent woman. Like Philander, he illustrates how traitors and murderers can again appear in "splendor at Court."

Behn's texts are examples of the ways writers can influence public affairs and of new literary forms and lines of action that evolved in a time when existing forms seemed inadequate for the experiences of living people and old resolutions and ideologies unsatisfactory. Her fictions show judgments of public and private people to be, like capitalistic relations, always in process, continuous, and expansive in their transactions. Thus, Behn did more than exploit the aspects of these forms that locate them within public discourse. She continued her experimentation with ways to write women's experiences and women's nature and constructed position into history. Her texts leave a record of unreconciled public and private conflicts, social ruptures, and contradictions. We see in her work the justice of one of Edward Said's criticisms of Foucault's model of power for allowing no space for "emergent movements and none for revolutions, counter-hegemony, or historical blocks. For in human history there is always something beyond the reach of dominating systems, no matter how deeply they saturate society, and this is obviously what makes change possible."[101]

Although more women published poetry than fiction in the eighteenth century, the novel became their major form of public participation. It came to be recognized as a print space in which they held almost equal influence. Over the same time period, it was "established as the major literary form for dissemination of the image and ideology of the nation, and writers knew it."[102] Anna Letitia Barbauld wrote, "[Novels] take a tincture from the learning and politics of the times, and are made use of successfully to attack or recommend *the prevailing systems of the day*" (emphasis mine).[103] And editions of *Love in Excess, Robinson Crusoe, Pamela, Tristram Shandy,* and scores of other novels sold and sold to the widest range of readers of any genre.

Fredric Jameson has insisted that the first question for literary critics should be "not how we go about interpreting a text properly, but rather why we should even have to do so."[104] Behn's texts, like Jameson's question, make problematic accepted hegemonic readings and reading habits. In resisting the society's tendencies to naturalize and appropriate their characters and plot lines, women writers continued to introduce new interpretative codes into the literature and the life of the culture. In this section, I shall look at some representative texts and episodes that have resisted interpretation and then argue that they resemble Behn's discourses and are united by strategies that force judgment and by attempts to make readers competent interpreters. In order to focus this section, I concentrate on one of the early novel's favorite subjects, courtship as quest for happy marriage; and, because Anglo-American culture represents the body of the opposite sex as the reward for successful sexual negotiations, I concentrate on bodies.

Courtship, a highly ritualized social experience and the subject of a substantial and conventionalized body of literature, was also a crucially important issue for women. In spite of the fact that women writers came to assume the position of instructors on matters of love, they were highly conscious of the locus of real power and the nature of courtship rituals. They would agree with Erving Goffman, who has noted that "the courtship process leads the male to press his pursuit, first in finding some reason for opening of a state of talk, and second, in overcoming the social distance initially maintained therein. Breaching of existing distance . . . is, then, a standard part of the male's contribution to cross-sex dealings. . . . And it is in the nature of his view of these dealings that they know no season or place."[105]

The power to "press his pursuit," to "find an opening," to "overcome" and "breach" social distance, and to propose marriage were the man's. As Foucault observed, whenever power relations exist, they "have an immediate hold on the [body]: they invest it, mark it, train it, torture it, force it to carry out tasks, to perform ceremonies, to emit signs." This process is "useful only when a productive and subjected body" results, and this state is usually attained through violence or ideology.[106] And violence is necessary, for it is during courtship that women are made synonymous with the category of sex that will be their identity for the rest of their lives. They learn that *"they* are sex, *the* sex, and sex they have been made in their minds, bodies, acts, and gestures."[107] As Mary Wollstonecraft wrote in *A Vindication of the Rights of Woman,* "Every thing [women] see or hear serves to fix impressions, call forth emotions, and associate ideas, that give a sexual character to the mind. False notions of beauty and delicacy stop the growth of their limbs and produce a sickly soreness."[108] During the courtship years, society imprints the text that is woman, for she learns to change the way she walks, moves, and functions in the world.

Courtship was a time of intense scrutiny for women, and men, who often had few unchaperoned opportunities to talk to the woman, "read" and set a value upon the text offered them. Tobias Smollett gives a crude but usefully frank description of the process at its worst in *Humphrey Clinker.* Lydia describes Tabitha Bramble's attempts to "market her charms." Jerry Melfort writes that Tabitha, "at every place where we halted, did mount the stage, and flourished her rusty arms, without being able to make one conquest." "She was grave and gay by turns—she moralized and methodized—she laughed, romped, and danced, and sung, and sighed, and ogled, and lisped, and fluttered, and flattered." Tabby here presents a pathetic picture of a woman inviting men to write her character; she offers herself to be whatever is desired.

Interpretation here is easy, as it is in less blatant presentations of heroines such as Sophia Western's introduction into *Tom Jones* and of her activities, which include playing and singing for her father and Tom and titillating falls from horses. In such scenes, looking—by characters and readers, who I believe must almost necessarily slip into reading from the dominant male's perspective—has far more to do with domination than with seeing.[109] Women writers, in order to foster a different kind of reading, must produce resisting texts, texts that demand interpretation and demand that we ask why they require interpretation, and feminist critics have developed a rich body of literature on the ways women writers have attempted to "educate the male reader in the recognition and interpretation of women's texts, while [providing] the woman reader with the gratification of discovering, recovering, and validating her own experience."[110] In order to make concrete a few of the strategies of resistance and to bring them to bear upon issues of the continued development of the novel, I shall analyze in some detail a representative text, Eliza Haywood's *The British Recluse.*

Published in 1722, it is the 138-page recital of two young women's unhappy love affairs. Cleomira, the recluse, relates her story, which includes the stillbirth of her illegitimate child. Then Belinda, her auditor, tells Cleomira of her own unfortunate passion for Courtal, which motivates her rejection of the allegorically named Worthly, who marries her sister. The young women, and the reader, discover that Cleomira's Lysander is the same man as Belinda's Courtal, and his equally unhappy or unpromising relationships with three other women are incidentally sketched in. Bellamy (his "real" name) becomes, through what traditional critics might label the improbability of his ubiquity, a trope for the aristocratic male.

For all of these women, Bellamy is the representation of the object of desire. Each enumerates his attractive qualities, which notably include "enchanting Graces" and "seeming sweetness of Disposition."[111] Cleomira recalls, "[I] saw a Form which appear'd more than *Man,* and nothing inferior to those Idea's we conceive of *Angels;* his Air! . . . Miriads of lightning Glories darted from his Eyes . . . yet temper'd with such a streaming Sweetness!" (18) Although his physical appearance is important, the temperament that would be the cornerstone of "middle-class love, the stuff that modern families are made of" receives the most extended praise and comment.[112] Bellamy, however, is a force, and each woman experiences him as such.

Roland Barthes writes of meaning as "a force which tries to subjugate other forces, other meanings. . . . The force of meaning depends on its degree of systematization: the most powerful meaning [seeming] to encompass everything notable in the semantic universe."[113] As trope, Bellamy functions as the structuring force that leads readers to experience a problem that calls out for resolution. As Emile Durkheim observed, a powerful representation is "a force which raises around itself a turbulence of organic and psychical phenomena."[114] Bellamy's sexual energy infects them, and none, regardless of bad treatment and reason's counsel, has overcome her obsession with him. That this sexuality is a metaphor for ambition and desire for power manifests itself overtly in Bellamy and more symbolically in the women, who express it in their contempt for "boring men" and country life. The narrative makes it clear that Bellamy cannot be contained by the law, any moral code, or human affection. Instrumental, for instance, in robbing Cleomira of her fortune, he cannot be determined to be responsible, and no law could be invoked to punish him for seducing her.[115] Of Richardson's Lovelace, who is the same kind of character, Anna Howe remarks, "To have *Money,* and *Will,* and *Head,* to be a villain, is too much for the rest of the world, when they meet in one man" (*Clarissa,* 6:145).

The text cannot contain Bellamy either. Unlike many contemporaneous with it but written by men, this text does not solve the problem of the aristocratic male (and the ideology he represents and still had great power to impose) by either domesticating him (as Richardson would later in *Pamela*)[116] or criminalizing him (as Richardson would in *Clarissa*).[117] Rather, it, like many of the other early texts by women, lays bare the co-existence of residual and emergent structures of feeling and of an unresolved problem in the larger society.[118] The resolution, which of course is no cultural resolution at all, is for Cleomira and Belinda to form a nation of two, a new society seventy miles from London.

The structure of *The British Recluse,* which has been seen as repetitious, old-fashioned, and even inept, in fact captures the moment in literary history brilliantly. At such an early stage in the development of novelistic narrative strategies, the double-telling becomes a form of self-examination and reflection, which might be seen as one manifestation of the way diaries and journals empowered women's writing.[119] As such, it exists as an example of the novel's move toward its psychological, introspective character. More important, however, is the fact that Cleomira's story is the child of the multivolume romance, and Belinda's the relative of the infant novel. Complete with somewhat stilted, luxuriant language, vividly erotic descriptions, extravagant love letters quoted in their entirety, and plots with new lovers' stories growing out of stories, Cleomira's story follows the pattern of the "fallen woman" plot. Belinda's, which is much more fast-paced and written in more straightforward prose, represents a more active, independent heroine.

Both content and form reflect that Belinda carries emergent structures of feeling and Cleomira residual ones. As the woman capable of being an independent economic unit, Belinda displaces the plot of the seduced and abandoned maiden whose worth is defined and determined in relation to a man. In both recitals, the retrospective first person is broken by other time frames. The interpolated letters give Cleomira's immediacy, and Belinda's frequent references to the "present"—to Bellamy's married life, Worthly's health and marriage, and even to her own resolutions—are far more like the experienced narrative time of *Moll Flanders* than that of the romances.[120]

Rachel Blau DuPlessis convincingly argues that the romance plot in narrative is a powerful gendering process and that romance is a trope for the sex-gender system as a whole. She points out how forcefully it bears the message of external intimidation threatening loss of love.[121] Cleomira's story acts out this idea, for she is reduced to the most gendered, retiring, passive female. Each recital represents an ideology of love and of womanhood, and Haywood later developed the core of Belinda's story into a full-length prose fiction, *The History of Miss Betsy Thoughtless* (London, 1751). In spite of the contrasts, however, the point is unmistakable and is reinforced by the incidental accounts of Melissa, Miranda, and Semanthe: the reader learns to recognize the universality of female experience and "conceives in some fashion" the reality of patriarchy.[122]

The positioning of Belinda's narrative disrupts easy interpretation of the text and opposes the available, traditional set of roles for women (misunderstood flirt, censorious prude, fallen woman, lascivious widow) with their accompanying (his)stories.[123] Because of Belinda's story, Cleomira is not experienced as defined by her sexual fall. It is an accident that Belinda, not she, escaped, and the women define themselves over time and go away to make a happy life together. No one ostracizes, taunts, or sees the women as fallen or cast-off mistresses.

Jean E. Kennard has distinguished between conventions that are agreements on the meaning of symbolic gestures and those that are agreements to use a specific interpretative strategy in order to find "metaphorical coherence."[124] Haywood, Behn, and many other women writers include some of the most powerful conventional gestures in our culture (giving birth to an illegitimate baby and being executed as a criminal) and yet manage to forbid the simple experiencing of their heroines as fallen women, sinners, criminals. Judgment is shifted from classifiable plot lines, conventional sex-character roles, and symbolic gestures to the reader as reader of circumstances, human motives, and character. The perspective, relentlessly subjective and relentlessly female, insists upon factoring such human traits as generosity, integrity, and passion (even sexual arousal) into situations conventionally set up to make chastity and virtue, passivity and womanhood, synonyms. By doing so, texts such as these continued the development of one of the novel's special features: the construction of the position of the reader as simultaneously reader of narrative and literary conventions, dialogic player, and judge.

These writers repeatedly provide characters who "read" the heroines against the grain of convention. Belinda and Cleomira, of course, read each other, but so do the landlady, the nurse, and half a dozen apparently perceptive and ordinary people. The bodies of the heroines in *The British Recluse* are social texts. Defined even more schematically than Bellamy as the culture's objects of desire, Cleomira symbolizes her loss of this position and her future as a disqualified relational being by neglecting to dress her hair or herself for day.

Within her narrative, too, are the special signs of the female, attacks of spectacle and theater of catharsis. Deployed to represent the extreme consequences of the stressful, artificial experience that courtship is and the savagery of the double standard, Cleomira and a number of other heroines created by early women writers play out what Catherine Clément has called "an attack of spectacle, a crisis of suffering." In order to "escape the misfortune of their economic and familial exploitation, [these women] chose to suffer spectacularly before an audience of men," Clément says. Clément also recognizes the attack of spectacle as "a festival, a celebration of their guilt used as a weapon, a story of seduction."[125] During these attacks, the woman becomes category as well as spectacle, and the people who see themselves as the representatives of society separate themselves from her by adopting the role of being the community from which the woman has alienated herself.[126] By her behavior she has laid bare the contradictions all women experience and has, therefore, committed a transgression. She has exposed the truth that male/female are categories that conceal the fact that social differences always belong to an economic and ideological order, that there is a system of domination, and that men know that they are trained to dominate. As Teresa de Lauretis says, "The historical fact of gender, . . . that it has concrete existence in cultural forms and actual weight in social relations, makes gender a political issue that cannot be evaded or wished away. . . . We cannot deny that [it] finally positions women and men in an antagonistic and asymmetrical relation."[127] Cleomira's letters become those of the hysterical sufferer, and her extravagant language and broken syntax become a carnival of guilt and suffering.[128] Finally, as hysteric she loses the power of rational speech altogether (71). Back in London, she tries to get Lysander to recognize "what he owes her" and to reclaim her fortune from her "guardian" Marvir. In neither economy does she have power, nor, as she is quickly told, any legal recourse. Her place in the ideological order is clear.[129] Soon after, she rains curses on Lysander and describes herself as becoming a fiend, able to "smile at Mischief" (73–74).

Catharsis for Cleomira comes after an attack of raving madness culminating in a suicide attempt. Here she participates in a classic example of what Clément calls the theater of catharsis.[130] She turns her claustro-phobic dwelling into theater as she gives her nurse instructions, writes a final letter, and promises if denied her easy method to use "knives or Cords—my Garters . . . dashing out my brains against the Wall." Her revenge fantasies and her extended meditation on suicide are the kinds of representations of alienation and destructive control of the body that theorists have described and that are common in early texts by women. Jane Barker, for instance, makes Galesia's revenge fantasy theater of catharsis (*Love Intrigues,* 1713). Galesia imagines killing Bosvil with a machete and seeing a statue of herself erected by grateful women. Para-doxically, even as her fantasy reveals guilt as her culture would assign it, as well as intense suffering, it forges a bond with women readers and is the incident that frees Galesia to get on with her life.

The greatest violence inscribed in these novels is the presentation of the chasm between honest feelings and external behavior imposed on women by social codes. Belinda, like Galesia, seethes with emotion and conflict. Their situation makes clear the three systems in play: personal feeling, "the game of love," and the discourse that depends on parental prerogative and leads to marriage and settlement contracts. Both resort to stammers, blushes, and the game-of-love code in attempts to commu-nicate their genuine feelings in acceptable ways. Unwilling to cross the boundaries of propriety or to utter empty, dishonest lines, they represent both the fact that women have no acceptable language and the unsatisfac-tory nature of eighteenth-century courtship rituals. These texts prefigure persistent themes in women's writings. From their creators writers learned to express the pain of the ruptures between feelings and both social codes and to make art of the distinction between manners that are morals and manners that are mere empty behaviors (and often hypocriti-cal, unkind, or even destructive ones). The concentration on a protago-nist's inner life and the divorce between feeling and expression, between the promptings of the heart and social demands, became the content of the English novel, and writers learned to move smoothly between de-scriptions of the exterior world and renderings of an inner existence.

In the hands of men, courtship novels were powerful means of gen-dering. In women's hands, however, they are revealed for what they are—novels of inscription and conscription.[131] Women's attempts to control the body during courtship represent the truth of this statement. The female body seems to both sexes always on the edge of becoming grotesque through awkward gesture, through violation of social boundaries, or even through calling attention to biological reality (for pregnant, aging, and sexually aroused bodies were often represented as grotesque). Standing in contrast to the "classical body, which is monumental, static, closed, and sleek," the grotesque body is "protruding," asserting, "the body of becoming, process, and change."[132] Clément's description of the attack of spectacle comes from her essay, "The Guilty One," and if the woman participating in courtship is not exactly guilty, she is, at least, on trial.

In the novels by women, the control of the body and its presentation is of paramount importance, and loss of control inevitably leads to judgment. When two people look intensely at each other, there is a moment of appraisal, challenge, and recognition. As Behn has Willmore say in *The Rover,* "I will gaze, to let you see my strength" (2:73). When the woman modestly drops her eyes or smiles while letting her eyes go blank, the man has controlled and dominated and is then free to evaluate without fear of the woman watching him doing it or returning his look and evaluating him. Such an interchange works against the possibility that looking will be seeing. Upon analysis it reveals that one sex, female, is valued for her aesthetic appeal—and that appeal is usually, as Roland Barthes says, based upon the reproduction of classical (or ideological) beauty. Simultaneously, the other sex, male, has become a mysterious, unknown body.

Narratives that show courtship going awry suggest that the differences between male and female bodies, which may be a source of powerful human fascination with the intriguingly different, may be exaggerated and expressed in the representation of the other as radically unknowable, unattractive, and even grotesque. In Eliza Haywood's novel *Fantomina* (1725), Beauplaisir does not recognize Fantomina in any of her various disguises—or presumably without them in a series of bedrooms.[133] At the end of the novel, Fantomina, who has seen, not merely looked at Beauplaisir, rejoices that her "Arts" kept him "always raving, wild, impatient, longing, dying"—in short, grotesque. The hero of Charlotte Lennox's *Life of Harriot Stuart* (1750) becomes unrecognizable to the woman who loves him. Disguised as an Indian, Belmein has so brutalized and intimidated Harriot that she is amazed to discover who he is and struggles to reconcile her opinion of him with his treatment of her.

Many novels by women show a self-conscious awareness of women's desires to control their own bodies. Galesia notes that she kept her

"Words close Prisoners" and "always stay'd in his Company, heard him, laugh'd, fool'd, and jested with him; yet not so freely as to transgress good Manners."[134] And the women smile and smile, that sign, in Collete Guillaumin's words, that is "the traditional accompaniment of submission, obligatory and demanded of female children and domestics."[135] Rage, frustration, bewilderment, illness, grief, even exuberant joy, must be hidden by the temperate, complying smile. Sarah Scott, who can imagine women free, creates a home in *Millenium Hall* where a poor woman is never "obliged to stay a minute longer in company than she chooses."

Not only her physical attractiveness but her health and "shape" matter, for she is being assessed as a brood mare is. Recent studies by Carol Gilligan document what an important part a growing sense of uncertain control of the body plays in the diminishing sense of power, confidence, and even happiness that occurs in girls between the ages of eleven and sixteen. Coincidentally, Jane Barker has Galesia identify the years between ten and fifteen as her happiest; after that, she experiences frequent periods when "my Sleep forsook me, and I relish'd not my Food."[136] She looks in a mirror for an explanation of why Bosvil's behavior toward her has changed in only three weeks, as does Alovisa to understand D'Elmont in Haywood's *Love in Excess* (1719). As Lilly Daché says, "Every little girl starts looking in the mirror almost as soon as she can walk. When [she] . . . sees ugliness reflected back . . . what she is actually experiencing is the value that her society has placed upon her gender category, that she has no value."[137] Courtship also foreshadows the realities of pregnancy and childbirth and, perhaps, the prospect of forced or unsatisfying intercourse. For instance, Sarah Scott's Mrs. Morgan is described as suffering less from her husband's brutal temper "than from his nauseous fondness."[138] Mary Davys' heroines are often coerced into marriage or raped and then married; one of her heroines describes her honeymoon: "I embraced him with the same desire, I shou'd have done a Serpent, and went to his Bed with more loathing, than I shou'd have gone to a stinking Dungeon."[139] For Mary Russo, both "radical negation, silence, withdrawal, and invisibility" and "the bold affirmations of feminine performance, imposture, and masquerade" are grotesque transformations of the body ("Female Grotesques," 213).

Caroline Bynum has pointed out that "women's food practices" have often functioned as control strategies;[140] in these novels, some characters refuse to eat. Far less sanguine (and more true to the courtship novels of the eighteenth century) is the argument in *The Madwoman in the Attic:* "Patriarchal socialization literally makes women sick, both physically and mentally," and, in "learning to be a beautiful object, the girl learns anxiety about—perhaps even loathing of—her own flesh."[141] Delarivière Manley gives us a depressingly detailed picture of the extent to which women had internalized the patriarchy's hierarchy of assessment. She describes "Rivella's" appearance for several pages and includes a question/answer period in which the young chevalier asks such things as, "How are Her Teeth and Lips?" She describes love as a disease and characterizes the female sufferer as being unable to eat or sleep and becoming "Hecktick."[142]

A number of feminist critics, including Susan Suleiman and Mary Russo, have demonstrated that attempts to control one's own body can extend to extremely self-destructive behavior. The last and completely desperate attempts to control the body are self-mutilation and suicide. Rather than see herself raped, one of Penelope Aubin's characters in *The Noble Slaves* (1722) tears out her own eyes. In Frances Burney's *Wanderer* (1814), women characters make it clear that they see Juliet's transformations as mutilation. Elinor calls her "maimed and defaced," and Mrs. Ireton catalogues the violence to the self that Juliet has displayed— "bruised and beaten," "wounded"—and asks if she will further disfigure herself by "dwindling into a dwarf" or "shooting up into a giantess." Lennox's Harriot Stuart attempts suicide rather than submit to a gang rape, her "punishment" for stabbing the sea captain who attempted to rape her.

Texts that defy reader expectations demand interpretations. When the pregnant Fantomina refuses Beauplaisir, when the courtship of Galesia and Bosvil falls apart, when a disguise as a savage Indian appears a more accurate portrait of an English gentleman than his usual dress, the reader experiences characters as texts rather than as symbolic characters in a patterned story. Women writers show remarkable self-consciousness as they have their heroines seize control of their stories and, thereby, of their representations and, by extension, of their identities. Equally notable is their awareness of the implications of available structures. Cleomira's choice of romance proves to be self-effacing and obliterating, while Belinda's is exploratory and regenerative, appropriate for the newer form she chooses. McKeon has hypothesized that employing "romance in novelistic narrative is characteristically framed by the self-conscious sense of its instrumentality *as* romance, marking the space between it and something else."[143] Certainly the juxtaposition of the two stories makes readers feel that neither the forms and conventions of prose fiction nor the labels and categories of society are adequate to the presentation of the text that is courted woman.[144]

Like Haywood, who rewrote Belinda's story in *Miss Betsy Thoughtless* in order to contain some of its unresolved issues, Barker revised Galesia's story. Galesia, whose identity as a poet is reinforced not only in the text of *Love Intrigues* but in revisions of it, says she intends to write her story and conclude "the tragedy." By the 1719 edition, however, the ambivalence felt between marriage and poetry is unapologetically a significant theme and has led at least one critic to call the text "a tale of success."[145]

The stakes have always been clear for women writers: movement, free movement, freedom of movement, control of the body, control of the story. By creating characters that resist appropriation into patriarchal plots and categories, women writers manage to create characters that survive as texts and, thereby, demand interpretation. Thus, women begin to create and establish ways of exploring and elucidating themes and subjects of vital importance to themselves within commercially viable forms. As a student in my seminar said, they have created the "inexpressible role," a life moving through time that is not defined by the moment of its marriage or sexual fall or by its relationship to a man.

Analysis of Behn's work and these texts highlights the reality of the negotiating *process* at work in all cultures, the impact of new groups rising to deliberative status, and the fact that social relationships, no matter how private and personal, are always power relationships. The evolution of Behn's political and revisionary expressions into prose fiction has enormous social and literary significance, and part of that significance is the direct effect of her sex. Her work assured that the novel would be a major hegemonic apparatus, and her sex's perspective, coming at the historical moment identified with the formation of an individual sense of selfhood, set the novel on its subversive course. Pope would praise literature that was "what oft is thought but ne'er so well expressed." Behn was praised for making previously "inarticulated strings to speak" and for finding "new discover'd Mines."[146] Pope's work focuses readers' attention on aesthetics within literary conventions: how genre, form, actors, writer measure up to culturally determined performance standards. The novel pushes readers into judging in a new zone in which they are in contact with the world, with morals, motives, and actions. Language is tested in two quite different zones.

Historically, women's writing has deconstructed male conventions and embodied the possibility of other desires and other lines of action— what Fredric Jameson has called the utopian potential of meaningful literature. Accessible to reader and writer as no existing literary form had been, the novel released this utopian element to a wide audience and became more absorbing and more seductive than other literary forms. In doing so, it actualized another quality that Bakhtin has identified with its zone of contact: its special closeness to the future. Claudine Herrman has pointed out that women's fiction often attempts "to invent the man of the future."[147] Over and over, women's texts argue that the body and emotions are as important as the rational and economic, and they express longings for better courtship rituals and for men who had traveled, had liberal educations that had cultivated their tastes and sensibilities, had managerial and often legal experience, and were bold men able to take the initiative and think on their feet. The reasons for this outline of the utopian man are obvious—not only did women need economic security, but men opened the world to them. Conversations, libraries, and shared cultural artifacts educated them, and women's hopes and expectations for their educations were rising with their hopes for improved marriages.

As a woman and a writing woman, Behn was Other, sure to feel the dissonance between the empirical self and the immanence of being more strongly than most men, and it is this dissonance that Lukács has identified with modernity and with the novel.[148] John Richetti has identified "the real movement" in Daniel Defoe's novels as "not simply towards the determinants of character but rather towards the depiction of a dialectic between self and other which has as its end a covert but triumphant assertion of the self." In much the same position as this Nonconformist— a persecuted minority often stigmatized for their enthusiastic (emotional), rebellious (needing control) "natures"—women writers wrote into their fiction their desire to define themselves and, in Richetti's words about the novelistic narrator, "to supply the perception which supplies being."[149] They also wrote in the contradictions and ruptures they saw and experienced in ideology, and the novel came to be praised and damned for its open-endedness and its sprawling formlessness.

These texts, and many women's novels, have been frequently criticized for lacking satisfactory resolutions. Closure, however, is in the interest of the hegemony, and the "conclusions" of novelistic works are eloquent testimony to this truth. The dissident can emphasize that at this moment there are no satisfactory resolutions to problems. She can dramatize demands for equality and justice within marriage even as domestic harmony seemed to depend upon the subordination of the wife.[150] She can make obvious the hypocrisies of a system that returns Lord Grey to court "in splendour" and makes Bellamy exempt from any criminal or civil penalty. She can create an ending so alien and alienating that it lingers in the mind, tantalizing the reader to seek other resolutions, as *Oroonoko* does. She can impose a conclusion so formulaic as to deconstruct the formula. She can participate in and even initiate and accelerate "organic changes," those changes Gramsci recognized as permanent and aimed at a new collective will.

PART THREE

Gothic Drama and National Crisis

OTHIC DRAMA REACHED ITS CREATIVE AND POP-
ular peak at a time when a number of political orders
were being renegotiated and being complicated by almost unprecedented national and international crises. A
few of the major events of the last quarter of the eighteenth century were the American Revolution, the Gordon Riots, the
Regency Crisis, the French Revolution, the Reign of Terror, and the
beginning of the Napoleonic Wars. In addition, Britain had to absorb the
massive physical and social dislocations of the agrarian and industrial
revolutions, navy mutinies, Irish unrest, and the arming of British citizens in preparation for a French invasion in the winter of 1797–98.[1]
Economic pressures from bad harvests and new taxation, unsettling
radical educational tracts by and for women, and waves of political
pressures propagated through reformist societies and their publications
increased the people's sense of insecurity and turmoil. By the end of
1793, Thomas Paine's *The Rights of Man* had sold two hundred thousand
copies. Even traditional conceptions of the family and gender were un-
dergoing drastic revision.

During the tumultous 1780s, the gothic drama became a recognized
and popular literary mode; in the 1790s it became a mania, as did the
gothic novel. The gothic suited the times, for it challenges the limits of

the predictable, the "natural," the possible. If borders and limits do not hold, then the assumptions that determine our interpretations of phenomena and behavior are threatened. The public and private, the affectionate, the social, and the political become areas of uncertainty and insecurity, and every person and every event is capable of arousing dread.

Gothic drama, surely one of the most denigrated and neglected forms in the entire history of drama, is an especially rich field for the study of literature as hegemonic apparatus. In addition to offering a third kind of case study for the analysis of how some forms of literature function in times of social crisis characterized by competing ideologies, it also contributes to strains of intellectual and social history presented in parts 1 and 2 of this book.

As the size of the London theaters increased, as the number of provincial theaters rose sharply, and as published plays and novels became ever more inexpensive and accessible, the gothic became available to a very broad spectrum of society. Indeed, it may be the earliest indisputable example of what we call mass culture. Although individual works of literature, including John Dryden's *Absalom and Achitophel* and Daniel Defoe's *True-Born Englishman,* had attracted mass audiences, and a few literary kinds, such as multivolume romances, travel books, and she-tragedies, had had sustained appeal, the gothic drama marks a new stage. It offers a paradigm for the study of the artistic and social dynamics that give rise to those wonders of cultural history that are modern mass culture: an artistic configuration that becomes formulaic and has mass appeal, that engages the attention of a very large, very diverse audience, and that stands up to repetition, not only of new examples of the type but of production of individual plays. As such, it offers a way to extend the exploration of several questions raised earlier: Why at some moments in a nation's life do strikingly large numbers of the population give themselves over to an art form? What in the experiencing of that form captivates and gratifies that audience? When that form is judged to be inferior, not only by subsequent ages but even by its major creators and practitioners and by professional critics, as the gothic drama has been, these questions become even more intriguing. It seems likely that greater understanding of why certain forms come to have mass appeal in modern Western societies will emerge from such inquiries.

Inscribed in the gothic drama are two other major concerns of my study: sex as political category and public opinion. By this time, women and women writers had learned that their acceptance and even authority—at least what authority they were permitted—depended upon their conforming to a female script. The gendered spheres so eloquently documented by Jane Spencer, Janet Todd, Nancy Armstrong, and Mary Poovey were firmly in place and available as a simple symbolic code. Gothic dramatists, therefore, could use sex as binary opposition in order to schematize philosophical and political systems. By this time, too, public opinion as a legitimate and legitimating political force had been almost universally accepted. Those in power had been brought to say with Charles Fox that "he had contended, and he ever would contend, that no ministers who acted independent of the public opinion, ought to be employed. The public opinion alone was the basis, in his mind, on which an administration should be formed." Increasingly large numbers of people from all social orders felt competent to make and express political opinions and even to believe in their ability to influence their nation's history. As Pierre Bourdieu observed, "The propensity to speak politically . . . is strictly proportionate to the sense of having the right to speak" (411).

Unlike the creators of coronation year events and of *Love-Letters between a Nobleman and His Sister,* the writers of gothic drama did not see themselves primarily as participating in a political discourse when they wrote gothic drama.[2] Unlike playwrights like Howard and the women novelists, they were not feeling in opposition, seeking ways to "say the unsayable," or creating a new space for newly deliberative groups to write themselves and their perspectives into history. These playwrights, however, no less than the other writers in this study, were innovators and deeply engaged in hegemonic processes.

Chapter 5 demonstrates how they gradually precipitated out technical and ideological elements that captured and spoke to the most pressing anxieties and needs of their time and how their plays, like Behn's text, used visible, orchestrated languages. This chapter thereby identifies the aspects and operation of gothic drama that ally it with popular mass art and made it successful. Chapter 6 extends the analysis of the ways gothic drama exercised, released, and then contained the major personal and social anxieties of the time. It reveals the political dynamic symbolized by male, female, and crowd that allowed the gothic to articulate conflict and then to deny it. Eighteenth- and early nineteenth-century gothic drama is a huge subject. My concerns here are with its rise from plays such as Miles Peter Andrews's *Enchanted Castle,* on the one hand, and John Home's *Douglas,* on the other; and with its participation in the events and anxieties of 1780–98 and the ways it became one of the many hegemonic apparatuses that negotiated the world-view that allowed England to defeat Napoleon. Although I include references to late eighteenth-century plays that signal the diverse modes of related drama popular in the new century and to Matthew Lewis's *Castle Spectre,* which exemplifies the beginning of the process of deconstructing the gothic, I do not analyze any of them in detail.

5

POPULAR ART

A YOUNG WIFE HEARS A MUFFLED GROAN FROM BEHIND A locked door; responsive to "the accent of distress" and the duty of "humanity to succour a wretched soul," she uses her husband's key to unlock the door. Rather than swinging open, it drops down into the floor "with a tremendous crash." Revealed is a room streaked with "vivid streams" of blood containing tombs "in the midst of which ghastly and supernatural forms are seen—some in motion, some fix'd—In the centre is a large Skeleton seated on a tomb."

A heroine dies bravely between the two virtuous, heroic men who have loved her. They weep copiously. The villain, who has poisoned her, throws himself off a cliff onto the rocks in the sea far below.

These are typical scenes from early gothic drama. It is hard to find an eighteenth-century gothic play that did not have a respectable initial run and regular revivals, and many had truly phenomenal success.[1] And the London theaters had become very large. By the 1792–93 season, Covent Garden held 3,013; by the spring of 1794, Drury Lane held 3,611, and the gothics were equally popular at the increasingly numerous provincial theaters.[2] James Cobb's *Haunted Tower* (1789), with eighty-four performances in the first two seasons, was the most successful opera staged by Drury Lane in the entire century. George Colman the Younger's *Battle of Hexham* had twenty performances at the Haymarket in 1789, sixteen the next season, eleven the next, fifteen the next, and so it went. His *Blue-Beard* (1798) ran sixty-four nights in its first season, the longest first run of any play produced between 1776 and 1800; his *Iron Chest* (1796) ran almost annually until 1879. Theaters staged John Burgoyne's *Richard Coeur de Lion* (1786), which was one of the ten most performed plays in the last quarter of the century, produced 123 times in fourteen years. Among the most successful plays of the 1794–95 season were the gothics, *The Mountaineers* (1793), *The Mysteries of the Castle* (1795), *The Secret Tribunal* (1795), *The Count of Narbonne* (1781), *Fontainville Forest* (1794), and *The Battle of Hexham*. The seasons of 1797–98 and 1798–99 included even more gothic plays, and, again, among the most successful were *The Battle of Hexham, The Iron Chest* (1796), and *The Italian Monk* (1797), and the premiers of *The Castle Spectre* (1797), *Blue-Beard,* and *Aurelio and Miranda* (1798).

Gothic plays are quite diverse, and it is not possible to construct a definitive, "pure" list of them. Indeed, gothic elements were markedly present in English drama at least as early as the production of John Home's *Douglas* (Edinburgh, 1756; London, 1757); in fact, critics beginning with Samuel Johnson have located similar strategies, characters, and themes in the plays of John Dryden, Thomas Otway, and their contemporaries. Of Dryden's scenes for Almanzor, for example, Johnson wrote, "They exhibit a kind of illustrious depravity and majestick madness: such as, if it is sometimes despised, is often reverenced, and in which the ridiculous is mingled with the astonishing."[3] As early as the 1740s, the structures of feeling that would animate the gothic were beginning to appear in architecture; an example is the duke of Cumberland's artificial ruin, Virginia Water (1746), which had transported, ancient columns augmented by constructed, complementary parts and was set over a wide, somewhat barren area. In 1759, William Chambers added an imitation gothic "cathedral" to Kew Gardens.[4] By the 1780s, characteristics that we usually associate with the gothic had been incorporated in many kinds of plays. The use of archaic settings and attempts to portray the terrifying as well as the presence of such icons as skulls, shrouds, bones of limbs or rib cages, daggers, moving curtains, and flickering lights had become ubiquitous.

Yet some generalizations about gothic drama can be made and a group of plays identified as belonging to a category of literary kind that we can safely classify as English gothic drama. In the decade of the 1780s, with a few exceptions such as *The Count of Narbonne,* gothic drama

The duke of Cumberland's artificial ruin, Virginia Water, captured the gothic mood. (Photo courtesy of Dr. Richard P. Wunder, Washington, D.C.)

depended primarily upon the conventions of English comic opera and even pantomime. Among these plays were Miles Peter Andrews's *Enchanted Castle* (1786), which was a true pantomime with Harlequin and Colombine; James Cobb's comic opera, *The Haunted Tower* (1789); and George Colman the Younger's *Battle of Hexham,* which he called a comedy. In the nineties, although the plays of the eighties remained extremely popular and others like them became hits, gothic drama drew primarily upon the conventions of post-1670s English tragedy with its strong elements of melodrama. The variety of these plays can be surmised from the forms with which their titles allied them. Lewis called *The Castle Spectre* "a drama," and Andrews styled his *Mysteries of the Castle* (1795), which was based on Laetitia Aikin's *Fragment of Sir Bertrand* (1774)[5] and on Horace Walpole's *Castle of Otranto,* "a dramatic tale." Colman intended *Blue-Beard* to be the Christmas pantomime for Drury Lane, and he called it "a Dramatick Romance."[6] Robert Jephson had called *The Count of Narbonne,* which was also loosely based on Walpole's *Castle of Otranto,* a tragedy. By midcentury, "A Play" became the conventional choice.

In spite of the diversity of the plays, that gothic drama became a formulaic type is indisputable. Like all formula literature, it had come to promise its consumers a definite setting, a particular cast of characters (which in this case implied predictable casting decisions and acting styles), a restricted repertoire of highly readable cultural icons, and a limited number of what John Cawelti has called "lines of action." Matthew Lewis, one of the most perceptive analysts of the late eighteenth-century gothic, described the dramatic "formula" in the prologue to his *Castle Spectre;* first he mentioned such elements of setting as the "dungeons damp, / Drear forests, ruin'd aisles, and haunted towers," the howling storms, and the sound of surf on rocks; then he continued,

> Next choosing from great Shakespeare's comic school,
> The gossip crone, gross friar, and gibing fool—
> These, with a virgin fair and lover brave,
> To our young author's care the enchantress gave;[7]
> But charged him, ere he bless'd the brave and fair,
> To lay the exulting villain's bosom bare,
> And by the torments of his conscience show,
> That prosperous vice is but triumphant woe!

Lewis captures setting, repertory of characters, and plot well. The configuration of characters determines the plot. Basically, the villain, who is the protagonist, menaces a beautiful, virtuous woman who will be happily married to an admirable, stable man. Desire for property, not love or sex, motivates the villain, who, as Lewis notes, has a tortured conscience. The romance line is strongly subordinated to the story of removing the threat emanating from the protagonist, who always repents or dies.

Modern theorists of the gothic have gone beyond these concrete elements to argue that the form, in all its manifestations, is best distinguished by the experience its readers or spectators have, and it is now widely accepted as an expression of dissatisfaction with the possibilities of conventional literary realism.[8] In his prologue, Lewis had cast "Romance," "the moon-struck child of genius, and of woe" as the Muse, and numerous gothic playwrights added "romance" to their titles. Thus, they signaled their freedom from the referential, veridical world of realist texts and allied themselves with a highly symbolic art, often reaching for a higher reality or a deeper psychology. Tzvetan Todorov quotes Pierre Mabille: "Beyond entertainment, beyond curiosity, beyond all the emotions such narratives and legends afford, beyond the need to divert, to forget, or to achieve delightful or terrifying sensations, the real goal of the marvelous journey is the total exploration of universal reality" (57). Peter Brooks, in "Virtue and Terror," calls "the Gothic emotion" "a delectation in chiaroscuro, in the experience of ruin, mystery, awe—in order to imply the capacity and aptitude of the natural world to receive and produce the supernatural" (255), and David Punter notes that "the world, at least in some aspects, is very much more inexplicable—or mysterious, or terrifying, or violent" than realism allows (407). This sense of the unknown, the unpredictable, the essentially threatening nature of the world, and especially of the possibilities for familiar limits to collapse underlies the gothic experience. "It is a fear of shadows and unseen dangers in the night" (Keech, 132). It is the fear of what might happen, of what human beings, even a friend or relative, might suddenly do.

In the 1770s and 1780s, gothic drama brought threatening, mythical archetypes into dynamic contact with contemporary preoccupations. The social ruptures that would be fought out in every aspect of nineteenth-century British life were becoming painfully evident,[9] and the signs of competing ideologies challenging the dominant order are manifest in the Gordon Riots, the reformist societies, and the radical educational tracts by and for women. In 1788 King George III had his first extended attack of porphyria, and his physicians' reports and the Regency Crisis astonished the nation. *The Castle of Otranto,* often considered the first gothic novel, appeared shortly after John Wilkes was expelled from Parliament,[10] and *The Count of Narbonne* in the year after the Gordon Riots; in the 1790s, the decade in which the ramifications of the French Revolution and the horrors of the Napoleonic War became clear, the gothic drama and novel became a public mania that lasted well into the nineteenth century. In the 1760s, the second largest group of chapbooks dealt with the supernatural and religion,[11] and by 1790 critics were saying that gothic drama was threatening to drive all other plays off the stage. Between 1764 and 1820, four thousand gothic novels were published in England, and the Minerva Press books, which began in 1790, made cheap editions widely available.

The time was right for the gothic. Writers felt its spirit in the times. Charlotte Smith began *The Romance of Real Life* (1787), "It has been asserted, that there is in human nature a propensity to every kind of evil; and that persons of the best disposition, and most liberal education, may find themselves in situations as will, if their passions are suffered to predominate, betray them in the most frightful excesses, into crimes which cannot be related without horror" (1). The Marquis de Sade commented perceptively,

> For anyone familiar with the full range of misfortunes wherewith evil-doers can beset mankind, the novel became as difficult to write as monotonous to read. There was not a man alive who had not experienced in the short span of four or five years more misfortunes than the most celebrated novelist could portray in a century. Thus, to compose works of interest, one had to call upon the aid of hell itself. [12]

In 1793, Frances Burney, who had lived at court, conversed with George III at the onset of his illness, and walked in the garden with the "mad" king, wrote: "Already we look back on the [recent] past as on a dream . . . wild in its horrors." [13] Pent up in this drama were the signs of the cultural crisis.

It is now common to locate the gothic impulse in the French Revolution, but it seems to me that the great gothic impetus was born in an English crisis and, from its inception to its demise, reflected British events and structures of feeling at least as much as it did any winds that blew across the channel to England. [14] Between the time of the adaptation of Walpole's *Castle of Otranto* for the stage in 1781 and the first adaptation of one of Anne Radcliffe's novels in 1794, there was more than a decade during which gothic drama rose in popularity and took shape. That decade's gothic drama has largely been ignored.

Something as simple as comparing the sets for these plays with the new palace under construction at Kew suggests the fanciful and romantic cast of this early gothic and its relationship to the king. In 1783, the king engaged James Wyatt to build a royal residence large enough for his family; from then until into the next decade, construction on the "Gothic" or "Castellated Palace" continued. Sir N. Wraxall came to call it a "most singular monument of eccentricity" and an "image of distempered reason." [15] In 1783, James Wyatt was a sensationally successful young architect. Only thirty-seven years old and elected an associate to the Royal Academy at age twenty-four, he had dazzled London with his Pantheon in Oxford Street (designed 1769, opened 1772). [16] Between 1770 and 1799, he exhibited designs at the Royal Academy no fewer than thirty-five times and established himself as an architect of elegant, imaginative, and pleasurable rooms graced with exquisite and often unexpected yet harmonious details. By 1780, he was abandoning such influ-

A number of gothic theater sets resemble the "castellated palace" being constructed for the king and his family at Kew. *Top.* James Wyatt's castellated palace for the king. (From John Brooke, *King George III.* © 1972, McGraw-Hill.) *Bottom.* This construction for *Richard Coeur de Lion* is a typical gothic theater setting with workable bridges and towers and "sublime" mountain scenery in the background. (Courtesy of the Harvard Theatre Collection.)

ences as the Hagia Sophia in Constantinople, which was the model for the Pantheon, and the classical for the gothic, a style he is sometimes credited with having made fashionable.[17] As the *DNB* says, "There is scarcely a county or large town in which Wyatt did not erect some public or private building." Although detractors compared Kew Palace to the Bastille, pointed out that its chief "prospect" was "the dirty town of Brentford," and pronounced it "highly inconvenient and uncomfortable,"[18] public interest ran high. The *Times* for 27 August 1805, for instance, reported:

> His Majesty's *chateau* at Kew, is proceeding as fast as possible. By the erection of a castellated range of buildings . . . with a Gothic gateway in the centre, the disagreeable appearance of Brentford is nearly hidden. . . . Great alterations are making in the gardens. . . . Most of the temples have been recently repaired and painted, and a fosse is now digging in a semi-circular direction, which will enclose the house from that part of the gardens in which the public may be permitted to walk. From various parts of the grounds the new building forms a very picturesque object. (3)

In the king, too, were the hints of the Janus-faced gothic protagonist. By 1771 political essayists, including Junius, were depicting George III as the "virtual director of a neo-Stuart attempt to impose tyranny on Britain."[19] It was during the decade of the '80s that George III's strong demands for respect for royal prerogative and his willing assertion of the power of the throne came to be well known. In fact, in 1780, Commons had passed a motion stating that "the influence of the Crown has increased, is increasing, and ought to be diminished."[20] In the midst of the Gordon Riots he brought the troops, both horse and foot, into London and ordered them as a last resort to shoot rioters without pausing to read the Riot Act and even asserted that he was willing to lead the Horse Guards himself if necessary.[21] During the debate over the India Bill in 1783, the king ruthlessly pressured the members of the House of Lords, including the archbishop of Canterbury, to vote as he desired.

The "plot" of the king's life and the standard gothic story had many points of similarity. Before his illness, George III had first been in opposition to his own ministers, including the popular Pitt-Newcastle "broadbottom" coalition, and had then been the object of resolutions passed in Parliament condemning the increase in his exercise of power. In the autumn of 1788, he suffered a severe attack of porphyria, one that led his chief physician to write on 6 November that the king had "lost his reason." It would be late February before his recovery was certain.[22] Among the most violent signs of his illness were violent mood changes, eruptions of impatience and rage, pathetic evidence of self-awareness, and great agitation accompanied by multiple and contradictory orders.[23] One of the most embarrassing symptoms of his illness was his delusion that he was married to a youthful sweetheart, Elizabeth Pembroke, rather than to his queen. At other moments, he would say that he planned to become a Lutheran in order to divorce Charlotte and marry Elizabeth.[24]

Simultaneously, George III was "Farmer George," the king who mingled freely with his subjects, talked on mundane matters with them, and headed a "cult of domestic virtue, a cult in which he was not to be surpassed even by his grand-daughter."[25] Even his youngest children attended his drawing rooms, and the precedent-setting division he made between them and his audiences, between his home and his court, Queen's House (the former Buckingham House) and St. James, contributed to the establishment of the nineteenth-century conception of private and public. Prints depicted him taking tea with his daughters or toasting muffins while the queen fried sprats. A few months before he fell ill, he and his wife walked the streets of Cheltenham hand in hand and even visited in private homes; they would do the same in Weymouth during the king's recovery in June 1789.[26] He and his family were frequently at Windsor after 1780, and, since the grounds were open, he often met his subjects while he was engaged in mundane actions.

To some extent, all monarchs provide stability to a nation, and George's firm adherence to such traditional institutions as the Church of England, the family, and a strong, patriarchal monarchy increased the illusion of security that his people drew from him. His illness, accompanied by shocking reports of his behavior and treatment and by political intrigue, threw the entire nation into distress. His recovery in 1789 occasioned extravagant national rejoicing, and George seemed to have become a more sympathetic monarch. During the time when his illness was abating, he wanted to set up a new order with the motto "Rex Populo non separandus."[27] A man who saw him often, Lord Auckland, remarked that the king "is a quite altered man, and not what you knew him even before his illness; his manner is gentle, quiet, and, when he is pleased, quite cordial."[28] In spite of lingering weakness, he insisted upon attending the five-hour St. George's Day thanksgiving that began with a service at St. Paul's and concluded with a *feu de joie* from the Guards

under the windows at Buckingham Palace. He tirelessly greeted his subjects in every village he went through. In late August, he began a three-
week progress where "one constant mob" turned out for him.[29]

By 1788, George III was also "the distressed father of the wicked
Prince of Wales," frustrated by his rebellious son and the rebellious
Americans.[30] The nation knew that they were not eager to see the Prince
of Wales, George Augustus Frederick, ascend the throne. He had been
scandalously involved in an expensive relationship with an actress, Mary
Robinson, and soon came to be known for excessive indulgence in what
many considered the vices of the *ton:* heavy drinking, gambling, mas-
querades, and sexual assignations. His extravagance was common
knowledge. By then, too, he was deeply involved with the opposition and
especially with the Fox-North-Portland coalition.

When George III began making public appearances in 1789, the
signs of his illness could not be ignored, for he was extremely thin,
persistently hoarse, and some even noted that he became upset more
obviously and quickly. Burney recorded a conversation in which he
expressed sentiments of great benevolence and "sweetness" and yet
became "animated almost into a rage" and said he was going to "rule
with a rod of iron" (4:247, 249). His subjects would never be able to
forget that he had been mad and, therefore, always feared that he would
be so again. In these first fragile weeks of his public emergence, the
French Revolution began. At first regarded with detachment and even
approval, it would be nearly two years before such events in France as the
abolition of all titles, the arrest of Louis XVI, and the invasion of the
southern Netherlands began to change public opinion. Pitt, for instance,
had expected that France would be less warlike under a constitution
more like England's.[31] By 1791, however, events in France, demands for
reform in England, and riots, such as those in Birmingham and Manchester that required the dragoons to end them, had English anxieties high.

The heart of gothic drama in the nineties is an authority figure gone
mad, or at least seriously obsessive and neurotically moody. Here is the
face of authority in England after 1788:

> Such rapid fluctuations between great excitement and compara-
> tive calm, between insight that his mind was playing tricks and a con-
> viction that his hallucinations were reality and building false beliefs
> on them, between rational behavior and impulsive inappropriate
> actions . . .

> To these gentler workings of a disordered mind, [there] often
> succeeded sad transports of vehemence and agitation.[32]

These descriptions of King George III's first descent into madness could
be descriptions of the protagonists of almost all gothic plays. Moreover,
other powerful people exhibited similar troubling behavior. Edmund
Burke's conduct, for instance, was described as irrational, "violent almost to madness," and as "confirm[ing] the suspicions which many of
his contemporaries entertained regarding his mental stability"; George
Selwyn mused, "Burke walking at large and [the king] in a strait waist-
coat!"[33] Soon the Reign of Terror and Napoleon would provide mind-
boggling images of the face of authority.

This man, and it seems always to be a man, is "gothic" because he is
pushing the absolute limits of what the audience imagines to be possible
in nature. He is subject to cataclysmic passions, has committed or is
contemplating unspeakable crimes that reek of ancient, sacred taboos,
and is engaged in a magnificent struggle with himself. Like Colman's
Mortimer, he can horrify with his rapid changes: "I will crush thee!
pulverise thy frame! . . . Ha, ha ha!—I will not harm thee, boy—O,
agony!" (*Iron Chest,* 32). Narbonne, Octavian (*The Mountaineers*),
Rawbold, Mortimer (both *Iron Chest*), and many others experience periods of madness; other characters, Ferrand in *The Castle of Otranto*[34] and
Schedoni (*Italian Monk*), describe their brains as "on fire." Abomelique,
Bulcazin Muley, and Mortimer are passionate, agitated, and subject to
rapid mood changes.

Because the plays are usually set in feudal times and in isolated parts
of familiar nations, the characters are few and palpably isolated. Therefore, the protagonist's influence—both political and emotional—is vast
and permeates every aspect of the portrayed world. Because of this man,
the gothic settings are completely appropriate. They develop his character and influence but also carry subliminally the other messages essential
to the gothic. Secret chambers, locked rooms, sealed vaults, dungeons,
and underground catacombs—places available as reminders of his guilt
or locations for future atrocities—express the most obvious possibilities
for such a man. He is also capable of assuring that a woodland glen will
be a threatening, dark forest where conversations may be overheard and
assassins hide.

What has gone berserk in this world, of course, is power. And British
people felt they lived in such a place. By creating a claustrophobic world
with this kind of single authority figure, the playwright found a way to

make power prevail everywhere and to embody an ideological struggle. The audience sensed what Foucault has identified as the true nature of power, that it is very widely disseminated and penetrates everywhere. Foucault saw that power had come to work on the mind as well as the body and to permeate into private spaces, private places, even into the soul. When power transferred its pressure from the body to the mind, it gained the power to "modify, use, consume, or destroy" the subject that the British mind identified as the "true self." Many of the most effective episodes in gothic art and literature make the audience acutely aware of the multiple sources of power and the fragility of the restraints on these forces. In human beings the British saw new capacity for evil, for the perverted use of authority. In official forms of authority they saw the ability to put under surveillance, to coerce, to confine, and to silence, and they saw the church and the state colluding. In landscapes and the theater's special effects, they saw the power of nature, sensed the omnipotent force behind it, remembered its superhuman and unpredictable power, and realized that such power could make it seem crushingly malevolent. Such awareness of the reality, dissemination, and potential of power is painful and frightening.

The protagonist of a gothic play represented the ideology of feudal privilege, and in some plays specifically as it manifested itself in the period Alexis de Tocqueville called "the ancien régime." Insisting upon the absolute right of prerogative even as he recognized this stance as threatened, the protagonist is the sign of aggressive, individualistic behavior, which objectifies, commodifies, and consumes. He was a particularly effective carrier of threat, because of feudalism's similarities and contrasts to bourgeois and capitalist ideologies.[35] Like these, ancien régime feudalism emphasized the solitary actor and tended to glorify aggressive, individualistic energy. As economic historians have noted, feudal lords exploited people and lands in ways we now consider capitalistic, although significant differences in philosophy and values existed.[36] For instance, rather than insisting upon "natural rights" as higher laws as capitalists often did, feudal lords saw themselves as the law and, therefore, were willing to deny all other legal claims. Representing the demand for obedience based upon obligation to status, they denied any claims of rational self-interest and any legitimacy to voluntary contractual community.

As J.G.A. Pocock points out, England can be seen as an ancien régime because it was doing modern things—commercially, imperially, and intellectually under the authority of the ancient institutions of monarchy, aristocracy, and church.[37] In some gothic plays, the king intervened, usually through an emissary, to check or correct the actions of a nobleman. In *Thoughts on the Cause of the Present Discontents,* Edmund Burke had argued against "a phantom of tyranny in the nobles" but almost simultaneously Horace Walpole "hoped the Crown can reduce the exorbitance of the peers."[38] The ideal of Polybian mixed government with its checks and balances runs deep in English discourses, and in the last quarter of the century the king could be seen as the best hope of controlling the excesses and abuses of both capitalistic power from wealth and aristocratic power based on traditional "rights." It is no coincidence that playwrights made the gothic protagonist an aristocrat, but one corrupt and in decline and never the legitimate possessor of his estate. Raymond, Count of Narbonne, announces, "My will's the law." Austin, the priest, exclaims, "A venerable law! / The law by which the tyger tears the lamb." He asks Raymond if, when he is called to answer in heaven's court, "Will that supremacy accept the pleas, / *I did commit foul murder, for I might?*"

His basic drive is to secure his claim, and that claim is rapidly embodied in or transformed into a young woman. Like Otranto, who wants to maintain and bequeath his fiefdom and whose story Ronald Paulson calls a fable of the ancien régime,[39] these characters are not like the modern bourgeois dictator who often claims to be "enlightened" and dedicated to "supposedly emancipatory values of freedom, justice, and fraternity, the abolition of social hierarchies and privileged authority."[40] Unlike bourgeois ideology, it lacks commitment to humanism, "progress," or even the crucial importance of the individual's interiority.

Even relatively early gothics, such as *Narbonne,* state explicitly the assumption of the privileges of power depicted in gothic protagonists and even in a few minor characters who imitate these aristocrats in kind if not magnitude. Collectively they recall the aggressive and oppressive old order, the violence of the past, and its lingering power over the present. Lamotte in *Fontainville Forest* explains, "My means for ever sunk below my wishes—/ I lanquish'd still for splendour out of reach, / Never by industry to be obtain'd" (52). He resorts to fraud and then robbery. Another thief, Rawbold in *The Iron Chest,* says, "Fortune has thrust me forth to prowl, like the wolf" (8). Other passages in these plays briefly raise the possibility that such individualism is "natural" and, thereby, suggest that the ideological conflict represented by the characters extends to nature. For instance, the marquis in *Fontainville Forest* explains, "The savage unperverted follows nature, / And stabs his unsuspecting enemy, / Pursues occasion of secure revenge, / And strikes the blow, when harmless to himself" (54).

The marquis's will to power becomes a desire for Adeline, his murdered brother's child, and then transforms itself again into the desire for her murder. Like Osmond in Lewis's *Castle Spectre,* he desires the daughter because she resembles her mother, the woman originally loved and lost, and because she, as the legitimate heir, would secure the usurped property. Like Raymond, these men want to possess the woman in the same way they want the land: utterly, permanently—consuming both and obliterating all possibility of rivals. They display the conservative, restrictive interests of finance capital rather than the capitalistic drive to expand and compete in an open market, a difference Foucault characterized as knowledge of wealth rather than knowledge of production.[41] They are completely willing to kill again and to violate the most prohibited taboos. Incest is almost always planned, and that they constantly threaten rape, entombment, and murder introduces hints of cannibalism and necrophilia as well.

The Regency Crisis brought the nature of authority, its fragility, and the implications of it painfully to the attention of a nation that was already engaging such issues. Gothic drama concentrated these anxieties in the protagonist and encoded other structures of feeling as well. In modern times of crisis, popular literature serves major hegemonic functions. Its potential for strengthening the status quo has long been recognized; more important, however, than its alleged ability to forestall independent thinking and to become Thorstein Veblen's anesthetizing technology for managing consensus or Theodor Adorno and Max Horkheimer's "irrefutable prophet of the prevailing order"[42] is its existence as a mediator between lived experience and utopian desires. As Fredric Jameson says of all memorable art, "[It] proves to unite a lived experience of some kind, as its content, with an implied question as to the very possibilities of Experience itself, as its form."[43]

To become mass art, literature must appeal enough to become popular; to do this, it must speak to the hopes and fears of its audience at a particular moment in their history even as it does what popular art always does: entertain. Evidence suggests that most satisfying entertainment literature indulges deep fantasies and fears; that it enthralls—often by providing superficial delights to the senses—but finally delivers the satisfactions of poetic justice. In times of turmoil and stress, above all, it must exercise, release, and contain powerful feelings. This last sequence helps explain the pleasure of repetition, the secret to drawing the same individuals time after time to the same play with the same cast. It is certainly necessary for literature to become popular before it can be a highly effective modern hegemonic apparatus, and it may also be necessary for it to become formulaic.

Gothic drama undoubtedly succeeded as mass art so prodigiously because it managed to unite nearly unprecedented spectacle and excitement with the elements we now know consumers find most satisfying in entertainment art. It depended upon spectacular settings, mood music, and acting in specific styles as much—or even more than—it did upon a predictable set of characters, conflicts, icons, and resolutions. These plays could be deeply appreciated by the lover of English theatrical music, by the devotée of great actors and actresses, by the student of landscape painting, and by the fan of melodrama and other popular dramatic forms. The audience in the late eighteenth century included true connoisseurs, able by experience and even study to be highly discriminating in all of these aspects. Even the least educated of the audience had been conditioned to react to many of the effects in sophisticated ways. Most of the audience would share the enjoyment of what Martin Meisel calls "the wonder of the machinery and the enchantment of the transformations," but it is surely more accurate to think in terms of Bernard Bergonzi's participants in a "field of force" than of Adorno's passive consumers in whom consciousness has become mindless conformity. Bergonzi imagines a model in which author, genre, the ideology of the author's group, and other factors are on a parity with the audience's desires, expectations, and ideology and in which all constitute the text.[44] As such, it can actualize literature's potential to become a hegemonic apparatus through its artful strategies of exercise and containment.

In many ways, gothic drama, like the novel, was a new literary kind born of the orchestrated languages of other popular forms. These recognizable traces enhanced the form's ability to please and to soothe its audience. *The Battle of Hexham* is a good example, and because it is in the first wave of gothic plays highly instructive. Colman called it a comedy, but it begins with the defeat of Henry VI and Queen Margaret by Edward IV, and this familiar history and the opening scene would have been experienced as historical romance or even tragedy. One of Adeline's first expositions reads, "My house is wretchedness—The wars I seek have made it so—they have robb'd me of my husband—comfort now is lost to me, My very children, whose pretty frolic round our hearth, charm'd even time and made the lagging winter's night fly . . . I kiss them thro' my tears. . . . Oh Gondibert, too faithful to weak cause" (6). An early scene between Margaret and a Shakespeare-style tragic fool whose wit is caustic and worldly marks the play's antecedents, but other scenes involving Margaret are even more sentimental than Adeline's speech. Recalling the historical time, the despair and dark forests of Home's *Douglas, Hexham* brings the fear of unknown places, of storms, discomfort, violence, robbery, and death before the audience through scene changes and special effects. In a touch foreshadowing the gothic novel to come, all of the characters imagine and describe far worse things than they experience. The bandit lord talks of how "imagination discovers to the dull and feverous sense mishapen forms ghastly and horrible" (50). Colman also included many of the conventions of comic opera, and he may have used the word "comedy" to prepare the audience for the excessive sentiment, for bandits that are soon revealed to be more picturesque and miserable than threatening, and especially for the number and variety of the songs. The improbable happy ending is sealed with a patriotic speech and a rousing chorus celebrating the end of wars. Today this play with its mixture of carefully coordinated if contrasting forms is often inappropriately located as early melodrama rather than within the strain of pre-1790s gothic literature, an emergent form composed of re-accentuated art forms.

Before turning to a discussion of the encoded philosophical issues and the political dynamic beneath the surface of these plays, I shall attempt to illustrate what the major components of gothic drama were like and how its dramaturgy participated in the exercise, release, and containment of personal and social anxieties. I shall organize the rest of this chapter by some of the plays' components and limit it by focusing primarily upon the aspects likely to be least familiar to modern readers and upon the stress most fully integrated and openly expressed in gothic drama—the sense of power gone berserk.

Unfortunately, gothic drama is almost as difficult as street pageants to reconstruct, and more difficult still for modern *readers* to integrate imaginatively so that effects appear before the mind's eye. To understand this drama, its success, and how it contained the most pressing fears and hopes of its audience, modern readers must recognize the coordinated art forms and bring perspectives from them all to bear simultaneously upon the printed text. To a large extent, this theater did depend upon the bombardment of the senses and the use of techniques that fixed manipulative tableaux in the audiences' memories. Thus, just as exercise and containment alternate, so do periods of intense activity with "freeze-frames." The playwrights gave precedence to form over reality and even plausibility, and charges that gothic drama was low on narrative and high on iconic manipulation are legitimate. It did, however, express people's legitimate concerns as they encountered the world, fulfilled needs and desires ranging from entertainment to education, and came to give pleasure as ritual and repetition.[45] The modern student of this drama, then, must exercise unusual re-creative imagination.

Horror art has always called for technical innovation, and today some of the men who designed the sets are better known than the playwrights. The intention was to create *Stimmung,* "moments when a landscape seems charged with alien meaning," the experience of what came to be Romantic epiphany,[46] most often to remind the audience of nature's moodiness and awesome power and to create scenes that reflected and dwarfed the protagonist's awesome and changing nature. Opening scenes made power, loneliness, desolation, and threat visceral. Contemporary witnesses record that certain scenes infallibly elicited gasps of wonder and appreciation from the audience. On stages as large as 108 feet high, 83 feet wide, and 92 feet long (Drury Lane after 1791), designers were able to produce landscapes accurately called "sublime," some based on familiar illustrations to which members of the audience had already learned "appropriate" responses.[47] Some scenes, like the "strong dismantled lonely Fort upon the Sea-side" in *The Italian Monk* and the "View of the City of *Messina,* the *Bay,* Mount AETNA, &c. &c." in *The Mysteries of the Castle,* are archetypally sublime. Nature's awesome power and beauty provide the background for constructions of buildings, many of which are depicted as crumbling. Thus, for instance, the disintegrating *manmade* buildings, in spite of their vast and massive size, provide a contrast to the divinely created, apparently immutable Italian Alps and are reminders of nature's great and potentially destructive power as the mountains are of its strength and permanence.

Major advances in set building, stage machinery, special effects, and lighting allowed designers like Philippe De Loutherberg, William Capon, and Thomas Greenwood the Younger to go somewhat beyond participating in the audience's willing acceptance of the premises of the play to offering an impressive demonstration of sublime art in its own right. Mountain landscapes, massive castles, and vast forests emphasized human weakness and insignificance; as early as 1770 playgoers commented on the skill with which they could be lit to show, for instance, the gradual coming of dawn, storms with lightning and thunder, and eerily foggy twilight. Jean Georges Noverre explained, "The art lies in knowing how to distribute the lamps in uneven groups, so as to bring out the parts which require full lighting and to leave in shadow or darkness . . . the other parts."[48]

At least by the 1770s English people had rejected the discipline of French art in favor of the "extravagantly heroic and sublime *Sturm und Drang* movement"; gothic sets showed the influence of the Neapolitan, "savage" Salvator Rosa, as James Thomson described him, over the very popular Claude Lorraine and Nicolas Poussin. Robert Rosenblum points out that English art came to be characterized by a blending of pictorial realism and "a style of visionary fantasy,"[49] and set designers learned to give the impression of fog with lights and reflectors and to produce dreamlike sequences against a background that might have come from an artist's on-site sketchbook. In the best plays, scenery and props contribute greatly to the mood of each segment of the play and even express the situation or mood of major characters. Colman's *Blue-Beard* has a "brilliantly and fancifully illuminated" garden with a working fountain. His set using the Sierra de Ronda in *The Mountaineers* is not unpredictable but seems to intensify the characters' mingled feelings of danger and exodus.

Many of these scenes with blended realism and nightmare join nature's dangers with man's evil in order to evoke elemental fears: confinement, perpetual surveillance, and death, especially in horrible ways such as falling great distances onto rocks or starvation in an underground vault. One of the best gothic sets is the one Sophia Lee devised for *Almeyda, Queen of Granada* (1796). The villain, Abdallah, has a "dark vault irregularly hewn in a rock, extending out of sight on one side, in a vista of rude imperfect pillars.—A small gate leads on the other side, through an enormous crag of the rock" (40). Abdallah tells him that beneath a large stone is a "chasm / Thro' jagged rocks—imperious— horrible—/ A stream, oblivious as the fabled Lethe, / Washes to many an undiscover'd hollow, / The victims of my will" (41). He chains Alonzo there, and throughout the next scenes the sound of the rushing water is a constant reminder of the danger. The stage directions for *The*

Castle Spectre were especially lavish and are memorable even for a modern reader. One of the most famous reads:

> A gloomy subterraneous Dungeon, wide and lofty: The upper part of it has in several places fallen in, and left large chasms. On one side are various passages leading to other Caverns: On the other is an Iron Door with steps leading to it. . . . Reginald, pale and emaciated, in coarse garments, his hair hanging wildly about his face, and a chain bound round his body, lies sleeping upon a bed of straw. (88)

Eternal imprisonment in a kind of labyrinth, human loneliness and vulnerability, the fears of midnight and of nightmares are given concrete expression in the "wide and lofty" set that dwarfs the chained being whose thin frame and wild hair show the ravages upon body and mind.

As is characteristic of the gothic—and, indeed, of much popular art—the suspense and dread are pleasurable partly because the audience has always at hand ways to remind themselves that the danger is art they can give themselves to or pull back from. The means of containing anxiety at least equal those allowing the exercise of fear. Playwrights and designers composed pastoral, picturesque scenes—the beautiful—as carefully as they did the sublime.[50] Lovely open fields and neat rural cottages shown at dawn or in daylight break the gloom and storm of convents, caves, and jagged mountains. Act 3 of *The Battle of Hexham* opens with a village that gradually displaces the image of the dark groves and robbers' cave. Scenes that call attention to the Sierra de Ronda alternate with those featuring the goatherds and their simple cottage in *The Mountaineers*. These juxtapositions regulated the intensity of the mood and reminded the audience of the gentle side of nature, but more importantly they captured the Janus-face of the world that seemed gothic. In replying to a friend recently bereaved, Walpole wrote, "Life seems to me as if we were dancing on a sunny plain on the edge of a gloomy forest, where we pass in a moment from glare to gloom to darkness."[51]

The plays and sets were, after all, manmade. In fact, in contrast to playgoers who may have wanted maximum illusion, playwrights seem to have shared the desire of eighteenth-century novelists for analytical and reflective auditors; James Boaden, for example, wrote, "It would not be desirable that the spectator should lose his senses to the point of forgetting that he is in a regular theatre, and enjoying a work of art invented for his amusement and instruction by a poet, and acted by another artist of corresponding talent called a player."[52] Spectators at any production periodically remember that they are watching a play and then give themselves over again to the experience, and aspects of eighteenth-century production made it quite difficult to sustain extended illusions. The proscenium arch stage framed the production, and therefore distanced the audience from the action. As late as the mid-nineteenth century, a playgoer complained that he could see "the broken portions" of a tower designed to crumble and fall "working smoothly on a hinge."[53] That hearty workmen changed the sets without closing the curtains and that such machinery as runners in the floor were clearly visible also worked against audience absorption in the mood.[54]

There is even evidence that some members of the audience believed that the sets were educational, and this mind-set would have inclined audiences to study the sets in a somewhat detached, analytical mode. One theatergoer is reputed to have said, "There is nothing like a playhouse for fine prospects; and . . . without fatigue, and trouble, one can see all Europe, *well lighted for a shilling*."[55] These plays were performed at the time when the delight in picturesque landscapes and some of the ideas in books such as Edmund Burke's *Philosophical Inquiry into the Origins of our Ideas of the Sublime and the Beautiful* (1757) had reached large segments of the population. Sets done in the styles of Rosa, Poussin, or Gaspar would have been recognized as such by some people. Middle-class people collected reproductions of landscape paintings, and the fact that even cheap, everyday household utensils and working-class taverns were decorated with famous scenes proves that such pleasures were not open to the educated alone.[56] Periodical reviews record the fact that people enjoyed and attended for the scenery in its own right; a *Morning Chronicle* article for 1776 noted, "Those who delight in a representation teeming with instances of the sublime, the beautiful, and the surprising in scenery and machinery, will be highly entertained."[57] Others could have compared Michael Angelo Rooker's famous paintings of architectural ruins with his theatrical scenes of the same places. In fact, it was common for scene designers to use familiar, published travel literature as models, and their creations were clearly recognizable. Some members of the audience would certainly have evaluated Inigo Richards's model of Netley Abbey or William Capon's re-creations of real ruins and, for *The Iron Chest,* of the vaulting from St. Stephens Westminster. As early as 1772, *Harlequin in Ireland* had carefully reproduced a set of impressive local landscapes, Killarney, Turk Mountain, and the Glena Mountains among them. Even the numerous bandit bands found in these plays had an artistic counterpoint: the popular paintings and drawings of them by John Henry Mortimer.[58]

Among its major orchestrated voices, especially in gothic drama's early years, was pantomime. Beginning in the mid-1720s, the landscape painter George Lambert had designed sets for pantomimes at Lincoln's Inn Fields and Covent Garden that put on stage erupting volcanoes and thick woods opening to lighted, open fields. In one of his designs for *Harlequin Sorcerer* (1753), "a scene drops and gives us a prospect of ruinous rugged cliffs, with two trees hanging over them." De Loutherbourg's first pantomime, *A Christmas Tale* (1773), had "forbidding mountains, [a] distant view of a romantic ruined castle perched on a crag, and a broken foreground of rocks."[59] Surely gothic theatergoers' reactions to scenery and effects were conditioned by the debt gothic design owed pantomime, and that would have tended to work against absorption in a gothic universe. Managers trotted out the same sets for comedies and tragedies, but pantomimes and the gothic often included elaborate original sets. Pantomime habitually mingled the mythic, the grotesque, and the magic. It routinely included a "dark scene," in which Harlequin lost his magic wand and the young couple became vulnerable to phantasmagorical horrors.[60] As early as 1727, hell rose from below in one of Lambert's sets for *The Rape of Proserpine,* heaven descended to dance on earth, a palace collapsed, and a cornfield was set afire and burned to ashes on stage. Eruptions of volcanoes, spectacular storms, and ascendable mountains were easily within the designers' and machinists' abilities.[61] Through all of this, the audience could trust the happy ending, the gardens, and the lighted meadows as well as the threatening gloom.

Similarly, gothic drama used music in sophisticated ways to engage the senses while subliminally both exercising and containing anxieties. One of the most popular scenes in all of gothic drama, a famous moment in Lewis's *Castle Spectre,* depended entirely upon music and pantomime:

> The set scene had an oratory with a perforated door of pure Gothic . . . , and Mrs. Jordan, who played Angela, being on the stage, a brilliant illumination suddenly took place, and the doors of the oratory opened—the light was perfectly celestial, and a majestic and lovely, but melancholy image stood before us; at this moment, in a low but sweet and thrilling harmony, the band played the strain of Jomelli's *Chaconne,* in his celebrated overture in three flats. . . . And the figure

began slowly to advance; it was the spirit of Angela's mother, Mrs. Powell, in all her beauty.

A spectator wrote that "no other scene of the kind ever made" the impression that that one had with "the solemn music to which she moved slowly forward to give a silent blessing to her kneeling daughter" and with the scene's closing chorus of female voices chanting, "Jubilate."[62] Audiences could expect ominous background music as well as such special effects as lightning and thunder cued to the music at crucial moments. The coordination of effects enthralled audiences. Some plays established musical themes for major characters. In the last scene of Thomas Holcroft's *Life of Mystery* (1802), Romaldi, the villain, enters accompanied by his ominous, mournful music, "pursued as it were by the storm." The *Monthly Mirror* reviewer wrote, "The last scene . . . has a most striking effect; the trees are represented in actual motion from the storm which, with the accompanying music, is well suited to Romaldi's state of mind, whose dreadful guilt has made him a fit object of both earthly and divine vengeance." His soliloquy is broken by intervals of music and the sounds of the storm. When the simple, good Michelli enters, the music becomes "a cheerful pastorale."[63] Michelli's music displacing Romaldi's mirrors the reliability of the favorable balance between good and evil in the theatrical gothic world and the certainty of the pleasing resolution. In some of the plays, the music is the first and primary means of containing the fears called up and exercised. The songs in *The Battle of Hexham* decisively contradict the early genre signals. Adeline, Gregory, and the soldiers all have songs in the first act that defuse the anxiety raised by civil war and the women's circumstances. The soldiers, for instance, sing, "Fight away for the cause of the jolly red rose; / Never flinch while you live, shou'd you meet with your death / There's no fear that you'll run, you'll be quite out of breath" (13).

As one of the observers of *The Haunted Tower* remarked, composers and librettists had learned to tell "the story of the *scene* in music" (emphasis mine, Fiske 505). Music, like painting, had become a fashionable leisure time activity and object of study. Sociable recitals, Catch Clubs, Harmonic Societies, and musical dinner party entertainment flourished, and audiences were prepared to enjoy music of high quality and rich variety. The music in plays such as Colman the Younger's *Blue-Beard* and Lewis's *Castle Spectre* included haunting love songs, stirring marches, and intricate duets and quartets. Andrews's *Mysteries of the Castle* opens with a chorus accompanied by Sicilian instruments that is worthy of Gilbert and Sullivan: "Gaily tripping to and fro'/ We village maids to market go" (5). *The Haunted Tower* included an aria with oboe obbligato, the Mozartian "Be mine, tender passion," and a rendition of the ever-popular "Roast Beef of Old England" (Fiske, 501–5).

In *The Iron Chest* the robbers sing a long ensemble: "Listen, it is the owl that hoots upon the mouldering tower." This song moves from the gloomy opening to become a rowdy drinking song as robbers enter at intervals to augment the singers. Several of Barbara's songs in the same work develop important aspects of the play or carry the weight of character development. For instance, she and her brother Samson have several highly original duets that blend his innocent stupidity with her domestic good-heartedness; one is sung to the accompaniment and interruption of the younger children crying for food (12–14). She also has a haunting ballad that begins,

It was a time when the quality of each theatrical house's music frequently came in for critical comment. People practiced and sang the songs they heard; the songs from *The Haunted Tower* were sung all over Great Britain and America for half a century. Some songs are still being sung; an example is Shield's "Lord, Dismiss us with Thy Blessing" from *The Mysteries of the Castle*.

The acting was a major part of any late eighteenth-century play, and many of the most effective leading men had experience in pantomime. Perhaps surprising to the modern reader is the fact that the techniques of pantomime had by the last quarter of the eighteenth century blended with great tragic acting. Indeed, some of the existing conventions of both became essential to gothic drama. From the time of David Garrick and the leading tragic actresses of his time, Hannah Pritchard and Mary Ann Yates, audiences expected emotional performances. To voice modulation, facial expressiveness, and gesture, the players added strong body language. Especially in the parts of Shakespeare's greatest tragic heroes and villains, actors came to exploit opportunities to express intense emotions and, in a development that would especially benefit gothic drama, to extend the time within and between speeches to portray through pantomime techniques a succession of strong passions. Masters of pantomime, especially Christopher Rich, had perfected a style that was "so perfectly expressive of his meaning that every motion of his hand or head, or of any part of his body, was a kind of dumb eloquence that was readily understood by the audience." Such great actors as Henry Woodward and Edmund Kean had been Harlequins.⁶⁴

As John Mullan has demonstrated, it was an age that believed that the body acted out emotions and had greater representative powers than words.⁶⁵ One contemporary observed, "You heard what they spoke, but you learned more from the agitation of mind displayed in their action and deportment."⁶⁶ John Genest described Garrick: "The passions rose in rapid succession, and, before he uttered a word, were legible in every feature of that various face—his look, his voice, his attitude changed with every sentiment" (4:14). The power of Sarah Siddons became legendary. Like Garrick's Lear, her Lady Macbeth could hypnotize an audience. James Sheridan Knowles recalled her movements and gestures more vividly than any spoken lines:

> Though pit, gallery, and boxes were crowded to suffocation, the
> chill of the grave seemed about you while you looked on her;—there
> was the hush and the damp of the charnel-house at midnight; you
> had a feeling as if you and the medical attendant, and lady-in-waiting,
> were alone with her; your flesh crept and your breathing became
> uneasy.

"I smelt blood! I swear I smelt blood!" he wrote (Sprague, 67).

Players also came to assume picturesque poses, thereby freezing a moment of particular significance or emotional resonance. They assumed "readable configurations visually conceived" that encapsulated a charged moment and made the theatrical experience one of "achieved situations."⁶⁷ The masterful conclusion of Lewis's *Castle Spectre* manages just this effect. Reginald is asleep on his straw, as described above. He awakens and walks about, then hears Angela and the priest who are escaping through the dungeons. The father runs away from the sight of Reginald. When Angela sees Reginald with his wild hair and the chain around his body, she gazes. He thinks she is the ghost of his beloved, murdered wife. He gazes. They recognize each other, embrace, and hold that position for an instant. They hear Osmond, and Reginald hides Angela and assumes his sleeping position on the straw. Osmond enters and stares at Reginald for a moment and then says, "Wake, Reginald." And so the act proceeds until the final tableau when all of the characters surround and gaze upon Osmond, now bleeding on the ground.

The playwrights of the eighties and nineties took this acting style for granted and built their reliance on it into their plays. Colman's outraged attack on John Philip Kemble, who played Edward Mortimer in the premiere of *The Iron Chest,* gives a good idea of the kind of performance expected. Colman expected "a man of whom it might be said, 'There's something in his soul / O'er which his melancholy sits, and broods.' " He wanted "passion over-leaping it's [*sic*] customary bound, movements of the soul, sullen, or violent, very rarely seen in the common course of things, yet still *may* be seen" (viii–ix). Colman insisted that he had provided scenes that "afford an opportunity to the Performer of playing off his mimick emotions, his transitions of passion, his starts, and all the trickeries of his trade" (xvii). The part of Wilford in the same play was also written to exploit the ability of actors like Bannister to make riveting the scene in which he hesitates, shows fear, horror, and compelling curiosity, and then, in spite of solemn orders and threats, opens Edward Mortimer's iron chest. Innumerable speeches were constructed to be broken, as Garrick had Richard III's and Charles Macklin had Shylock's, and to be accompanied by the pantomime of wild swings in emotion and rapid transitions from mood to mood.

In this age of great actors and actresses, playwrights usually wrote parts with specific performers in mind, and audiences could "read" the story by the assignment of parts as surely as by the ages, social classes, and opening speeches of the characters. Rather ironically, the very power and distinctiveness of leading performers' styles acted to contain the gothic in the plays. Like some of the sets and music, they became art in their own right and drew the attention of connoisseurs. Anecdotes about people who praise one actor for three acts of a play and then explain their

James Boaden wrote that Fuseli's *Hamlet and the Ghost* was the "sublimest of painting" and demanded that his gothic ghosts be costumed like them. (Kunsthaus, Zurich.)

preference for another actor's interpretation of the final two acts, making specific, detailed comparisons, suggest the degree of expertise extant. Seeing Mrs. Powell, Mr. Kemble, Miss De Camp, or Mr. Suett competed with seeing "Mortimer," "the spectre," "Judith," or "Samson," and the characters came in and out of focus. Therefore, the drama marshaled yet another fashionable social and aesthetic experience that audiences had been conditioned to read and experience in specific ways.

English preferences in painting influenced acting as well as set design. De Loutherbourg conceived his sets as pictures, and many dramatists and technicians of the time described their achieved effects that way. Noverre discussed his idea of the stage as a "picture in which the actors were the moving figures."[68] Boaden wrote that "the sublimest of painting" is Fuseli's *Hamlet and The Ghost,* which he believed he had duplicated successfully in the staging of *Fontainville Forest.* He explained Fuseli's success as "recollecting some of the known principles of the sublime. By the artifices of the pallet; by keeping down all too positive indications of substance; by the choice of a cold slaty prevalent colour, touched slightly with the pale silvery tone of moonlight . . . and action of the most venerable dignity and command." For the performance, Boaden even demanded that the tall, thin John Follet replace the short, stocky James Thompson as the ghost, that the armor be made close-fitting, and that an additional gauze screen be erected.[69]

The proscenium arch provided the frame, and the contemporary acting style and direction with its frequent tableaux contributed to the impression that the gothic world was safely contained. The audience would have been at least subliminally aware of director, designer, play-wright, and performers cooperatively creating a work of art that at individual moments became a "still" and deliberately resembled popular painting subjects and styles; at times they would have been insistently brought to admire its art. As Michael Wilson has pointed out in "Columbine's Picturesque Passage," "Dramatic action could be conceived as a sequence of sustained, emotionally-charged pictorial situations whose voyeuristic qualities were sublimated in the mutual testing by character and audience of aesthetic sensibilities, converting the sensual to the sensuous for the gaze of the connoisseur" (205).

At the same time that spectacle overwhelmed the intellect and assured times of unified, powerful effect, the tableaux acted to summarize each segment of the play and to superimpose themselves on the tableaux experienced before. These tableaux represented relationships among characters and among their symbolic meanings and reinforced deep structures in the texts that were being presented as the nature of the universe. Like the Restoration street pageants, they drew upon and reinforced symbolic "landscapes," stories, and cultural myths that people were currently using to organize and interpret experience—in short, to construct reality. From Kenneth Burke's conception of the "fog of symbols" that " 'locates' the various aspects of experience," they sorted out social and ethical values.[70] Boaden's *Aurelio and Miranda,* for example, concludes with the brothers and sisters (Lorenzo and Agnes; Miranda and Christoval), the loyal friends (Raymond and Lorenzo), the reunited lovers (Raymond and Agnes), and the new lovers (Aurelio and Miranda) foregrounded. Previously each has been the center of a set piece, as Agnes was beside her infant in the sepulcher and as Miranda was in disguise as Eugenio with a basket of flowers in the door to Aurelio's cell. The sets carefully enhance each mood; in a rather Radcliffean construction, Aurelio searches for "firmness and tranquillity" in the garden with a "rustic hermitage" on one side and the abbey in the distance, and his retreat to his cell symbolizes his painful awareness that his actions have imprisoned and isolated him.

This play presents a panoply of human suffering. Antonia and Aurelio are orphans; Agnes has been forced into a convent, and Raymond and Lorenzo fear that Agnes is dead. This suffering caused by dislocation and loss spoke directly to the experiences and anxieties of many in the audience. As the Marquis de Sade said, ordinary people felt that they had experienced more misfortune in a few years than novelists could portray in dozens of books. The ideas that they held about the nature of the world and the probable experiences of human existence were under stress. It has been argued that the universe that the gothic novel relentlessly creates and re-creates is amoral at best and evil at worst.[71] In contrast to the novel, the gothic drama represents a world that can be suspected of allowing hideous suffering and unrequited virtuous and villainous acts but finally reassures audiences that a benign order infuses every aspect of the universe and, incidentally, provides the poetic justice that consumers of popular literature demand.

Among the most obvious strategies of containment aimed at presenting a safely ordered world are the happy endings (and almost all gothic plays have them) and the use of comedy. Dramatists almost entirely avoid complications resulting from accidents and coincidences, those strategies so important in tragedy and so much a part of our experiencing the world as beyond our control. In a number of them, the protagonist repents as Schedoni, Bulcazin, Lamotte, and Aurelio do. In other plays, armies arrive led by the romantic hero or, more frequently, an older male relative of a female character. In *Fontainville Forest,* Nemours, an ideally virtuous man who clearly knows the economic and political affairs of the world, appears and resolves everything, including the redemption of Lamotte. Plays characteristically end with scenes of great activity, often fights or entrances of armies, but conclude with a tableau that fixes relationships in an orderly world. Most important, in almost every case, the heroine marries a brave young hero, the poor are given good employment, and long-suffering, good servants are rewarded; Lewis's formula holds, and every part of the audience is gratified.

Plot and characterization are as important to comedy as acting styles are to tragedy and pantomime. One of the most reliable ways that readers and spectators can anticipate the experience that literature will give them is to determine the tone or the mode of the work. That gothic playwrights include numerous comic elements, many not there simply as comic relief or as parody of any aspect of the form, works to contain those elements of the plot that express contemporary anxieties and to reassure the audience about the nature of the world (at least the "world" of that play). Much of the comedy comes from character types. Following the publication of Horace Walpole's *Castle of Otranto,* it was a commonplace to include characters modeled on Shakespeare's low characters, a fact that Lewis's prologue also acknowledges. Even in the gothic plays that are not comedies or musical romances, such characters abound. Their functions, however, are different from Shakespeare's. These characters express fear at the same time their higher-ranked or more intelligent companions obviously feel it. Thus, they articulate that which contributes to the physiological experience, the feeling James Twitchell has identified in *Dreadful Pleasures* as "horripilation," the zoological term for the response that causes gooseflesh or even nape hair "standing on end," and is associated with the moment when the person is poised "between fight and flight" (10–11).

Gregory in *The Battle of Hexham* is the epitome of such characters; a typical reaction occurs when he sees the tents massed before a battle and tells his mistress, "I cou'd turn about again directly, and walk back brisker by half than I came" (*Hexham,* 8). Similarly, Hilario freely expresses fear as he and Carlos approach the castle in Andrews's play. Such characters usually have realistic fears but exhibit them in such inappropriate settings or in such rustic or idiomatic language that we laugh. These low characters may also voice elemental feelings in undignified terms; for instance, Christoval certainly speaks for Raymond and Lorenzo when he exclaims, "My joy's worth a million times the damage." In his hurry to give good news, he confesses he may have done such things as rolled an old woman into a kennel (*Aurelio and Miranda,* 46).

Other comic characters manifest their fears in terms of basic human needs or comment on the villain's lack of charity, and thereby represent and express anxieties held by at least some of the audience. The servant Valoury in *The Mysteries of the Castle,* for instance, often worries about food. Such moments work to contain horror, first by locating it in statements of basic physical desires and consequences rather than in expressions of spiritual or social threat and, second, by providing one of the most common releases for fear. After all, what do children in the dark or adults at a horror movie laugh at more often than at the member of the group whose fear is most obvious and extreme? By identifying someone more afraid, the others once again feel themselves within tolerable limits and, therefore, in control.

Comic characters add dimensions to the anti-aristocratic bias common to these plays. Martin in *The Castle of Otranto* rebukes a gatekeeper for asking their business: "We've no business, fellow, we're gentlemen." Colman's Fool in *Hexham* explains that "your true court-bred fool always cuts the cloth of his conscience to the fashion of the times," and the robbers agree on a toast that "suits your soldier, your tithe-parson, your lawyer, your politician, just as well as your robber," and it is "Plunder!" The Rawbold family in *The Iron Chest* provides humor of this type, but they are decidedly unsettling. Samson explains, "The cottage was blown down—the barn fired—father undone—Well, landlords are flinty hearted—no help!" He and his father are "up early, and down late, in the exercise of our industry," which is to "purloin every single thing" that the family has.

Many comic characters are neither servants nor poor. Acted by the greatest performers of their time, they satirize the acquisitive, authoritarian ideology of the villain. For example, Quick played Fractioso, the heroine's father, in *The Mysteries of the Castle*. His small size and squeaky voice must have made his self-important posturing as he orders his daughters about hilarious. Ibrahim, who is too dense to see that the husband he has chosen for his daughter is a serial killer, optimistically begs a place in Bluebeard's court and spouts what he thinks is the wisdom of the world: "Throw Riches and Power into the scale, and . . . Merit soon kicks the beam" (3). Because the comic elements are so carefully integrated, they work subliminally to signal to the audience that there is no lasting threat.

The songs and activities of these characters and others often act as counterpoint to the protagonist's fretted world. They draw a contrast common to eighteenth-century poetry between the lives and unquiet minds of the ambitious and the untroubled sleep of those "far from the madding crowd." Their brief scenes open other possibilities for experience in this world and prevent the claustrophobic gloom of many gothic novels. These dramatists were not afraid to use some farce and slapstick as comic effects. Both Andrews and Lewis stage excellent scenes in which characters fall or jump in and out of windows. Lewis's Percy, the romantic hero played by John Philip Kemble, not only jumped from a window but, in this uncharacteristically farcical and undignified part, had to flop back and forth on a sofa in order to delude his guards. That this scene is played out in a situation highly suggestive of possible murderous violence when two of Osmond's slaves gamble for their captive's money suggests the sophistication of these playwrights' use of juxtaposition.

The final structural means of containing the idea of evil in the world that I want to discuss is, perhaps, the most likely orchestrated language to be ignored today. It is the author's self-conscious, deliberate linking of gothic drama with children's nursery tales. Colman says that he took the plot for *Blue-Beard* from "the celebrated Mrs. GOOSE" (in fact, from Charles Perrault's *Histoires ou contes du temps passé avec des moralités,* 1697), and most of the early gothic playwrights at one time or another deliberately brought the visceral recollection of nursery tales to the audience. Lamotte asks if "A school-boy's terror" should make him shrink from opportunity; when Sophia Lee's Alonzo is chained in an underground vault, he exclaims, "By heav'n I feel an infant once again, / When thus insulted with an infant's terrors!" (*Almeyda,* 42); Gondibert, in Cowley's *Albina,* observes, "How dark the night! . . . And dismal fancy, in yon shadowy ailes, / Might conjure up an hundred phantoms. / How strong th'impression of our dawning years! / The tales . . . that did awe / My infancy, all rush upon my mind, / And, spite of haughty reason, make it shrink" (40). Andrews, too, reminds his audience of the vestiges "of Enthusiasm or Superstition . . . which Reason smiles at, but cannot prevail over" (preface, *The Enchanted Castle,* iv–v). So steady a character as Paullo denies superstition but admits to "a certain odd sympathy of the nerves, which the vulgar would call trembling." He says, "The place itself makes a man rummage among the relics of the nursery . . . and such desolation as Paluzzi, make a child of me". (*The Italian Monk,* 7). This canny recognition of the limits of reason served the dramatists well.

In *Spectator* no. 419, Joseph Addison had recognized the value of playing upon recollections of terror; he recommended that writers know "Legends and Fables, antiquated Romances, and the Traditions of Nurses and old Women, that he may fall in with our natural Prejudices, and humour those Notions which we have imbibed in our Infancy."[72] Addison goes on to say that these stories draw their power from "those secret Terrours and Apprehensions to which the Mind of Man is naturally subject." He finds correlative primeval fears aroused by some of Shakespeare's writing ("something so wild and yet so solemn") and in such personifications as Milton's Sin and Death and Ovid's Hunger and Envy. This recognition of the relationship between nursery tales and the attempts to represent the lurking evil and passion behind the human face increasingly found expression in the late century gothic.

The kind of nursery experience eighteenth-century people meant has probably been widely misunderstood. Rather than full-fledged lengthy ghost stories, perhaps of the kind the modern scholar associates with Defoe's *Mrs. Veal,* they meant "spooky stories," which were short and dependent upon a sudden shock. Some of them were for very young children and involved the teller's fingers "creeping" around the toddler's body until suddenly the teller cried, "Gotcha" and pinched or tickled the child. Others used the icons of gothic horror and might involve a person going through a dark wood to a dark house with a dark room with a dark cupboard holding a closed box; then the teller says, "In that box was a—" and yells, for example, "Skull!" *Bluebeard* is a classic example of the forbidden room holding a horrible secret. As Vita Sackville-West noted, "Baby had been taught to fear everything he possibly could, tangible and intangible." Among the rhymes she collected is one about a lady who went to church where

> She saw a dead man on the ground,
> And from his nose unto his chin
> The worms crawled out, the worms crawled in.
> Then she unto the parson said
> Shall I be so when I am dead?
> Oh yes! oh yes! the parson said,
> You will be so when you are dead.[73]

Many nursery tales encode the sexual fears that inform the gothic; in one, a young girl hears or dreams that if she goes to a nearby large, ornate house, she could get "a treasure" simply by asking for it. She goes to the house and knocks on the door; the door swings open, she enters, and she sees a man seated at a large desk. She asks if he has a treasure for her. The man looks up at her; he has dark, intense eyes, and he says, "YES!" The final confrontation in Perrault's "Little Red Riding Hood" is similarly structured. The little girl has been invited to "come up on the bed with me" by the wolf-grandma. The wolf tells her to undress. As Red Riding Hood removes each garment, she asks what to do with it and is told to throw it in the fire because she won't need it again. Once there, she remarks, "What big eyes you have, Grandma." "The better to see you

with," the disguised wolf answers. "What big ears you have, Grandma
. . ." "The better to hear . . ." And so on, until—delivered in the same
innocent tone—what has been anticipated with dreadful expectation:
"What big teeth you have, Grandma." Then the answer and the leap,
"The better to eat you with!"[74] The thrill of these stories is in the waiting
for the inevitable shock; that it was coming, but that the exact moment
and content could not be predicted, kept the listeners tense and fearful.

In many ways, Colman's *Blue-Beard* is the archetypal gothic drama.
Still bearing some of the zaniness of Walpole's novel, a text in which, as
Inverso says, Conrad is born to be squashed, *Blue-Beard* carried its
viewers on a Disney-style ride through suspenseful dread, romance, magic, and comic opera. What is distinctive about the gothic is that its
orchestrated languages come from dramaturgy as well as text. Tragic
acting styles, pantomime forests, theatrical songstyles, Shakespearean
low characters, and landscape painting are reaccentuated and absorbed
as surely as are the elements of pathetic tragedy and nursery tales. Colman mentions Mother Goose, Johnston—whom he calls "a *classical
Machinist*"—pantomime, the composer Michael Kelly, and the scene
painter Greenwood; and he calls his play "dramatick romance," "Mag-
ick," "an Enchantment," and "my Syllabub."

The play begins with the scene of a "romantick, mountainous country" beyond a village, in which Selim and Fatima are singing a lovers'
duet. It ends with a sunrise and a grand cavalcade across the mountains;
stage directions show that the sound of the martial music was to grow
stronger as Abomelique and his "magnificent train" draw nearer. Contemporary descriptions show that great pains were taken to have the
group appear larger as they approach and that the scene was constructed
so that they would occasionally be "lost to the sight" and would even
cross footbridges. This procession took half an hour. In early productions, clever figures by Johnston were used; later, extras of varying
heights were recruited, and the shortest crossed the stage in the distance
to be gradually replaced by the taller; later yet, live animals were added to
the procession and to the battle scenes. Careful coordination of text,
scenes, and music contribute to each mood and turn in the plot.

The discovery of the blue room delivers the most extravagant fears of
the forbidden room:

> The Blue Chamber appears streaked with vivid streams of Blood. The
> figures in the Picture, over the door, change their position, and

> Abomelique is represented in the action of beheading the Beauty he
> was, before, supplicating. The Pictures, and Devices, of Love, change
> to subjects of Horror and Death. The interior apartment . . . exhibits
> various Tombs, in a sepulchral building;—in the midst of which
> ghastly and supernatural forms are seen;—some in motion, some
> fix'd—In the centre, is a large Skeleton seated on a tomb, (with a
> Dart in his hand). (17)

That Abomelique and Shacabac (who dreads but has seen the room
before) visit the room before the two young women increases the suspense and makes the horror dreadfully predictable.[75] As in nursery tales,
sex and death are strongly identified. The room has pictures showing
lovers in conventional poses shift to execution scenes, and the juxtaposition of the consummation of marriage and murder is constantly reinforced. Later, as Abomelique repeatedly moves toward and then post-
pones entering Fatima's room, the audience is not sure if he intends to
consummate the marriage (and thereby rape her) or to kill her. One of
the songs includes the line, "When he falls on her Neck, 'tis to cut off her
head" (22).

Colman and his contemporaries praised the players' performances.
The comic Dicky Suett as Ibrahim "punned, shivered, and ran away,"
and Bannister as Shacabac vacillated between heroic indignation at his
master's murders and comic fear.[76] Palmer and Mrs. Crouch, veterans of
tragedy and melodrama, played Abomelique and Fatima, and playgoers
like the Countess of Bessborough cried as DeCamp as Irene stood on the
castle tower and sang of her hope for rescue.[77] Crammed in are dances
and songs, spectacular processions of actors and extras in exotic costumes. The conclusion featured the skeleton killing Abomelique, crash-
ing walls, and the blue room swallowed "beneath the earth" with a
"volume of Flame" arising as the "earth closes." By 1811, John Philip
Kemble punched up the excitement with camels, horses, and elephants
from Astley's Amphitheatre, and Hazlitt described the conclusion as
filled with dismounted warriors fighting across the horses' bodies,
"drums, trumpets, smoke, and confusion."[78]

The content and the experience of nursery tales were familiar and
"safe"; as well as the dread, the stories evoked where the tales were
told—in a safe place, in the nurse's lap, in front of a warm fire, in a
nurturing, mothering place. Gothic fiction, however, developed strategies for horrifying readers out of violations of nursery tale patterns. In

The cover of the music for *Blue-Beard* shows De Camp as Irene in the emotional scene immediately before the women's rescue. (By permission of the British Library.)

Charles Maturin's *Melmoth the Wanderer,* the patriarchs are hideously transformed into monsters, and one "with horrid unnatural force" tears food from his starving grandchildren's hands, gobbles it, and leers at them. A child asks him, "Are you the wolf?" In contrast, gothic drama followed nursery tales more closely but provided happy endings, thereby returning the auditor to an ordered and safe world. Unlike the readers of gothic novels, playgoers could trust dramatic gothic strategies to deliver thrills and yet contain and dissolve the fear.

Spectacular staging, legendary acting, and high-quality music combined with the promise of comic characters, a mesmerizing yet defeated villain, and ideal lovers united in the resolution: the superficial appeal is obvious. Critical reception of these early plays was decidedly mixed. Special effects, individual performances, and technical aspects received praise that often implicitly damned what we think of as "the play." A representative review said that the best that could be said of *Blue-Beard*, "the very worst of Colman's very worst productions . . . a patchwork of buffoonery and bombast," was that "the author, who had little in view beyond manufacturing a convenient vehicle for the display of gorgeous scenery and shewy processions, has effected his intention with a cleverness, which many who think meanly of the performance, would find some difficulty in equalling."[79]

Were gothic plays mere show, they would have become like circuses—dependent on new spectators and static in form and content. Bakhtin has observed that the more mature and complex a form becomes, the better it remembers its past. "Its past" is also the national skilled readers' *langue,* and playwrights could use its systems and the nature of other forms to do new things and create genuinely original texts. They were able to reaccentuate the orchestrated languages and each new group of gothic plays, and these plays evolved into several popular literary forms that have survived into our time. The gothic plays can be used to show that, in these times of stress, from the beginning consumers of mass culture have not been passive objects of manipulation but have recognized a transformational work that performs an urgent social function.[80] It is this aspect of the drama that assured its almost addictive appeal and, with its deeper personal and political elements, is the subject of the next chapter.

6

MEN, WOMEN, AND THE CROWD

THE GOTHIC PLOT CAME TO HAVE INCREASINGLY URGENT
work to do. The years 1780–95 laid bare just how many strains were
being put upon the dominant structures of feeling that upheld British
political orders—family and village as well as national. If gothic novels
are "fables of sexual identity,"[1] then the plays are fables of social identity.
As is common to all popular literature, the crisis and its issues are articulated in personalized terms housed in individual characters and cultural
icons that are quite simple in comparison to the complex weaving of plot,
character, episode, and strategies of authorial commentary characteristic
of the novel of ideas.

These plays dreamed and re-dreamed the particular nightmares of
the fragile sanity of leaders and of power present everywhere and gone
berserk. As James Twitchell says, "Horror stories, like nightmares, never
end; they are just re-dreamed" (72). By the middle of the last decade of
the century, the plays had sharpened the presentation of the major characters and had invested them with urgent political and philosophical
symbolism. Not only did the anxieties—the horrors—that drove them
become more obvious but so did the collective fantasies that offered
relief and hope and even participated in the processes that brought the
British people temporarily together enough to defeat Napoleon.

The gothic protagonist continued to be the heart of these plays and

Arthur Atherley's *Portrait of an Etonian* shows the intense
eyes and moody sky of the gothic and romantic age. (Los
Angeles County Museum.)

the concentrated locus of anxieties about power and authority. His was a
nightmare version of the face of authority and the sign of human reason.
One result of the very public discussion of George III's porphyria was
that even ordinary people came to know a great deal about contemporary
theories of madness and the treatment of it. Numerous general and
specialized medical discussions appeared simultaneously with and for
years after the "news" published about the king's condition and progress.[2] Out of this literature emerged a reaccentuation of the eye as the
window to the soul, the part of the male body valorized and scrutinized.

     In addition to the eye as frightening confirmation of a wild, unsettled,
mad intellect, the eye held special, now largely forgotten significance.

John Palmer starred in many gothic plays and was recognized for his ability to communicate with gesture and gaze. Here he is playing the part of Don Carlos in *Ximena*. (Courtesy of the Harvard Theatre Collection.)

Gothic and tragic actors of the period perfected conveying a wild interior life. This is a representation of Edmund Kean.

One of the treatments for madness was "the eye," and practitioners such as Francis Willis and William Pargeter used it as a major form of control. The work of Franz Anton Mesmer had been known in England since the early 1780s, and people were fascinated with "mesmerism," or "animal magnetism," which was identified as hypnotic power over the will *and nervous system* of the subject. A contemporary described Willis's power: "His piercing eye seemed to read their hearts and divine their thoughts as they formed and before they were even uttered."[3] Some practitioners insisted that the eye could express every judgment "from the highest degree of sternness, down to the mildest degree of benignity" and could "secure minute changes in the patient's behavior."[4] Not only did such claims focus attention on the power and expressiveness of the eyes, but they helped establish what Foucault has called the age of surveillance.

Mortimer horrifies Wilford with his gaze in *The Iron Chest* and intends Wilford's punishment to be eternal residence with the watching Mortimer.

In contrast to the man's eye, the audience of gothic drama is directed to the heroine's breast, the sign of nurturing sexuality and the feeling heart. In *The Castle Spectre* Evelina enters dressed in flowing white robes; there is a bright wound "upon her bosom" and her garments are spotted with blood oozing from it. The breast, unlike the horrifyingly unstable face of authority, was long-suffering and eternally constant. Illustrations of scenes habitually show the heroine with a low-cut, loosely puffy, white bodice, often with a jewel to emphasize her cleavage. She is frequently shown leaning her body forward slightly even as her head tilts back as though recoiling or resisting what she is seeing; this position emphasizes the bosom and shows a long, vulnerable neck. The illustration of Elizabeth Younge as Hortensia in *The Count of Narbonne* is typical. In it, Younge appears to look back in fear even as her forward and slightly downward motion thrusts her chest slightly outward. Henry Fuseli's famous painting, *The Nightmare* (1781, exhibited at the Royal Academy in 1782), positions the woman so that her head is hanging off the pallet, stretching her neck and rounded breasts, pushing them into the most prominent position in the picture.

Climactic scenes on the stage usually invoke a confrontation of eye and breast. *The Italian Monk* provides a paradigmatic scene: Schedoni enters the cell in which Ellena sleeps "upon a wretched Pallet-bed." He holds his lamp over her, and, as he gives a speech meant to be broken for interludes of pantomime, he hesitates. In order to make a clean target so he can stab her neatly, he opens her robe. The stage directions read: "He looks at her Breast, and seeing a Picture starts; then eagerly detatches it, drops the Dagger, and shuddering draws back in an Agony of Horror" (51). The part, played by John Palmer, a man whom contemporaries described as having "a majestic figure" and known as one of the greatest and perhaps the most flexible actor of his time,[5] had already established Schedoni's terrible looks and piercing gazes. The eyes on her breast, then on the picture (which is Ellena's mother's of himself) make the implications of the selection of these sites obvious. Schedoni had intended to stab Ellena, as he had stabbed his wife. Here, as in other gothic plays, the selection of weapon and the supine position of the intended victim underscore the mingling of acts of violence intended to secure property and expressions of more or less repressed sexual passion also aimed at

The frontispiece to *The Count of Narbonne* shows some
typical gothic icons and a conventionally posed heroine.
This is Mrs. Younge as Hortensia.

possession. Below the surface of the unfolding scene is Schedoni's near-
ness to incest or to the murder of his own daughter.

What the fiction often hints, the gothic suggests viscerally: "[Sched-
oni] had a dagger concealed beneath his Monk's habit; as he had also an
assassin's heart shrouded by his garments" (*The Italian,* 224). Lewis in
The Monk states explicitly that, with Antonia, Ambrosio's "desires were
raised to that frantic height by which brutes are agitated." Jean Hagstrum has recognized that in Radcliffe's novels fear and terror are located
"in that part of the civilized psyche where sexual love and sexual encounters are anticipated but never formulated in direct and unequivocal
terms or images." Emily, for instance, in *The Mysteries of Udolpho* does

not know if Valancourt is robber or lover—or both.[6] The novels exploit the confusions of categories, thereby making sexual *love* uncertain and risky. Gothic plays situate the mingling and possibilities of love and violence directed at the heroine within the protagonist, not within the exploration of mutual attraction. Because so much is unstated, the imagined possibilities multiply as they do in the novel, but the heroine is passive recipient, potential victim. In the fiction, women's bodies command center stage. They are confined, badgered, pursued. Readers are made hyperconscious of their vulnerable bodies and that the body is synonymous with their vulnerable sex. The plays approach psychomachia in which at one level a man's mind is the battle ground and at stake is what is often seen as the feminine, the benevolent, part of himself.

The villain's idea of victory depends upon the sexual possession of the heroine; his final act of violence is to offer to stab her. In fact, what happens to the protagonist in the plays and some novels conforms to Freud's description of sadomasochism in "Instincts and Their Vicissitudes"; the act of sadism, the exercise of power upon someone else, becomes a struggle to master the self, and then the instinct turns back to an external object, whom the villain feels sympathy toward or allows to master him. For instance, Caleb in Godwin's novel says, "I have a secret foreboding as if I should never again be master of myself."[7] The plays begin by establishing the tyrannical personality against whom almost all other characters (and groups) are opposed. He is the "problem" the play must resolve, and he must be brought back within the community or expunged from the universe in order to allow the harmonious natural order that the play represents as its conclusion. Therefore, the villain's true victory would be that of the community—redemption and reintegration. In this chapter, I consider the political dynamic beneath the surface, especially as it is represented by the symbolism of male and female and of "the crowd."

The heroines' function in gothic plays is complex, perhaps more complex than that of the male protagonist. Like him, they represent an ideology, but theirs must appear "natural," "the way the world is." They are associated with the sublime's companion, the beautiful. They embody sensibility, often in its purest, most idealistic form. The philosophy of sensibility as transmitted through the work of Anthony Ashley Cooper, third earl of Shaftesbury, Francis Hutcheson, and David Hume explored the idea that human beings had an innate "moral sense" that existed even without religion.[8] In its popularized form, the basic tenets were that human beings were essentially good and possessed "sensibility" in more or less developed degrees. Sensibility produced feeling and analysis in association, which was never to be confused with instinctual emotion, maudlin pity for an unworthy object, or pure intellectual reasoning. Such heroines, then, exhibited "rational feeling" and were neither unintelligent, unperceptive, nor weak.

In spite of this more important philosophical position, they are objects, while the male protagonists are memorable, complex, and occasionally nearly novelistic subjects. Analysis reveals that although the heroines appear to be the narrative opponent and ideological contrast to the protagonist, they are not; they are vessels and agents. Their will is directed toward virtue, but of a rather narrowly focused kind: usually their own chastity and charity toward others. They seek relationships, especially with mothers and fathers. Most are unaware of their claims to property or positions of influence and when informed hardly notice. Many of their speeches make clear the ideological contrasts offered to the protagonist. Andrews's descriptions set typical oppositions: Julia, the heroine of *The Mysteries of the Castle,* loves Carlos, and "love's soft wishes were sanctified by reason." Her father's "avarice and ambition," however, led him to marry her to Montoni, a man "with large possessions, and extended power." This play, which is very loosely based on Radcliffe's *Mysteries of Udolpho,* uses Julia and her heritage in entirely formulaic, and therefore low-key, ways; in contrast, Radcliffe's Emily and her aunt, Mme. Cheron, stubbornly defend their legal rights to their property.[9] In Andrews's play, Julia *is* property; in Radcliffe's novel, she *has* property.

The heroine had to be as strongly gendered as the protagonist,[10] and by emphasizing her chastity the playwrights actually foregrounded and constructed a sexualized subject in an eroticized world. Like the popular *castrati* of the period, what heroines will not or cannot do opens up "a resonant space for the amplification of sexuality, a hollowness at the center which is an incitement."[11] Characters often respond as Raymond in *Aurelio and Miranda* does when angered by Austin and reveal the sexual nature of their world:

> The frail and fair make you their oracles;
> Pent in your close confessionals you sit,

Bending your reverend ears to luscious secrets;
While they sigh out each amorous wish;
Till flesh and spirit, mingling flame with flame,
Their glowing senses fix at last on man,
And priests may quench the fire a lover kindled. (27)

Similarly, when Lamotte must describe the murder he was engaged to perform for the Marquis, he says, "Would you had seen her then? In rage I rush'd, / Enring'd these fingers in her golden hair, / And plung'd the thirsting poniard in her breast; / She struggled not—forgave me—and expir'd" (*Fontainville Forest,* 61). Procreation becomes a charged political field.[12] Julia in *Mysteries of the Castle* has chosen to be imprisoned and thought dead rather than allow Montoni to consummate their marriage. Aurelio takes Agnes's pregnancy as an act of rebellion deserving death.

In addition, playwrights selected characteristics from the emerging conception of woman as essentially "different in every conceivable respect of body and soul, in every physical and moral aspect."[13] This woman was the product of the eighteenth century's reinterpretation of reproductive biology, which extended to redesigning the female skeleton so that the skulls were small, the limbs short and childlike, and the pelvises extremely wide.[14] She was less the displayer of aristocratic power (always accompanied by troops of servants), name (often her name had been the same as that of an estate or a parliamentary district), and fortune (rich fabrics, jewelry, and fashionable "heads" made wealth conspicuous) and less sexually alive, for female orgasm had been discovered to be unimportant for conception. Adeline in *Fontainville Forest,* for instance, says her "worthless outside" is what has attracted the Marquis and that "purity within . . . gives the whole / Its harmony and grace" (31). Editha, who longs for wealth and position, and Albina, who is virtuous and hopes for a companionate love, explicitly discuss these ideologies (*Albina,* 16–17).

Depictions of heroines always define the object of desire that is "woman," and those of the gothic heroine largely conform to those Kate Ellis, Nancy Armstrong, and others have identified with the rise of the "domestic woman."[15] Praise for domesticity in general is common. For instance, Barbara listens to her brother recount the work that she does daily (including "trim the faggots, nurse thy mother, . . . kill the poultry, cure the hogs, . . . and comb the children") and comments, "Many might think that no small charge" (*Iron Chest,* 3). Gondibert in *The Battle of Hexham* nearly breaks down as he describes the domestic life he has lost (50–52). Moreover, the plays inscribe the process by which "a woman's virtue . . . overcomes sexual aggression and transforms male desire into middle-class love, the stuff that modern families are made of" (Armstrong, 6).

The heroines' most important function is to bring out the latent benevolence of the protagonist. Their conduct, their words, and their looks can awaken the feelings of the villain. That it is their looks, and specifically their resemblance to the villain's sexual love object (their mothers), suggests that they are not individuals and that they are icons, not mimetic characters. By locating a traditional feminine power in appearance as opposed to, for example, words or actions, the dramatists reinforce women's status as cultural objects. Spalatro and Schedoni in *The Italian Monk* and Osmond in *The Castle Spectre* are struck by the resemblances of the heroines to women they loved and become incapable of murder. In *Fontainville Forest,* both his wife and Adeline can soften Lamotte. Virolet says to the heroine Zorayda, "Thou may'st preach, / When rigid Schoolmen fail, and win with gentleness; / Cause even shame to spread the proud man's cheek, / And make the world in love with charity!" (*Mountaineers,* 32). Woman, keeper of the flame of virtue and bearer of the moral values of the culture, can make even those villains too hardened for redemption recall their youthful moral sense.

Conditioned to recognize sensibility by the heroine's speeches and scenes such as these in which moral feeling emerges in the villain, the audience is prepared to see that almost every gothic villain's character includes elements of benevolence, and, significantly, that these feelings can be evoked *without the heroine.* Colman's Bulcazin says, "I have now a something working here / Does urge me to requite thee—trust me, Christian, / The rough and dusky bosom of a Moor / Does carry feeling in it" (*Mountaineers,* 59).

At the conclusions of plays by men, the heroines are rewards, not enforcers, and the hegemonic process that is the point of gothic drama is to renegotiate the meaning of "male," not "female."[16] The repentance of the father or the maturation of the lover brings about a new contract between the authority figure and his family and, by extension with his community, which is society. When this process occurs, characters are reinscribed in gendered spheres, and few scenes are harder for the feminist to swallow than the hideously mistreated wife's pledge to her monster-husband. In a 1793 *Castle of Otranto,* Ferrand has kept his wife (known only as "Lady") in a cell in the rocks. At the end he is defeated in battle and goes mad out of frustration; in spite of her years of imprisonment, "Lady" says, "By heaven I swear in sickness and in health to prove your constant, tend'rest Comforter." First, the tyrant has inscribed, disciplined her body, and then the play reveals that Foucault is correct: cultural and social mores diffuse power and mark, shape, the body and mind more drastically than any single "ruler" can.[17]

The reformed protagonist or the matured lover is always a sensibility character, and explicit statements contrast him to the individualistic tyrant. For instance, Fatima in *Blue-Beard* says, "When virtuous men have gold they purchase their own happiness, by making others happy:—Heap treasure on the vicious, they strengthen their injustice with the sweet means of Charity, and turn the poor man's blessing to a curse" (21). Angela scornfully compares her beloved Percy to Osmond: "What peasant names you his benefactor? What beggar has been comforted by your bounty? Your breast is unmoved by woe [while] the gates of Alnwic Castle . . . are open as their owner's heart" (*Castle Spectre,* 54).

In the hands of these dramatists and the performers whom they called their "fellow artists," the heroines became highly effective vehicles for the exercise and containment of the deepest anxieties and longings of the 1790s. They expressed vulnerability, beleaguered virtue, and beauty, and they were in a world in which their situation had suddenly changed, one that threatened moral and political chaos. Poignantly, they have become vulnerable partly because they loved and obeyed, and the audience feels how fragile are beauty and goodness in this world. At times they seem bewildered and without ideas for meaningful action. As social subjects they are positioned, motivated, constrained within (subject to) social networks and cultural codes that exceed their comprehension or control.[18]

The gothic contains this discomforting situation, too. Objects are not felt to suffer. Like violence to characters in nursery tales, the coercive attacks on the heroine are not perceived as individual incidents but as part of the pattern in which the representation of virtue is tested and rewarded and the personification of evil is destroyed.[19] Because of the conventions of the fashionable theater, the audience is secure; performers rarely touched each other, and suffering was picturesque as well as part of a ritual pattern—the heroine or even a family of beggars positioned themselves on the scenic stage and within a meaningful collective story. They became part of the spectacle. As in nursery tales, it is not the heroine's suffering that the audience was to remember. They might remember the protagonist's pain; after all, he was an extraordinary or a good man made victim of his uncontrollable passions. But more likely, they simply remembered the experienced happy ending, for gothic drama is a consumable art, and it is the story, not individual characters, with which the audience pleasurably identified.

For benevolence to influence the hegemonic process and to triumph, it cannot be depicted as a female virtue; instead, it must be universal in humankind. It must be the way the species is. Therefore, an agent other than the heroine must be responsible for the triumph of the ideology of sensibility, and the women must be denied ultimate agency and subjectivity. Even their strongest speeches fail to move men, as when Hortensia appeals to the Marquis's and Lamotte's consciences and concludes, "I charge thee, see thou wound not innocence / Pure as the shrines of saints." The Marquis says coldly, "Bear off the women!" (*Fontainville Forest,* 63). When the villains choose their better selves, they are choosing what is already within them. The moral sense is indeed universal, and the audience saw an ideal self-image.

As the incarnations of the most elemental of male desires, economic and political as well as sexual, the heroines are objectified. This strategy of objectification appears to be necessary to the success of the gothic drama, and this surmise is reinforced by the fact that there may be no gothic plays written by women. At the time of the gothic craze, several experienced and highly successful women had reached the peaks of their careers, and they had all written tragedies or melodramas. They earned their livings as playwrights and had already established their abilities to exploit fads and to adapt popular English and Continental works. Some of their plays definitely approach the gothic, and others, such as Hannah Cowley's *Albina,* helped make gothic elements and story lines available, but the contrasts in female characters, in lines of action, in experienced atmosphere, and in structures of feeling separate them from true gothic plays.[20]

The ways that gothic drama contrasts to tragedy and to melodrama underscore the differences between these plays by women and gothic plays. In melodrama, the protagonist is pitted against an external adversary, which may be accident or natural calamity (the breadwinner breaks a leg; there is a shipwreck). Opposing forces are outside the protagonist, who is a unified character. The gothic divides the male protagonist just as it spreads the potential sources of evil among human, natural, and super-natural actions. Ordinary mortals may be the victims of any of these, and the atmosphere created is one of ontological insecurity. Even in the most romantic gothic plays, the laws of causality are suspended or made arbi-trary and the reasons for the evil impulses—the "demons" within—left tantalizingly mysterious. The effect is that the possibility of hideous surprises and unanticipated behavior is left open; therefore, the gothic sustains the atmosphere of dread and tension that is synonymous with it.

The gothic protagonist, of course, is a deeply divided character. In many cases, the forces of tyranny and benevolence fight within him. The tragic hero is also a divided figure, but many theorists insist that the forces contending within him are equally legitimate, his possibilities for action equally justified or impossible, and his choices almost equally combining good and evil. Hamlet, for instance, cannot revenge his fa-ther's death without committing murder. Robert Heilman argues per-ceptively that in tragedy, the issue is the reordering of the self, while in melodrama it is "the reordering of one's relations with others, with the world of people."[21] In melodrama, characters tend to be good *or* evil. As Peter Brooks says, good and evil "inhabit persons who have no psycho-logical complexity but who are strongly characterized." These plays bring about the recognition of virtue, which has been misprized, while the gothic concentrates attention on the soul in agony, one at war with itself.[22]

Every tragedy is about limits; every melodrama is about virtue; and every gothic is about power. Tragedy makes a statement about the nature of the metaphysical universe; melodrama about human nature and social relations. In fact, melodrama often reforms the old society and unites young and old characters in symbolic scenes. The gothic implicitly re-lates human nature to "the way the world is," but is more secular than tragedy and more metaphysical than melodrama. The tragic universe is frightening, and human destiny with the built-in tragic flaw arouses pity and terror in an audience that contemplates what it means to be human. In melodrama, natural or social misfortune comes to blameless people who may be entirely good, and the audience pities the characters and themselves as "victims." The gothic concentrates on the human mind and the mysteries of reason and control, and the audience experiences horror at its hidden depths, potential for evil, and possible impact on the ordinary world. The gothic is fascinated by the hidden, "the realm of inner imperatives and demons." It brings this "occult" "into man's wak-

ing, social existence, of saying its meaning and acting out its force."
Moral ambiguities in melodrama turn out to be "the result of plotting,
evil, conscious obfuscation; they are not inherent to morality itself"
(Brooks, 19, 32), as they are in tragedy nor inherent in the human mind,
as they are in the gothic.

The contrasts between the gothic plays by men and plays with
marked gothic elements by women are illuminating. In Hannah Cowley's
Albina and Sophia Lee's *Almeyda*,[23] the heroines are active, even complex, forces; their dilemmas and sufferings compete successfully for
attention with the male protagonists' ambitions for attention. Two men,
Gondibert and Edward, want to marry Albina, widow of the hero Rai-
mond, who was Gondibert's brother. Edward is the conventional virtuous, heroic, honorable man, and Gondibert has the gothic energy, ambition, capacity for evil, mercurial temperament, and desire for possession.
When he hears that Edward and Albina will marry, he exclaims, "But
shall she to another yield her heart—/ Yield her whole self!—/ Earth
open first, and swallow me!" (20) In this love plot, Albina is the ideally
virtuous woman who is wronged; Cowley, however, includes a foil, Editha, who is as evil as George Lillo's Millwood (*The London Merchant,*
1731). Editha schemes to regain her power and position through marriage to Edward and ruthlessly uses Gondibert. Gondibert, whose internal struggle is mirrored in the conflicting advice of Editha and the loyal
Egbert, is finally driven to despair and attempts to stab Albina rather
than lose her to Edward.

Albina and Editha represent the competing ideologies usually
housed in the plays' resolutions and the male protagonist: domestic order, community, love, and procreation versus ambition, self-
aggrandizement, and disordered energy. Edward and Gondibert are
pawns. Editha insists, "The fire which animates / My breast, is a true
flame—'tis bright ambition!" Albina counters, "A sweeter province Nature gave to us—/—As a fond parent to its last-born child, / For woman
she reserv'd her choicest gift, / And call'd the blessing—Love—" (16).
Editha's passionate outbursts and clever manipulations that drive Gondibert from sin to sin somewhat overshadow Albina's scenes, but Albina's anguish and then outrage over Edward's gullibility and her horror at
the combat between her champion, the aged Westmoreland, and Edward give the impression that she has the power to choose, that she has
subjectivity.

Lee's Almeyda is even less a gothic heroine. From the beginning she is established as a woman whose beauty "Is lost—absorpt in mind" and disdains the behavior that makes most women "Domestic, artificial beings" (18). Her adversary is her uncle Abdallah, who intends to usurp her kingdom. When she defies him, he threatens her with true gothic horrors such as confinement "in a fortress, / Where tongueless ministers perform my will, / Amid the murky horrors of the night, / And hollow rocks inter the nameless victim! /—Ev'n now death yawns beneath thy feet, a *word,* / A *look,* of mine, consigns thee to oblivion!" (32).

Much of the conflict and its language is highly gendered; for instance, Almeyda describes Abdallah's eyes as having "a black penetration, which deep-pierces / Thro' virtue's thin and variable complexion" (23). Providence (or accident) had united the lovers in *Albina,* and Lee's play also insists upon God's power more than most gothic plays. Almeyda says, *"Kings* can give *crowns,* my lord, and *sires commands,* / Yet nature sometimes gives the heart a pow'r / To rest self-poiz'd, ev'en as the globe we tread on, / Dependant on no breath but our Creator's" (24–25). Here Lee unites the feminine breast and heart with "breath," an image recalling God's creation of the earth and the Holy Spirit. When she urges a servant to act virtuously, she says, "Oh! then be warn'd! and as thou die in peace, / List to the voice of heav'n that speaks thro' me" (38). Throughout the play she works and influences by such threats of heavenly judgment and invokes the supreme ordering power in the universe, God.

A marvelous vehicle for a great actress, the part of Almeyda demanded every emotion portrayed passionately and in rapid succession. From a rather headstrong girl Almeyda grows into a truly regal queen. In spite of three strong male parts, she absorbs the audience's attention. Lee and Harriet Lee's prologue had invoked Shakespeare, Rowe, and Otway, and indeed the play is more similar to the old she-tragedies than it is to the gothic plays. Passions such as Abdallah's, after all, recall Samuel Johnson's description of Almanzor in Dryden's *Conquest of Granada* as "above all laws . . . exempt from all restraints . . . exhibit[ing] a kind of illustrious depravity and majestick madness: such as, if it is sometimes despised, is often reverenced" (1:348–49).

Like Nicholas Rowe's Jane Shore, Almeyda's sex and relationship to powerful men determine much that happens to her; but her position as queen is her fate, and it is her tragic destiny that is the subject of the play. Sophia Lee treats the heroine's sex differently from Rowe. Under pressure Almeyda goes mad temporarily, and Abdallah brings her before her country's governing council in order to have her deposed. Male play-wrights, as Southerne had done with Behn's *Fair Vowbreaker,* frequently used this device at points of action when heroines might have asserted themselves and attempted to assume control or might have submitted to some dishonorable action; the device, thus, serves to remove respon-sibility for immoral, "unfeminine," or effective action. Almeyda asks, "Why . . . am I dragg'd forth, a spectacle?" She is a spectacle, of course, but simultaneously she resists complete spectacalization. In fact, Lee self-consciously constructs an example of Catherine Clément's "attack of spectacle, a crisis of suffering." Rather than foregrounding the "escape" from the misfortune of their exploitation that Clément says such attacks can be, Lee emphasizes her recognition of the attack of spectacle as "a festival, a celebration of their guilt used as a weapon, a story of seduc-tion." For Clément, the woman indulges herself in this behavior and is simultaneously psychopath, hysteric, and sorceress, and a new power is generated. The members of the council, like Clément's audience of in-quisitors, magistrates, and doctors, surround Almeyda and are hypno-tized and immobilized by her. For a moment, fields of power are held in stasis. At the last moment before she is forced to abdicate, she assumes her former demeanor and says, "I am not mad, but miserable!" She draws back from submitting and becomes again a speaking subject. In plays by men, the female mortal body does usually subsume and cancel out all other roles; in Lee's play, the mortal and regal bodies are once again united.

There was an actress whom modern critics have described as capable of investing any part with the "true gothic," and the part of Almeyda was created for her by Lee: Sarah Siddons.[24] In fact, Siddons's career reveals important, distinctive things about gothic drama—most notably how crucial the objectification of the heroine is and how gendered gothic power is. The great serious actresses of the last quarter of the century can be divided into two groups based upon their frequency and success in the parts of gothic heroines. Mary Ann Yates and Sarah Siddons are in one group and Elizabeth Younge, Maria Theresa De Camp (Kemble), and Jane Powell in the other. Neither Siddons nor Yates played the parts of gothic heroines as often as Younge; Maria Theresa De Camp, who starred in singing parts such as Irene in *Blue-Beard* and Judith in *The Iron Chest* and was the original Ellena in *The Italian Monk;* and Jane Powell, who was the original Agnes in *Aurelio and Miranda* and Evelina in *The Castle Spectre.* (No actresses achieved the starring consistency of Palmer, John

Philip Kemble, William Barrymore, Richard Wroughton, and Charles Kemble, all of whom came to be cast in predictable ways in dozens of gothic plays.) Of Siddons's Hortensia in *Narbonne,* Thomas Campbell, her usually worshipful biographer, says only, "the part . . . was by no means worthy of Mrs. Siddons's powers." The production of *Aurelio and Miranda* in which she played Miranda was unappreciated by an audience that "would not learn their parts."[25]

It appears that playwrights' conceptions of the actresses who would create the roles were in harmony with their strengths. In addition to Lee's Almeyda, Joanna Baillie's Jane de Monfort in *De Monfort* (1800) was written for Siddons, and Campbell says that the description of Jane in Act 2, scene 1, is "a perfect picture of the actress," "So queenly, so commanding, and so noble."[26] These characters are in the tradition of English tragedy, and the plays' lines of action and configurations have almost nothing in common with the gothic formula. Hannah Cowley intended Albina for Mary Ann Yates and Editha for Mrs. Younge, the actresses who had played, respectively, Jane Shore and Alicia and Andromache and Hermione in 1776. At the height of her powers, Yates was also playing Calista in *The Fair Penitent* and Medea, both parts that would be triumphs for Siddons as well. Younge would go on to create the part of Hortensia in *The Count of Narbonne* and eclipse Siddons as Hortensia[27] and as Miranda in *Aurelio and Miranda.*

Although Younge, De Camp, and Powell were very good actresses, they never truly rivaled Siddons or Yates. The fact that critics usually described their looks and Siddons's and Yates's performances suggests that they better served the purposes of gothic dramatists who needed to objectify the heroine. Younge's "elegance," De Camp's stunning figure, and Powell's "majestic" beauty and "dignity" were often mentioned. Younge, "not an absolute beauty" and inclined to repeat the same gestures and histrionics, never developed interpretative depth.[28] In a telling passage, Thomas Gilliland describes how De Camp put herself "through a regular course of studies" and made "the deportment of her person . . . one of the subjects of her sedulous attention, which . . . was soon brought obedient to every rule of grace from the finest example of the antique figure."[29] In contrast, Siddons once remarked that, unlike her brother, she was willing to allow her hair and dress to become disordered during passionate scenes.

Younge, De Camp, and perhaps especially Powell, who was tall and elegant, contributed to the moving, picturesque effect desired by playwrights and managers. The evidence for Siddons's probable contrast to these actresses can be found in passages in her "Memoranda" as well as in surviving contemporary descriptions and published reviews. Elizabeth Inchbald, actress and successful playwright, identified her with intelligence: "Who will allege, that mental powers have no charm in the female sex? Mrs. Siddons performed . . . in the prime of youth and bloom of beauty, yet was totally neglected; She came a few years after, with judgment for her aid, and was enthusiastically worshipped."[30] The detailed analysis of Lady Macbeth suggests how much she brought to the part, and her conception of some scenes breaks radically with other eighteenth-century interpretations and argues the pervasiveness of her conception of herself as speaking subject. She is fully aware of her originality:

> It is now the time to inform you of an idea which I have conceived of *Lady Macbeth's* character, which perhaps will appear as fanciful as that which I have adopted respecting the style of her beauty; and . . . must carry you back to the scene immediately preceding the banquet. . . . I have imagined that the last appearance of *Banquo's* ghost became no less visible to her eyes than it became to those of her husband. Yes, the spirit of the noble *Banquo* has smilingly filled up, even to overflowing, and now commends to her own lips the ingredients of her poisoned chalice.
>
> Behold her now, with wasted form, with wan and haggard countenance. (Campbell, 182)

Siddons notes that Lady Macbeth calls upon "the power of hell to unsex her" and displays characteristics and tendencies that are perceived as strongly "masculine," even as she insists that Lady Macbeth must have had the qualities "allowed to be most captivating to the other sex,—fair, feminine, nay, perhaps, even fragile."

William Hazlitt wrote of Siddons, "Power was seated on her brow, passion emanated from her breast"; and Boaden commented that "before us [stood] the true and perfect image of . . . a *fiend-like* woman."[31] Many descriptions and reviews fall back on "sublime" to describe her performances, especially of individual scenes. A poem inspired by two of Siddons's performances that was published in the *Monthly Mirror* for June 1798 singles out as the most singular and impressive aspect of her art: "But who shall paint that energy of soul / Which animates the wonders of that form, / Beyond all colours radiantly sublime."[32] Com-

These sketches of Sarah Siddons by George
Romney and by Thomas Lawrence (courtesy of the Harvard Theatre Collection)
return the viewer's gaze and contrast
to the more conventional representation shown in the portrait of
Mrs. Younge as the Countess
of Narbonne (courtesy of the
Lewis Walpole Library,
Yale University).

bined with her self-conscious inclusion of both-sex gendered behavior, these descriptions suggest that she recalled the gothic protagonist, not the heroine. Her greatest triumphs were in plays in which the heroines acted out strong, conflicting inner drives and even compulsions and in which love relationships broke down conventional sex roles and even had some masochistic traces. Among these were Lady Macbeth, Belvidera in Otway's *Venice Preserved,* in which she was described as displaying "amazing versatility of countenance," "increasing wildness of her eyes," and delivering lines with "a horror that chill'd one's blood," and Zara in Congreve's *Mourning Bride,* in which her "transition from love to rage" and "horrid tranquillity" were consistently praised.[33] Yates also could be "commanding," and the *Theatrical Biography* remarked that "where *rage* and *domineering* are called for, she has no equal."[34]

Siddons may have resisted becoming object and spectacle in the ways that Richard Dyer, Andrew Britton, and Judith Mayne ascribe to Marlene Dietrich and Katharine Hepburn. To some extent, all stage players are spectacles and resist becoming objects, because they undeniably move and speak. Moreover, they assert their own presence as well as the imagined or projected presence. Some expose the contradictions within and between ideologies even when the roles they play are highly ideological with closed resolutions; at times they may even reveal an alternative or oppositional ideological position.[35] Widespread recognition of Dietrich's "sexual ambiguity . . . in the sense of her androgynous beauty . . . and of her transgression of heterosexual boundaries" exists, and portraits of her catch her alleged ability to "return the look."[36]

As Campbell says, some actresses were unquestionably more willing "to meet the gaze of spectators in impassioned parts" (55). Pritchard, who had begun her career at Bartholomew Fair; Yates, who had presented herself to the managers of Drury Lane as "Moll G." and never entirely avoided occasional moments of "vulgarity"; and Siddons, daughter of a strolling manager, may have been among this group. Sketches of Siddons often show her full face, looking directly forward as though meeting the gaze of the painter and, therefore, of the viewer of the portrait. The George Romney and Thomas Lawrence sketches of Siddons contrast markedly to the sweet and pensive face of Younge in the Harding print and to "The late Mrs. Pope as Juliet," a likeness of "figure and expression" Boaden declared "perfect."[37] In the Briggs painting of Mrs. Siddons and Mrs. Kemble, Mrs. Kemble is looking down and left and is holding an open book; although Siddons is painted with a three-

This detail from Sir Joshua Reynolds's painting of Sarah Siddons as the Tragic Muse casts her in the conventional pose that emphasizes the long, vulnerable neck and the snowy breasts.

quarter face to the right, her direct gaze is striking. In thirty-three portraits of Siddons as herself, eleven show her returning the viewer's gaze.[38] In comparison, while six of sixteen of her in theatrical roles represent an extended throat, none show the return of the gaze. Of fourteen of Maria De Camp, none do; De Camp's "hourglass" figure is emphasized, and in two engravings she is bursting out of her costume in breeches parts (Aladdin and Julio).[39] Portraits, especially those of her in emblematic or

Most theatrical illustrators used plates of earlier engravings and made a few small changes. This illustration of Siddons as Constance in *King John* was one of the most frequently used, but it shows some modifications designed to bring out her dark eyes and intense performance style. (Courtesy of the Harvard Theatre Collection.)

theatrical roles, often produced conventional positions. For instance, in spite of numerous full-face sketches, when Reynolds painted her as the tragic muse, he emphasized a long, slender neck, elongated yet more by her slightly uptilted head, and clustered pearls at her breast, thereby emphasizing them and the traditional symbol of purity and value.

Depictions of her in theatrical roles are even more conventional, as might be expected, since many engravers simply took older engravings of

This illustration, too, was frequently used; here again, however,
the engraver managed to bring out Siddons's striking eyes and the
emotional energy she brought to familiar parts. Here she plays Isabella
in the Garrick adaptation of Behn's novel *The History of the Nun; or,
the Fair Vowbreaker.* (Courtesy of the Harvard Theatre Collection.)

other actresses and made very superficial changes, as comparisons of
Yates and Siddons as Calista and as Isabella show.[40] The 1783 engraving
of her as Isabella calls attention to her maternity by her position and the
prominent mention of her son. Other actresses had been depicted in this
role in very similar positions and costumes, and the engraving of her as
Constance in *King John* is probably an old print minimally reworked.
Comparison to illustrations of Mrs. Hartley as Almeyda (*Don Sebastian*)

Unlike the reworked plates used to produce the two former illustrations, this engraving is an original made to represent Siddons in performance. Made for the *Lady's Magazine,* it shows her returning the gaze. (Courtesy of the Harvard Theatre Collection.)

or Mrs. Yates as Calista in Bell's 1776–81 edition and especially to Ann Barry as Constance shows the kinds of changes engravers made.[41] Only a few theatrical representations of Siddons, such as the 1783 *Lady's Magazine* illustration of her as Euphrasia in *The Grecian Daughter,* catch her meeting the gaze of the audience. Some, including those of her as Calista and the princess Katharine, foreground the vulnerable throat, but engravers seem to have touched up the eyes in order to catch their well-known "wildness." A series of *Grecian Daughter* engravings captures the

These three illustrations of Siddons as Euphrasia in *The Grecian Daughter* made over several years show changes in representation that correspond to the development of her career and reputation. (Courtesy of the Harvard Theatre Collection.)

public's perspective on Siddons. She is in a very conventional pose, but the series shows both signs of age and the darkening of her character. She becomes heavier, and the feminine figure and slender neck give way to the heavy arms and neck of the final print. Successive versions show darker eyes, a more determined expression, a more obviously bloody dagger, and a more rugged landscape sketched in between the columns. Later illustrations of her as Isabella show her alone and in white, the color associated with feminine madness. She wears a turban, and her eyes are dark and focused intently and slightly to the viewer's left.

This wildness, gestures and postures that became "signatures," and the fact that she was often shown carrying a dagger tended to cancel out the impression of vulnerability in her pose.[42] In the Lady Macbeth depiction, one muscular arm ends in a fist, and the other, in one of Siddons's familiar gestures, is at her chest, thereby covering part of her strong neck. The pose shows little femininity in face or body. Siddons often wore a headdress with a wide band below her chin; this style tended to break the line of throat to breast and also appeared to protect the throat.

Of Siddons, however, it is unquestionably clear that she surpassed all other actresses in resisting confinement in the "symbolic space" reserved for women, who in theater are always perceived as some variant on the category of "love interest." As Teresa de Lauretis says, the resistance comes from disturbing or perverting that space, making trouble or seeking to exceed its boundary, which, in theater as in film, must be done visually as well as narratively.[43] One of the most subversive things that a player can do in a highly gendered society is to resist the patriarchal binary opposition of either/or. Mayne suggests that Dietrich is so powerful an image because she projects through her roles that she is both contained by patriarchal representation and resistant to it, " 'both/and,' rather than 'either/or' " (41). Siddons's interpretation of Lady Macbeth as being both the most captivating kind of woman and "unsexed" and even masculine partakes of this possibility, and some representations of Siddons do emphasize physical strength or even masculinity. In some pictures from the 1790s, her arms and neck are enormous, nearly as large and firm as those of modern football players. A number of representations are decidedly masculine. The Lawrence portrait of her as Zara emphasizes her strong features and her resemblance to her brother; the same face engraved above a military costume genders yet more the representation as male.[44] The satiric print of her as Tragedy puts a discordant face on the pose used repeatedly in Bell's engravings. In another satiric print, "Melpomene in the Dumps," a fat Siddons wearing a laurel wreath is beside a table stacked high with books such as *The Rights of Woman* and *The Duty of Man*.[45]

That many of the qualities she developed in Lady Macbeth are of intellect, what Siddons calls "a naturally higher toned mind," and demanded a subtlety of interpretation designed to show the audience that she perceives more quickly and fully than Macbeth and leads and manipulates is but one example of her revisionary, androgynous interpretation. This "energy of soul," which is impossible to capture in words or paint, raised Siddons above "mere woman" and associated her with a select group of mortals whose sensibilities seemed to contemporaries to escape the usual limitations associated with sex and gender. Like the gothic protagonist, she strained and extended the limits of human nature and achieved moments of sublime transcendence.[46] Aphra Behn had referred to her "masculine part," the poet within her, and Siddons and her audiences had no other way to conceive of the "energy of soul" and "fire" that Siddons brought to the stage. Yet there was something horrible, some threatening transformation occurring, that allied Siddons with the gothic at its most primitive level. Her performance, her body, became a Foucauldian site for the representation of warring sexualities and powers.[47] She makes the possibilities of "both/and" fascinating and dangerous.

In fact, Siddons's performances were less contained than the stories of gothic heroines. Julia Lesage and Judith Mayne have pointed out that even when the actress successfully resists becoming an object of spectacle (thereby defying the patriarchy), the role is almost invariably reabsorbed into the male plot structure.[48] Almeyda triumphs and retains her crown, but the play ends with her death as the two men who have loved her watch helplessly. In the plays by women, the heroines may be reabsorbed into the male plot structure, as Almeyda is here, but they are not often reabsorbed into the patriarchy. In gothic plays by men, there are few incidents of the resisting spectacle, and the heroine need not be reabsorbed into the patriarchy or the male plot structure because she is always a harmonious part. Most significantly, the plays by women do not conclude with a tableau foregrounding female suffering, either as sympathetic subject or as magnificent spectacle, but with an idealized image of an integrated community.

These three representations of Sarah Siddons show the tendency of artists to give Siddons's strong features a masculine cast. (Courtesy of the Harvard Theatre Collection.)

It has been said that the gothic world is inhabited only by victims and tyrants,[49] but this is not true of gothic drama. A third "character" inhabits the stage world, one that became almost as mammoth and brooding as the sublime natural universe invoked by music and spectacle. This is the crowd, "the mob," "the people." Before the modern period, this group often served as the Other, the binary opposition to "man." Bakhtin, for example, interpreted Rabelais by contrasting the mass body to the classical. Like woman's body, the mass or material body was in process, sensual, sexual, protuberant, riotous, excessive, fecund, and identified with the grotesque, "the world of becoming." The classical body, like the government set up by noblemen, was ordered, impenetrable, determined, idealized, finished, smooth, immutable, detached, and cold.[50] In many discourses generated in the last quarter of the eighteenth century, "mobs" were often projected as this Other. Societies, riots, and other mass political demonstrations gave a nightmarish quality to the eternal awareness that, in Lucia Folena's words, "The Other is constantly threatening to break through and break down the boundaries/definitions of the Same."[51]

In gothic plays, masses of largely nameless characters congregate, apparently spontaneously, at crucial moments and are symbolic representations of "the people" and "public opinion."[52] This drama, therefore, offers a kind of mini-history of the rise of public opinion and of the hegemony's apprehension of its nature, significance, and usefulness. As Tony Davies has pointed out, "A historical reading of a [popular genre] suggests that [apparently stereotypical] character-types and their positions within the textual hierarchy are changing continually in small but significant ways, and that the visual, phonetic and cultural codes through which they are generated are engaged in an unceasing intertextual transaction between the already constituted genre and the historically shifting registers of class."[53] In an extremely suggestive tract, Horace Twiss writes that the institutions from which public opinion sprang had gained their importance within living memory and "to spell out the effects of the phenomenon 'would be to retrace the whole history of our times.'"[54]

In 1764, Walpole's representation of "the common people" was distinctly unflattering. He aligned himself with the tradition, loosely associated with Shakespeare, of portraying servants and lower-class people as comic, foolish, easily influenced, and superstitious, but he added some of the elements that would shortly be invoked to limit the political power of ordinary people. Some percentage of the British people had been consistently seen as lacking the finer rational powers that made the recognition and contemplation of general truth, common good, and what Joshua Reynolds called "general beauty" possible. The reasons for this perceived deficiency were variously explained. Locke, Hume, and others described them as existing in the "animal" condition because of their economic deprivation. Locke explained that their struggle for "bare subsistence" never allowed "time, or opportunity to raise their thoughts." Reynolds said that man "in his lowest state, has . . . no wants but those of appetite; . . . those whom their superiority sets free from labour, begin to look for intellectual entertainments."[55] Adam Smith summarized the phenomenon:

> The man whose whole life is spent in performing a few simple operations, of which the effects too are, perhaps always the same, or very nearly the same, has no occasion to exert his understanding, or to exercise his invention in finding out expedients for removing difficulties which never occur. He naturally loses, therefore, the habit of such exertion, and generally becomes as stupid and ignorant as it is possible for a human creature to become. The torpor of his mind renders him, not only incapable of relishing or bearing a part in any rational conversation, but of conceiving any generous, noble, or tender sentiment, and consequently of forming any just judgment concerning many even of the ordinary duties of private life.[56]

Taste, understanding, and education seemed to draw a line dividing "popular or base men" and those suited to govern. Burke ratified the idea that "the people, however erroneous at times, must always govern the legislature," but he insisted emphatically that "it was sometimes the duty of the better informed and more enlightened part of the community to resist the sense of the people."[57] Hume's *Essays* express the hope that taste and manners will be guards against immoderate passion and motivate the right kinds of public spirit.[58]

Reynolds consistently argued that "refined taste is the consequence of education and habit" and required leisure; he, like other thinkers of his time, valued abstraction and perspective over the immediate. "Whatever abstracts the thoughts from sensual gratifications . . . must advance in some measure the dignity of our nature," he wrote; and Samuel Johnson once said that "whatever makes the past, the distant, or the future predominate over the present advances us in the dignity of thinking beings."[59] One sign of the intellectual limitations of Walpole's "lower orders" is their inability to conceive of and act upon anything but the present moment. When ordered to search for Isabella, for instance, they leave their prisoner Theodore completely unguarded and scatter like field mice. Other gothic plays incorporate both the Shakespearean comic characters and the low characters whose memories and imaginations are severely limited. In *The Iron Chest,* for example, Samson, the robber Helen has agreed to employ, exclaims, "Virtuous and a livery, all in a few seconds!" (56)

Narbonne, following the Gordon Riots, as *The Castle of Otranto* had the hysteria over Wilkes and the Massacre of St. George's Field, raises a different specter of the lower orders: the possibility of mob action. Adelaide, one of the most virtuous and sympathetic characters, says, "The castle is beset; / The superstitious, fierce, inconstant people, / Madder than storms, with weapons caught in haste, / Menace my father's life" (44). Her words play a variant of the theme of her father's contemptuous references to the people's superstitiousness and, in his opinion, disloyal nature. The count insists that they had to have an instigator and suspects that Austin has been it; the count's opinion is that of the conservative nobility: "But was't not poor, / Unlike the generous strain of Godfrey's lineage, / To stir the rabble up in nobles' quarrels?" (45). Jephson's text also refers to the power of the church, for the count remarks that the priest's words had more effect than his use of force. Even Theodore, the romantic hero and legitimate heir, has joined with the count and the priest in suppressing "the mob." That the people want Godfrey, whose claim is legal, is obscured in the text, and the resolution is the effect of providential (or coincidental) action.

Here collected are the stereotypes and nervous prejudices against the masses. As Raymond Williams has said, "Masses are other people. There are in fact no masses; there are only ways of seeing people as masses." The transmogrification from "the people" to "the masses" to "the mob" seemed to occur more easily in the 1780s. "The people" might theoretically mean "the people as a whole," all of the inhabitants of a nation, Samuel Johnson's "very heterogeneous and confused mass of the wealthy and the poor, the wise and the foolish, the good and the bad," but it was generally used to mean "the commonalty" or even the ignorant.[60] Walpole had assigned a lack of insight and perspective; Jephson adds recklessness and a lack of discretion. Many Englishmen would have shared the count's belief that the people had to have an instigator, and that made their fickleness more frightening. In a nation aware of the importance of theatricality to the maintenance of power, "instigators" with the wit to stage progresses as Monmouth had or to speak and write brilliantly as Paine did were immediately recognized as threats. Burke concluded his caution that "the better informed" needed to resist the sense of the people "when it appeared that [they] were deceived or misled" (3:10). Modern historians tend to agree with J.A.W. Gunn's statement: "An awareness that the public was easily imposed upon hangs like a dark cloud over the British radicals of the revolutionary period."[61] Gothic drama refines and exploits this insight.

By the end of the 1780s and into the 1790s, the "lower orders" are usually portrayed more sympathetically than Walpole or Jephson did but as outside the central action and largely powerless. They are, however, represented as rather reliable indices to national well-being, good and evil, and social stability.[62] The good queen in Colman's *Battle of Hexham* (1788) expresses the ideal, "Thy king unites his people to his confidence, and his commanding virtues, mild, yet kingly, shall draw the breath of rapturous loyalty from the [gilt] palace to the clay-built cottage, then will thy realm indeed be enviable" (57). A year later, "the whole village" in Cobb's *Haunted Tower* joins in scouring helmets and armor and unites with the soldiers in restoring Palamede to his rightful estate. Seven years later in *Blue-Beard,* one of Colman's heroes says, "When Power is respected, it's [*sic*] basis must be Justice. 'Tis then an edifice that gives the humble shelter and they reverence it:—But 'tis a hated shallow fabrick, that rears itself upon oppression:—the breath of the discontented swells into a gale around it, 'till it totters" (8). The common people and the slaves join him in overthrowing the tyrant.

In this same eight-year period, Boaden, who was the son of a merchant, represents the lower orders as judges, as public opinion, and as potential enforcers. As outsiders who are instinctual and admirable, they gossip and speculate, and by doing so suggest the demand for information endlessly repeated by the societies and associations.[63] In *Aurelio and Miranda,* the outraged people surround the walls of the convent until they know Agnes is safe. These plays reflect the fact that the number and nature of those conceived as the masses had changed significantly between the time of Locke and of Hume and that more writers were willing to recognize taste, refinement, and sensibility as possibly occurring "naturally" in members of the lower orders. Hannah More, for instance, observed that Anna Yearsley, the "milkmaid poet," seemed to have these qualities. By the end of the century, something like one-third of the population could be considered middle class.[64]

More than anything else, the growth of the periodical press and the uses of it by politicians had changed the influence of the people. With access to information and because they were addressed directly as thinking, evaluating beings in pamphlets and papers, they conceived of themselves as "public opinion" and were ripe for such self-images as those offered by people like Edmund Burke, who insisted that they were establishing "this double House of Commons, . . . the Commons of England in parliament assembled, and the Commons of England in corporations and county meetings dispersed."[65] One of the most revolutionary changes in a people engaged in organic social change is the increase in the number of people who believe that they are competent to make and express political opinions and even have the ability to affect at least in some small measure the course of events. As Pierre Bourdieu pointed out, "The propensity to speak politically, even in the most rudimentary way . . . is strictly proportionate to the sense of having the right to speak." At this time, increasing numbers of people carried out the act of asserting themselves as "parties to the debate, entitled to express an authorized, authoritative opinion, to voice the performative utterance of a legitimate pressure group."[66]

Inseparable from this effort was the drive for information, to be educated in political discussion. The Sheffield Society for Constitutional Information, for instance, listed as its chief objectives "the acquirement of useful knowledge, and to spread the same." "Considering, as we do, that the want of knowledge and information in the general mass of the People has exposed them to numberless impositions and abuses," it continued, and praised Tom Paine for the clarity and usefulness of both parts of his *Rights of Man*.[67] As early as the Exclusion Crisis, the Whigs had systematically collected opinion and used the press (and patronage) to influence it. Robert Harley and Robert Walpole had spent fortunes on their efforts to control the press and buy writers. Received opinion is that "the development of public opinion [is] a stage in the emergence of modern societies characterized both by growing literacy and political awareness and by institutions—such as elected politicians and an unfettered press," and it is clear that public opinion became a significant and recognized force in this part of the eighteenth century.

When dramatists such as Colman and Boaden depicted the people as judging aright but being outside of the central action, they were tapping into the Norman Yoke myth, reinforcing the ideal of the people as bearers of the innate sense of "liberty." Dramatically, they were conjuring up an opposition also deep in English history, one stated in the title of William Thomas's discourses to Edward VI: "Whether it be better for a Commonwealth that the power be in the Nobility or in the Commonalty."[68] Literary and political discourses often told a fable of a nobility prone to assuming tyrannical power, and an oppressed people who were alternately cast as those who remembered their ancient rights and as potential anarchists. On the one hand, the people are identified with a national consciousness and identity that legitimates authority and its actions and, on the other, with a threatening Other that cannot be depended upon to possess sensibility and good judgment and to act rationally. The first perception is that of John Locke and a series of "Whig" thinkers that produced such works as Daniel Defoe's stirring *The Original Power of the Collective Body of the People of England* (1702) and Charles Davenant's 1701 "opinion is the sole foundation of power."[69] The second is that of those who feared "King Mob" and a group in need of restraining, firm discipline.

Events in the latter half of the century brought opinions about "the people" into the forefront of British consciousness, and they became bitterly contested, deliberately exploited, and widely disseminated in the major discourses of the culture. At the same time that the drama was presenting this idealized self-image of the crowd as possessing sensibility, representing exemplary public opinion, and being obedient to an effective legal system, quite contradictory incidents were occurring and opinions about the masses were becoming more extreme and conflicted. The duke of Norfolk was dismissed from his lord lieutenancy for toasting "Our Sovereign, the People," and Fox is reported to have said that he had been dismissed for "an opinion which to have controverted in the times of the first two Georges would have been deemed a symptom of disaffection."[70] "The people" met one of Gramsci's criteria for provoking a crisis of the ruling class and hegemony in that they had passed rather "suddenly from a state of political passivity to a certain activity, and put forward demands which taken together, albeit not organically formulated, add up to a revolution" (210). As G.D.H. Cole and Raymond Postgate describe events,

> The new King, George III, had determined to recover for himself the power which was nominally his, but which his predecessors had aban-

doned. The control of Parliament being a marketable thing, haggled over by well-to-do aristocrats, he had seen that it was perfectly possible for himself, an individual richer and more highly placed than any Duke, to enter into the competition and by the use of the same methods as the Whig dignitaries to outbid them and control Parliament for himself.[71]

Petitions to Parliament, subsidized or free publications, and the threat of riots became identified with public meetings and the associations and societies that grew out of them. To offset associations such as the Society for Constitutional Information, groups established such organizations as the Society for the Preservation of Liberty and Property against Republicans and Levellers. Control of public opinion became the way to "haggle over" control of the ministry and of Parliament.

At the same time, citizens used such things as advertised "football matches" to organize protests. An announcement in *The Northampton Mercury* of a match called for "all Gentlemen Gamesters and Well-Wishers to the Cause now in Hand" to attend, and a subsequent news item reported that "a great number of People" assembled there "formed themselves into a tumultuous Mob, and pulled up and burnt the Fences designed for the Inclosure of that Field." Other groups attacked mills and shops they believed were charging inflationary prices; the *Adams Weekly Courant* reported, "In most places they behaved remarkably well, taking only corn, and leaving the value of it in money at a moderate price."[72] Even women were arrested for destroying fences enclosing commons.

After 1760, opposition newspapers had higher circulation figures than those firmly supportive of the government, and by the 1790s the government had to respond: powerful officials and M.P.'s invested heavily in newspapers, pamphlets, and periodicals again.[73] Wilkes's chief tactic had been to encourage public meetings "as a method of expressing opinion and influencing the Government,"[74] and the threat of riots became identified with these meetings and the associations and societies that grew out of them. Burke referred to "the swinish multitude" in *Reflections on the Revolution in France,* and *A Plan proposed for arming the Inhabitants of the Metropolis* wanted property owners armed and trained in "loading and firing quickly" so that they could defend London against the French but also could "overawe the populace who may be excited to commit outrages upon property in a moment of alarm."[75] By 1818, Hazlitt could convey the same split vision but with weary insight gained from thirty years of struggle over public opinion; he complained of the ways "prejudice or fashion" shaped opinion and continued, "Neither are the opinions of the people their own, when they have been bribed or bullied into them by a mob of Lords and Gentlemen. . . . The *vox populi* is the *vox Dei* only when it springs from the individual, unbiassed feelings, and unfettered, independent opinion of the people."[76]

As early as 1727, there was a government periodical named *The Free Briton: or, The Opinion of the People,* and throughout his life Defoe appealed to the people and to the concept of the people, as did other journalists of his time. As we have seen, the dual notion that the people legitimated authority but that their "opinion" could be harnessed, or even shaped and then harnessed, seems to have been embedded in the nation's sensibility at least as early as the Restoration and to be an outgrowth of the nation's experience from at least the time of the Civil War. The first image is the sturdy English yeoman, the second the football yob. From that time, both perspectives figured significantly into English politics and social life, and assessments such as one by a Gloucestershire sheriff were far from uncommon: the mobs of 1766 had committed many acts of violence, "some of wantoness and excess; and in other instances some acts of courage, prudence, justice."[77]

Gothic plays came to strengthen the most persistent themes of the Anglican hegemony. Examination of what appears to be a persistent anti-aristocratic strain in gothic drama reveals an endorsement of the true aristocracy (those with proper lineage, property, and conduct) and a condemnation of those who tried to assume an aristocratic position. Matilda, for instance, in *Richard Coeur de Lion* sounds a common theme when she tells Lauretta to beware of knights "of high descent": "when they seem most devoted to your beauty, they are least forgetful of their own rank." The lines of action invariably work to reveal the contrast between the usurper who has assumed position and prerogatives (and would take advantage of the Laurettas of the world) and the virtuous, *noble* man. The plays tie clashing ideologies to class and gender symbols that are usually blatantly obvious. Adela in *The Haunted Tower* says that "fine folks have fine names for bad actions," and the usurper is suspected partly because he prefers ale to wine. The marquis in *Fontainville Forest* threatens Lamotte: "Thou wretched fool, who will believe thee? / When grac'd with all the eloquence of rank, / I stand to answer the sullied charge / Made by an outlaw'd gambler" (62). Adeline explains that a

"tranquil bosom" is the prize of virtue and "when wealth / Courts her
. . . / She spurns it, and remains in peace." Almost invariably the
usurper is an opportunist, often a younger brother or a person able to
purchase his position. The words of Palamede in *The Haunted Tower* are
typical: "I scorn to owe my title to force; I am confirmed by my sovereign
. . . in the estates of my father" (54). The conclusion to many of these
plays is the reproduction of the fable of the king as the mediator between
the wealthy's will to tyrannize and the people's gravitation to anarchy.

In plays that invoked the idealized image and also kept the crowds
uninformed of the details and outside the central action, growing fears
about the masses were exercised but strongly contained. Year by year,
the plays show stronger and stronger strategies of containment. In *Aurelio and Miranda* (1799), the crowd's action is parallel in important ways
to the invasion of the monastery by Christoval, Raymond, Lorenzo, and
others, yet even the reformed Aurelio joins the other upper-class characters in insisting upon the end of the mob action at the convent. In this
play and most others, the law exists as a form of power that is both good
and available upon appeal. In fact, playwrights use it as an intervening
force in the ways that Providence is used in other dramatic forms. Laval's
entrance at the end of *Fontainville Forest* functions this way, and Aurelio
states firmly as he leaves to end the attack on the convent, "Though there
is virtue in their sympathy, / Yet violence is not the march of justice. /
Where there are laws, the laws alone should punish" (64). As reliably
virtuous as their instincts are, they are always depicted as outside—of the
law, of informed circles, and of the positions in which decisions are made
and resolutions effected. Ellena, a character more closely modeled on a
fictional heroine than most dramatic figures, makes some of the most
eloquent statements on this theme. She insists that "no one is born too
low for justice" and that the wealthy parents of her suitor have "no right,
but such as power gives; / A tyrant's power, that's wrested from the
laws, / And violates the confidence of life" (25). This 1797 play seems to
endorse the rights associated with revolutionary reform since 1688—to
life and property.

Just as the Church and King demonstrations insisted upon the deeply
conservative linking of the monarchy with the established church, so the
gothic drama mingled divine and earthly laws with "natural order." In
both cases, these institutions and concepts became inseparable and indistinguishable. Civil discourses of the period are filled with such state-

ments. As the revisionist historian J.C.D. Clark says, "Anglicanism was a natural thing, almost universal; taken for granted; inherited; acquired like one's nationality."[78] Impassioned defenses of the idea that religious and political duty are inseparable abound in the hegemony's statements. Edmund Burke, for instance, said in 1792, "In a Christian Commonwealth the church and the state are one and the same thing, being different integral parts of the same whole."

By the end of the century, the concept of public opinion as a permanent part of government had been established, and more and more people were stating that it was "the only legitimate" authority for government. Consent and even collaboration had replaced prerogative and coercion. J.A.W. Gunn suggests that Fox serves as a guide to the positions that politicians could take. In 1770, Gunn says, Fox "had denied the value of consulting the people outside Parliament. By 1783 Fox's words were recorded to the effect that 'he had contended, and he ever would contend, that no ministers who acted independent of the public opinion, ought to be employed. The public opinion alone was the basis, in his mind, on which an administration should be formed.'" Thomas Bentley shrewdly observed, "Governments, I suspect, cannot any longer be maintained, under the new and peculiar exigencies of these times, by the old maxims they have found in their offices, or the political testaments of their predecessors. The public has drawn nearer to them, the middle space has been contracted, and the common interests and union of the people and the state are become more intimate and visible."[79]

One of the reactions to this recognition was indeed the narrowing of the space allowed for "the people," the middle space between the elite and those whose lives were nothing more than a struggle for subsistence. Goldsmith had referred to those between "the very rich and the very rabble; those men who are possest of too large fortunes to submit to the neighbouring man in power, and yet are too poor to set up for tyranny themselves. This order alone is known to be the true preserver of freedom, and may be called the people."[80] Goldsmith's text invokes property, and that came to be more important than possessing taste or understanding. Over and over those with membership and stakes in the dominant economic and social orders were separated from the "unthinking multitude." Property, credit, industry, and respect in the community or some combination of these become a litany of requirements for membership in "the people."[81] Such circumscription might allow people to disquality others' opinions, but it could not deny them the ability to form and express them. By decreasing the number of the "people," they increased the size and therefore the threat of the mob.

The later gothic plays consistently include the lower orders as a massed throng with opinions that can flare into forces that must be dissipated because they cannot be ignored or even discredited. Twiss described public opinion's "subtle, unembodied spirit [as] present everywhere, piercing, and watchful, and swift, and searching the very hearts of men."[82] This perception distributes power into a sphere in which Renaissance English people had seldom located it and comes close to realizing Foucault's definition of power as widely dispersed and ubiquitous. Moreover, Twiss reproduces the metaphors of surveillance and intrusion. Horror depends on a fear of violation, usually an invasion of the body, and the late century's double vision of the common people partook of the structures of feeling in the culture and created two fears: tyrannical invasion of the people's rights, "the body politic," and the possibility of the people's penetration and violation of class order and the spaces represented by that order.

By using women as the Other, gothic playwrights could use the vulnerability to rape as symbol.[83] Woman's identification with house, social values, and human relationships elevated the protagonist's threat. British people felt that even more was at stake, however, and the villain violated the "natural rights" of the people, penetrating Locke's "property, liberty, and pursuit of happiness." Although the protagonist threatens the heroine in this way, because she is a woman and because she is the focus of other powerful and more elemental desires and anxieties, a different Other is needed if this theme is to be actualized. By using crowds, the plays pit coercion in various forms against consent, which had become the dominant form of control in England. The French Revolution, which was a crisis of legitimacy, made frightening what the mob *and* those in positions of authority could do, and it also made obvious the need and ability of rulers to "produce" authority.[84] These anxieties, too, the gothic moved to contain.

Even more significant than gothic drama's existence as one of the discourses in which public opinion as a force is examined is its example as mass culture. The Other plays a crucial part in defining the dominant and, therefore, in bringing into existence and defining the culture. One of the primary tasks of the hegemony is to liquidate, absorb, or assimilate its challenges. At its most effective, those in power organize the situation of disorder to its advantage and are able to create a new balance of political forces and alliances that will reestablish its dominance and leave state and private institutions basically intact.[85] To a considerable degree the Regency crisis, the execution of Louis XVI, and the French declaration of war on Great Britain interrupted the organic crisis under way and created a situation in which the British people urgently needed to unite.[86]

Among the culture's most urgent tasks was to write a story of unification and within that story to write a place for the masses of people who were joining associations, societies, and unions—those who were a newly influential deliberative body. Theater is always a three-way communication between the play, the individual, and the collective audience, and it has the potential for being received as reinforcement or revision of Kenneth Burke's "vast symbolic synthesis, a rationale of imaginative and conceptual imagery that 'locates' the various aspects of experience [and] . . . guides social purpose."[87] Gothic drama was available as a hegemonic apparatus, a mechanism for the negotiation of a system of knowing and believing—an ideology. Surely gothic drama succeeded in becoming a mass art and as hegemonic apparatus partly because it is consumable. Its aim was to appeal to emotion through unmediated sensation, a strategy that made the plays theater of identification. It brought so many arts together in order to bring direct pressure on all of the senses simultaneously. And it excluded carefully. One convention was that no one had to kill anyone else. Even when confronted by armies, the villain repents, goes mad, or kills himself. In one case, a skeleton does the deed after the romantic hero has defeated the villain in single combat. Thus the young man remains innocent. Plays adapted from novels often omit the protagonists' past crimes. For instance, in *The Italian,* Ellena's aunt, not her mother, has given her the picture of Schedoni and told her that the man is her father (as he is in the play); in the novel, her father is Schedoni's elder brother, whom he murdered. The slaves and servants in *Blue-Beard, The Castle Spectre,* and other plays stand ready to help the virtuous and smile approval and pledge loyalty when the tyrant is overthrown.

In these plays, the complex ambiguities stemming from the sources of madness and evil and from conflicts over authority and power give way to a benevolent, humanly oriented moral order. The conclusion, because often presented as vividly schematic, tableau representations of this moral order, sums up the experience of the play and contributes to its nature as consumable art. "The tensions . . . concentrate toward a last over-whelming tableau, a final stasis beyond which one must not think." Indeed, it is possible that members of the audience could identify with the story rather than the hero, heroine, or any other character(s). After seeing enough gothic plays, they could find pleasure in anticipating satisfaction from the story/fantasy and its conclusion.[88] The plays' reso-lution also involves domesticating concepts that were at the center of controversy and anxiety even as others are carefully excluded.[89] "Pas-sion," for instance, would be explained in the resolution; the last speech (spoken by a man, of course) in *Aurelio and Miranda* concludes, "Our passions are the fairest gifts of Heav'n! / Their just indulgence is our proper joy: / 'Tis their perversion only makes us wretched" (67). Sim-ilarly, "sensibility" partakes of none of the dispute between the reform-ists who claimed it and the "conservatives" who feared that it led to moral relativism but appropriated it as expressing their philosophy for "softer feelings" nurtured in the ideal home.

The different purposes and strategies of gothic drama are high-lighted by contrasts to the novel. The novel, for instance, was creating truly frightening crowds. Matthew Lewis's *The Monk* and Hogg's *Confes-sions* include ferocious, completely bestial mobs that tear human beings into pieces and trample them into pulp. The crowd has evolved from exercising legitimate public opinion to mindless violence; it has become a rapacious monster. Judith Wilt points out that crowds share "the same lightning shifts of mood as the hero" and that the novels "celebrate riot."[90] The novels also immerse the reader in an alien world in which the perspective is that of a haunted mind; the plays restore a benign harmony of mind in the world, the characters, and the spectators.

With its reliance upon unmediated sensation and its obvious insis-tence upon social, moral judgments of individual actions, the gothic theater attempted to integrate the spectator into the world of the play, and its effectiveness at doing so was greatly increased by the way the theater audience of the time was socialized to behave. In fact, the theater audience seems strikingly similar to the crowds in the plays. Dwellers in Bakhtin's world of "sweating and sneezing," most of the spectators sat on benches and were so packed in that they touched each other. The size and shape of the theaters manipulated the audience into feeling a strong sense of communion. Cowley's prologue to *Albina* addresses those who "crowd it here, to pant, and sob, and cry, / Whilst Madmen swagger."

They expressed their emotions and opinions audibly. They cheered

good deeds and applauded often. They seem to have been personifications of Jürgen Habermas's "public opinion." Like the audience, Habermas's public has rationally considered the actions of the authorities and,
acting as private persons, believe that their judgments of situations are
valid. As Habermas says, a public sphere had developed in which private
people cast themselves as a "forum" and came together to form a public
ready to compel public authority to legitimate itself before "public opinion."[91] By projection, the audience, like the dramatized crowd, recognized virtue and stood ready to champion it. There was no illusion that
the stage world was to be kept inviolate; they stopped performances to
hear speeches or even short episodes repeated, they burst into patriotic
songs or called for songs, and sometimes they even addressed the performers, who answered or obeyed their directions.

Contemporary witnesses record that both men and women wept
freely and that women screamed and sometimes fainted. Boaden wrote,
"I well remember (how is it possible I should ever forget?) the *sobs,* the
shrieks among the tenderer part of [Mrs. Siddons's] audiences; or those
tears, which manhood, at first, struggled to suppress, but at length grew
proud of indulging." The actor Brereton was so overcome by Siddons's
performance of Euphrasia in *The Grecian Daughter* that he "burst into
tears" and was hardly able to finish the scene. A reviewer mentioned that
he had "seldom ever witnessed more tears shed in a theatre" as he had at
The Surrender of Calais in 1791.[92]

The experience of sitting in a crowded theater and sharing strong,
approved emotions enhanced the intense and immediate excitement and
gratification.[93] Bernard Beckerman theorizes, "The play projects doubly,
to each member of the audience as an individual . . . and to the audience
as a whole, in that distinctive configuration it has assumed for a particular occasion."[94] Like the home crowds at football games, the theater
audience participated in a collective ritual that brought them together.
The plays addressed the spectators both individually and as members of
a social group, and the plays made clear they were also addressed as a
specific culture and country. Thus, they were drawn into patterns and
possibilities of identification.[95]

As J.C.D. Clark has pointed out, the longstanding stability that came
from the interlocking system of beliefs and institutions based upon the
nation's conception of the Church of England and the Constitution had
begun to disintegrate rapidly, and such things as the bills for annual
Parliaments and universal suffrage and demands for repeal of the Test

and Corporation Acts, for the repeal of legislation directed against Roman Catholics, and for parliamentary reform were its unmistakable signs. Since the plays repeatedly and clearly articulated and reaffirmed primary cultural values of benevolence, civic virtue, legitimate property possession, romantic love, domestic harmony, and transparent goodness, the theater functioned as patriotic street pageants or Easter religious services did. Notably, after the 1790s, "repeal" did not appear in reformists' demands until 1828.[96] Years later, the melodramas of the French playwright Pixerécourt were described as "the morality of the revolution": "At that difficult time, when the only place where the people could recommence their religious and social education was at the theatre, there was in the application of melodrama to the development of principles fundamental to all types of civilization, a providential purpose."[97] Something of the same thing could be said of the English gothic plays.

They propagated a comforting vision of community, of human nature, and of a providential, benignly ordered world. As Marybeth Inverso perceptively notes, two of the most significant contrasts between the gothic novel and gothic drama are the drama's "resolute banishment" of the nonthetic and of what many gothic theorists join her in describing as the novel's amoral or hostile, even evil universe.[98] At a time when the hegemony could not resolve the conflicts in the nation, the best that could be expected of gothic drama was that it contain some of the major contradictions and ruptures, and it did. Its formulaic structure and its concluding harmonious tableaux created symbolic order and momentarily gave the illusion of a kind of unity and wholeness that seemed applicable to the individual and the national life.

A common function of art is to provide structures, and, in times of crisis, the more rigid the better. The need is always for forms that "exorcise the fear that we may lose control—indeed that we are not really in control at all. . . . In placing such images within culturally accepted categories of representation, within 'art,' we present them as a social reality, bounded by a parallel fantasy of the validity of 'art' to present a controlled image of the world."[99] Ernesto Laclau has pointed out that one of the most effective ways hegemony works is to define difference and then appropriate it: "A class is hegemonic not so much to the extent that it is able to impose a uniform conception of the world on the rest of society, but to the extent that it can articulate different visions of the world in such a way that their potential antagonism is neutralized."[100] By eliminating the gothic tyrant (or the tyrannical aspects of his personality) and uniting the heroine, the romantic hero, and the common people within a common ideology, these plays deny class differences and competing interests and construct an Other that unites across these destructive lines. By constructing an ideal universe of consent, the plays elide the realities of how much authority rulers have over the governed, husbands over wives, and masters over workers.

In performing this function, some of the most frequently criticized aspects of mass culture can be discerned. In large theaters built with seating and operated with a price structure that reinforced class differences, the ideology of these plays acted as Gramsci posited they could, fostering forms of consciousness which led to the acceptance of positions of subordination. The plays are strongly ideological and invite spectators' complicity in viewing the world in that manner. Thus, the spectator has responded to what Althusser calls the "hailing" and becomes the "subject" of the text whose ideological work can then be performed. It was Althusser who emphasized that ideology could be false consciousness, could be "the representation of the *imaginary* relationship of individuals to their real condition of existence,"[101] and the gothic drama delivers what they wanted to believe about themselves and even the universe as they faced evil, disruption, and poverty.

Hazlitt wrote that popular feeling arises "out of the immediate wants and wishes of the great mass of people," and that it and public opinion are the "collective sense" of their inherited instructions and hopes.[102] Popular feeling creates mass art. By acting out repressed anxieties and hopes in overt and symbolic representations, the plays released tensions and made social contradictions momentarily innocuous. Social antagonism became opportunities to demonstrate the idealized British self-image and to confirm that no revolution was needed in their country. The plays and audience responses, which included frequent requests for group singing of "God Save the King" and "Rule Britannia," mirrored the King and Constitution processions, feasts, and speeches being conducted throughout England.[103] The aristocrats could be restrained and the poor would be taken care of.[104] The heroine gives a criminal a job in *The Iron Chest,* and he is a model of gratitude and dedicated service. Sentiments such as Zorayda's are ubiquitous: "I do see no cause, / Why I shou'd blush in feeling for the lowly" (*Mountaineers,* 32). The spectator-crowds could identify the moral sense within themselves that was universal in humankind. Conflict became spectacle, a containable and consumable product.

"That Restless, Resistless Power"

 NTHRALLING LITERATURE PRODUCES, IN PIERRE Macherey's words, "magic resolutions" to problems that the culture feels, perhaps only senses, and often can not yet name, either because they are so threatening or because they are so new.[1] Such literature is a powerful fusion of daydream and nightmare held together and rendered satisfying because for a brief time it articulates a fantasy-story that is a collective wish. At every moment, it is unstable, tangibly fragile, and always in danger of deconstructing itself. Thus, it requires its spectators to collaborate in sustaining its fiction. Neither its creators nor the people are yet able explicitly to confront the ideological inadequacies and contradictions being felt within that historical moment, and so they exercise them through cultural symbols and threatened violations of social and genre mores.

Nightmares are fears of limits and powerlessness; daydreams are fantasies of the ability to order and control. Nightmares make us victims, and daydreams make us heroes. Popular literature builds a double structure from these forms of experience and thereby pits the culture's idealized self-image against the thing it fears most. It uses formulaic character types, plot lines, and resolutions—ideological simplicities—to communicate and satisfy. It speaks simply and directly to the people as a whole, reaffirming not only what they want to believe in but also what they believe they are. Because both the image and the fear come from the dominant ideology and the hegemonic processes always at work in the society, the art form can appropriate, neutralize, and finally integrate structures of feeling, thereby becoming an active participant in hegemonic processes.

Experiencing such works of art in groups as communal events and even rituals (entering, taking up a place to view the event, leaving, comparing the experience and its meaning) reinforces every important aspect of art as civic discourse. Indeed, it fosters "collective artistic behavior," as well as "collective fantasy." Although it is true that in a culture in which art is always at least partly supported by consumers there will be an "inevitable tendency toward standardization . . . if only because one successful work will inspire a number of imitations by producers hoping to share in the profits,"[2] more than this happens. It has to continue to satisfy and to adapt, or it would stop selling. Hegemonic texts *are* social relationships, and reality is "a product of the application of human will to the society of things."[3] The writers, like the spectators and readers, become part of an ad hoc collective consciousness, desiring to find meaning in the plays and to hold onto and use that meaning in their individual and social consciousnesses. Together they *will* a reality in which they can live and work.

Street pageants, best-seller novels, gothic plays—all are examples of mass culture. It is clear, however, that they are neither culture industry nor indigenous folk art, neither the self-conscious *tour de force* of the dedicated (and probably privileged) man of letters nor the naive repetition of ideology by the writer doomed to produce commercially tested formulae. Each has been refined within the dynamic relationship between classes and in the crucible of the simultaneous pressures of residual, dominant, and emergent structures of feeling until it becomes a transformative and empowering work for a large number of people, regardless of class.

It is true, of course, that it may transform and empower in different ways. As Gramsci explains, meaning is negotiated between text and reader in relation to social experience, which differs by class and by sex and gender. Popular forms and the history of their reception reveal that they are one of the sites of the constant struggle between the dominant culture and the "resistances" within the society. Pierre Bourdieu is surely right to say that "art and cultural consumption are predisposed, consciously and deliberately or not, to fulfill a social function of legitimating social differences,"[4] but as the triumph of bourgeois ideology in the late seventeenth-century theater shows, representation and even celebration of social differences may not have had the outcome the playwrights and the powerful desired. Malcolm Smuts gives a good example from his analysis of royal entries in "Public Ceremony and Royal Charisma":

> An ordinary Londoner who witnessed a royal entry would therefore be forcefully reminded of his subordination to a massive, multi-layered system of authority, ascending from his wealthier liveried neighbours and employers, through the Lord Mayor and aldermen, to the resplendent royal court and half-deified monarch. From this vantage-point royal entries appear as classic examples of rituals which demonstrate and define power and status. Such a conclusion is tempered, however, if we turn our attention to the behaviour of the crowd of ordinary Londoners and people up from the country. . . . We should expect the crowd to have assumed a passive and deferential posture. Instead it always aggressively asserted its presence, treating the monarch less as an awesome symbol of authority than as a popular hero. (74)

Every comparison of eyewitness accounts with text and with the explications of those like Ogilby and Walker who created the texts discovers again the wide discrepancy between reception and intended transmission. For instance, Thomas Rugge, although an Oxford man, describes the streamers, pendants, and young boys in special uniforms at the first coronation arch and the "very great Lion and Unicorn made by great Art" at the Fleet Street pageant rather than any of the classical or historical emblems and myths. As Campbell complained in one of his descriptions of Siddons's performances, the spectators "would not learn their parts."

We sometimes forget that works of art are agencies of knowledge, pleasure, energy, power—important means of creating new kinds of desire, satisfaction, and truth. Even the most analytical of us seldom thinks about what characteristics and factors open the possibility for a work to become popular, that condition that opens the way for it to become hegemonic apparatus and mass culture. The most important are probably penetration to the dominant moods and concerns of an era, the reinforcement of the basic values of a culture, and technical displays. Although often denigrated and mistrusted,[5] innovative and masterful technological aspects contribute in crucial ways to a literary text's becoming popular. Pyrotechnics give an intense and immediate kind of stimulation and gratification that delivers excitement and relieves boredom. Such effects often "carry" a large part of the fantasy and bear great responsibility for absorbing the spectator in its "world," thereby contributing to the necessary condition of the spectators' experiencing the imaginary world without continually comparing it to their own lived experience or "reality."[6] At a deeper level they are evidence to the spectators of the author's skill and control, signs that they can "trust" and put themselves in the creator's hands.

Each of the cases in this book considers literature that became a hegemonic apparatus. Created in times of social crisis, the texts participated in the negotiations that would assimilate change and reestablish ideological, and therefore social, stability. In order to do so, they helped resolve tensions and ambiguities, named and confined the Other, and confirmed or helped create a new moral order with an idealized English self-image. In other words, they helped the entire culture agree on what its people were like, what their shared aspirations were, what "community" would mean, and what the nature of the universe was.

That these cases involve literary kinds, groups of texts or even performances, rather than individual works underscores the importance of the evolution of a formula to the process that allows literature to become a hegemonic apparatus. The authors' imaginations, the orchestrated languages available, and the demands and expectations of all of those involved in the creation, production, and reception of the work refine and fix the basic pattern and its elements. It then has created its own world, and the audience becomes familiar with it through repetition. At this point, the pattern is available not only for confirmation and reassurance but also for allowing a testing of the boundary between the permitted and the forbidden, the temporary and the impossible. The reactions shared by people in a group experience become collective consciousness, which reaffirms borders and limits. It finally delivers the predictable and reassures about communal norms, social relations, and natural and political order. Thus, royal progresses, popular gothic plays, and novels that resemble a charivari reaffirm the moral values that make a people a society; and they act, like the recitation of a religious creed, to renew the culture's devotion to those values.

We have also seen how the cases that I have examined also carry messages about power, about its location in relationships and the ways that it is produced. The first two chapters examine a case from the public, political sphere. The last two chapters explore a case represented in the increasingly clearly conceived private sphere. The middle two eloquently testify to the fact that the private is the public and political. All three cases illustrate how power is diffused through a civil society. In the pageants and plays of 1660–1664, the dependencies and interrelationships between Gramsci's political and civil societies are evident.[7] The king attempted to dominate the coercive mechanisms of political society such as the military, legal, and taxation systems. Even the family was appropriated, as Cromwell's was, and turned into the rhetoric and theatrics of power production.

But civil society, that "ensemble of organisms" that Gramsci put at the heart of understanding hegemonic processes, was tangibly producing power and authority, too. It is this latter sphere that primarily engaged Behn and the playwrights. As women, they were especially and deeply concerned with the ways people are grouped together and with the ways that such things as sex, age, and conduct are assigned value and influence. As political thinkers and writers, they were concerned about other groupings such as regions, religions, parties, and national rivalries. Gramsci considered the family a major organization and institution within this category and was aware of the subtleties of exploitation and oppression inherent in the male-privileged structure. In fact, his terms for women, broodmares and dollies, are horrifyingly accurate descriptions of the roles that women play in many Restoration comedies,[8] and in Behn's plays as well as those by the women of 1696, the category of "dolly," the sexual object for sport, is contested and its boundaries perverted and disrupted.

One of the achievements of *Love-Letters* is that Behn so fully mingles Gramsci's two spheres. The community, the moral consensus that erupted in "rough music" and charivaris, judges Philander, Sylvia, and even Mary Berkeley and their families. This community seems coherent and even cast as readers with whom we are invited to join. Simultaneously, Philander's politics and the implications of his and others' actions are placed on the stage. As such, they challenge and arouse the coercive forces available in the political society as they had the censoring and collaborative forces in the civil society. Thus, we can see the reality of the "integral state" and of the diffusion and penetration of power into every conceivable institution, relationship, and private life.

The gothic plays show continued movement toward full awareness of individual selfhood and its vulnerability; once again, coercive power, this time embodied in a sign of illegitimate authority, is portrayed beside collective civil society, represented by, finally, all of the other characters. Gothic drama shows how apt the terms "political" and "civil" society are and yet how integral is the state, for the weapons in the protagonists' hands are, at first, state institutions and apparatuses—the law, the hired churchman, and the administrative functions such as taxation and charity—while the civil society's ultimate success depends on the kind of intellectual and moral consent, consensus, and majority that Gramsci argued always finally determines the existence of a stable ideology. Conclusions produce tableaux that represent both private and public, that translate the family relationships of reunited lovers, brothers and sisters, loyal friends, and new couples into symbols of consolidated, legitimate power over estates and kingdoms.

Within all of these texts and cases, the struggle for intellectual, moral, and philosophical dominance is visible and rendered into art. The movement of cultural symbols from the social world into genre and back into the social shows how imposed and indigenous symbols play a part in organic change. In the first case, symbols that were not indigenous and proved false to the experiences and desires of the people were rejected. In the third, deeply indigenous symbols were reinvested with reassurances and embraced. In the second case, the plays by women, the symbols were equally deeply indigenous, but the difference of their meanings for men and women and for Whigs and Tories underscored the fact that times of Caesarism are always political, moral, and linguistic crises. Some of the most basic categories of the society—love, marriage, and commerce among them—were critiqued, reconsidered, and adjusted.[9]

Each incidence shows the demands for alternative styles of social relations[10] and challenges some of the basic conceptions from which reality is created: "sovereign," "male/female," "sane." For example, anxieties about sex, sexual identity, and sexual roles are evident in all three cases. Each teases out the fact that there is "male" and "female" in ourselves, and then considers how society contributes to and judges that fact. In the first two cases, the anxieties about the destructive and weakening effects of the woman within are often revealed to be tropes and prejudices, not the reigning opinion about sex or gender. In the third case, finding and expressing the woman within, the tender sentiments, is essential for even the most powerful man. In all three, even in the plays by women, woman is most often a sign of something else, of "difference," but in the second case, new concerns and a new perspective increased the tensions between the changing reality of people's lives, courtship rituals, and marriages and the dominant expectations of what men and women are and how they are supposed to feel and behave.

Ross Chambers argues that readers and spectators are influenced when their desires are changed: "to change what people desire is, in the long run, the way to change without violence the way things are" (*Room for Maneuver,* xii). Equally important, however, is the balance of power among desiring groups. Each of these cases involves such a time of shifting balances and desires, and each is characterized by an awareness of new groups of people as mobilized, deliberative bodies. Between 1660 and 1662 the City commercial people, many of whom were Nonconformists, in 1695 middle-class women, and between 1788 and 1793 "the masses" challenged the dominant political order and its ideology. As Howard Twiss said, "Within the personal recollection of many who are yet alive,—has sprung that restless, resistless power, which men call Public Opinion."[11] Each pair of chapters considers the establishment of the concept of public opinion and shows that Habermas's location of this important force should be pushed back earlier in history. When this concept and the awareness of individual selfhood are considered together, it is clear that Bakhtin is correct to see that "a new, concrete, and realistic historic awareness was born and took form: not abstract thought about the future but the living sense that each man belongs to the immortal people who create history."[12] Throughout the period, literature assisted in the processes of individual and group awareness and of resisting or assimilating change.

At every level, these cases show a struggle for the control of representation. How people imagine themselves and their "stories" is always the issue. In these examples, we can see how writing can be a civil discourse and a mode of imaginative exploration and radical discovery. More important, we can see how examining texts produced during periods of turmoil and instability reveals new things about literature and its social contexts, how writers' new orchestrations of literary languages can create radically original and culturally important texts, and how literature functions in a free society. We can even begin to see some of the necessary conditions for the transformation of a literary kind into mass culture and hegemonic apparatus.

NOTES

INTRODUCTION

1. The term *hegemony* is Antonio Gramsci's and is usefully explained by Raymond Williams in *Marxism and Literature,* 108–14; see also *ideology,* 55–71. In this book, I use *ideology* to refer to a stable system of concepts, values, opinions, attitudes, and structures that represents a vision of the world that has been recognized, named, and at least partially defined *in modern times.* I use *hegemony* and *hegemonic process* to refer to the dynamic process that is what Gramsci calls "a moving equilibrium" and that emphasizes the fact that the dominant culture is, in Williams's words, always in the state of being "resisted, limited, altered, challenged" (112). My study is in many ways an extension and application of some of the theories of Gramsci and of a configuration of social and literary theoretical works, the most important of which are Gramsci's *Selections from the Prison Notebooks* (hereafter identified as *Prison Notebooks*), Raymond Williams's *Marxism and Literature,* Fredric Jameson's *Political Unconscious* and "Metacommentary," and Mikhail Bakhtin's *Dialogic Imagination.*

2. Quoted from Gilbert White's journal in Paulson, *Representations of Revolution*, 1.

3. Esslin, *Anatomy of Drama*, 28.

4. De Marinis, "Dramaturgy of the Spectator," 108.

5. Gunn, *Beyond Liberty and Property*, 260. Jürgen Habermas locates the time when the public sphere began to function in the political realm at the beginning of the eighteenth century (*Structural Transformation of the Public Sphere*, 56 et passim).

6. See *Structural Transformation of the Public Sphere*, 29–30, 38–43, 57.

7. See, for instance, Levy, "How Information Spread among the Gentry," 11–14, 20–21, 34; Holmes, "The County Community in Stuart Historiography," 54–73; Houlbrooke, "Women's Social Life and Common Action," 171; Tim Harris, *London Crowds*, 98–108 et passim; Alice Clark, *Working Life of Women*, 107–9.

8. Paulson, *Popular and Polite Art in the Age of Hogarth and Fielding*, x.

9. Tim Harris summarizes the superiority of this position in *London Crowds*. One study that he cites notes that 18 percent of London apprentices were sons of the gentry, 23 percent sons of yeomen, and 43 percent were sons of artisans, professionals, traders, and wealthy merchants. Apprenticeship often led to being made free of the City and therefore eligible to become Lord Mayor (15–27). In literature, critics have shown that amateur Cavaliers, dissident courtier dramatists, professional court and City playwrights, and country dramatists all wrote critical, revisionary political drama in the 1730s and 1740s (Tricomi, *Anticourt Drama*, 167–89).

10. Damrosch, *Fictions of Reality*, 78.

11. Jameson, *Political Unconscious*, 286–92, and "Metacommentary," 15–17.

12. The term is John Richetti's, in *Popular Fiction before Richardson*, 9–10.

13. Nancy K. Miller summarizes the case against them well in *Subject to Change*, 25–26, 38–45, 85–86, 99n. 14.

PART ONE. CHARLES II'S LONDON AS NATIONAL THEATER

1. J. R. Jones, *Country and Court*, 132–33.

2. The pulpit, which might have been a competitor, could not be trusted because of religious factions and distrust for Charles. In fact, the churches were sites for some of the most radical interpretations of the monarchy. Moreover, scholars have demonstrated that far too few parish churches existed, many charged prohibitive pew fees, and snobbery, pluralism (clergy assigned a church in London and one in the country), and absenteeism contributed to the lower classes having lower religious exposure than was previously thought. See Keith Thomas, *Religion and the Decline of Magic*, 151, 159–66; and Malcolmson, *Life and Labour*, 81–93.

3. Gombrich, "Renaissance and Golden Age," 307.

4. A month after the request on 14 March 1662, the City had but £60,000 pledged. Another month later, even after a determined effort spurred by an annoyed letter from Charles, the City had raised only £100,000. CLRO Letter Book UU, fol. 125, and Sharpe, *London and the Kingdom*, 2:399, 403.

CHAPTER I. THE CONSOLIDATION OF POWER

1. "The Earl of Newcastle's Letter of Instructions to Prince Charles for His Studies, Conduct, and Behaviour," in *Original Letters, Illustrative of English History,* 3:290.

2. On Louis's political uses of spectacle, see Hanley, *Lit de Justice,* especially 307–28. Strong points out that there was "a vast explosion" of court spectacle that lasted for nearly two centuries, and that there was "profound belief in the power and efficacy of such spectacles" (*Splendor at Court,* 21). Margaret Rich Greer points out that court spectacles actually became more frequent and elaborate as "absolutism became the dominant political form in Europe in the sixteenth and seventeenth centuries" ("Art and Power," 337n. 1).

3. See Lawrence M. Bryant, *King and the City,* 23–24, 119–20, 205, and 208–14. This book also describes some of the symbolism associated with French pageants (cf. 126–30), as does Hanley, *Lit de Justice,* 329–44, and Landwehr, *Splendid Ceremonies.*

4. Quoted in Greenblatt, "Invisible Bullets," 57. See Withington, *English Pageantry,* for descriptions of some seventeenth-century royal spectacles (1:232–39). Louis XIV's *Mémoires for the Instruction of the Dauphin* (1661–68) offers indisputable evidence of the European monarchies' awareness of the uses of ceremony and spectacle. I am grateful to Kevin Cope of Louisiana State University for bringing this document and the work of Bob Robinson on it to my attention.

5. See Geertz, "Centers, Kings, and Charisma," 154–57. For descriptions of Elizabeth's coronation progress, see Anglo, *Spectacle Pageantry* [*sic*], 346–57; Withington, *English Pageantry,* 198–202; and Strong, *Splendor at Court,* 25. The quotation is from Mullaney's *Place of the Stage,* 11.

6. Quoted in Orgel, *Illusion of Power,* 42. Roy Strong has carried this further to argue that the court masque as it developed under James was the exposition of the divine right of kings intended to be an acting out and a visual realization of the king's "part" in the world (*Art and Power,* 159). Nancy K. Maguire points out that Charles I used the emblems of kingship and left a legacy of useful symbols for Charles II ("Theatrical Mask/Masque of Politics," 1–22).

7. Quoted from *A Short View of the Life and Reign of King Charles* (1658), in Smuts, "Public Ceremony and Royal Charisma," 90.

8. Reprinted in "The Royal Standard of Our Country" (London, 1803).

9. Smuts, "Public Ceremony and Royal Charisma," 93.

10. Two other studies that consider from very different angles Charles's use of the theater are MacLean, "King on Trial," 375–88; and Deborah C. Payne, "Rewriting the Restoration of the London Stage" (Paper given at the American Society for Eighteenth-Century Studies Annual Meeting, New Orleans, La., 1989).

11. "The Prologue to his Majestie At the first PLAY presented at the Cock-pit in Whitehall, Being part of that Noble Entertainment which Their Majesties received *November* 19. from his Grace the Duke of ALBEMARLE" (1660).

12. Thomas Rugge, "Mercurius Politicus Redivivus. A Collection of the most material Occurances and Transactions in Public Affaires Since . . . 1659." BL Add. MS. 10116, p. 87. The manuscript is continued in Add. MS. 10117.

13. Walker, *Circumstantial Account,* 19, 29–32. Many of the payments for these pieces are recorded in PRO SP 38/20 for June 1661; among them were a new St. Edward's crown and scepter, globes, and "the Collar of Gold." The total cost was £20,000.

14. Clarendon, *Edward Earl of Clarendon,* 1:455 and 407, respectively. Charles had to borrow £60,000 of it.See PRO SP 38/20 and SP 44/3, fol. 40, for 31 October 1661; the king rewarded Sir Thomas Player, Chamberlain of the City of London, with £500 for "his paines" in securing the loan.

15. PRO SP 44/48, fol. 20; GH ExGLMS 290, nos. 19 and 34; *DNB,* drawing on Ashmolean MS. 857. Because Ogilby had the exclusive patent to publish descriptions of the entertainment and was such a master of self-aggrandizement, he has obscured Walker's part, and some modern scholars (including Knowles) have given Ogilby primary credit for the arches and show. See also Walker's own account in *Circumstantial Account.*

16. The *Iliad* had been licensed on 18 April 1656 but was not published until 1660. Ogilby would go on to be the king's cosmographer and geographic printer and, with the king's warrant, would replace Davenant as Master of Revels for Ireland the month after the coronation, May 1660 (*Stationers' Register;* Knowles, "Introduction" to Ogilby, *Entertainment of Charles II,* 9; Edmond, *Rare Sir William Davenant,* 118).

17. The pageants are best compared to what we would call tableaux and were often mounted on modern parade floats or barges. They were set up at symbolic locations, thereby having enhanced emblematic richness.

18. Clothworkers' Company, Orders of Courts 1649–1665, fol. 168, for 11 April 1661; in Ogilby's *Relation of His Majesties Entertainment.* Mills is listed on a final unnumbered page with "another" who wished to be anonymous; this could be Edward Walker, whose position would make listing him here inappropriate, or it could be the other City Surveyor, Edward Jermyn (or Jarman).

19. Orders of Courts 1649–1665, fol. 168.

20. The Grocers' Company Minute Book uses "design," "contrive," and "complete" and orders various committees to "consult with" or "deal with" the surveyors; these words are routine. Cf. entries for 2 and 22 October 1661. Anglo describes such collaboration and the appointment of two men for each of the six stations for the entry of Katharine of Aragon; they were to "supervise the construction and decoration of the sets, disburse the money for artists, craftsmen, and labourers, and generally to see that everything went according to plan" (*Spectacle Pageantry,* 58). William Morgan, Ogilby's assistant, published an account of the affair many years later in which he says that the City of London built the four arches (*King's Coronation,* 1).

21. Richards, "Restoration Pageants of John Tatham," 51 and 53; *Lord Mayors' Pageants,* 2:83; *Neptune's Address To his Most Sacred Majesty Charls* [sic] *the Second,* 8.

22. Knowles, "Introduction" to Ogilby, *Entertainment of Charles II,* 16. Knowles mentions that the king intervened. The declaration by Walker is reprinted at the beginning of the facsimile *Entertainment* in this volume. A number of printed accounts of the coronation survive, and even those published by Ogilby in 1661 differ. Collation shows that *The Relation of His Majesties Entertainment Passing through the City of London* is a completely different book from the editions of *The Entertainment*

of Charles II and that significant differences between the Mariot and Dring (BL L.R. 294 d.15) and the Roycroft (BL 140. h.17) editions exist. The Mariot and Dring version, for instance, gives a rather full account of the altercation between the footmen and the barons. Walker's detailed description, *A Circumstantial Account,* was not published until 1820. For an account of his conduct and Ogilby's opportunistic publications of descriptions of the coronation, see Halfpenny, "Citie's Loyalty Display'd."

23. The *Nazeby* became the *Charles;* the *Richard,* the *James;* the *Speaker,* the *Mary;* the *Bradford,* the *Success,* and so on (Pepys, *Diary,* 23 May 1660).

24. Shoemaker, "London 'Mob,'" 293; Tim Harris, *London Crowds,* 39.

25. Modern accounts tend to emphasize the razing of the cross as though the event were a lamentable Puritan desecration of art; in fact, beginning at least as early as 1581, the monument had been repeatedly defaced and mutilated. It seems that vandals especially enjoyed stealing the baby Jesus and hacking up the Virgin Mary (Thornbury, *Old and New London,* 1:333–35).

26. Edwards, *London,* 231.

27. Walford, *Westminster and the Western Suburbs,* 3:123–30; *The London Encyclopedia,* ed. Ben Weinreb and Christopher Hibbert, s.v. "Charing Cross"; Edwards, *London,* 229–34; Walford, *Old and New London,* 3:123–28.

28. Quoted in Tim Harris, *London Crowds,* 39.

29. Foucault, *Discipline and Punish,* 216.

30. Foucault, *Discipline and Punish,* 227.

31. Howell, *Complete Collection of State Trials,* 5:1079.

32. Information about the public displays of Charles's first year's reign comes from Richards, "Restoration Pageants of John Tatham," 49–73; Harris, *London Crowds,* 36–61; Morrah, *1660;* and Rugge, "Mercurius Politicus Redivivus." Margaret Greer notes, "Wherever the court spectacular developed, one of its primary purposes was to publish a Machiavellian message of the monarch's glory and power, to dazzle with a display of wealth any potential sources of opposition, internal or external" ("Art and Power," 329).

33. Clothworkers' Company, Orders of Courts 1649–1665, for 11 May 1660; Skinners' Court Book no. 4, 21 May 1660; Haberdashers' Court of Assistants' Minutes, GH Library MS. 15,842, vol. 2, fol. 73 for 19 May 1660.

34. CLRO, Remembrancia, 9:13.

35. Geertz, "Centers, Kings, and Charisma," 152–53. See also Brewer, *Party Ideology,* 34–35.

36. Knowles, quoting Francisco Giavarina, in *Entertainment of Charles II,* 14–15.

37. Rugge notes that the bonfires were decorated and that one in Southwark was higher than any house in London ("Mercurius Politicus Redivivus," 97).

38. Bodleian Wood 537 (18), "The Citie's Loyalty Display'd," quoted in part in Halfpenny, "Citie's Loyalty Display'd." Nicholas Rogers describes the way public behavior was "orchestrated from above" (*Whigs and Cities,* 357–58, 361, and 368–69). On financing bonfires and street symbols, see Tim Harris, *London Crowds,* 26, 38–39.

39. Quoted in Fairholt, *Lord Mayors' Pageants,* 10:59 (pt. 1).

40. Louis XIV, *Mémoires*, 193.

41. See Halfpenny, "Citie's Loyalty Displayed," [8], and Anglo, *Spectacle Pageantry*, 82, 94.

42. On Charles's efforts, including his trips to Parliament, see J. R. Jones, *Country and Court*, 135–36; Arthur Bryant, *King Charles II*, 115–17; and Clarendon, *Edward Earl of Clarendon*, 1:398–403, 447–48.

43. Clarendon, *Edward Earl of Clarendon*, 1:458; Clarendon, *History of the Rebellion*, 1:278; Clode, *London during the Great Rebellion*, 23; Emberton, *Skippon's Brave Boys*, 63–70, 81.

44. Walker, *Circumstantial Account*, 19; Eric Halfpenny notes that Walker believed a gaffe was committed in Westminster when the Head Bailiff and High Constable rode before the Sword but argues that "within their own liberty" their right was equal or greater ("Citie's Loyalty Display'd").

45. Clarendon and others state that the coronation was originally scheduled for the beginning of May (*Edward Earl of Clarendon*, 1:455).

46. Knowles, "Introduction" to *Entertainment of Charles II*, 15.

47. Ferdinand had become the governor of the Spanish Netherlands, and Antwerp hoped for more favorable trade concessions; for descriptions of the entry, see Martin, *Decorations for the Pompa Introitus Ferdinandi;* Erlanger, *Louis XIV*, 93. Walker had been at the Hague and in the Netherlands for extended periods beginning in 1649 and with Charles in Cologne and in France (*DNB*).

48. Pepys, *Diary*, 2:82. For his error about the procession but his correct surmise, see n. 7. It is important to note that the modern editor has concluded that large parts of the *Diary* consist of Evelyn's transcripts of his notes rather than his original notes. After 1688, the *Diary*'s sources become less privileged (Evelyn, *Diary*, 121, 128–29).

49. Evelyn, *Diary*, 3:278–80; see also Rugge, "Mercurius Politicus Redivivus," 326–29; and J. R. Jones, *Country and Court*, 133.

50. Knowles, "Introduction" to *Entertainment of Charles II*, 17; see also Pepys, *Diary*, 2:79; and Rugge, "Mercurius Politicus Redivivus," 336. The king's saddle and furniture for his horse cost but £2,395.17.5 (PRO AO1 2022/5A).

51. Knowles, *Entertainment of Charles II*, 2–6.

52. Anglo, *Spectacle Pageantry*, 58, 96–97.

53. Withington, *English Pageantry*, 1:xvi. Information on the pageants comes from this two-volume work and from Strong, *Splendor at Court*, 23–48.

54. Strong, *Splendor at Court*, 33–36.

55. Withington's account summarizes the integration of living people among the represented figures and the use of music, stages, and streets usefully (*English Pageantry*, 1:244–47).

56. Compare Reedy, "Mystical Politics," 19–42.

57. See Strong, *Splendor at Court*, 156–57 and fig. 21; and Hanley, *Lit de Justice*, 231, 329. Although Tommaso Campanella, perhaps the first to hail Louis by the title of Sun King, had used the term to express his hopes for religious and political unity in Europe, Louis suggests that he felt he had chosen the symbol after the building of the Carrousel de Paris: "Ce fut la que je commencai à preude celle que j'ai toujours gardée depuis" (196). The quotation in the text is also from *Mémoires*, 124–25.

58. Lines 285–91, *Poems on Affairs of State*, 1:5–6.

59. Orgel, *Illusion of Power,* 70–77.

60. Two of "the verie best" actors played the parts of the Tritons, and Richard Burbage, the great King's Company actor, performed the speeches (Munday, *London's Love,* 11; Withington, *English Pageants,* 1:230–32).

61. Withington, *English Pageants,* 1:243.

62. Fairholt, *Lord Mayors' Pageants,* pt. 2:81–85.

63. Ogilby, *Entertainment of Charles II,* 126–30.

64. PRO AO1/2433, roll 85.

65. Pepys, *Diary,* 2:83–84; Ogilby, *Entertainment of Charles II,* 172–73.

66. Lawrence M. Bryant notes the same change in perception and discourse about kingship in France as absolute monarchy replaced the older notions of a union of disparate authorities (*King and the City,* 213, 217–18); see also Butwin, "French Revolution as *Theatrum Mundi,*" 141–52.

67. Geertz, "Centers, Kings, and Charisma," 153. He has changed the quotation from Wallace Stevens's "Theory" slightly: "Women understand this. / One is not duchess / A hundred yards from a carriage." I am grateful to Professor Catherine Neal Parke for the identification of this line.

68. Debord, *Society of the Spectacle,* par. 12.

69. The relationship between City pageants and court masques is greater than that between the pageants and the theater. Familiarity with, for instance, the function of setting in the masques makes this point and suggests that an extended study of the pageants as masque and antimasque would be productive. On setting and the construction of symbolic spectacle in the masque, see Cooper, "Location and Meaning," 135–48. She does not discuss street pageants at all but concludes that masque settings could create complex images of "moral action, good government, the symbolic and mythic dimensions of everyday living." See also Butler, *Theatre and Crisis,* on the king as "soul of his kingdom" (252).

70. It is not certain that they succeeded in obliterating all traces of Cromwell's body. Stories survive that it was successfully stolen and buried; the skull is preserved at Sidney Sussex College, Cambridge (Fraser, *Cromwell,* 695–97).

71. Bruce A. McConachie points out that both Antonio Gramsci and Kenneth Burke argue that human beings "by nature respond to symbols" and demonstrate how language and ritual help establish a "hegemonic we"; see "Concept of Cultural Hegemony," 37–58. Burke writes that rhetoric is "rooted in . . . the use of language as a symbolic means of inducing cooperation in beings that by nature respond to symbols" (*Rhetoric of Motives,* 43–46). See also Burke's *Attitudes toward History,* 179–215; the quotation is from p. 179.

72. This description of the welcoming pageant and the speeches are in *The Dramatic Works of John Tatham,* 293–304.

73. Charles referred to "the general distraction and confusion which is spread over the whole kingdom" and the "long misery and sufferings" of the people (*Parliamentary History,* 4:16).

74. Tatham, in *Several Speeches,* says that the scenes were presented on water and land on 25 October, and the speeches were added as part of the procession on the twenty-ninth.

75. Tatham, *Several Speeches,* 4.

76. Tatham, *Royal Oake.*

77. Richards, "Restoration Pageants of John Tatham," 51; CLRO Cash Accounts 1/10, fol. 212. The account books of the Companies show that each paid approximately £230 toward the entertainment.

78. Jordan, "Speech Composed to Welcome Charles the Second," 10.

79. The 1660 title page of *The Rump* reads, "Acted many times with great applause at the Private House in Dorset Court." The play is printed in *The Dramatic Works of John Tatham* with the characters' names as they were in the first edition (i.e., "Bertlam" for "Lambert," "Woodfleet" for "Fleetwood," etc.). It was registered with the Stationers' Company on 23 August 1660.

80. Abraham Cowley, Preface to *Cutter of Coleman-Street.*

81. Cromwell, *Letters and Speeches,* 2:169; Fraser, *Cromwell,* 462.

82. Pepys, *Diary,* 7 Jan. 1660/61. Kynaston may not have played this role very long; Downes's cast for the play lists Mrs. Knep as Epicoene (*Roscius Anglicanus,* 13).

83. *A Biographical Dictionary of Actors, Actresses,* s.v. "Kynaston."

84. The quotation is from the Introduction to *The Court and Kitchin of Elizabeth, Commonly called Joan Cromwell.*

85. Shesgreen, *Criers and Hawkers of London.* See illustration and commentary, 154–55.

86. Fraser, *Cromwell,* 26–28, 193, 477, and 687. See also *The Court and Kitchin of Elizabeth, Commonly Called Joan Cromwell,* esp. pp. 32, 37–38, and the recipe collection at the end of the pamphlet.

87. Besant, *London in the Eighteenth Century,* 274.

CHAPTER 2. MEN, WOMEN, AND RESISTANCE

1. *Parliamentary History of England,* 4:16–17.

2. Gramsci describes the tension between "the dialectical revolution/ restoration" and the characteristics of progressive and reactionary Caesarism ("a situation in which the forces in conflict balance each other in a catastrophic manner") in *Prison Notebooks,* 219–20.

3. Quoted in George, *Women in the First Capitalist Society,* 27.

4. Cibber, *Apology,* 66.

5. Nicholas Rogers concludes that decades of party strife had broadened politics to encompass "petty artisans, servants, and labourers" and that the people cannot be relegated to a marginal position (*Whigs and Cities,* 367, 385). Defoe, *Original Power; Address of Thanks* quotation from Schwoerer, "Women and the Glorious Revolution," 208. A number of other social historians have found and described incidents that show the rise of popular opinion as political force this early; see, for example, Holmes, "Drainers and Fenman," 166–95, and especially Gunn, *Beyond Liberty and Property,* 260–79.

6. Peter Burke, "Popular Culture in Seventeenth-Century London," 47.

7. Atkyns, "Epistle to the King," prefacing *The Original and Growth of Printing* (1664).

8. Quoted in Rogers, *Whigs and Cities,* 387.

9. Watt, *Rise of the Novel,* 61.

10. Clarendon, *Edward Earl of Clarendon,* 1:268–69. Of course, many people

had not wanted the restoration of the king; petitions such as one from "Gentlemen, Freeholders, and Inhabitants of Kent and Canterbury" against a "monarchy or oligarchy" survive (4 June 1659, GH Broadside 18.45).

11. See Brewer, *Sinews of Power*, 168–70 and 257n. 94. Among the key dates he gives are those of the Dutch Wars (beginning in 1652) and the Navigation Acts (the first in 1651).

12. See PRO SP 29/57, 25, 42, 57, 70, 72 et passim. Most of these are dated midsummer 1662.

13. Gramsci, *Prison Notebooks*, 57–61. Charles faced a situation similar to that described in the discussion of reconstructing the hegemonic apparatus of a ruling group (228–29).

14. Geertz, *Interpretation of Cultures*, 317–18; Raymond Williams, *Culture and Society*, 301–6.

15. Ralph, *History of England*, 1:9.

16. See Anglo, *Spectacle Pageantry*, 357–58.

17. Auden, *Criterion Book of Modern American Verse*, 17.

18. Enough evidence survives to conclude that the Lord Mayor's Day pageants regularly included morally and politically instructive speeches intended to "enumerate the virtues that the mayor should seek" (Bergeron, *Thomas Heywood's Pageants*, 6–7; Withington, *English Pageantry*, 2:199–202).

19. Clothworkers' Company, Orders of Courts 1649–1665 for 28 February 16$\frac{59}{60}$, and Brome, *Speech to the Lord General Monk*, 199–202.

20. Broadside dated 4 June 1659, "Gentlemen, Freeholders and Inhabitants of Kent and Canterbury." Dozens of these petitions for a free Parliament are preserved in the Public Record Office and Guildhall; many mention the need to encourage trade. Cf. "The Declaration of the Nobility, Gentry, Ministry, and Commonalty of . . . Kent . . . Canterbury . . . Rochester and parts within the County" [1660] and "A Declaration of the Nobility and Gentry of the County of Worcester Adhering to the late King." Tim Harris discusses the free Parliament sentiment in *London Crowds*, 42–49.

21. The play was registered by the Stationers' Company on 23 August 1660; its title page reads, "Acted many times with great applause at the Private House in Dorset Court." On the possibility of Charles seeing it, see Love, "State Affairs," 1–2; and Freehafer, "Formation of the London Patent Companies," 9–12. The conclusions of the latter have been disputed.

22. Grocers' Company, Calendar to the Minute Book, vol. 4, pt. 3:764, 768–70, and 772.

23. CLRO, Repertories, vol. 67, fol. 330 for 25 October 1659.

24. Mullaney, *Place of the Stage*, 16.

25. Rugge, "Mercurius Politicus Redivivus," BL Add. MS. 10116, 163–64.

26. Tatham, *London's Glory Represented*, 2, 3, 4, 6, 8.

27. The king agreed to attend on 7 June 1660; Grocers' Company, Calendar to the Minute Book, 800–801, 811; Thornbury, *Old and New London*, 1:315.

28. Payments made to painters, joyners, and carpenters always dwarfed those to the poet. The Skinners paid the joyner £43 and the painter £56 in 1658 (Receipts and Payments, 492).

29. Tatham, *London's Tryumph, Presented by Industry and Honour;* Grocers'

Company, Calendar to the Minute Book, bk. 4, pt. 4, 912–13 for 22 August 1662.

30. Hiring professional actors seems to have been rare. The Skinners, however, hired no less an actor than Walter Clunn (along with several others) for £15 in 1657 and for £20 in 1658. They also hired "2 Negros," a "Gyant," and tumblers ("Receipts and Payments," fols. 448 and 492).

31. *London's Triumph: Presented in several Delightfull Scenes,* 17–18.

32. ExGLMS MS. 289, fol. 3. The Clothworkers paid £165, the Merchant Taylors £200, and the Skinners £226 (see Court Book no. 4 for 26 June 1660).

33. Minutes often include appointment of a committee and simultaneous direction to consult Jerman "about the design of the pageantry"; see, for instance, Grocers' Company, Calendar to the Minute Book, vol. 4, pt. 4, 875. Scholars now agree that the court masques were parallel in that the principal "inventor" was the surveyor—for instance, Inigo Jones, whose work took primacy over the poet's text. Cf. Edmond, *Rare Sir William Davenant,* 65.

34. A detailed description of the building is in Thornbury, *Old and New London,* 1:501–3 and 2:4.

35. Cf. Grocers' Company, Calendar to the Minute Book, vol. 4, pt. 3, 764, and vol. 4, pt. 4, 880; Clothworkers' Company, Orders of Courts 1649–1665, 212; GH MS. 15,869. L. J. Morrissey calls "German" "the architect" in his "Theatrical Records of the London Guilds," 102.

36. GH MS. 15,869, Triumph's Accounts 1604–1699 (Haberdashers' Company); Clothworkers' Company, Quarter and Renter Warden's Accounts 1649–1699 for 1658–59 and Orders of Courts 1649–1665 for 12 April 1659; GH MS. 11,571, "Payments and Charges for Lord Mayors Day." Only the Haberdashers record payment to a poet except for copies of printed books describing the entertainment. Morrissey notes that earlier Settle received the same £12 as Tatham ("Theatrical Records of the London Guilds," 105). In 1638 and 1639, the Drapers paid John and Mathias Christmas for the pageants and left it for them to pay the poet Heywood (Calendar of Dramatic Records, xliii).

37. Sir John Robinson added a pageant on his own initiative in 1662. See Clothworkers' Company, Orders of Courts 1649–1665 for December and January 1662–63.

38. PRO PC 2/55, 74.

39. CLRO, Remembrancia, vol. 9, MS. 35c, fol. 4.

40. Arthur Bryant, *King Charles II,* 134–35, 138.

41. Grocers' Company, Calendar to the Minute Book, vol. 4, pt. 4, 912–13; Clothworkers' Company, Orders of Courts 1649–1665, 199.

42. The Clothworkers responded to the Lord Mayor's directive on 16 August with the report that they were "very willing but because of the short time they could not repair or hav in readiness any thing of Padgentry," and they ordered the Company Court to "take no further notice" of the request. The Court of Aldermen, however, wrote "to will and require you forthwith to prepare and have then attending on your Barge something of Pagentrie . . . you are not to fayle but to observe" (Orders of Courts 1649–1665, for 1 August–19 August 1662).

43. CLRO Cast Accounts 1/11 for 20 September 1661–10 September 1662.

44. Hutton, *Charles the Second,* 163.

45. When he finally renewed it two years later (June 1663), he went so far as to remove William Love, one of the City's M.P.'s (PRO PC 2/55, 407; Sharpe, *London and the Kingdom,* 2:396 and 403).

46. CLRO Letter Book UU, fol. 125; Sharpe, 2:399.

47. Hutton, *Charles the Second,* 195.

48. She processed from Greenwich to the Tower; the barges and pageants and the crowd's reactions are described in Anglo, *Spectacle Pageantry,* 247–48.

49. Hutton, *Charles the Second,* 166.

50. The illustration omits the barges carrying the livery; the text of Tatham's *Aqua Triumphalis* and Company minutes confirm that the pageants were in front.

51. Petrides, *State Barges on the Thames,* 19 and illustrations. Some of the companies wanted special music. The Clothworkers, whose minutes show more interest in music than any others I have read, asked a member to try to furnish the Company "with a Consorte of strange musicke for the credit and accommodation of the livery in the barge" and instructed him, if he failed, not to hire any string music (Orders of Courts 1649–1665, 197, for 6 August 1662).

52. Rugge, "Mercurius Politicus Redivivus," 372–74.

53. Tatham, *Aqua Triumphalis,* not paginated.

54. CLRO Repertory 68, fol. 166 for 31 July 1662.

55. Tatham, *Aqua Triumphalis,* 2.

56. Defoe, *Complete English Tradesman,* 3:128; and see Backscheider, *Daniel Defoe,* 510–15.

57. Reedy, "Mystical Politics," 28. On the Commonwealth and later conception of naval power and commercial wealth as inseparable, see Brewer, *Sinews of Power,* 168–69.

58. *London's Triumph: Presented in several Delightfull Scenes.* I have found but one copy of this show (in the British Library). The writing and design styles seem quite different from Tatham's. This author writes in the dedication to Robinson that "the *Employment* it self was so wholly *Strange* to me, that it never till now fell within my Disquisition"; although Tatham used the obligatory apologies, he could not, and in other places did not, say the work was "strange" to him. Moreover, Tatham usually signs his work, and the printer is Brome, one he was not known to use. There is no reason to assign this pageant to Tatham.

59. The phrase is from Thomas Fuller, *The History of the Worthies of England,* 1:137; see also the subtitle of Thomas Deloney's *The Pleasant Historie of John Winchcomb,* originally published 1597, in the tenth edition by 1626 and twelfth in 1662. Quotations are from the Oxford, Clarendon edition, 1912, edited by Francis Mann. I am grateful to my colleague Rosemary Kegl for sharing her work on Jack of Newbury.

60. The publication date of the chapbook is not certain; Tias printed copies to sell at 2d, for 500 copies were inventoried with his estate for the Orphans Court (Spufford, *Small Books and Pleasant Histories,* 259). Another edition became the property of Cluer Dicey, who inherited his father's printing business in 1736 and about the same time acquired John Cluer's Bow Church Yard business. I am grateful to Jan Fergus of Lehigh University for advice and assistance with this note.

61. In Deloney's text he says, "Let me rest in my russet coate" (38).

62. See Jack's final speeches for the poet's explication of his symbolism. Indeed, the poet says he has brought the characters back together for this purpose (19).

63. Davenant's spectacular revival of Shakespeare's *Henry VIII* in December 1663 is a typical example and may also include covert criticisms of the king's lifestyle.

64. See Bergeron, *Thomas Heywood's Pageants,* especially 6–9. Bradbrook finds Catherine "very surprisingly resurrected" ("Politics of Pageantry," 71).

65. Tatham, *London's Triumph Celebrated the Twenty-ninth of October 1664,* 6–8. Bergeron says that only Heywood regularly incorporated the patron saint of the sponsoring guild; St. Catherine of the Haberdashers had given important speeches in 1631 and 1632 (*Thomas Heywood's Pageants,* 6–7).

66. Fuller, *History of the Worthies of England,* 1:137; see also *Victoria History of the Counties of England,* 4:149–50.

67. Although the account books of the companies are hard to interpret, I offer a few comparative figures: in 1659, the Drapers' Warden's Minutes cites £132.17.8 for pageants and other related charges; the Haberdashers' Triumph's Accounts 1604–1699 gives £549.10 for the pageants and the costumes of the figures on them (GH MS. 15,869); the Grocers' Company Calendar to the Minute Book records that Jermyn gave £400 as the whole charge for the pageants and actors. Unless otherwise noted, records are still kept by the companies.

68. Orders of Courts 1649–1665, 6 and 24 October 1662 and 20, 27 January, and 16 March 1662/63; and Quarter and Renter Wardens' Accounts for 1662–1663. I am grateful to the Company for use of the manuscripts and permission to quote. In 1664, the Haberdashers paid Jerman £30, the painters £104, and Cleere and other workmen £549 (GH MS. 15,869, fols. 36–37; CSPD, 537–38). Complaints about Robinson continued to be made; in 1665, for instance, a prisoner lodged a formal charge that he received £3 per day from the prisoners in the Tower and kept it as personal profit (CSPD for August 1665).

69. Information on St. Paul's is from Weinreb and Hibbert, *The London Encyclopedia;* Thornbury, *Old and New London;* and Benham, *Old St. Paul's Cathedral.* The quotation is from *The London Encyclopedia,* s.v. "St. Paul's."

70. On 3 October 1660, a sixty-ounce piece of plate was sent Robinson as a christening gift for his child (PRO LC 5/137).

71. *His Majesties Commission Concerning the Reparation,* 12–13.

72. Reresby, *Memoirs,* 35. Sir John Reresby, son of a Royalist, became part of Queen Henrietta Maria's entourage at the Palais Royal and the special friend of Princess Henrietta Maria. At the Restoration he was "much at the King's Court, and often at the Queen Mothers"; he was finally preferred to the position of governor of York (27–32, 35–36). By 31 December, even Pepys was pronouncing the court "sad, vicious, negligent."

73. J. R. Jones, *Country and Court,* 142; Arthur Bryant, *King Charles II,* 148–55.

74. Arthur Bryant, *King Charles II,* 158–60; J. R. Jones, *Country and Court,* 147, 157–58. Jones says that the Act of May 1662 "permanently divided the nation" (148).

75. Tatham, *London's Triumph Celebrated In Honour of . . . Sir Anthony Bateman.*

76. Hutton, *Charles the Second,* 140, 168–70; J. R. Jones, *Country and Court,* 143–45.

77. Cibber, *Apology,* 63, 65–66.

78. Thompson, "Moral Economy of the English Crowd," 78. Compare Habermas, *Structural Transformation of the Public Sphere,* 54–58, 64–67.

79. For a full discussion of this myth and Steele's periodical and its voice, see Kathy Ivey, "My Persona, My Self," University of Rochester doctoral dissertation, 1991. The best discussion of the historical roots and significance of the myth is in Hill, *Puritanism and Revolution,* 57–74, 87–93.

80. Quoted in Mitchell, *Iconology, Image, Text, Ideology,* 140–41. Mitchell points out that this opinion shaped Burke's reaction to Paine's demand that the Constitution must be written.

81. Hill, *Intellectual Origins of the English Revolution,* 193.

82. Shoemaker, "London 'Mob' in the Early Eighteenth Century," 282; see also 286–87, 298, and 301.

83. Shoemaker, "London 'Mob' in the Early Eighteenth Century," 293; Rogers, *Whigs and Cities,* 354–55. Hill cites a study that argues that the legend arose as urban resistance to feudal lords (*Puritanism and Revolution,* 59), and notes its appeal to merchants and gentry who felt their property endangered (67–69).

84. Mullaney, *Place of the Stage;* Mullaney is speaking primarily of Stow's *Survey,* which, he says, is organized by the course of Elizabeth's precoronal progress (15–18).

85. These dates are certain, as is the fact that he did not attend in 1662, although the City prepared a collation for him at the usual private house. It is not clear whether he attended in 1663, but it is unlikely because of the queen's dangerous illness. In 1661, the refreshments cost the City £68.5.7; in 1664, the cost was £112.15.0 (CLRO 36B Royal Entertainment, book for 1714–27; CLRO Misc MS. 237.5 and Small MS. Box 15, no. 7; CLRO Repertory 68, fol. 219, shows that the king was expected in 1662; Arthur Bryant, *King Charles II,* 168).

86. Information about Howard's life is from Oliver, *Sir Robert Howard,* and from Thurber's introduction to *Sir Robert Howard's Comedy.*

87. Pepys, *Diary,* 8 December 1666. Among Howard's offices were Clerk of the Patents in Chancery and Serjeant Painter (CSPD, and *Diary,* 20 February 1668, respectively).

88. Robert Hume describes these elements of the play as "clichéd," in *Development of English Drama,* 112.

89. Robert Hume, *Development of English Drama,* 114; A. H. Scouten, "Plays and Playwrights," in *The Revels History of Drama in English,* 5:166–69.

90. Staves, *Players' Scepters,* 203.

91. It was usual, of course, for women to manage the home and the estate during times when the husband was absent. Moreover, it was common for women to be sent to work with the Committee of Sequestration; in fact, men advised other men to send their wives. See George, *Women in the First Capitalist Society,* 30, 37–39; Thomas Knyvett's letters reprinted in Lamont and Oldfield, *Politics, Religion, and Literature in the Seventeenth Century,* 95–96; and Hilda Smith, *Reason's Disciples,* 54–55. Women's armed defenses of their estates were not unknown; cf. George, 192–93. The position of feminist scholars and historians as a group coincides with that of Phyllis Mack, who says that "the burgeoning feminism of the seventeenth century" was "squelched" by "the cult of sentimentalism" and the "rise of the domestic

woman" ("History of Women in Early Modern Britain," 719).

92. Historians often comment on the rigid behavior of both sides; Arthur Bryant, for instance, says, "The Cavaliers in Parliament in no way shared their sovereign's capacity for forgetting the past" (*King Charles II,* 140).

93. Harbage, *Cavalier Drama,* 188.

94. Quoted in Hilda Smith, *Reason's Disciples,* 54–55.

95. Behn, *Love-Letters between a Nobleman and His Sister,* 117–18.

96. Abraham Cowley, *Cutter of Coleman-Street,* 261; *London Stage,* 1:44. According to Downes, however, it ran "a whole Week with a full Audience" (*Roscius Anglicanus,* 57).

97. John Wilson, *The Cheats,* 11; Burnet, *History of His Own Time,* 1:178. Pepys liked Howard's play better in 1668 than he had in 1662, and it did seem to grow in popularity.

98. Durfey made his heroine the daughter of a Roundhead, and Kinglove rejects her until he discovers this act of loyalty. The longing for unity and national harmony is part of this blatantly Tory play.

99. Jameson, *The Political Unconscious,* 286–92, and "Metacommentary," 15–17.

100. PRO LC 5/137 for 6 November 1662. Another typical entry is £149 for painting and gilding the king's barge (18 December 1660, fols. 392 and 64, respectively).

101. A famous example is Farquhar's *Beaux's Stratagem.*

102. Dryden, *Conquest of Granada,* 3:[15].

103. Pepys, *Diary,* 8 May 1668; Thurber, *Sir Robert Howard's Comedy,* 13–15; Robert Hume, *Development of English Drama,* 259–60.

104. Chesterfield's speech on the stage licensing bill, May 1737, in *The Works of Lord Chesterfield,* lxvii.

105. On its publication and production, see Thurber, *Sir Robert Howard's Comedy,* 39 and 133; it was "canonized" in the eighteenth century by being included in many collections of plays and in being selected for repertories, including one that went to America (Marion Jones, "Actors and Repertory," *Revels,* 5:156).

106. Morrice's "Entring Book," 24 July 1686, Dr. Williams Library MS. 31.P, fol. 580; I am grateful to them for permission to quote.

107. *Spectator,* 25 March 1712; quoted in Oliver, *Sir Robert Howard,* 52. Tim Harris gives numerous examples of the "association of puritans" with Catholics in *London Crowds,* 33–34.

108. *Poetical Register* (17$\frac{19}{20}$), 1:143; quoted in Oliver, *Sir Robert Howard,* 52–53. The play was acted at least eleven times at both theaters in 1718–19 and eight in 1719–20. The only record of a banned play that I can find is early July 1719 at Lincoln Inn's Fields, but the reference does not seem to be to *The Committee.* See Milhous and Hume, *Register of English Theatrical Documents,* 2:611–12.

109. Cf. Milhous and Hume, *Register of English Theatrical Documents,* 2:594, which quotes Theobald's *Censor* as saying people find political meanings that the author never intended.

110. Jauss, *Toward an Aesthetic of Reception,* 22–23, 25.

111. Marinis, "Dramaturgy of the Spectator," 100–114. See Lois Potter, "The

Plays and the Playwrights, 1642–60," on the "curious double view of Tatham's *Distracted State*" as tragedy and satire (*Revels*, 4:273), and Staves on *Hudibras*, in *Players' Sceptres*, 207. Potter discusses a fascinating example of this kind of play, John Rowe's *Mercurius Britannicus* (1641), which, she says, is deliberately left incomplete (*Secret Rites and Secret Writing*, 85). In his discussion of Interregnum political romances, Paul Salzman identifies several that lack resolution (*Argenis, Theophania*) and comments that one "ends on the note of uncertainty which one might expect from a royalist romance written in 1645" (*English Prose Fiction*, 148–56).

112. These questions, of course, came to dominate the work of John Locke and a series of great English philosophical thinkers.

113. Geertz, *Interpretation of Cultures*, 311–18.

114. See Habermas, *Structural Transformation of the Public Sphere*, 52–53, 57–67. Notably he locates the birth of this change in the controversy over the principle of absolute sovereignty.

115. Kenneth Burke, *Attitudes toward History*, 179.

116. I think not only of print, and especially of the newspaper, periodical, and novel, but also of the sporadic struggle of the theater to reach a large, diverse audience (the 1730s, for example).

117. Habermas, *Structural Transformation of the Public Sphere*, 29, 51, et passim.

118. Margaret Greer says, "The conspicuous presence of the ruling figures, given the appropriate cues in the drama, would almost inevitably result in a political construct" ("Art and Power," 333).

119. Butler, *Theatre and Crisis*, especially 49–82, 135–36, and 220–28; Albert Tricomi, *Anticourt Drama in England*, 167–89.

120. Butler, *Theatre and Crisis*, 227–28.

121. Tatham, *The Distracted State*, in *Works*, 52 and 66.

122. Martin Butler (*Theatre and Crisis*) discusses in some detail the parallels between some dramatic strategies and both the prose of Puritan political controversy and the ballads and pamphlets of burlesque news. Although he is writing about literature immediately before the Restoration, much of what he says applies equally well to 1660; see, for example, 232–48.

123. See Rogers, "The Crowd in Urban Politics," in *Whigs and Cities*, 347–89; and J. B. Williams, *History of English Journalism*, vi–vii, 30.

124. Geertz, *Interpretation of Cultures*, 318.

PART TWO. NEGOTIATING THE TEXT

1. Barbauld, "On the Origin and Progress of Novel-Writing," 62.

2. Woolf, *A Room of One's Own*, 68.

3. Weimann, "Text, Author-Function, and Appropriation," 435.

4. For studies of how writing became respectable again see especially Spencer, *Rise of the Woman Novelist;* Todd, *Sign of Angellica;* and Armstrong, *Desire and Domestic Fiction*. Late Renaissance critics such as Margaret Ezell argue that manuscript "publication" and the writing of noncreative literature was respectable earlier (*Patriarch's Wife*).

5. Staves, "Where Is History?" 141.

6. The term is Michel Foucault's. See "What Is an Author?" especially pp. 121–127, 130–31. Foucault notes that the author function "refers to the *status* of this discourse within a society and a culture" (emphasis mine) (123).

CHAPTER 3. REPRESENTATION AND POWER

1. Jordan and Love, Introduction to *Oroonoko, The Works of Thomas Southerne,* 2:90–91. The other was Cibber's *Love's Last Shift;* Pix's *Ibrahim* and *The Spanish Wives* were moderately successful and became repertory pieces. Trotter's *Agnes de Castro* was, according to Jacqueline Pearson, a "modest success" (*Prostituted Muse,* 181). F. P. Lock notes that one-third of the total new plays that season were by women, "probably the highest proportion ever" ("Astrea's 'Vacant Throne,'" 30). In that same year, *Poems on Several Occasions,* by Elizabeth Singer Rowe, was published with a "Preface to the Reader" that celebrated female achievement. Also that year, Briscoe published *The Histories and Novels of the Late Ingenious Mrs. Behn* with a biographical sketch. In the summer of 1992, Ariadne's *She Ventures* was performed at the Man-in-the-Moon Theatre in Chelsea, and plays by both Pix and Trotter were also produced in London.

2. A good account of these events is in Judith Milhous, *Thomas Betterton,* 51–112.

3. Robert Hume, *Development of English Drama,* 809; Milhous, *Thomas Betterton,* 68–72, 75–79, 97–98.

4. Prologue to *She Ventures, and He Wins.* On the nature of the competitive climate, see Milhous, *Thomas Betterton,* 80, 88–94.

5. Laclau, *Politics and Ideology,* 148; see Gramsci, who says that a crisis in the ruling class's hegemony may occur when "huge masses . . . have passed from a state of political passivity to a certain activity" (*Prison Notebooks,* 210–11). The recognition of this aspect of the period is now generally accepted: see Alice Clark, *Working Life of Women.* And David Roberts makes a cogent argument for women's deliberative behavior (*The Ladies,* 133–44, 157–65). Various impetuses for it have been posited; Susan Staves and others find it in Protestantism and in changes in political power (see Staves, *Players' Scepters,* 184–89). The works of the feminist controversy are too well known to require discussion; among the major works by women were Mary Astell's *A Serious Proposal to the Ladies* (1694) and Judith Drake's *An Essay in Defence of the Female Sex* (1696).

6. John Crowne, John Banks, and Thomas Southerne were among the playwrights who were reputed to take women's tastes into careful consideration. On women's power in the theater, see Roberts, *The Ladies;* Milhous, *Thomas Betterton,* 76; Pearson, *Prostituted Muse,* 49; and Robert Hume, "Marital Discord in English Comedy," 248–72.

7. "To Mrs. Manley, upon her Tragedy called *The Royal Mischief,*" one of the prefatory poems to Manley's *The Royal Mischief* (1696).

8. Critics have called this play a comedy of intrigue; but in structure, character configuration, language, and outcome it conforms to the "wit" comedies of the period. As Linda Payne points out, "None of the intrigues that are *hinted at* are actually executed" (emphasis mine) ("Delarivière Manley," in *Dictionary of Literary Biography* 80: 129).

9. The Cotterell edition begins with the Restoration courtier poems and a few addressed to male friends, but the great number, and the most praised then as now, are on Philips's private friendships and experiences, especially with women.

10. Preface to *The Lost Lover* (1696).

11. Behn's *Agnes de Castro* is, in fact, a translation of the novella by J. B. de Brilhac. Gary Kelly explains that it is based upon but differs from the lives of actual people ("'Intrigue' and 'Gallantry,'" 187–88). Jeslyn Medoff points out that Trotter did not acknowledge her debt to Behn, but Behn's translation was so well known that it may not have been necessary ("Daughters of Behn," 40).

12. Philips's most serious competitor, one who is often given precedence over her, is Anne Finch, countess of Winchilsea. Statistical studies of women's writing show that poetry was the most frequently chosen genre for women; for 1660–1800 Judith Stanton has counted 263 poets, 201 novelists, and 71 playwrights ("Statistical Profile of Women Writing in English," 247–54).

13. Harriette Andreadis notes that as late as 1817 John Keats used Philips as "the female standard of excellence toward which other women ought to aspire" ("Sapphic-Platonics of Katherine Philips," 34 and 34n. 1). For a summary of her present-day reputation, see this essay, 35–36; Hobby, *Virtue of Necessity*, 128–35; and Roger Lund, "*Bibliotecha* and 'the British Dames,'" 100–104.

14. Preface to posthumous edition of Philips's poems, reprinted in Saintsbury, *Minor Poets of the Caroline Period*, 1:490. Hobby points out that "before the widespread use of printed books," manuscript circulation was "the normal way to make writing public" (*Virtue of Necessity*, 129). Hobby's use of "public" is different from mine; I would date "widespread use" somewhat earlier than she. See Ezell, *Patriarch's Wife*, especially 62–100.

15. Joan DeJean notes that "hyperbolic affirmations of female . . . advancement beyond previous norms" were *de rigueur* and points out that Mme. de Lafayette was "usually called 'the Incomparable'" ("Lafayette's Ellipses," 899). Paul Hunter is typical, however, in believing that Philips was "rather patronizingly" so-called (*Before Novels*, 369n. 10).

16. Other poems by Cowley are not so fulsome. His "Ode. On *Orinda*'s Poems" is a strange, rather offensive poem filled with fertility imagery: "'Twere shame and pity, *Orinda*, if in thee / A Spirit so rich . . . / Should unmanur'd, or barren lye"; and "That like the *Holland* Countess thou may'st bear / A Child for every day of all the fertile year."

17. Lund, "*Bibliotecha* and 'the British Dames,'" 100. See also Souers, *Matchless Orinda*, 248–49.

18. The fullest discussion of this topic is in Gerald MacLean, "What Is a Restoration Poem?" 330–34, although it is present in almost all studies of Philips. Lillian Faderman concludes in *Surpassing the Love of Men* that "romantic friendships" such as those Philips described do not have to be "genital" to be lesbian: "women who identify themselves as lesbian generally do not view lesbianism as a sexual phenomenon first and foremost. What romantic friends wanted was to share their lives, to confide and trust and depend upon each other, to be there always for each other" (142; and see especially 15–18, 27–29, 45–46, 68–72, 115–18, 125, 411–12). David Roberts cites evidence that one of the Mothers of the Duchess's Maids was forced to resign because of her "fondness" for the "fair sex" (*The Ladies,* 106).

19. De Beauvoir, *The Second Sex,* 604–7.

20. Jane Barker includes a vision of "Orinda" on a throne "as Queen of Female Writers," in her *Lining of the Patch-Work Screen,* 174; Ruth Perry argues persuasively that celibacy was physiological emancipation, which "spared life and health" ("Veil of Chastity," 141–58). One of Jane Barker's poems asks, "Why was I . . . a Female born / Or did I not with Teeth, or Rickets die" (*Amours of Bosvil and Galesia,* 40). Janet Todd, too, discusses the "praise of spinsterhood and celibacy"; I do not agree with her that it is "peculiar" to the seventeenth and early eighteenth centuries or that it is more common in poetry (*Sign of Angellica,* 29–30, 42).

21. Elizabeth Carter, "To———. Occasioned by an Ode Written by Mrs. Catherine Philips" (1762), and Eliza Tuite, "To a Friend Written, 1782" (1796), in Fullard, *British Women Poets,* 81 and 84, respectively.

22. Several good recent books, primarily about the novel, have traced this constraining movement in the century. See Jane Spencer's *Rise of the Woman Writer;* Nancy Armstrong's *Desire and Domestic Fiction;* and Janet Todd's *Sign of Angellica.* Spencer points out that Philips contributed to the "transference of the status of literary heroine" to literary women ("Creating the Woman Writer," 168). Pearson notes that Pix, Trotter, and Manley "illustrate the range of different ways in which a woman writer could work and be perceived" (*Prostituted Muse,* 171–201).

23. Nancy Cotton summarizes some of the translations and their performances in *Women Playwrights in England,* 28–43. Orrery also knew the adventurous and rather liberal William Davenant, who had put actresses on the London stage in 1656, and Queen Henrietta Maria, who performed in court masques and pastorals. Maureen Mulvihill gives an excellent summary of the contributions made to her production ("Feminist Link," 82–95).

24. Information about her life is from Elaine Hobby, *Virtue of Necessity;* Fidelis Morgan, *Female Wits,* 3–11; Patrick Thomas, *Katherine Philips (Orinda);* and Philip Souers, *Matchless Orinda.* Souers also notes the romantic and exaggerated reputation she gained. Thomas quotes Aubrey as identifying Mrs. Salmon as "a famous schoolmistris, Presbyterian" (3).

25. Philips, *Letters from Orinda to Poliarchus* (1705); on the Herringman dispute, see Mambretti, "Orinda on the Restoration Stage," 244–45; Philips, *Letters from Orinda to Poliarchus,* 127–28 (for 15 April 1663); and Mulvihill, 71–104.

26. So that Philips could "explain them as I thought fit," she asked Poliarchus (Cottrell) to "make use of [Italian] in whatever you intend should be private" (25–26).

27. See *Letters,* 142, 149, 169–70, and 192–94.

28. See *Letters,* 112, 122–23, and 142–43.

29. Mulvihill, "Feminist Link," 73.

30. Quoted in Hobby, *Virtue of Necessity,* 140–41.

31. On these publications and her notoriety as a writer, see Hobby, *Virtue of Necessity,* 129; and Patrick Thomas, *Katherine Philips,* 9–12.

32. It should be noted that until recently Cotterell's interpretation of Philips's distress has been accepted uncritically. Recently Hobby has pointed out that Philips's objections to the corrupt, published texts of her poems were well-founded (*Virtue of Necessity,* 132–33, 221n. 11), and Mulvihill notes that some of the poems were not hers ("Feminist Link," 91–92).

33. Ezell, *Patriarch's Wife,* especially 62–100. The quotation is from p. 100.

34. Such disclaimers were, of course, conventional; see Hobby, *Virtue of Necessity,* 130–31.

35. *Horace,* completed by John Denham, was performed at court by amateurs in February 1668 and at Killigrew's Theatre Royal the next year (Mambretti, "Orinda on the Restoration Stage," 249; Pearson, *Prostituted Muse,* 288). Pearson also discusses her plays briefly (122–23).

36. Ballard quoting Aubrey, who was the cousin of her dear friend Mary Aubrey ("Rosania" in her poems); Anne Killigrew, "Upon the Saying That My Verses Were Made by Another," in Fullard, *British Women Poets,* 22.

37. Abraham Cowley, "Upon Mrs. Philips her Poems," in Saintsbury, *Minor Poets of the Caroline Period,* 1:495. Keats and others to the present day have continued to assume her beauty; see Andreadis, "Sapphic-Platonics of Katherine Philips," 34n. 1.

38. Granger, *Biographical History of England,* 3:194; and compare to Granger's opinions of Cavendish, 4:61, and Behn, 4:59 and 172.

39. Ballard, *Memoirs of Several Ladies,* 269. Later books, such as Colman and Thornton's *Poems by Eminent Ladies,* uncritically repeated these judgments: see 2:214.

40. Ballard, *Memoirs of Several Ladies,* 269; Souers describes Philips's economic affairs in *Matchless Orinda,* 157–58, 210–11.

41. Philips's essays are mentioned in the preface to her poems (Saintsbury, *Minor Poets of the Caroline Period,* 492).

42. On her "ever more scandalous reputation," see Pearson, *Prostituted Muse,* 21. Carol Barash notes that the first anthologies of "women's poetry," which she dates to the 1750s, tended to exclude her, a sign that the process of replacing the complex woman with the author function that we know was well under way ("Political Possibilities of Desire," 165).

43. Reeve, "Address to the Reader," xi.

44. "A Pindarick to Mrs. Behn on her Poem on the Coronation. Written by a Lady" (published 1688), in Germaine Greer et al., *Kissing the Rod,* 262–63. Jane Spencer says unequivocally that "most" early women writers saw their work "as part of a feminine tradition" (*Rise of the Woman Novelist,* 63).

45. Reeve, *Progress of Romance,* 1:117–19. Reeve blames the times for the licentiousness she acknowledges to be in Behn's work and concludes, "Let us do justice to her merits, and cast the veil of compassion over her faults" (118).

46. Manley's cousin and legal guardian, John Manley, posed as a widower long enough to marry her and squander her inheritance. She was about fourteen years old, he over thirty. Swift called John Manley a "beast" (Fidelis Morgan, *Woman of No Character,* 41, 47).

47. Mulvihill claims that Philips was important for showing the possibilities for a public career and identifies some relatives who may have served as literary models for her ("Feminist Link," 72 and 79–81).

48. "To the Reader," *Sir Patient Fancy,* in *Works of Aphra Behn,* 4:7. Farm and domestic work, the most available labor, required considerable physical strength and stamina. Some women could work in the cloth trade or as shopgirls; only heavy, arduous needlework such as stitching stays, quilting, and binding shoes with cloth

paid a living wage. Middle-class women, regardless of their need, were often turned away with apparently well-intentioned and short-sighted rebuffs when they applied for work perceived as "beneath them" (George, *Women in the First Capitalist Society,* 207–8, 362nn. 91 and 92). In the dedication to Lord Maitland in *Oroonoko,* Behn referred to the "Fruits" of "my Industry."

49. In 1670, the year in which Behn's first play was produced, she, like Manley, was one of several women attempting to begin careers as playwrights. Her *Forced Marriage* opened at Lincoln's Inn Fields on 20 September; Elizabeth Polwhele's *Faithful Virgins,* licensed and probably produced, would also have been at Lincoln's Inn Fields, and Frances Boothby's *Marcelia* had premiered at Bridges Street, probably in the summer of 1669. Boothby's play, a tragi-comic exploration of domination and submission, failed and seems to have been her only performed play. Polwhele probably wrote two, perhaps three, plays, two of which survive and were probably performed (Milhous and Hume, "Two Plays by Elizabeth Polwhele"; Pearson, *Prostituted Muse,* 133–35 and 137–39).

50. Cixous, "Laugh of the Medusa," 245.

51. Woolf, *A Room of One's Own,* 69 and 68, respectively. Technically, Philips was middle class, yet she married into the gentry class and became the friend of courtiers and the nobility.

52. Foucault, *Power/Knowledge,* 198. Compare Gramsci on civil society and the family in *Prison Notebooks.*

53. Although *The Lucky Chance* was licensed on 23 April and entered in the Stationers' Register on 8 May, it does not appear in the Term Catalogues until 11 February 1687; Milhous and Hume speculate that there was an April production but publication (and perhaps the composition of this preface) was in 1687 ("Dating Play Premieres," 392–93).

54. Hannah Cowley expresses this latter sentiment vividly: "They will allow me, indeed to draw strong character, but it must be without speaking its language. I may give vulgar or low bred persons, but they must converse in a stile of elegance" ("An Address," *A School for Greybeards,* in *Plays of Hannah Cowley,* 2:vi). Katharine Rogers describes Finch as "a woman imprisoned in man-made conventions," in *Selected Poems of Anne Finch,* xv. Margaret Homans's *Bearing the Word* is a searching examination of the "collisions" between women's experiences and the language theories that underlie these positions: see especially xi–xiii, 4–5, 16–22, 32–33.

55. Years later, Samuel Richardson could have Clarissa say, "To be given up to a strange man; To be engrafted into a strange family; To give up her very Name, as a mark of her becoming his absolute and dependent property; To be obliged to prefer this strange man to Father, Mother,—to every body:—And his humours to all her own. . . . To go no-whither: To make acquaintance: to give up acquaintance: To renounce even the strictest friendships perhaps; all at his pleasure, whether she think it reasonable to do so or not . . ." (*Clarissa,* 1:207).

56. Bakhtin, *Dialogic Imagination,* 411.

57. "Plot patterns" may be those of the dominant ideology (pregnancy as the unmarried woman's punishment) or of the achievement of what Jonathan Culler has called "literary competence" (*Structuralist Poetics,* 113–30). I use "archetype" here as John Cawelti does, as story patterns that appeal in many different cultures (*Adven-*

ture, Mystery, and Romance, 5–6, 37–39). On reading women's texts, see Schweickart, "Reading Ourselves," 31–62; and Miller, *Subject to Change,* 83–90, 126–27.

58. The standard work on this subject is Elizabeth L. Eisenstein, *The Printing Press as an Agent of Change;* see also Louis B. Wright, *Middle Class Culture in Elizabethan England,* and Richard D. Altick, *The English Common Reader.* George Thomason, a London bookseller, collected over twenty-three thousand books and pamphlets between 1641 and 1660; in 1660, when Charles II tried to control the press by limiting the number of printing houses to twenty, there were at least thirty-four that had been prosperous enough to have posted the required £300 surety a few years earlier. My forthcoming book, *Novel/Drama: The Transforming Imagination,* develops the implications of the expansion of publishing opportunities.

59. These quotations are from, respectively, Damrosch, *God's Plot and Man's Stories,* 244; and Heilbrun, *Hamlet's Mother,* 109.

60. See, for example, Pearson, *Prostituted Muse,* 149–68; Diamond, "*Gestus* and Signature," 519–41; Zimbardo, "Aphra Behn," Kavenik, "Aphra Behn," and Cotton, "Aphra Behn and the Pattern Hero," all in *Curtain Calls,* 371–82. I do not intend to deny the important part that male dramatists played in these hegemonic processes; my focus here, however, is on a single feminist contribution.

61. Another example, but from a later period, is Hannah Cowley's *School for Greybeards,* an adaptation of Behn's *Lucky Chance.* Cowley calls Behn "a poet of the drama, once highly celebrated."

62. Candace Katz points out that Manley uses similar reversals in *The Lost Lover* ("Deserted Mistress Motif," 35).

63. Kristeva, "Oscillation between Power and Denial," 165.

64. Marie-Madeleine Pioche de la Vergne de Lafayette, *The Princess de Clèves,* 49 and 67, respectively. Quotations are from this edition.

65. Irigaray, *This Sex Which Is Not One,* 23–33; Cixous, "Laugh of the Medusa," 245–64.

66. Woodcock, *Aphra Behn,* 121; Williamson, *Raising Their Voices,* 213; Würzbach, *Novel in Letters,* 200.

67. Behn and other women writers came to use a double plot, with the plots made dialogic because of the contrast in foregrounded, orchestrated language; Chapter 4 discusses an example at some length. Later, Elizabeth Inchbald was to use a similar doubled plot in *A Simple Story* (1791). Margaret Homans reads *Wuthering Heights* as such a text and concludes that the first Cathy's story is a "refusal to enter . . . the Lacanian symbolic order," and that the second Cathy's story is the entry into the Law of the Father (*Bearing the Word,* 68 et passim). Independently, James Gill, in private correspondence, has made the intriguing argument that in *The History of the Nun* Isabella's husbands represent the "two aspects of mankind" and "recombine the law and pleasure of the father."

68. Howe, *Politics and the Novel,* 22–23. I am grateful to one of my former graduate students, Edward Katz, for calling my attention to this quotation.

69. Manley surely has Aphra Behn's powerful Angellica Bianca and La Nuche from the two parts of *The Rover* in mind; in part 2, Behn's Willmore marries La Nuche, the courtesan. See Pearson, *Prostituted Muse,* for the usual treatment of "ruined" women (73, 92–93). Among her conclusions is that marriage usually makes

"full reparation" to the woman (99). Richardson has Lovelace say in crude, blunt words, "MARRIAGE . . . thou seest, Jack, is an Atonement for all we can do to them. A true Dramatic Recompence!" (*Clarissa*, 6:227). For a discussion of the contrasts between several Restoration "cast mistresses" and Manley's character, see Katz, "Deserted Mistress Motif," 28–34.

70. Pearson, *Prostituted Muse*, 154.

71. Novak, "Closing of Lincoln's Inn Fields Theatre," 51. Southerne's *Wives' Excuse* includes a joke involving a play to be written called "Cuckolds make themselves" that is declared "likely to be 'popular among the women' and 'true among the men,'" thus suggesting that jokes turned on men held economic risks; quoted in Roberts, *The Ladies*, 151. *The Wives' Excuse* failed.

72. Blackstone, *Commentaries on the Laws of England*, 1:439–40. See also *The Forced Marriage* (1670), Erminia and Philander; *The Town Fop* (1676), Clarinda and Bellmour. Susan Staves discusses such "divorces" in *Players' Scepters* and defines some important similarities between Behn's and her contemporaries' marriage plays (160–74, 185–88). The most extended discussion of the validity of these marriages and possibilities for separation, annulment, and divorce is in Gellert S. Alleman, *Matrimonial Law;* see especially 6–8, 24, 26–27, 125–28. He points out that this play is one of several in which the characters "regard the contract as marriage and the marriage which violates the contract as adultery" (17).

73. *Ibrahim*, 25. Lurid descriptions of rape were something of a fad on the English stage; one of the most infamous is in Nathaniel Lee's *Lucius Junius Brutus* (1680). Pix has another in her *Conquest of Spain* (1705). Behn's are less sensational, but this female fear is realistically presented in her plays as well. For instance, Florinda in *The Rover* faces several men intent on forcing her to have sex.

74. Raymond Williams lists among these oppositional and alternative elements new meanings, values, practices, relationships, and kinds of relationships. He mentions perceptions of excluded human areas and the "coming to consciousness of a new class" as sources for the creation of these things. I would extend the second to include women, who can be accurately described in Williams's defining terms as a group, a rank, and a formation (*Marxism and Literature*, 113–14 and 123–27; *Keywords*, 60–69).

75. *Oroonoko* became "a repertory piece" in periodicals and in collections of novels. Both the *Oxford Magazine* (1736) and *The Ladies Magazine* (1753) serialized it at the request of "female correspondents" (Mayo, *Magazine Novel in the Magazines*, 211–12, 273, 404–5; Wiles, *Serial Publication in England*, 69); and Elizabeth Griffith included it in her *Collection of Novels*, calling it "long so popular, that the Editor . . . could not be excused from admitting it" ("Character of Oroonoko, and Anecdotes of its Author").

76. The poet wrote, "The Poetess *Afra,* next shew'd her sweet Face, / And swore by her Poetry, and her black *Ace,* / The Lawrel by a double Right was her own, / For the Plays she had writ, and the Conquests she had Won: / *Apollo* acknowledg'd 'twas hard to deny her . . ." (*Miscellaneous Works of His Grace George, Late Duke of Buckingham*, 48). Internal evidence suggests a composition date in the 1670s. The authorship of the poem is disputed; for a cogent account, see Vieth, *Attribution in Restoration Poetry*, 296–321. I am grateful to Robert Hume for this reference.

77. "To His Grace, William Duke of Devonshire," dedication of *Oroonoko* by Thomas Southerne (*Works of Thomas Southerne*, 2:102).

78. *Oroonoko*, 78.

79. Southerne's Widow Lackitt is also eager to marry.

80. *Oroonoko;* see 46 and 47. See also Robert Chibka on the narrator's liminal position ("'Oh! Do Not Fear a Woman's Invention,'" 510–37).

81. The friendship between Agnes de Castro and the princess has been cited as scarcely credible by reviewers, but later critics explain that it violates plot expectations for artistic purposes and "embodies dissent from the dominant tradition." See Miller, *Subject to Change*, 8; and Kendall, "Finding the Good Parts," 168. Kendall says that Trotter's play and others by women during the reign of Anne "forced [her] to imagine another sexual universe"; on the play, see 170–71. The historical Agnes became Don Pedro's mistress, then his second wife, and bore him several children (Gary Kelly, "'Intrigue' and 'Gallantry,'" 186–88).

82. See, for instance, "To my Excellent Lucasia, on our Friendship": "For thou art all that I can prize, / My Joy, my Life, my Rest. / No bridegroom's nor crown-conqueror's mirth / To mine compar'd can be: / They have but pieces of this Earth, / I've all the World in thee"; "To Mrs. Mary Awbrey": "How happy are we now, whose souls are grown, / By an incomparable mixture, one"; and "A Friend" (Saintsbury, *Minor Poets of the Caroline Period*, 1:537, 548, and 561–63, respectively).

83. Southerne may have made Imoinda white so that the governor's lust and willingness to rape her, a conventional stage tyrant-villain's action, would be more credible to the audience.

84. Keyssar, *Feminist Theatre;* see especially xii, 2–3, 22, and 33. Compare Nancy K. Miller's definition of feminist writing in *Subject to Change* (8).

85. This usage is well documented. See Todd, *Sign of Angellica*, 15, 27, 28, 218; Marsden, "Pathos and Passivity," 73–74, 78; and Goreau, who gives some examples, including the familiar "all women are born slaves" (Mary Astell) (*Reconstructing Aphra*, 290).

86. Chibka points out that he is whipped partly because the narrator does not trust him, although she still expects him to trust her ("'Oh! Do Not Fear a Woman's Invention,'" 523).

87. Other interesting adaptations include a series of *Oroonoko* plays: *Oroonoko: A Tragedy* (1759), by John Hawkesworth, and *Oroonoko, or The Royal Slave* (1760), by Francis Gentleman; the latter was performed in Edinburgh. George Canning and John Frere's *The Rovers; or, the Double Arrangement* (1798) is a parody of late century tastes and claims to be an adaptation of two German plays; it is not, as is occasionally said, an adaptation of Behn's *Rovers*. The Canning and Frere piece is the inspiration for *The Quadrupeds of Quedlinburgh* (1811), by George Colman the Younger. Jessica Munn finds the 1986 John Barton RSC revival of *The Rover* a similar kind of appropriation, in that Barton "simplifies" Behn's play and "obscures" Behn's exploration of the relationship between sex, love, and money and the issues involved in choices about life styles and sexual styles ("Barton and Behn's *Rover*," 11–22).

88. In order to shorten the play, Kemble cut such things as second sentences in

many speeches and Blunt's soliloquy. Typical excised Cavalier lines are those that say characters "suffer with the best of Kings."

89. Cf. Behn's essay on translation, prefixed to her translation of Fontenelle's *A Discovery of New Worlds*. Angeline Goreau cites this and other examples in *Reconstructing Aphra* (292); see also Maureen Duffy, *Passionate Shepherdess*, 271–75.

90. See especially "To the Reader," the epilogue to *Sir Patient Fancy*, and her preface to *The Lucky Chance*.

91. Several recent articles discuss Behn as constructing herself but disagree on what she was modeling herself upon and on the verbal motifs that she was using to speak of herself. Among them are Jessica Munn's " 'I by a Double Right Thy Bounties Claim'"; Frances Kavenik's "Aphra Behn: The Playwright as 'Breeches Part' "; and Catherine Gallagher's "Who Was That Masked Woman?"

92. Rebecca Gibson says she knows of "only two occurrences of the word 'labour' in the early prefaces," but she is concerned with poetry only; admissions of "labour," I believe, are as rare in drama (" 'My Want of Skill,'" 82). This article identifies some important features of women's prefaces, and my discussion has benefited from her categories.

93. Although my emphasis and point are different, I agree with Deborah Payne that Behn offers us a chance to do something needed: "examining more closely the construction of gender in cultures that do not offer women means of artistic self-representation outside of patriarchal models" and with her conclusions that we should not be surprised that "the only words available" to Behn were "My Masculine Part the Poet in me" (" 'And Poets Shall by Patron-Princes Live,' " 117).

94. Quoted in Milhous and Hume, "Two Plays by Elizabeth Polwhele," 1, 3. It would be the last part of the eighteenth century before women began to mock such statements. Hannah Cowley wrote, "I wrote merely to appease my sensation" (quoted in Gibson, " 'My Want of Skill,' " 82).

95. This protest, however, may be a convention; Linda Kauffman points out that Phaedra speaks of "writing as a compulsion; it overpowers all taboos, all modesty, and all injunctions" and equates it with love, "thus achieving what speech makes impossible . . . what modesty forbade to say, love has commanded me to write" (*Discourses of Desire*, 35). Frances Burney has one of her characters describe the urge to write coming "from within, over which she had no control . . . issuing from her vitals" (quoted from *Camilla* by Julia Epstein, in *The Iron Pen*, 19). The author of "The Lady Novelists" broods about "some hereditary organic tendency, stronger even than the domestic," 73; George Eliot or G. H. Lewis is the writer.

96. *The Lucky Chance* is, however, full of political allusions and comments. Among them are references to the quo warranto proceedings against the City (3), a dig at the Commonwealth (6), ridicule of those gullible about plots, and sustained satire of City attitudes.

97. *The Lucky Chance* play is political in that it continues the attack on City Whigs, and Behn may have had in mind the faction that worked to prevent its success.

98. Charles sent James abroad before Parliament met in 1679; later James went to Edinburgh (J. R. Jones, *Country and Court*, 204–5 and 210–11).

99. Deborah Payne describes Behn's dedication to James and also suggests that

Behn "subtly equates the battle between playhouse factions with the hardships endured by the roving cavaliers" ("Restoration Dramatic Dedication," 32–34). Behn often points to commendable conduct and aligns herself with good people in her dedications, as she does in *Oroonoko* to the earl of Rochester, and in *The Roundheads* to the duke of Grafton. Laurence Hyde, earl of Rochester and the son of Edward Hyde, earl of Clarendon, was the most effective director of royal finances before Sidney Godolphin; he served from 1679 to 1685 and was King James's Lord Treasurer (1685–86) (J. R. Jones, *Country and Court*, 48–49, 63–64).

100. Behn's play was probably acted in December 1681, and 1682 began the years sometimes labeled the "Stuart revenge," because of such royal initiatives as the quo warranto actions, the persecution of the Dissenters, and the purging of Whigs from government employment. The Whigs finally lost control of the City in the election of September 1682. The sheriffs of London and Middlesex, however, had been able to pack grand juries and prevent the prosecution of Shaftesbury and Francis Rouse. Both cases were dismissed by an *ignoramus* verdict, to which Behn refers in her dedication (J. R. Jones, *Country and Court*, 217–22).

101. "To Astrea on her Poems," in Behn's *Miscellany, Being a Collection of Poems by several Hands;* the author identifies himself as a country curate (89 and 87); "Upon These and Other Excellent Works of the Incomparable Astraea," in her *Poems upon Several Occasions,* respectively. "An Elegy Upon the Death of Mrs. A. Behn; The Incomparable Astrea. By a Young Lady of Quality" (licensed 22 April 1689) says, "Her Royal Master she has follow'd home / Nor would endure the World when he had lost his Throne." "To Madam A. Behn on the Publication of her Poems," by F.N.W., praises her: "Wou'd you the pattern see / Of spotless and untainted Loyalty / . . . Reade you then *Astrea*'s lines" (*Poems upon Several Occasions*).

102. Both Robert Hume and David Roberts cite evidence that a faction worked against Behn's play (Roberts, *The Ladies,* 31–32, 107–9, 128–29, and 129n. 5). Contemporary evidence to support Roberts's point is abundant; *The Reasons of Mr. Bays Changing his Religion* says Bays has "railed at Matrimony to ingratiate with the superannuated Maids of Honor" (24).

CHAPTER 4. WOMEN, MEN, AND THE INEXPRESSIBLE ROLE

1. I do not intend to deny all financial exigency; in the dedication to *Emperor of the Moon,* Behn complains that the "Town" is not able to support even one playhouse (*Works of Aphra Behn,* 3:391–92).

2. De Krey, "London Whigs," 462–63.

3. Schwoerer, "Propaganda in the Revolution of 1688–89," 843–74. Efforts to use drama as Charles had were rebuffed, as James's disastrous visit to the Artillery Company at Merchant Taylors' Hall in October 1679 showed. *A True Account of the Invitation and Entertainment of the Duke of York* asserts that he gave £200 toward the entertainment. There is also evidence that James paid playwrights, as he did Crowne for *Sir Courtly Nice.* See LC 5/148, fol. 195, which reads, "from His Majty" (9 January 16$\frac{87}{88}$).

4. "A Lenten Prologue refus'd by the Players," 1682.

5. Dryden's play was permitted to go into rehearsal in October and Crowne's in

December (PRO LC 5/144, for 15 and 26 June, 18 July, 29 October, 18 December). Lee and Dryden's play was performed on 30 November, and Crowne's on 19 January 1683. Five days after the opening, Crowne was severely beaten. Shadwell wrote of *The Duke of Guise* that it "insinuated by false Colours into the People, and as much as in him lies into the *King* a hatred to the Capital City . . . an aversion and contempt of the House of Commons . . . and seems chiefly to be written [to assassinate] a *Gallant* and *Innocent Prince*" (*Some Reflections,* 20–21). James A. Winn speculates that references to Monmouth and the sheriffs were behind the Lord Chamberlain's action and points out that the audience never heard some of them (*John Dryden and His World,* 370–71 and 381–83). Prologues that were approved and sold as propaganda included lines such as, "Kings can forgive if Rebels can but sue. . . . The Father yearns in the true Prince's Breast" (Dryden, "Prologue to his Royal Highness. Upon his first appearance at the Duke's Theatre since his return from Scotland" [London, 1682], GH Broadsheet, 16.91).

6. I can find no evidence that Behn or the actress named with her on the Lord Chamberlain's order to the messenger were detained, committed to prison, or indicted. Robert Hume gives the *Newdigate Newsletters* as the source for his statement that they "were thrown in jail," by which he means confined in the "porter's lodge" (*Development of English Drama,* 362n. 2). The order reads in part, "Whereas the Lady Slingsby Comedian and Mrs. Aphra Behen have by acting and writing at the Royall Highnesse Theatre comitted Severall Misdemeanors & made abusive reflections upon persons of Quality, & have written & spoaken Scandalous Speeches without any Lycense or Approba[t]ion of those that ought to peruse & authorize the same These are therefore to require you to take into y^r Custody the said Lady Slingby & Mrs. Aphra Behn & bring them before me to answer the said Offenses" (PRO LC 5/191, fol. 100, for 12 August 1682). James Derriman and I have also searched the box of "original warrants" in LC 5 (recognizance rolls), in LC 4/88 and LC 5/101 and 115, in the CLRO Sessions of Peace and of Oyer and Terminer, and, as a farfetched possibility, in the Pye Books, the indices of defendants in London and Middlesex indictments. I am grateful for his help.

7. According to Paul Salzman, *The Fugitive Statesman* is *Absalom and Achitophel* adapted into a novel (*"Absalom and Achitophel,"* 11–13).

8. McKeon, *Origins of the English Novel,* 268. In 1689, Behn wrote,

> While my sad Muse the darkest Covert Sought,
> To give a loose to Melancholy Thought;
> Opprest, and sighing with the Heavy Weight
> Of an Unhappy dear Lov'd *Monarch's* Fate;
> A lone retreat, on *Thames's* Brink she found,
>
> . . . .
> All of a suddain thro' the Woods there Rung,
> Loud Sounds of Joy that *Jo Peans* [*sic*] Sung.
> *Maria!* Blest *Maria!* was the Theam
>
> . . . .
> The Muses all upon this Theam Divine,
> Tun'd their best Lays, the Muses all, but mine,
> Sullen with Stubborn Loyalty she lay.

The poem goes on to pay tribute to Mary as bearing her father's "face" and reconciling the English people ("A Congratulatory Poem to her Sacred Majesty Queen Mary upon her Arrival in England" [1689], in *Uncollected Verse*, 159–60).

9. "Prologue to *Romulus* . . . Written by Mrs. Behn" and "Epilogue to the Same."

10. Mikhail Bakhtin describes this condition as distinctive to the novel form: see *Dialogic Imagination*, 31.

11. The phrase is J.M.S. Tompkins's and is quoted in Spacks, *Desire and Truth*, 175.

12. See, for example, John Mullan, *Sentiment and Sociability*, 100–101. I have modified his sentence slightly.

13. *Loyal Protestant and True Domestick Intelligence*, 26 August and 12 September 1682.

14. See *Loyal Protestant and True Domestick Intelligence*, 12 September, and *London Mercury*, 29 September–3 October 1682, for typical reports.

15. Price, *Cold Caleb*, 14. My account of Grey's life is largely based on this book and on the historical account in J. R. Jones, *Country and Court*. The accounts of the events of 1682–85 are augmented by the *London Gazette* and Morrice's "Entring Book," Dr. Williams Library MS. 31.P. As late as 1749, accounts of the trial were still being published; see, for example, *Whoredom, Fornication and Adultery, detected and laid open*, which was cited in the *Monthly Review* (September 1749) as "a copy of the proceedings at law, in the affair betwixt lord *Grey* and lady *Harriet Berkeley*, and her family; in the reign of K. *James* II. This is that nobleman and lady whose amours occasioned the publication of those two celebrated volumes, entitled love-letters betwixt a nobleman and his sister; with the history of their adventures." The notice also mentions that *Love-Letters* was "generally" attributed to Behn (394).

16. The *London Gazette, Benskin's Domestick Intelligence*, the *London Mercury*, the *Observator*, and the *Loyal Protestant and True Domestick Intelligence* all printed advertisements and news about the scandal. See, for instance, Lord Berkeley's advertisements in *London Gazette*, 21–25 and 25–28 September 1682 and *Loyal Protestant*, 3 October 1682; trial accounts in *Loyal Protestant*, 24 October and 14 November 1682.

17. Price, *Cold Caleb*, 24–26, 30–31, 48–49, and 55–58.

18. A disreputable informer, William Bedloe, was the first to implicate the queen, but it was not until Oates claimed that he had seen letters of thanks for large sums of money to her from the Jesuits and that she had known of a plan to poison the king that the Whigs began to try to discredit her (Mackay, *Catherine of Braganza*, 208–28; Hutton, *Charles the Second*, 362–63, 377–78).

19. Grey's fine was one of the four largest. Fines for the other twelve ranged from 100 to 500 marks (*London Gazette*, 25–28 June 1683).

20. *Love-Letters*, 112. All quotations are from the Penguin-Virago edition.

21. Price, *Cold Caleb*, 147.

22. In *The Lucky Chance*, she was to turn the City's gullibility about rumors of plots into high comedy.

23. Turner is identified in Morrice's "Entring Book," Dr. Williams Library MS. 31.P for 23, 25, and 28 November 1682. Behn says that Turner fought at Sedgmoor and escaped to Flanders (*Love-Letters*, 461).

24. It is important to remember that the authority and veracity of even the "newspaper" press was affected by the prominence of the families, their political positions, and the partisan nature of the press. The *London Gazette* carried Lord Berkeley's advertisement and brief notices about the trial. A few years later, Congreve's Mrs. Marwood describes how "Short-hand Writers" take notes at trials and give them "to the publick Press; and from thence be transferr'd to the Hands nay into the Throats and Lungs of Hawkers, with Voices more licentious than the loud *Flounderman's,* or the Woman that cries Grey-pease" (*Way of the World,* Act 5, ll. 214–20).

25. Robert Adams Day says that Behn's *Love-Letters* was "the first original piece of long fiction in English entirely in letters" (*Told in Letters,* 241).

26. On the publication history of *Lettres portugaises,* controversies over its authorship (perhaps Gabriel de Lavergne Guilleraques), and its importance to the literary history of the novel, see R. A. Day, *Told in Letters,* 32–38, and Kauffman, *Discourses of Desire,* 18–19, 19n. 3, 92–117. Day says that Behn "took over the Nun's method wholesale" and does not comment on the propaganda value of the work (37). Kauffman notes that "to write 'à la portugaise' became a veritable code for a certain style" (95); see also her citing of publication figures for imitations (95–96). On the publication history of *Five Love Letters,* see Day, 240n. 18.

27. See bibliographies in R. A. Day, *Told in Letters,* 239–41. Another extremely popular prose fiction was *Abelard to Eloisa,* of which two editions in Latin were published in 1616. Behn probably knew Jacques Allius's version of the story, *Les amours d'Abelard et d'Heloise* (Grenoble, 1676; first English translation 1714). In 1687, Bussy-Rabutin sent Mme. de Sévigné his version of three of the love letters in French; he added invented incidents, but this text appears not to have been printed until 1697 (see McLeod, *Héloïse,* appended bibliography). Alain Viala argues that the birth of French epistolary fiction proper can be dated to 1550–80, and that the decade 1650–60 is "plenitude du genre." He argues that the public was conscious of differences in kinds and practices within the genre and that writers such as Racine wrote all three (galante, polémique, moral) ("Genése des formes epistolaires," 168–83).

28. Behn mentions Marten in *Oroonoko,* and George Marteen is a sympathetic character in her *Younger Brother.*

29. Years later, Behn's own political novel would be issued as "Lord Grey's Incomparable Love-Letters to his Sister the Lady Harriot Barclay" in the *Oxford Journal* (1736) and as *The Several Love Letters that passed between a Nobleman and his Sister* (published in four installments in 1735 by T. Read) (Wiles, *Serial Publication in England,* 69, 216–17; and Mayo, *English Novel,* 211–12 and 273).

30. The quotation is from the preface to Gilbert Burnet's *History of His Own Time,* 1:5.

31. The postscript addressed to the reader explains the reasons for the duchess's coming to England; it and "The Letter" testify to the authenticity of the Memoirs and describe her physical appearance, personality, and deportment. Behn dedicated her *History of a Nun* to the duchess.

32. Hutton, *Charles the Second,* 336.

33. See Hutton on the king's reputation for philandering; I have relied on his

account for information about the duchess (335–38). The translator of the text was Henry Oldenburg, a German who had attended Oxford and had become one of the original members and the first secretary of the Royal Society. In 1667 he had been briefly imprisoned, probably because of his extensive foreign correspondence, and was living by translating in 1676 (*DNB*). There is no reason to think that he was not loyal to the king.

34. Gary Kelly correctly notes that Behn's other fictions, including the translations, are indebted to the French *nouvelle* ("'Intrigue' and 'Gallantry,'" 184–94). He does not discuss *Love-Letters*.

35. Ray, *Story and History,* 24 and 44n. 4; Haviland, "*Roman de Longue Haleine,*" 72–74. R. A. Day, *Told in Letters,* mentions that *Cléopâtre* has twenty-two histories and *Artamenes* thirty-two (216n. 22).

36. See, for example, Clavel, *General Catalogue of Books Printed in England,* which extended his *Catalogue of all the Books printed in England.* In this classified list, *The History of the Late Wars in Denmark* appears beside *Cassandra* and *Cleopatra.* The same is true of the third edition.

37. The Druid in *Astrea,* for instance, tells Silvia that she can learn to be armed "against the forces" of love, "lest being too secure in your opinion of that which you judge impossible, you should be surprised before you be prepared" (1:157).

38. "To the Reader," *Artamenes* (1691). Compare Humphrey Moseley's similar statement in "The Stationer to the Reader" in his edition of *Artamenes* (London, 1653): "our Author in this hath so laid his Sceans, as to touch upon the greatest Affairs of our Times: for, Designs of War and Peace are better hinted and cut open by a *Romance,* than by down-right Histories; which, being bare-fac'd, are forc'd to be often too modest and sparing; when these disguiz'd Discourses, freely personating every man and no man, have liberty to speak out" (quoted in Reed, "Humphrey Moseley," 94). Bakhtin calls it a roman à clef (*Dialogic Imagination,* 96).

39. Readers would have "met" "familiar situations and incidents . . . at every turn" in *Astrea* (Upham, *French Influence in English Literature,* 310). For a still-useful discussion of some of the historical elements of the romances, see Haviland, "*Roman de Longue Haleine,*" 70, 72–75, and 100–116. Haviland calls *Panthalia* a thinly disguised history of England (110–11). See also Salzman, *English Prose Fiction,* on the political and French romances (148–201).

40. See, for instance, Honoré D'Urfé's "To the Reader" prefixed to part 1, book 1, of *Astrea,* "Translated by a Person of Quality." These fictions were extremely popular in England at this time. In addition to the publication of new editions of La Calprenède's and de Scudery's romances, new ones such as the anonymous *Heliodorus* (1686), *Adelaide* (1686), and *Cynthia* (1687) were appearing.

41. *Astrea,* vol. 2, "To the Reader."

42. This quotation is from the work of one of Behn's biographers, George Woodcock ("Founding Mother of the English Novel," 32); it is not by any means atypical. In addition to the examples cited in the text, other aristocrats, including Sir William Sales, Sir Percy Herbert, and Lady Mary Wroth, wrote romances. Philips's confidant, Sir Charles Cotterell, translated part or all of La Calprenède's *Cassandra.* Eliza Haywood's *Love in Excess* (1719) is a misunderstood example of the French romance and was enormously popular, outselling all early eighteenth-century prose fictions

except *Robinson Crusoe* and *Gulliver's Travels*. *Parthenissa* (1654), by Roger Boyle, earl of Orrery, was in the fourth edition in 1676.

43. Manley, preface to *The Secret History of Queen Zarah* (1705). Southey and Coleridge were still enjoying *Argenis* (Salzman, *English Prose Fiction,* 149–50).

44. See Jameson, *Political Unconscious,* 204. The reasons for this change are many and complex. Among the most obvious are the breakdown in sumptuary laws, stratified fashions, and increased social mobility, which resulted from the rise of the merchant and commercial classes. Londa Schiebinger points out that anatomists in the eighteenth century came increasingly to "play down differences among males or females in order to heighten the contrast between the sexes," even as they were rejecting qualities associated with children or the lower classes ("unpolished roughness") in constructing the ideal male model (*Mind Has No Sex?* 201–2). See also Sennett, *Fall of Public Man,* 65–66; and Laqueur, *Making Sex,* 22, 135, and chapter 6.

45. Barthes, *A Lover's Discourse;* quoted in Kauffman, *Discourses of Desire,* 60.

46. *Five Love-Letters written by a Cavalier* may have appeared too late to have influenced Behn's work; however, she may have seen it in manuscript, for there is evidence that she and L'Estrange were friends: see "A Poem to Sir Roger L'Estrange" (1688). Robert Adams Day notes that *Astrea* contains 129 letters, *Artamenes* 117, and *Clelia* 121 (*Told in Letters,* 216n. 23). This perception of gendered discourse became more generally accepted in the eighteenth century; Mary Wollstonecraft, for example, discusses a number of gendered, and incidentally hegemonic, language systems in *A Vindication of the Rights of Woman* (1792). She writes self-consciously of how she intends "to persuade by the force" of her arguments and to avoid women's "flowery diction" and discourse that creates "a kind of sickly delicacy" (Introduction; see also chap. 5, sec. 2).

47. Gustav Shpet called the novel "the contemporary form of moral propaganda" (quoted in Bakhtin, *Dialogic Imagination,* 268).

48. Cf. *Love-Letters,* 33–36.

49. In the introductory chapter of her discussion of women and language, Margaret Homans quotes Lacan, "The phallus is the privileged signifier of that mark in which the role of the logos is joined with the advent of desire" (*Bearing the Word,* 7).

50. For Behn's propagandistic retelling, see 280–81, 341, 347, and 447–60. In order to make it clear that this book was a new continuation, she titled it *The Amours of Philander and Sylvia.* The combined three-part edition was in the third edition by 1708, the sixth by 1735, and the eighth in 1765. It was serialized at least twice (O'Donnell, *Aphra Behn,* 417).

51. Price, *Cold Caleb,* 175–76, 184–85, 188–91; Behn, *Love-Letters,* 452–56; R. A. Jones, *Country and Court,* 229.

52. William Ray finds the "personal, emotional struggle" of the Princess de Clèves framed by "an ongoing semi-public drama of gossip and local reportage," "the public domain of politics and history" (*Story and History,* 25). Nathaniel Lee's *Princess of Cleve [sic]* had been produced in 1682 or 1683 and was printed in 1689. See also Lynch, "Conventions of Platonic Drama," 456–71.

53. Grey eventually received an earldom and became a member of King William's Privy Council.

54. Cesario in *Love-Letters* makes the same argument; see 334.

55. The stage history of *Venice Preserved* indicates how open to reinterpretation the major characters were. For a perceptive discussion, see Taylor, *Next to Shakespeare*.

56. Oroonoko continues to be willing to sell slaves: "he was every day treating with *Trefry* for his and *Clemene's* Liberty, and offer'd either Gold, or a vast quantity of Slaves" (45).

57. Laura Brown, "Romance of Empire," 56–58. I obviously disagree with her identification of Oroonoko with Charles I and with George Guffey (and others) who identify him with James II (Guffey, "Aphra Behn's *Oroonoko*," 16–18, 34–36).

58. Evelyn, *Diary*, 4:455–56. In 1682, Monmouth stayed at Henrietta's house in Bedfordshire until his father's anger subsided. He was captured without weapons in a ditch (Evelyn, *Diary*, 4:452).

59. J.A.W. Gunn usefully compares the French, German, and British traditions in *Beyond Liberty and Property*, 264–67.

60. Bakhtin, *Rabelais and His World*, 367.

61. Ray, *Story and History*, 33 and 50, respectively. See especially 24–50.

62. Tompkins, "Sentimental Power," 85.

63. Faller, *Turned to Account*, 73–116. See especially 84, 89–92; and note the similarity of the crowd reaction to Mary Blandy (1752) and the illustration of her hanging (111–14).

64. This section is informed by Jürgen Habermas, *Structural Transformation of the Public Sphere;* see especially 18–67, 89–102.

65. *Love-Letters*, 447. Lois Schwoerer documents women's activities during the period, noting that they petitioned and participated in "demonstrations," and even, sometimes, initiated them ("Women and the Glorious Revolution," 195–218).

66. Quoted in Goreau, *Reconstructing Aphra*, 249.

67. Behn may have known the print showing Queen Henrietta Maria doing penance over the graves of six executed priests at Tyburn. Originally published in 1628, it is reprinted in the British Museum's extra illustrated copy of Thomas Pennant, *Account of London* (1790), illustrated by Crowle. The distinctive royal coat of arms appears on the coach. The print was circulating as a satire of the Catholic queen.

68. If Lincoln Faller is correct about the seventeenth-century criminal narrative being written to "counter" rather than explain the etiology of crime, then Behn's text is experienced quite differently and as more uninterpretable by modern readers than it was in her time. See *Turned to Account*, 68, 89.

69. Patricia Meyer Spacks discusses this fear in relation to Burney (*Imagining a Self*, 158).

70. Habermas, *Structural Transformation of the Public Sphere*, 24; he also notes that "there was talk of 'public'" in England from the middle of the seventeenth century (26).

71. Keeble, *Literary Culture of Nonconformity*, 87.

72. Some evidence that Behn's texts were read aloud survives. Sir Walter Scott quotes his great aunt's comments on Behn's novels: "sixty years ago, I have heard [them] read aloud for the amusement of large circles, consisting of the first and most creditable society in London" ("To Lady Louisa Stuart," in *Memoirs*, 5:597).

73. Londa Schiebinger discusses the overlap in membership among salons, acad-

emies, and writers for the *Journal des Savants* and notes that Julie de Lespinasse's salon "has been called 'the laboratory of the *Encyclopédie'*" (*Mind Has No Sex?* 30–32). David Roberts argues that "the art of conversation was in a state of flux" and that there was "a new refusal to recognize traditional distinctions between male and female conversation" (*The Ladies,* 23–26).

74. The correspondence between Dorothy Osborne and William Temple in *The Letters of Dorothy Osborne to William Temple* provides telling evidence; see, for example, the section in which they join in the inquiry of who is the most unhappy in *Le Grand Cyrus* and which characters they like most (81–82). See also Charlotte Morgan, *Rise of the Novel of Manners,* 2; Salzman, *English Prose Fiction,* 178–82; Michaelson, "Women in the Reading Circle," 59–69; Haviland, *Roman de Longue Haleine,* 15–16, 21; and Roberts, *The Ladies,* 18–19. Joan DeJean gives a fascinating account of how the French paper *Mercure Galant* turned its readers into commentators and discussants of *La Princess de Clèves* ("Lafayette's Ellipses," 888–89).

75. See Kauffman's discussion in *Discourses of Desire,* 305–7 et passim.

76. Both Habermas and Foucault theorize that the "zone of continuous administrative contact became 'critical' . . . in the sense that it provoked the critical judgment of a public making use of its reason." The quotation is from Habermas, *Structural Transformation of the Public Sphere,* 24.

77. Thompson, "Eighteenth-Century Crime," 9–11. James Boswell once schemed to try to revive a man to be hanged for sheep stealing; the willingness and unwillingness of his fellow citizens is telling and substantiates the point that these people felt responsible for endorsing or intervening in acts of "justice" (Mark Harris, *Heart of Boswell,* 362–64, 367, and 382–87).

78. This stance has been associated with the Tories and can be contrasted with that described in Defoe by John Richetti in *Defoe's Narratives.* Dryden, for instance, was deeply committed to a vision of the state which took for granted an idealized role for monarchical absolutism (Myers, *Dryden,* 120).

79. The quotation is from Gérard Gennette's *Narrative Discourse.* Linda Kauffman applies it to Rosa Colfield in *Absalom, Absalom!* (*Discourses of Desire,* 24).

80. Behn may parody lines from John Crowne's *Calisto,* in which Lady Henrietta had performed. One of her lines went, "In my lost heart a strange uncommon flame; / A kindness I both fear and blush to name; / Nay, one for which no name I ever knew, / The passion is to me so strange, so new" (2:1). The line, spoken by a woman to a woman, had the power to create associations with transgressive love and court scandal (Roberts, *The Ladies,* 111).

81. Weimann, "Text, Author-Function, and Appropriation." The recognition of this aspect of the period is now generally accepted: David Roberts makes a cogent argument for women's deliberative behavior in *The Ladies,* 133–44, 157–65. Various impetuses for it have been posited; Susan Staves and others find it in Protestantism and in changes in political power. See Staves, *Players' Scepters,* 184–89.

82. There is evidence that writers were already quite self-conscious about the gendering of language. Dryden answers criticisms of one of his poems by writing, "I knew I address'd them to a Lady, and accordingly I affected the softness of expression, and the smoothness of measure, rather than the height of thought." Quoted in Winn, *"When Beauty Fires the Blood,"* 406.

83. Iser in Tompkins, *Reader-Response Criticism*, 65.

84. This section is based on Iser's essay, especially 65–68, and on Victor Nell, *Lost in a Book*. In Nell, see especially "imaginative involvement," 146 and 211–15.

85. This position is now common; see Teresa de Lauretis, "Desire in Narrative," in *Alice Doesn't*, 136–44, and Patrocinio Schweickart, "Reading Ourselves," especially 42–43, for two different approaches.

86. Kolodny, "Dancing through the Minefield," 153–55; Culler, *On Deconstruction*, 43–83.

87. Carol Barash points out that Behn has "dismantled" the Ovidian myth of Hermaphroditus; I am indebted to her subtle reading of this poem in "The Political Possibilities of Desire," 172–75.

88. Quoted in Pearson, *Prostituted Muse*, 157; Pearson has a substantial discussion of sex roles in Behn's plays (146–68).

89. Londa Schiebinger argues in *The Mind Has No Sex?* that the triumph of the theory of sexual complementarity based on the conception of men and women as fundamentally different provided a resolution of "problems" inherited from the seventeenth century. See especially chapter 8.

90. Samuel Pepys had once described Edward Kynaston as the prettiest woman and the handsomest man in the entire theater (*Diary*, 7 January 1660/61). When dressed as a man, Calista is described as "all lovely man," a near-oxymoron in its juxtaposition of culturally gendered language (*Love-Letters*, 317). See Marilyn Williamson's discussion of Behn's "libertine ideology" (*Raising Their Voices*, 212–17).

91. Kendall has done a detailed comparison of Behn's translation of the novel and Trotter's play in "From Lesbian Heroine to Devoted Wife," 9–22.

92. Quoted in Kauffman, *Discourses of Desire*, 288.

93. Quoted in Würzbach, *Novel in Letters*, 1.

94. I am grateful to Professor Brenda Meehan-Waters for sharing information from her forthcoming book on nuns.

95. I agree with Linda Kauffman that "the *Portuguese Letters* is not so much an authentic portrayal of feminine passion as a representation dependent on the codes of literature" (*Discourses of Desire*, 121).

96. Mish, *Restoration Prose Fiction, 1666–1700*, 41.

97. Miller, *Subject to Change*, 37; she cites Sylvère Lotringer's "La Structuration romanesque" as the source for this frequently repeated opinion.

98. The phrase is Estelle Jelinek's and is now widely used ("Discontinuity and Order: A Comparison of Women's and Men's Autobiographies," MLA convention paper, 1976).

99. Weinbrot, "New Eighteenth Century," 379. It should be noted that this quotation comes from a review rather than a standard scholarly article and that the review has a witty, carefully sustained tone quite different from most articles.

100. Chibka, " 'Oh! Do Not Fear a Woman's Invention,' " 510–37; the quotations are from 522 and 532. The last quotation is from Draine, "Refusing the Wisdom of Solomon," 167.

101. Said, "Travelling Theory," 66.

102. Gary Kelly, "Revolutionary and Romantic Feminism," 125.

103. Barbauld, "On the Origin and Progress of Novel-Writing."

104. Jameson, "Metacommentary," 10.

105. Goffman, "Arrangement between the Sexes," 328–29.

106. Foucault, *Discipline and Punish*, 25–26.

107. Wittig, "Category of Sex," 68. McKeon has found evidence that the patrimonial and patrilineal nature of English property law "argues that in the end, gender-based categories are prior even to status-based categories" (*Origins of the English Novel*, 379).

108. Wollstonecraft, *Vindication of the Rights of Woman*, 117.

109. Patricia Meyer Spacks points out that "the offhand manner in which [Sophia] is bestowed on [Tom] suggests that she constitutes an emblem of Tom's achieved position" ("Energies of Mind," 43).

110. Fetterley, "Reading about Reading," 154. Half facetiously, Rozsika Parker writes that "the construction of masculinity—the process that turns boy babies into men with the characteristics valued by our culture—does 'blind' men" ("Images of Men," 237). See also Kolodny, "Map for Rereading," 46–62; and Cixous, "Laugh of the Medusa," 250–57.

111. Haywood, *The British Recluse*, 96–97. All citations are to the 1722 edition.

112. Worthly has this personality; cf. *British Recluse*, 90, 92, and 97. The phrase is Nancy Armstrong's; see *Desire and Domestic Fiction*, 6.

113. Barthes, *S/Z*, 160.

114. Durkheim, *Division of Labor in Society*, 97.

115. After age fourteen, a young woman had the right to choose a guardian. "Stealing an heiress" was a felony, but Bellamy was innocent, since he had not taken her against her will for economic gain. For the legal basis of his innocence, see Blackstone, *Commentaries on the Laws of England*, 4:208.

116. Although Bellamy is not strictly an aristocrat, he subscribes to their ideology and their patriarchal code. Michael McKeon's discussion of the aristocracy, "status inconsistency," and the hegemonic process inherent in their attempts to maintain power usefully identifies the structures of feeling absorbed in the texts I discuss here (*Origins of the English Novel;* see especially 162–75 and 212–19). McKeon writes, "But for many contemporaries, the 'gentry' were a part of the 'aristocracy,' which was equivalent to the 'nobility'" (159).

117. McKeon notes the same impulse in the Mary Carleton narratives; he notes that when Mary is "telling her own story she resembles a self-constructed heroine more than an official example of the unregenerate. In the hands of her husband and her biographers, however, the story . . . is quite easily criminalized" (*Origins of the English Novel*, 100; see also 241, 243–44). Lincoln Faller demonstrates how the legal system, including execution, returns criminals to the community of citizens (*Turned to Account;* see especially 91, 166–67, and 196). His thesis works well with Defoe's *Moll Flanders* and could be applied as well to many other novels by men, including *Tom Jones.*

118. Richardson does this, of course, but he was writing more than twenty years later. As evidence from rape trials shows, the law was unlikely to protect the woman. Among the most famous examples is the trial of Lord Baltimore, who was acquitted of rape; see Flynn, *Samuel Richardson*, 112. This case, however, occurred later than these novels and *Clarissa*. A more likely echo for these writers is *The Tryal and*

Condemnation of Mervin, Lord Audley Earl of Castle-Haven (1699). In another famous case, Francis Charteris was convicted of the rape of Ann Bond, sentenced to death, but pardoned by the king. See Wagner, "Pornographer in the Courtroom," 126–27.

119. See Hunter, *Before Novels,* 303–13; he is not speaking specifically of women writers.

120. Bakhtin notes that such obsession with the present is characteristic of the novelistic moment (*Dialogic Imagination,* 30–31).

121. DuPlessis, "Breaking the Sentence," 481–87.

122. Kennard, "Convention Coverage," 79; Kennard is not writing about Haywood.

123. This section has benefited from Felicity Nussbaum's *Autobiographical Subject.* Much that she says about women writers such as Hester Piozzi and about scandalous memoirs could be applied to these women's novels: see especially 139–40, 179–82, and 187.

124. Kennard, "Convention Coverage," 72.

125. Clément, "The Guilty One," in Cixous and Clément, *Newly Born Woman,* 10.

126. Tanner, *Adultery in the Novel,* 21; Wittig, "Straight Mind," 105.

127. De Lauretis, "Violence of Rhetoric," 245. See also Mitchell's discussion of Lessing in *Iconology, Image, Text, Ideology,* 108–11; and Wittig, "Category of Sex," 64–65.

128. See *British Recluse,* 51–53, 59–61, 72–76.

129. Melissa also discovers that the "reward" for her infidelity is wretchedness (68). Economic language abounds and inscribes the ideology of sexual economy; for instance, Cleomira discovers she is outside any social order. She says she "suffered on his Account" and that she has "a Right I had so dearly purchased" (70, 72).

130. Clément, "The Guilty One," 14–17, 21–22.

131. Kristina Straub's wonderful conclusion about Burney's *Cecilia* might be applied to many women's lives and to many novels about women: "Cecilia's course-of-life plot is necessarily truncated by the ideological imperatives of romantic love in feminine life" (*Divided Fictions,* 142).

132. Russo, "Female Grotesques," 214 and 219; Bakhtin, *Rabelais and His World,* 303–67.

133. The rendering of the body as unrecognizable may be perceived as a matter of class as much as gender; in Arthur Blackamore's *Luck at Last* (1723), a visitor imagines he has seen Sylvia before, but, upon learning of her indigent background, "considering that one apple might be like another, he desisted . . . questions" (McBurney, *Four Before Richardson,* 43).

134. Barker, *Love Intrigues,* 40.

135. Guillaumin, "Question of Difference," 37.

136. Gilligan et al., *Making Connections,* 2–5, 62–64, 162–76, 323–28; Barker, *Love Intrigues,* 23.

137. Quoted in and commented upon by Dean MacCannell and Juliet Flower MacCannell, "The Beauty System," 214. Compare Catherine Steiner-Adair: "Perhaps on a *cultural* level, theirs [those with eating disorders] is a story about the

enormous difficulties of growing up female in a culture that does not value the feminine voice" ("The Body Politic," 176).

138. Sarah Scott, *Millenium Hall*, 120.

139. Davys, *The Cousins*, in *The Works of Mrs. Davys*, 2:226.

140. Bynum, *Holy Feast and Holy Fast;* see especially 220–21.

141. Gilbert and Gubar, *Madwoman in the Attic*, 53–54. Linda Merians has pointed out that Lady Louisa in Burney's *Evelina* may be an anorexic; I am grateful for this addition.

142. Manley, *Memoirs;* see especially 8–20.

143. McKeon, *Origins of the English Novel*, 241; see also 265–68 on the process of conflating truth and virtue.

144. Margaret Doody locates a possible and remarkable appropriation of *The British Recluse* in *Clarissa:* "It is as if Lovelace . . . had read *The British Recluse* with an ironic perception of 'sour grapes' in the feminist ending, and imagined such a situation of feminine defeat from the ego-satisfying view of the rake in the case" (*A Natural Passion*, 145–46).

145. According to Jane Spencer (*Rise of the Woman Novelist*, 65–66), the most accessible edition of *Love Intrigues* may be in *The Entertaining Novels of Mrs. Jane Barker* (London, 1719). See also the poem that survives in Magdalen College MS. 343 (Spencer, 73n. 40): "Then gentle Maid cast off thy Chain, / Which links thee to thy faithless Swain, / And vow a Virgin to remain. / Write, write . . ." (quoted in Spencer, 65).

146. Pope, "To Madam A. Behn on the Publication of her Poems."

147. Herrman, *Tongue Snatchers*, 23, 32–39; and see Backscheider, " 'The Woman's Part.' "

148. Lukács, *Theory of the Novel*, 84–93.

149. Richetti, *Defoe's Narratives*, 96 and 238, respectively.

150. Flynn, "Defoe's Idea of Conduct," 73–95.

PART THREE. GOTHIC DRAMA AND NATIONAL CRISIS

1. Typical news items read, "Friday a Meeting convened by the Lord Lieutenant of . . . Kent [recommended] an immediate invitation to all persons capable of bearing arms, to prepare themselves as Defenders of the country. Every person who has servants is desired to send a list of those who are able . . ." (*Times*, 28 March 1798); "Specimens of the accoutrements and cloathing for the use of persons who shall agree to be called into service, were brought for the inspection of the Council [of cabinet ministers], and the model of a pike, ten feet in length, with an iron spike at the end, for the use of the peasantry, was also exhibited" (*Times*, 4 April 1798); and, "Pikes for arming the Peasantry in the event of invasion were last week deposited in the barracks at Weymouth, Dorchester, Bridport, Wareham and other places along the Southern coast" (*Nottingham Journal*, 17 March 1798, quoted in Morsley, *News from the English Countryside*, 145).

2. Some dramatists of the period were highly active and even arrested for political acts; some of these, such as Thomas Holcroft, also wrote gothic drama.

CHAPTER 5. POPULAR ART

1. Production information is taken primarily from *The London Stage;* dates indicate initial production, not publication.

2. On the numbers of playhouses outside of London, see David Thomas, *Restoration and Georgian England*, 222–23 et passim, especially the map of the distribution of theaters in 1790, 4–5.

3. Johnson, *Lives of the English Poets*, 1:348–49. Joseph Donohue finds continuities with Fletcher's plays (*Dramatic Character in the English Romantic Age*).

4. Zucker, *Fascination of Decay*, 195–97, 206–7, 224–25.

5. *The Fragment of Sir Bertrand* was originally published in Aikin and Aikin, *Miscellaneous Pieces, in Prose* (London, 1773).

6. Production of *Blue-Beard* was delayed; see Colman's preface to the play (iii) and the title page as reproduced in *The Plays of George Colman the Younger.*

7. "Romance" was the Muse; prologue to the second edition of *The Castle Spectre.*

8. The most recent critical book devoted entirely to gothic drama is Bertrand Evans, *Gothic Drama from Walpole to Shelley.* Published in 1947, it is almost uselessly out of date. There are only a few recent articles and introductions to gothic plays. Paul Ranger's *"Terror and Pity reign in every Breast"* is largely a book of descriptive examples with valuable illustrations of performance practices drawn from the collection of reviews in the London Theatre Museum. Joseph Donohue discusses some gothic plays in *Dramatic Character*, but his enterprise is different from mine. Moreover, he tends to use setting too heavily to classify these plays and is concerned with features (suppressed information, the "soul sick" hero, opportunity) that I do not believe define the gothic: see, for instance, 27, 67, 69, and 88. Donohue calls the plays and the tradition he analyzes "the affective drama of situation." MaryBeth Inverso's *Gothic Impulse in Contemporary Drama* includes useful discussions of early gothic drama and correctly contrasts it to fiction; her interests are primarily in the nineteenth-century drama and in adaptations from novels.

Because so little exists on the drama, I have had to draw heavily upon and adapt work done on gothic fiction. Although he does not work with drama, David Punter is useful; he notes "a very disparate collection of works" now classified as gothic and their use of "elements drawn from diverse literary and subliterary traditions" (*Literature of Terror*, 8, 403). See also Linda Bayer-Berenbaum, *The Gothic Imagination*, 21 and 143–44; William Day, *In the Circles of Fear and Desire*, 4–5, 7–11, 13–15, 43–44, and 72; James Keech, "Survival of the Gothic Response," 132–36; and Judith Wilt, *Ghosts of the Gothic*, 12. Evans's definition of the gothic (7–12) is inadequate; Michael R. Booth attempts to distinguish the gothic drama from melodrama (*English Melodrama*).

9. On the social breakdown around 1800, see Roger Simon, *Gramsci's Political Thought*, 50–52; J.C.D. Clark, *English Society, 1688–1832*, 350 and 366; and also Gary Kelly, *English Fiction of the Romantic Period*, 24–25.

10. Wilkes refused to stand trial for seditious libel and left England in 1763. He returned in 1768 and was elected to Parliament from Middlesex, but was convicted on the seditious libel charge, sentenced to twenty-two months' imprisonment, and

expelled from Commons. Three years of "Wilkes and Liberty" riots ensued.

11. Valenze, "Prophecy and Popular Literature," 76–77.

12. Sade, "Reflections on the Novel," 109.

13. Burney is quoted in Doody, *Frances Burney,* 204.

14. This commonplace is usually traced to Ronald Paulson, but he wisely and correctly notes that the gothic had existed from the 1760s, and in "talking about a particular development in the 1790s, a specific plot . . . was either at hand for writers to use in the light of the French Revolution, or was in some sense projected by the Revolution and borrowed by writers who may or may not have wished to express anything specifically about the troubles in France" (*Representations of Revolution, 1789–1820,* 221; see also 37 and 219 for similar statements).

15. John Brooke quotes the king complaining on 26 September 1803 of the slow progress of construction (*King George III,* 284). By 1811, it was half finished and had cost £500,000. The palace was demolished in 1827–28 (Crook and Port, *History of the King's Works,* 6:356–59). Wraxall is quoted here (357).

16. Information on Wyatt is from *DLB;* Middleton and Watkin, *Neoclassical and Nineteenth-Century Architecture,* especially 168–71 and 320; and Robinson, *The Wyatts,* 57–89.

17. On the "long history" of the Gothic Revival, see Middleton and Watkin, *Neoclassical and Nineteenth-Century Architecture,* 316–20. Wyatt built William Beckford's Fonthill Abbey in Wiltshire (1796–1807).

18. Negative comments about Kew Palace are quoted in Brooke, *King George III,* 284.

19. Ayling, *George the Third,* 283, 305; Hibbert, *King Mob,* 91; Carretta, *George III and the Satirists,* 137, respectively; and see Carretta's chapter "The Royal Brute of Britain."

20. Vincent Carretta describes the contrasting sentiment of the 1760s when George III's subjects believed that "the major threat to the balanced constitution was the aristocracy, not the king, and that the monarch was the natural ally of the people in the struggle to avoid . . . 'tyranny in the nobles' " (*George III and the Satirists,* 47–48).

21. Hibbert, *King Mob,* 91.

22. Macalpine and Hunter, *George III and the Mad-Business,* xv, 23–24; they assert that he wrote a last note to his prime minister on 3 November and his next on 23 February.

23. Frances Burney describes these symptoms sympathetically. On at least two occasions she is terrified at meeting him and on one runs away with the sound of his "poor hoarse and altered voice" behind her (*Diary,* 4:120, 122, 191, 242–45).

24. There is evidence that some of these symptoms, including agitated impatience, lingered after his attack (Long, *George III,* 312–13).

25. White, *Age of George III,* 6; Brooke, *King George III,* 285–86, 298–99; Carretta, *George III and the Satirists,* 92–93. See the wealth of prints reproduced in the last-named.

26. White, *Age of George III,* 6–7; Brooke, *King George III,* 342–43.

27. Macalpine and Hunter, *George III and the Mad-Business,* 80.

28. Lord Auckland is quoted in Ayling (*George the Third,* 354).

29. Ayling, *George the Third*, 347, 350–51. Brooke tells of a band hidden in a bathing machine that played "God Save the King" when the king went in the water (*King George III*, 343).

30. White, *Age of George III*, 6.

31. Perceptions of the similarities between the English constitution and French ideals remain. In 1989, Margaret Thatcher commented that by 1688 England had peacefully accomplished the constitutional reforms that the French Revolution celebrations credited to France.

32. Macalpine and Hunter, *George III and the Mad-Business*, 41.

33. Derry, *Regency Crisis*, 154.

34. This interesting play was performed at the Newcastle-upon-Tyne Royal Theatre. The request to license was signed by Stephen Kemble; I have found it in manuscript only, as licensed by Larpent 13 November 1793. A copy is in the Larpent collection. Joseph Donohue notes the "near-insane rage," psychological inconsistency, and "perversion" of the norms of behavior in Fletcherian dramatic characters, but Fletcher's purposes and resolutions are different from the gothic (*Dramatic Character*, 21–24).

35. In a very different inquiry, Jon Stratton argues that feudal and capitalist "social structures and economic forms" combined in France at this time to make "desire for intercourse" rather than intercourse and the body important (*Virgin Text*, 72 ff.). Although capitalism is sometimes identified with the bourgeoisie, I do not think it can be in the eighteenth century; rather, the English bourgeois ideology seems to me to be descended from the London City structures of feeling associated with the "cits" in literary and political discourses.

36. See, for example, Douglas North and Robert Thomas, *The Rise of the Western World*. Other students of the gothic, including Judith Wilt and MaryBeth Inverso, have remarked upon the gothic hero's anachronistic exercise of power; see Inverso, *Gothic Impulse*, 59–61.

37. Pocock, review of John Brewer's *Sinews of Power*, 270–72.

38. Carretta, *George III*, 47.

39. Paulson, *Representation of Revolution*, 221.

40. See Ross Chambers's illuminating discussion of the contrasts between ancient and modern tyrannies in *Room for Maneuver*, 184–86.

41. Foucault, *Order of Things*, chap. 6. See also Jameson, who associates feudalism rather than capitalism with "relations of personal domination" (*Political Unconscious*, 89–90).

42. Adorno and Horkheimer's classic characterization appears in "The Culture Industry," 120–67.

43. Jameson, "Metacommentary," 17.

44. Meisel, *Realizations*, 33; Bergonzi, *Reading the Thirties*, 5.

45. See Jameson on repetition in "Reification and Utopia," 137.

46. Jameson, *Political Unconscious*, 135.

47. See also Michael S. Wilson's fine article, "Columbine's Picturesque Passage." I am grateful to him for sharing the manuscript with me. See also Hagstrum, "Pictures to the Heart," 436–37.

48. Noverre is quoted in Ranger, *"Terror and Pity reign in every Breast,"* 26. See

his useful chapter, appropriately titled "A World Untamed," 19–41.

49. Rosenblum, "British Art and the Continent," 12–15.

50. On the picturesque nature of the gothic stage, see Meisel, *Realizations,* 12, 38–39, 41–45, and 69–72; Rosenfeld, *Short History of Scene Design,* 87–90; and Russell Thomas, "Contemporary Taste." Paulson points out that the beautiful "is repose" (*Representations of Revolution,* 69).

51. Walpole is quoted in Morris, "Gothic Sublimity," 313.

52. Boaden is quoted in Russell Thomas, "Contemporary Taste," 71–72.

53. Quoted in Ranger, *"Terror and Pity reign in every Breast,"* 46.

54. Visser, "Scenery and Technical Design"; Rosenfeld, *Short History of Scene Design,* 85–93; *London Stage,* 5:1:lvi–lxvi.

55. The 1787 anecdote is quoted in Sutcliffe, *Plays by Colman and Morton,* 39.

56. On how common these reproductions were, see Paul Zucker, *Fascination of Decay,* 6; Neil McKendrick argues that purchasing power for such objects reached as low "as the skilled factory worker and the domestic servant class" ("Home Demand and Economic Growth," 172–73, 198 et passim). On the popularity of ruin hunting and viewing, see Ian Ousby, *Englishman's England,* 92–129.

57. The *Morning Chronicle* comment on theatrical scenery is quoted in Russell Thomas, "Contemporary Taste," 77.

58. Russell Thomas, "Contemporary Taste," 73–74; Rosenfeld, "Landscape in English Scenery," 174, and *Short History of Scene Design,* 97; Fiske, *English Theatre Music,* 454, 554.

59. Rosenfeld, "Landscape in English Scenery," 174.

60. Beaumont, *History of Harlequin,* 94.

61. Visser, "Scenery and Technical Design"; Rosenfeld, *Short History of Scene Design,* 69–70, 82; Niklaus, *Harlequin,* 142.

62. This contemporary spectator's reaction to *The Castle Spectre* is cited in Fiske, *English Theatre Music,* 572.

63. See Ranger, *"Terror and Pity reign in every Breast,"* 20–22. Quotations are from his discussion and the play.

64. Beaumont, *History of Harlequin,* 109. Donohue notes Kemble's "famous" use of pauses in *Dramatic Character,* 249–50; on contemporary acting styles, see 217–18 and 244–45.

65. Mullan, *Sentiment and Sociability,* especially chap. 5.

66. Davies, *Life of David Garrick,* 2:184.

67. Meisel, *Realizations,* 12, 38–39, 41.

68. Russell Thomas, "Contemporary Taste," 70.

69. Boaden's quotation appears in his *Life of John Philip Kemble,* 314. Boaden's demands are described in Reno, "Boaden's *Fontainville Forest,"* 99.

70. Bruce A. McConachie points out that both Antonio Gramsci and Kenneth Burke argue that human beings "by nature respond to symbols" and demonstrate that language and ritual help establish a "hegemonic we": see "Concept of Cultural Hegemony," 37–58. Burke writes that rhetoric is "rooted in . . . the use of language as a symbolic means of inducing cooperation in beings that by nature respond to symbols" (*Rhetoric of Motives,* 43–46). See also Burke's *Attitudes toward History,* 179–215; the quotation is from 179.

71. Inverso, *Gothic Impulse,* 1–3, 42.

72. Addison, for 1 July 1712; see also his *Spectator* no. 12 for 14 March 1711, which explains the long-lasting effect of such tales. David Punter says that horror "confronts" us with "the landscapes of childhood" ("Narrative and Psychology," 21). James B. Twitchell points out that four of the most popular modern horror writers were "all very successful camp counselors" (*Dreadful Pleasures,* 74), and Joseph Grixti confesses that "those of us who direct our storytelling into darker channels do so because we are . . . mindful . . . regarding our childhood confusions of identity, our conflicts with unpleasant realities and our traumatic encounters with imaginative terrors" (*Terrors of Uncertainty,* 181). Robert Le Tellier also discusses the "primitive impulses and sources" common to the gothic and to fairy tales (*Intensifying Vision of Evil,* 236–40).

73. Sackville-West, *Nursery Rhymes,* 15–16.

74. Perrault, *Tales of Passed Times by Mother Goose;* see also Opie, *Lore and Language of Schoolchildren,* 35–37; Alexander, *British Folklore,* 134–39; and Perrault, *Complete Fairy Tales,* 75–76.

75. In later productions, the blue room was not revealed until the women enter in Act 2, but Colman notes that he prefers his original composition and the opportunity to milk audience dread as well as surprise and horror.

76. Barry Sutcliffe quotes these descriptions from Adolphus in *Plays by Colman and Morton,* 40–41.

77. Cited in Ranger, *"Terror and Pity reign in every Breast,"* 78. Ranger says "Fatima," but this position is Irene's (47–48).

78. Ranger, *"Terror and Pity reign in every Breast,"* 79.

79. The review of *Blue-Beard* is quoted in Sutcliffe, *Plays by Colman and Morton,* 40.

80. Jameson, "Reification and Utopia," 144, 147.

CHAPTER 6. MEN, WOMEN, AND THE CROWD

1. The phrase is James Twitchell's (*Dreadful Pleasures,* 7); see also William Day's illuminating discussion of the thematic significance of sexual identity in the gothic novel (*Circles of Fear and Desire,* 5–17, 75).

2. The amount of information even ordinary people received about the king's health and behavior is simply amazing. In addition to daily bulletins, parliamentary reports appeared and attracted a huge readership. The official opinions of examining and consulting physicians were published by order of Parliament and even in one of "Bell's cheap editions," which was reprinted three times (Macalpine and Hunter, *George III,* 75–76 et passim).

3. Willis's contemporary is quoted in Macalpine and Hunter, *George III,* 270–72.

4. Scull, *Social Order/Mental Disorder,* 66.

5. Gilliland, *Dramatic Mirror,* 2:887–88; Palmer may have played more than 375 parts during his career.

6. Hagstrum, "Pictures to the Heart," 438–41; see also Morris, "Gothic Subliminity," 306–7.

7. Godwin, *Caleb Williams,* 316.

8. The moral sense is the capacity to experience feelings of approval and disapproval. Francis Hutcheson formulated a systematic theory, which was specifically opposed to the view that moral distinctions are made by reason. Hutcheson called the human capacity to act from disinterested motives "benevolence" (*Nature and Conduct*, 1728). David Hume used the word "sentiment" more commonly than "sense" and explained it as being the result of sympathy, thereby connecting the theory to a utilitarian approach to ethics (*Treatise of Human Nature*, 1740, esp. bk. 3). Shaftesbury and Hutcheson specifically linked the ethical with the aesthetic judgment. Claudia Johnson points out that "sensibility" became the "rallying cry of Burkean reactionaries who, anxious to discredit the presumptuous calculations of independent reason, cherish instead 'feelings' and 'affections' cultivated through the family" (*Jane Austen*, xxii).

9. Kate Ellis discusses the importance of women's claim to property and the ways Radcliffe's economic themes make her novels "female-centered" (*Contested Castle*, 112–24).

10. The gothic protagonist as "the masculine essence and its sexual force" is universally acknowledged; especially original discussions of the discourse are in James M. Keech, "Survival of the Gothic Response," 137, and Ann B. Snitow, "Mass Market Romance," 260–61.

11. See Joseph Roach's stimulating "Power's Body," 104. He describes the representation of Steele's Young Bevil in *The Conscious Lovers* as being in a position much like the one I argue the heroines occupy (111–15).

12. In *The History of Sexuality*, Foucault locates the socialization of procreative behavior as well as the hysterization of women's bodies in this epoch. James Twitchell remarks, "I don't believe there is a horror myth in the West that is not entangled with the theme of procreation . . . they are concerned with sex and reproduction" (*Dreadful Pleasures*, 66).

13. Opinion of Jacques Moreau de la Sarthe paraphrased in Laqueur, "Orgasm, Generation," 2.

14. Schiebinger, "Skeletons in the Closet."

15. Armstrong, *Desire and Domestic Fiction*, 3–7, 59–95; she argues that the redefinition of desire was "a decisive step in producing the densely interwoven fabric of common sense and sentimentality that even today ensures the ubiquity of middle-class power" (5). Doody remarks that "everyone in the 1790s seems to want some sort of 'new woman'" (*Frances Burney*, 206). See also Newton, *Women, Power, and Subversion*, 13 and 17–22.

16. Significantly, Kate Ellis reads *Caleb Williams* as a struggle between and among men and the ideologies of shame and guilt cultures (*Contested Castle*, 151–65).

17. Foucault, *History of Sexuality*, 1:139, and "Prison Talk," in *Power/Knowledge*, 39.

18. Montrose, "Renaissance Literary Studies," 9.

19. Cawelti, *Adventure, Mystery, and Romance*, 46; Le Tellier, *An Intensifying Vision*, 240.

20. Those critics who discuss such plays as gothic do so because of their sets or

even because of plot devices such as mistaken identity and disguise. Cf. Ranger, *"Terror and Pity reign in every Breast,"* 12–13; and Donohue, *Dramatic Character,* 82 et passim.

21. Heilman, "Tragedy and Melodrama," 256; this section on melodrama has been influenced by Inverso's illuminating discussion in *Gothic Impulse,* especially chap. 1.

22. Brooks, *Melodramatic Imagination,* 15, 27; Booth, *English Melodrama,* 80–83.

23. A third play that might logically be included in this group is Joanna Baillie's *De Montfort* (1798); I have omitted it, however, because it was performed only as John Philip Kemble's adaptation (Drury Lane, 1800). It is notable that Elizabeth Inchbald, whose *Lovers' Vows,* an adaptation of Kotzebue's *Das Kind der Liebe,* has gothic elements and who wrote original tragedies and melodramas, attempted no gothic play. These plays did, however, make gothic elements and story lines available. Cf. Ranger, *"Terror and Pity reign in every Breast,"* on *Albina* (12–13). Hester Lynch Piozzi's unpublished, unproduced "The Two Fountains" (1789–90) might be considered gothic in the style of the musical romantic type common to the 1780s; I learned of this play from Margaret Doody's paper given at the Johnson Society of the Midwest.

24. Barry Sutcliffe, for instance, says, "The crucial lever into the gothic frame of mind was the object of terror. In performance terms, Sarah Siddons . . . was herself that object" (*Plays by Colman and Morton,* 11).

25. Campbell, *Life of Mrs. Siddons,* 222 and 289, respectively. Campbell's interesting account of how the audience "laughed at the most tragic passages, and looked grave at the most comic" may suggest that Lewis's deconstructive energies resisted either Boaden's art or the conventions of the gothic theater.

26. Campbell, *Life of Mrs. Siddons,* 303. On this play's innovations, see Donohue, *Dramatic Character,* 78–82.

27. Younge played Hortensia in 1781, its premiere season, in which there were twenty-one performances; Siddons played the part for the first time in the 1786–87 season, in which there were two performances.

28. *Theatrical Biography; or, Memoirs of the Principal Performers,* 1:19.

29. Gilliland, *Dramatic Mirror,* 2:821–22; in another place, he compliments Sarah Siddons for her "classical and perfect possession" of the "antique figure" in painting and sculpture (2:972). I am grateful to Michael Wilson for this second reference.

30. Inchbald, *Remarks,* on Southerne's *Isabella.*

31. Hazlitt, *Hazlitt on the Theatre,* 94; Boaden is quoted in Sprague, *Shakespearean Players,* 62.

32. The poem celebrating Siddons is titled "Written on seeing Mrs. Siddons, As Mrs. Haller, in the Stranger, Friday the 25th, and as Isabella, in The Fatal Marriage, Monday 28th May, 1798," by C.L. (*Monthly Mirror,* June 1798, 363–64).

33. Roger Manvell has conveniently collected reviewers' comments in *Sarah Siddons,* 358–59.

34. This description of Yates was published in 1772, before Mrs. Siddons's career began (*Theatrical Biography; or, Memoirs,* 2:7).

35. Dyer is quoted in Mayne, "Marlene Dietrich," 29.

36. Mayne, "Marlene Dietrich," 29–31.

37. See also the Pope illustrations in *A Biographical Dictionary of Actors, Actresses,* s.v. "Elizabeth Pope."

38. Among the portraits of Siddons as herself that I examined are those by James Barry, Peter Contencin, John Henning, William Beechey, George Clint, A. E. Chalon, George Harlow, John Hayter, William Hamilton, John Downman, and Samuel DeWilde in the Harvard Theatre Collection, the National Portrait Gallery Archive, and the Theatre Museum, London. There is a quite remarkable one by Richard Cosway of Siddons at age twenty-seven looking directly out at the viewer but with a sweet expression. *A Biographical Dictionary of Actors, Actresses* reproduces some excellent portraits of this type, including Beechey's of Siddons with the emblems of tragedy (14:9) and others by Stuart and Lawrence (14:21 and 36).

39. In fact, it is common for illustrations of actresses in breeches parts to leave no doubt of their sex. Not only their chests but their lower bodies show the plump bulges of women.

40. Harvard Theatre Collection, Hall nos. 21, 22, 23, and 76. Both women wear the dark dress with its lace neckline; Master Pullen is with Yates.

41. The Ann Barry engraving is reproduced in *A Biographical Dictionary of Actors, Actresses* and is from the 1775 Bell's *Shakespeare;* the print is after James Roberts.

42. See Harvard Theatre Collection, Hall nos. 64, 72, and 106, Euphrasia (two illustrations) and Lady Macbeth.

43. De Lauretis, *Alice Doesn't,* 139. It should be noted that at the height of her career Siddons could pick and choose roles as most players could not.

44. Harvard Theatre Collection, Hall no. 35, executed in 1783.

45. Harvard Theatre Collection, extra-illustrated Kemble 6:380 and Dorn 4:351.

46. Patricia Meyer Spacks notes the importance of "energy of mind" in her "Energies of Mind." See also Ronald Paulson on the changing meaning of sublime (*Representations of Revolution,* 68–72).

47. Again, Roach's explication of the attractiveness and repulsiveness of the *castrati* is pertinent ("Power's Body," 103–5).

48. Lesage, "Women and Film," 90; Mayne, "Marlene Dietrich," 30.

49. Inverso cites Judith Wilt in *Gothic Impulse,* 59.

50. Bakhtin, *Dialogic Imagination,* 13–40, and *Rabelais and His World,* 303, 307–14, 317–20, 322n. 8. Significantly, Bakhtin locates the sources of the mass body in folklore, in the familiar and the colloquial (*Rabelais,* 341–57).

51. Folena, "Figures of Violence," 233.

52. Morag Shiach usefully points out how unstable usage of these terms was in the eighteenth century. "Popular government," for instance, could refer to "government with the consent of the people, sometimes government in the interests of the people, and sometimes, though always with fear, to government by the people" (*Discourse on Popular Culture,* 25; see also 22–34).

53. Davies, "Divided Gaze," 131.

54. Gunn, *Beyond Liberty and Property,* quoting Twiss, 292–93.

55. Reynolds, "Discourse IX," in *Discourses on Art,* 170.

56. A. Smith, *Inquiry into the Nature and the Cause of the Wealth of Nations,* 2:302–3.

57. E. Burke, *Speeches* (14 June 1784), 3:10.

58. See Shiach, *Discourse on Popular Culture,* 23–33; and Mullan, *Sentiment and Sociability,* 12, 223, 238–39 et passim.

59. Reynolds, *Discourses on Art,* 233 and 170, respectively; Johnson is quoted in Danziger and Brady, *Boswell,* 41.

60. Carretta, *George III and the Satirists,* 49; and see Shiach, *Discourse on Popular Culture,* 25–26.

61. Gunn, *Beyond Liberty and Property,* 304.

62. Social historians have found evidence that the people supported traditional rights or customs even when they participated in "disorder": see Thompson, "Moral Economy of the English Crowd," 78, 95, 108–10 et passim. Thompson argues that they were often "supported by the wider consensus of the community" and often based their actions upon some previous legitimating text such as the Elizabethan *Book of Orders.*

63. Cf. *Fontainville Forest,* 34–36.

64. See, for instance, Cole and Postgate, *Common People, 1746–1946,* 143–46, and the comparative graphs of the population, 70–71.

65. E. Burke, *Speeches* (14 June 1784), 3:12. Burke was condemning the development of "public opinion."

66. Bourdieu, *Distinction,* 398–99, 411.

67. Quotations from the Sheffield Society are reprinted in MacCoby, *English Radical Tradition,* 55–56.

68. The appendix to Strype's *Ecclesiastical Memorials* (1721). See also Shiach, *Discourse on Popular Culture,* 23–24.

69. Davenant is quoted in Gunn, who points out that the same words were used by a 1770 letter writer (*Beyond Liberty and Property,* 278).

70. Fox is quoted in Clark, *English Society, 1688–1832,* 357.

71. Cole and Postgate, *Common People, 1746–1946,* 99.

72. The item from the *Adams Weekly Courant* is cited in Morsley, *News from the English Countryside,* 52, 74, and 56–57, respectively. These and other similar items in his books are examples of what E. P. Thompson calls "the moral economy" of the English people and follow the ritualized patterns that he and others have identified.

73. Plumb, *First Four Georges,* 101; Gunn, *Beyond Liberty and Property,* 301–2; and see More, *Village Politics.*

74. Cole and Postgate, *Common People, 1746–1946,* 99.

75. *A Plan,* dated 17 April 1798, GH MS. 481.

76. Hazlitt, "What is the People?" 323.

77. The sheriff's opinion is quoted in E. P. Thompson, "Moral Economy of the English Crowd," 136.

78. J.C.D. Clark, *English Society, 1688–1832,* 375. Clark does, I believe, overestimate the influence of the church. Clark himself notes that in the half century after the American Revolution there was a "steady erosion of Anglicanism." However, he is

surely right to see the crucial significance of what he calls "this interlocking system of beliefs and institutions" (350) and the error of interpretations based upon the illusion of being able to separate politics and religion in the period.

79. Gunn, *Beyond Liberty and Property,* 260, 281, and 292, respectively. The Bentley quotation is from *Considerations upon the State of Public Affairs,* 46.

80. Goldsmith, *The Vicar of Wakefield* (1766), quoted in Carretta, *George III and the Satirists,* 49.

81. Carretta brings together a useful series of quotations in *George III and the Satirists,* 44–51; see also Shiach, *Discourse on Popular Culture,* 23–27.

82. Twiss, *Influence or Prerogative?* 14.

83. See Eugenia DeLamotte's stimulating discussion of women and violation in gothic novels in her chapter "Boundaries of the Self," in *Perils of the Night.*

84. See Chambers, *Room for Manuever,* 184–86.

85. Gramsci, *Prison Notebooks,* 210–11, 228–29, 235, 260.

86. The crisis broke out anew in the early nineteenth century as manifested in such events as the Luddite disturbances of 1811–17 and the Pentridge rising of 1817.

87. K. Burke, *Attitudes toward History,* 179.

88. See Cawelti's discussion of the operation of formula melodrama, in *Adventure, Mystery, and Romance,* 45–47 and chap. 9; see also Coward, *Female Desires,* 201–4. The quotation is from Sypher, "Aesthetic of Revolution," 262.

89. Caesarism requires that all sides lay claim to the most emotional ideological terms. Being contested was "passion," not "sensibility"; but "imagination" was of even more concern, and it is excluded from the plays. Edmund Burke, for example, writes, "There is a boundary to men's passions, when they act from feeling; none when they are under the influence of imagination" (*Appeal from the New to the Old Whigs,* 4:192). "Individualism" and "capitalism" are also almost entirely excluded, and "constitution" is never used. For their importance in gothic fiction, see Gary Kelly, *English Fiction,* 59 and 223–25. Modern discussions of "imagination" in the period are numerous; among the most interesting are Mullan, *Sentiment and Sociability,* 223–27, and Marshall Brown's in *Preromanticism.*

90. Wilt, *Ghosts of the Gothic,* 46–49; see also Inverso, *Gothic Impulse,* 64–66.

91. Habermas, *Structural Transformation of the Public Sphere,* 25–26, 64–66, 93; Bourdieu, *Distinction,* 398–99.

92. Sutcliffe, *Plays by Colman and Morton,* 8, 12, 29; Linda Kelly, *Kemble Era,* 21; *London Stage,* 5:1:cxcvi.

93. Here, too, there are similarities to nursery tales. Addison describes one tale-swapping and notes, "At the End of every Story the whole Company closed their Ranks and crouded about the Fire" (no. 12 for 14 March 1711).

94. Beckerman, *Dynamics of Drama,* 133.

95. Cawelti, *Adventure, Mystery, and Romance,* 91; De Lauretis, *Alice Doesn't,* 136.

96. J.C.D. Clark, *English Society, 1688–1832,* 350.

97. Charles Nodier, quoted in Hyslop, "Deviant and Dangerous Behavior," 66; Burke, quoted in Mitchell, *Iconology, Image, Text, Ideology,* 146.

98. Inverso, *Gothic Impulse,* 1–2, 5, 9.

99. Gilman, *Confusion of Realms,* n.p.

100. Laclau, *Politics and Ideology,* 161.

101. Althusser, *Lenin and Philosophy,* 162; emphasis mine.

102. Hazlitt, "What is the People?" 318–19.

103. Clifford Morsley notes that these events were "organized" and that their intention was to demonstrate that there would be no revolution in England and no answer to France's call to the republicans to help them (*News from the English Countryside,* 133–34).

104. At this time, the British were struggling to devise new ways to support the poor and to get the able-bodied into the labor force (Christie, *Wars and Revolutions,* 175–77, 209–12, 237–38). The Sheffield Society for Constitutional Information specifically thanked Paine for his "affectionate concern . . . in his Second Work in behalf of the poor, the infant, and the aged" (quoted in MacCoby, *English Radical Tradition,* 55–56).

CONCLUSION. "THAT RESTLESS, RESISTLESS POWER"

1. Macherey, *Theory of Literary Production;* Jameson, *Political Unconscious,* 79–84. See Ellis, *Contested Castle,* 167–78; and Kaplan, "Wild Nights," 167–78, who identify some pressing contradictions.

2. Cawelti, *Adventure, Mystery, and Romance,* 9. Art in Anglo-American culture is always supported by some combination of patronage, commodity production, and state subsidy.

3. Gramsci, *Prison Notebooks,* 171. Leopold Damrosch usefully reminds us that many Restoration and eighteenth-century writers "operate in an ambiguous zone between absolute reality and reality as perceived," that many are deeply engaged with "the problem of reality," and that there are both objects/events and community-preferred versions of reality at issue (*Fictions of Reality,* 4–5, 10).

4. Bourdieu, *Distinction,* 7.

5. See Adorno and Horkheimer, "The Culture Industry," in *Dialectic of Enlightenment,* 136–37.

6. Cawelti, *Adventure, Mystery, and Romance,* 10.

7. Gramsci, *Prison Notebooks,* 235–98; Simon, *Gramsci's Political Thought,* 68–73.

8. Gramsci, *Prison Notebooks,* 295.

9. This section has benefited from Macherey's discussion of Defoe's novels, especially of *Moll Flanders* (*Theory of Literary Production,* 242–47).

10. Raymond Williams identifies dominant visions of community as service, mutual responsibility, and the ladder (*Culture and Society,* 316–18).

11. Twiss, *Influence or Prerogative?* 14.

12. Bakhtin, *Rabelais and His World,* 367.

BIBLIOGRAPHY

PRIMARY SOURCES

Aikin, John, and A. L. Aikin. *Miscellaneous Pieces, in Prose.* London, 1773.
Andrews, Miles Peter. *The Songs, Recitatives, airs . . . of The Enchanted Castle.* London, 1786.
————. *The Mysteries of the Castle.* London, 1795.
Ariadne [pseud.]. *She Ventures and He Wins.* London, 1696.
Astell, Mary. *A Serious Proposal to the Ladies.* London, 1696.
Atkyns, Richard. *The Original and Growth of Printing.* London, 1664.
Baillie, Joanna. *De Montfort.* In *A Series of Plays.* 1798; Oxford: Woodstock, 1990.
Ballard, George. *Memoirs of Several Ladies of Great Britain.* Edited by Ruth Perry. 1752; Detroit: Wayne State UP, 1985.
Barbauld, Anna L. "On the Origin and Progress of Novel-Writing." University of North Carolina microfilm of the introductory essays in her 50-volume edition, *The British Novelists.* London, 1810.
Barker, Jane. *The Entertaining Novels of Mrs. Jane Barker.* London, 1719.
————. *The Lining of the Patch-Work Screen.* London, 1726.
————. *Love Intrigues.* London, 1713.
Behn, Aphra. *The Histories and Novels of the Late Ingenious Mrs. Behn.* London, 1696.

————. *Love-Letters between a Nobleman and His Sister.* London: Penguin-Virago, 1987.

————. *Miscellany, Being a Collection of Poems by several Hands.* London, 1685.

————. *The Novels of Mrs. Aphra Behn.* Westport, Conn.: Greenwood, 1969.

————. *Oroonoko.* New York: Norton, 1973.

————. *Poems upon Several Occasions with a Voyage to the Island of Love.* London, 1684.

————. "Prologue to *Romulus.* Spoken by Mrs. Butler. Written by Mrs. Behn" and "Epilogue to the Same, Spoken by the Lady Slingsby." London, 1682.

————. *The Rover.* Edited by Frederick M. Link. Lincoln: U of Nebraska P, 1967.

————. *The Uncollected Verse of Aphra Behn.* Edited by Germaine Greer. Stump Cross, Essex: Stump Cross, 1989.

————. *The Works of Aphra Behn.* Edited by Montague Summers. 6 vols. London: Heinemann, 1915.

Bentley, Thomas. *Considerations upon the State of Public Affairs, in the Year MDCCXCVIII, Part, the Third.* London, 1798.

Blackstone, William. *Commentaries on the Laws of England.* 4 vols. Philadelphia, 1862.

Boaden, James. *Memoirs of the Life of John Philip Kemble.* Philadelphia: Small, 1825.

————. *The Plays of James Boaden.* Edited by Steven Cohan. New York: Garland, 1980.

Brome, Alexander. *A Speech made to the Lord General Monk at the Clothworkers Hall in London (March 13, 1660).* In *Songs and Other Poems.* London, 1661.

Burke, Edmund. *Appeal from the New to the Old Whigs.* In *The Works of Edmund Burke,* edited by George Nichols. 12 vols. Boston: Little, 1865–67.

————. *The Speeches of the Right Honourable Edmund Burke, in the House of Commons.* 4 vols. London: Longman, Hurst, Rees, Orme, and Brown, 1816.

Burnet, Gilbert. *History of His Own Time.* 6 vols. Oxford: Clarendon, 1823.

Burney, Frances. *Diary and Letters of Madame D'Arblay.* Edited by Charlotte Barrett. 6 vols. London: Macmillan, 1905.

The Castle of Otranto. Manuscript licensed 13 November 1793, Newcastle upon Tyne, request by Stephen Kemble.

Cavendish, William. *Letter of Instructions to Prince Charles*. In *Original Letters, Illustrative of English History*, edited by Henry Ellis. London: Harding, Triphook, and Lepard, 1825.

Chesterfield, Philip Dormer Stanhope. *The Works of Lord Chesterfield*. New York: Harper, 1838.

Cibber, Colley. *An Apology for the Life of Colley Cibber*. Edited by Robert W. Lowe. 2 vols. 1740; New York: AMS, 1966.

———. *Love's Last Shift; or the Fool in Fashion*. London, 1696.

Clarendon, Edward Hyde, earl of. *The History of the Rebellion and Civil Wars in England*. 2 vols. Oxford: Oxford UP, 1840.

———. *The Life of Edward Earl of Clarendon . . . In Which is Included, A Continuation of his History of the Grand Rebellion*. Oxford: Oxford UP, 1857.

Clavel, Robert. *A Catalogue of all the Books printed in England since the Dreadful Fire of London, in 1666 To the End of Michaelmas Term, 1672*. London, 1673.

———. *The General Catalogue of Books Printed in England*. London, 1680.

Cobb, James. *The Haunted Tower*. London, 1790.

Colman, George. *The Plays of George Colman the Younger*. Edited by Peter Tasch. 2 vols. New York: Garland, 1981.

Colman, George, and B. Thornton, eds. *Poems by Eminent Ladies*. 2 vols. London, 1755.

Congreve, William. *The Way of the World*. Edited by Kathleen M. Lynch. Lincoln: U of Nebraska P, 1965.

The Court and Kitchin of Elizabeth, Commonly called Joan Cromwell, the Wife of the late Usurper. London, 1664.

Cowley, Abraham. *Cutter of Coleman-Street*. In *Essays, Plays and Sundry Verses*, edited by A. R. Waller. Cambridge: Cambridge UP, 1906.

Cowley, Hannah. *The Plays of Hannah Cowley*. Edited by Frederick N. Link. 2 vols. New York: Garland, 1979.

Cromwell, Oliver. *The Letters and Speeches of Oliver Cromwell*. Edited by S. C. Lomas. 3 vols. London: Methuen, 1904.

Davies, Thomas. *Memoirs of the Life of David Garrick*. 2 vols. London, 1780.

Davys, Mary. *The Works of Mrs. Davys: Consisting of Plays, Novels, Poems and Familiar Letters*. 2 vols. London, 1725.

Defoe, Daniel. *The Complete English Tradesman*. London, 1726.

———. *The Original Power of the Collective Body of the People of England*. London, 1702.

Deloney, Thomas. *The Pleasant Historie of John Winchcomb*. London, 1662.

Downes, John. *Roscius Anglicanus*. Edited by Judith Milhous and Robert D.

Hume. 1708; London: Society for Theater Research, 1987.

Drake, Judith. *An Essay in Defence of the Female Sex.* London, 1696.

Dryden, John. *The Conquest of Granada.* In *The Works of John Dryden,* edited by Edward N. Hooker and H. T. Swedenborg, Jr. 20 vols. Berkeley: U of California P, 1956–

D'Urfé, Honoré. *Astrea. A Romance, Written in French, by Messure Honoré D'Urfe; and Translated by a Person of Quality.* 2 vols. London, 1657.

Evelyn, John. *The Diary of John Evelyn.* Edited by E. S. de Beer. 6 vols. Oxford: Clarendon, 1955.

Farquhar, George. *The Works of George Farquhar.* Edited by Shirley S. Kenny. 2 vols. Oxford: Clarendon, 1988.

Finch, Anne. *Selected Poems of Anne Finch.* Edited by Katharine Rogers. New York: Ungar, 1979.

Fuller, Thomas. *The History of the Worthies of England.* 3 vols. London, 1840.

Gilliland, Thomas. *The Dramatic Mirror.* 2 vols. London, 1808.

Godwin, William. *Caleb Williams.* Oxford: Oxford UP, 1970.

Granger, James. *A Biographical History of England.* 3d ed. 4 vols. London, 1779.

Griffith, Elizabeth. *A Collection of Novels, from the Most Celebrated Writers.* 3 vols. London, 1777.

Haywood, Eliza. *The British Recluse.* London, 1722.

His Majesties Commission Concerning the Reparation of the Cathedral Church of St. Paul in London. London, 1663.

Howell, T. B., comp. *A Complete Collection of State Trials.* 34 vols. London, 1816–28.

Hume, David. *A Treatise of Human Nature.* London, 1740.

Hutcheson, Francis. *An Essay on the Nature and Conduct of the Passions and Affections.* London, 1728.

Inchbald, Elizabeth. *The Plays of Elizabeth Inchbald.* Edited by Paula R. Backscheider. 2 vols. New York: Garland, 1980.

———. *Remarks for The British Theatre (1806–1809).* Edited by Cecilia Macheski. Delmar, N.Y.: Scholars' Facsimiles, 1990.

———. *A Simple Story.* London, 1791.

Jephson, Robert. *The Plays of Robert Jephson.* Edited by Temple Maynard. New York: Garland, 1980.

Johnson, Samuel. *Lives of the English Poets.* Edited by George Birkbeck Hill. 3 vols. Oxford: Clarendon, 1905.

Jordan, Thomas. "A Speech Composed to Welcome to the English Shore, the most Sacred . . . Majesty of Charles the Second. In *A Royal Arbor of Loyal Poesie*. London, 1663.

Kemble, John Philip. *Love in Many Masks*. London, 1790.

"The Lady Novelists." *Westminster Review* (July 1852): 129–41.

Lafayette, Marie-Madeleine Pioche de la Vergne de. *The Princess de Clèves*. Translated by Nancy Mitford with revisions by Leonard Tancock. 1678; Harmondsworth, Middlesex: Penguin, 1978.

Lee, Sophia. *Almeyda, Queen of Granada*. Dublin, 1796.

"A Lenten Prologue refus'd by the Players." London, 1682.

Lewis, Matthew. *The Castle Spectre*. 2d ed. London, 1798.

London's Triumph: Presented in several Delightfull Scenes; both upon the Water and Land. London, 1662.

Louis XIV. *Mémoires de Louis XIV publiés avec une Introduction et des Notes par Jean Longnon*. Paris: Tallandier, 1927.

Manley, Delarivière. *The Lost Lover*. London, 1696.

———. *Memoirs of the Life of Mrs. Manley*. 3d ed. London, 1717.

———. *The Novels of Mary Delarivière Manley*. Edited by Patricia Köster. 2 vols. Gainesville, Fla.: Scholars' Facsimiles, 1971.

———. *The Royal Mischief*. London, 1696.

Miscellaneous Works of his Grace George, Late Duke of Buckingham. London, 1707.

More, Hannah. *Village Politics, by Will Chip, a Country Carpenter*. In *The Works of Hannah More*. 2 vols. London, 1801.

Morgan, William. *The King's Coronation: Being an Exact Account of the Cavalcade, with a Description of the Triumphal Arches*. London, 1685.

Munday, Antony. *London's Love to the Royal Prince Henrie*. London, 1610.

Ogilby, John. *The Entertainment of . . . Charles II*. Binghamton, N.Y.: Medieval and Renaissance Texts and Studies, 1988.

———. *The Relation of His Majesties Entertainment Passing through the City of London*. London: Roycroft, 1661.

Osborne, Dorothy. *The Letters of Dorothy Osborne to William Temple*. Edited by G. C. Moore-Smith. Oxford: Clarendon, 1928.

The Parliamentary History of England, from the Earliest Period to the Year 1803. 36 vols. London, 1808–20.

Pennant, Thomas. *Account of London*. "Illustrated by J. Chas. Crowle." London, 1790.

Pepys, Samuel. *The Diary of Samuel Pepys*. Edited by Robert Latham and William Matthews. 11 vols. Berkeley: U of California P, 1972–83.

Perrault, Charles. *Perrault's Complete Fairy Tales.* Translated by W. Heath Robinson. New York: Dodd, 1961.

———. *Tales of Passed Times by Mother Goose.* Translated by R. S. Gent. London, 1796.

Philips, Katherine. *Letters from Orinda to Poliarchus.* London, 1705.

———. *Poems By the Most Deservedly Admired Mrs. Katherine Philips, The Matchless Orinda.* In *Minor Poets of the Caroline Period,* edited by George Saintsbury. Oxford: Clarendon, 1905.

Pix, Mary. *The Plays of Mary Pix and Catharine Trotter.* Edited by Edna Steeves. 2 vols. New York: Garland, 1982.

"The Prologue to his Majestie At the first PLAY presented at the Cock-pit in Whitehall, Being part of that Noble Entertainment which their Majesties received *November* 19. from his Grace the Duke of ALBEMARLE." London, 1660.

Radcliffe, Ann. *The Italian.* London: Oxford UP, 1971.

Ralph, James. *The History of England during the reigns of King William, Queen Anne, and George I.* 2 vols. London, 1744.

The Reasons of Mr. Bays Changing his Religion. London, 1688.

Reeve, Clara. "An Address to the Reader." In *Original Poems on Several Occasions.* London, 1769.

———. *The Progress of Romance.* Colchester, 1785.

Reresby, John. *Memoirs of Sir John Reresby.* Edited by Andrew Browning. Glasgow, 1936.

Reynolds, Joshua. *Discourses on Art.* Edited by Robert R. Wark. New Haven: Yale UP, 1975.

Richardson, Samuel. *Clarissa.* 8 vols. 1751; New York: AMS, 1990.

Rowe, Elizabeth Singer. *Poems on Several Occasions.* London, 1696.

A Royal Arbor of Loyal Poesie. London, 1663.

"The Royal Standard of Our Country." London, 1803.

Rugge, Thomas. *"Mercurius Politicus Redivivus." A Collection of the most material Occurances and Transactions in Public Affairs.* BL Add. MSS. 10116 and 10117.

Sade, Marquis de. "Reflections on the Novel." In *The 120 Days of Sodom and Other Writings,* translated by Austryn Wainhouse and Richard Seaver. New York: Grove, 1966.

Scott, Sarah. *Millenium Hall.* New York: Penguin-Viking, 1986.

Scott, Walter. *Memoirs of the Life of Sir Walter Scott.* 5 vols. Boston: Houghton, 1902.

Scudéry, Madeleine de. *Artamenes; or, The Grand Cyrus, That Excellent Romance in Ten Parts.* Englished by F.G., Esq. London, 1691.

Shadwell, Thomas. *Some Reflections upon the Pretended Parallel in the Play called the Duke of Guise.* London, 1683.

"Silly Novels by Lady Novelists." *Westminster Review* (October 1856): 442–61.

Smith, Adam. *An Inquiry into the Nature and the Cause of the Wealth of Nations.* Edited by Edwin Cannan. 2 vols. Chicago: U of Chicago P, 1976.

Smith, Charlotte. *The Romance of Real Life.* London, 1787.

Southerne, Thomas. *The Works of Thomas Southerne.* Edited by Robert Jordan and Harold Love. 2 vols. Oxford: Clarendon, 1988.

Steele, Richard. *The Englishman.* Edited by Rae Blanchard. Oxford: Clarendon, 1955.

Steele, Richard, and Joseph Addison. *The Spectator.* Edited by Donald F. Bond. 5 vols. Oxford: Clarendon, 1965.

Tatham, John. *Aqua Triumphalis: Being a True Relation of the Honourable the City of Londons Entertaining their Sacred Majesties upon the River Thames.* London, 1662.

———. *The Dramatic Works of John Tatham.* Edited by James Maidment and W. H. Logan. Edinburgh: Paterson, 1878.

———. *London's Glory Represented by Time, Truth, and Fame: At the Magnificent Triumphs and Entertainment of his . . . Majesty . . . At Guildhall . . . being the 5th day of July 1660.* London, 1660.

———. *London's Triumph Celebrated In Honour of . . . Sir Anthony Bateman.* London, 1663.

———. *London's Triumph Celebrated the Twenty-ninth of October 1664.* London, 1664.

———. *London's Tryumph, Presented by Industry and Honour: with other Delightful Scaenes [sic].* London, 1658.

———. *Neptune's Address To his Most Sacred Majesty Charls [sic] the Second.* London, 1661.

———. *The Royal Oake: Being Twice as many Pageants and Speeches as have been formerly showen.* London, 1660.

———. *The Several Speeches Made to the Honourable Sir Richard Brown Lord Mayor of the City of London.* London, 1660.

Theatrical Biography; or, Memoirs of the Principal Performers. London, 1772.

Trotter, Catharine. *The Plays of Mary Pix and Catharine Trotter.* Edited by Edna Steeves. 2 vols. New York: Garland, 1982.

A True Account of the Invitation and Entertainment of the Duke of York. London, 1679.

The Tryal and Condemnation of Mervin, Lord Audley Earl of Castle-Haven.
　London, 1699.

Twiss, Horace. *Influence or Prerogative? being an attempt to Remove Popular
　Misconceptions, Respecting the Present State of the British Constitution
　and Government.* London, 1812.

Villiers, George. *The Miscellaneous Works of His Grace, George, Late Duke
　of Buckingham.* London, 1707.

Walker, Edward. *A Circumstantial Account of the Preparations for the Coro-
　nation of . . . Charles the Second.* London, 1820.

Walpole, Horace. *Horace Walpole's Correspondence with Sir Horace Mann
　and Sir Horace Mann the Younger.* Edited by W. S. Lewis, Warren Hunt-
　ing Smith, and George L. Lam. 27 vols. New Haven: Yale UP, 1954–71.

Whoredom, Fornication and Adultery, detected and laid open. London, 1749.

Wilson, John. *The Cheats.* London, 1663.

Wollstonecraft, Mary. *A Vindication of the Rights of Woman.* 1792; New
　York: Norton, 1975.

SECONDARY SOURCES

Adorno, Theodor W., and Max Horkheimer. *Dialectic of Enlightenment.*
　Translated by John Cumming. London: Lane, 1973.

Alexander, Marc. *British Folklore.* New York: Crescent, 1982.

Alleman, Gellert S. *Matrimonial Law and the Materials of Restoration Come-
　dy.* Wallingford, Pa.: U of Pennsylvania P, 1942.

Althusser, Louis A. *Lenin and Philosophy.* Translated by Ben Brewster.
　London: New Left, 1971.

Altick, Richard D. *The English Common Reader.* Chicago: U of Chicago P,
　1957.

Andreadis, Harriette. "The Sapphic-Platonics of Katherine Philips, 1632–
　1664." *Signs* 15 (1989): 34–60.

Anglo, Sydney. *Spectacle Pageantry, and Early Tudor Policy.* Oxford: Claren-
　don, 1969.

Armstrong, Nancy. *Desire and Domestic Fiction: A Political History of the
　Novel.* New York: Oxford UP, 1987.

Armstrong, Nancy, and Leonard Tennenhouse, eds. *The Ideology of Con-
　duct: Essays on Literature and the History of Sexuality.* London: Meth-
　uen, 1987.

―――. *The Violence of Representation: Literature and the History of Vio-
　lence.* London: Routledge, 1989.

Auden, W. H. *The Criterion Book of Modern American Verse*. New York: Criterion, 1956.

Ayling, Stanley. *George the Third*. New York: Knopf, 1972.

Backscheider, Paula R. *Daniel Defoe: His Life*. Baltimore: Johns Hopkins UP, 1989.

———. *Dictionary of Literary Biography: Restoration and Eighteenth-Century Drama*. 3 vols. Detroit: Gale, 1989–90.

———. " 'The Woman's Part': Richardson, Defoe, and the Horrors of Marriage." In *The Critical Controversy—New Commentaries,* edited by Edward Copeland and Carol H. Flynn. New York: AMS, 1993.

Bakhtin, Mikhail. *The Dialogic Imagination*. Translated by Caryl Emerson and Michael Holquist. Austin: U of Texas P, 1981.

———. *Rabelais and His World*. Translated by Hélène Iswolsky. Bloomington: Indiana UP, 1984.

Barash, Carol. "The Political Possibilities of Desire: Teaching the Erotic Poems of Behn." In *Teaching Eighteenth-Century Poetry,* edited by Christopher Fox. New York: AMS, 1990.

Barthes, Roland. *A Lover's Discourse: Fragments*. Translated by Richard Howard. New York: Hill, 1978.

———. *S/Z*. Paris: Seuil, 1970.

Bayer-Berenbaum, Linda. *The Gothic Imagination: Expansion in Gothic Literature and Art*. London: Assoc. Univ. Presses, 1982.

Beaumont, Cyril W. *The History of Harlequin*. 1926; New York: Blom, 1967.

Beckerman, Bernard. *Dynamics of Drama: Theory and Method of Analysis*. New York: Knopf, 1970.

Benham, William. *Old St. Paul's Cathedral*. London: Seeley, 1902.

Bergeron, David, ed. *Thomas Heywood's Pageants: A Critical Edition*. New York: Garland, 1986.

———. "Venetian State Papers and English Civic Pageantry, 1558–1642." *Renaissance Quarterly* 23 (1970): 37–47.

Bergonzi, Bernard. *Reading the Thirties*. London: Macmillan, 1978.

Besant, Walter. *London in the Eighteenth Century*. London: Black, 1903.

Booth, Michael R. *English Melodrama*. London: Jenkins, 1965.

Booth, Michael R., Richard Southern, Frederick Marker, Lise-Lone Marker, and Robertson Davies. *The Revels History of English Drama, 1750–1880*. London: Methuen, 1975.

Bourdieu, Pierre. *Distinction: A Social Critique of the Judgment of Taste*. Translated by Richard Nice. Cambridge: Harvard UP, 1984.

Bradbrook, M. C. "The Politics of Pageantry: Social Implications in Jacobean London." In *Poetry and Drama, 1570–1700,* edited by Antony Coleman and Antony Hammond. London: Methuen, 1981.

Brewer, John. *Party Ideology and Popular Politics at the Accession of George III.* London: Cambridge UP, 1976.

———. *The Sinews of Power.* New York: Knopf, 1989.

Bromley, Roger. "The Gentry, Bourgeois Hegemony, and Popular Fiction: *Rebecca* and *Rogue Male.*" In *Popular Fictions,* edited by Peter Humm, Paul Stigant, and Peter Widdowson. London: Methuen, 1986.

Brooke, John. *King George III.* New York: McGraw, 1972.

Brooks, Peter. *The Melodramatic Imagination.* New Haven: Yale UP, 1976.

———. "Virtue and Terror: *The Monk.*" *ELH* 40 (1973): 249–63.

Brown, Laura. "The Romance of Empire." In *The New Eighteenth Century.* *See* Nussbaum and Brown.

Brown, Marshall. *Preromanticism.* Stanford: Stanford UP, 1991.

Bryant, Arthur. *King Charles II.* London: Longmans, 1932.

Bryant, Lawrence M. *The King and the City in the Parisian Royal Entry Ceremony.* Geneva: Droz, 1986.

Burke, Kenneth. *Attitudes toward History.* 1937; Berkeley: U of California P, 1984.

———. *A Rhetoric of Motives.* New York: Prentice, 1950.

Burke, Peter. "Popular Culture in Seventeenth-Century London." In *Popular Culture in Seventeenth-Century London,* edited by Barry Reay. New York: St. Martin's, 1985.

Butler, Martin. *Theatre and Crisis.* Cambridge: Cambridge UP, 1984.

Butwin, Joseph. "The French Revolution as *Theatrum Mundi.*" *Research Studies* 43 (1975): 141–52.

Bynum, Caroline Walker. *Holy Feast and Holy Fast.* Berkeley: U of California P, 1987.

A Calendar of Dramatic Records in the Books of the Livery Companies of London, 1485–1640. Vol. 3. London: Oxford UP for the Malone Society, 1954.

Campbell, Thomas. *Life of Mrs. Siddons.* 1839; New York: Blom, 1972.

Canto, Monique. "The Politics of Women's Bodies: Reflections on Plato." In *The Female Body in Western Culture: Contemporary Perspectives,* edited by Susan R. Suleiman. 1985; Cambridge: Harvard UP, 1986.

Carretta, Vincent. *George III and the Satirists.* Athens: U of Georgia P, 1990.

Cawelti, John G. *Adventure, Mystery, and Romance: Formula Stories as Art and Popular Culture.* Chicago: U of Chicago P, 1976.

————. "The Concept of Formula in the Study of Popular Literature." In *The Study of Popular Fiction,* edited by Bob Ashley. Philadelphia: U of Pennsylvania P, 1989.

Chambers, Ross. *Room for Maneuver.* Chicago: U of Chicago P, 1991.

Chibka, Robert. " 'Oh! Do Not Fear a Woman's Invention': Truth, Falsehood, and Fiction in Aphra Behn's *Oroonoko.*" *TSLL* 30 (1988): 510–37.

Christie, Ian R. *Wars and Revolutions: Britain, 1760–1815.* Cambridge: Harvard UP, 1982.

Cixous, Hélène. "The Laugh of the Medusa." In *New French Feminisms. See* Marks and de Courtivron.

Clark, Alice. *The Working Life of Women in the Seventeenth Century.* 1919; New York: Kelley, 1968.

Clark, J.C.D. *English Society, 1688–1832: Ideology, Social Structure, and Political Practice during the Ancien Regime.* Cambridge: Cambridge UP, 1985.

Clément, Catherine. "The Guilty One." In *The Newly Born Woman,* edited by Hélène Cixous and Catherine Clément, translated by Betsy Wing. 1975; Minneapolis: U of Minnesota P, 1986.

Clode, Charles M. *London during the Great Rebellion.* Oxford: Oxford UP, 1840.

Cole, G.D.H., and Raymond Postgate. *The Common People, 1746–1946.* 1938; London: Methuen, 1966.

Cooper, Helen. "Location and Meaning in Masque, Morality, and Royal Entertainment." In *The Court Masque,* edited by David Lindley. Manchester: Manchester UP, 1984.

Cotton, Nancy. "Aphra Behn and the Pattern Hero." In *Curtain Calls. See* Schofield and Macheski.

————. *Women Playwrights in England.* Lewisburg, Pa.: Bucknell UP, 1980.

Coward, Rosalind. *Female Desires: How They Are Sought, Bought, and Packaged.* New York: Grove, 1985.

Crook, J. Mordaunt, and M. H. Port. *The History of the King's Works.* London: HMSO, 1973.

Culler, Jonathan. *On Deconstruction.* Ithaca: Cornell UP, 1982.

————. *A Structuralist Poetics.* Ithaca: Cornell UP, 1988.

Damrosch, Leopold. *Fictions of Reality in the Age of Hume and Johnson.* Madison: U of Wisconsin P, 1989.

————. *God's Plot and Man's Stories.* Chicago: U of Chicago P, 1985.

Danziger, Marlies K., and Frank Brady. *Boswell: The Great Biographer, 1789–1795.* New Haven: Yale UP, 1975.

Davies, Tony. "The Divided Gaze: Reflections on the Political Thriller." In *Gender, Genre, and Narrative Pleasure. See* Longman.

Day, Robert Adams. *Told in Letters.* Ann Arbor: U of Michigan P, 1966.

Day, William. *In the Circles of Fear and Desire.* Chicago: U of Chicago P, 1985.

de Beauvoir, Simone. *The Second Sex.* 1949; New York: Vintage, 1974.

De Krey, Gary S. "The London Whigs and the Exclusion Crisis Reconsidered." In *The First Modern Society,* edited by A. L. Beier, David Cannadine, and James M. Rosenheim. Cambridge: Cambridge UP, 1989.

De Lauretis, Teresa. *Alice Doesn't: Feminism, Semiotics, Cinema.* Bloomington: Indiana UP, 1984.

———, ed. *Feminist Studies/Critical Studies.* Bloomington: Indiana UP, 1986.

———. "The Violence of Rhetoric." In *The Violence of Representation. See* Armstrong and Tennenhouse 1989.

Debord, Guy. *Society of the Spectacle.* 1967; Detroit: Black and Red, 1983.

DeJean, Joan. "Lafayette's Ellipses: The Privileges of Anonymity." *PMLA* 99 (1984): 884–902.

DeLamotte, Eugenia. *Perils of the Night: A Feminist Study of the Nineteenth-Century Gothic.* Oxford: Oxford UP, 1990.

Derry, John W. *The Regency Crisis and the Whigs, 1788–1789.* Cambridge: Cambridge UP, 1963.

Diamond, Elin. "*Gestus* and Signature in Aphra Behn's *The Rover.*" *ELH* 56 (1989): 519–41.

Donohue, Joseph. *Dramatic Character in the English Romantic Age.* Princeton: Princeton UP, 1970.

Doody, Margaret Anne. *Frances Burney: The Life in the Works.* New Brunswick, N.J.: Rutgers UP, 1988.

———. *A Natural Passion: A Study of the Novels of Samuel Richardson.* Oxford: Clarendon, 1974.

Draine, Betsy. "Refusing the Wisdom of Solomon: Some Recent Feminist Literary Theory." *Signs* (1989): 144–70.

Duffy, Maureen. *The Passionate Shepherdess: Aphra Behn, 1640–1689.* London: Cape, 1977.

DuPlessis, Rachel B. "Breaking the Sentence; Breaking the Sequence." In *Essentials of the Theory of Fiction,* edited by Michael Hoffman and Patrick Murphy. Durham, N.C.: Duke UP, 1988.

Durkheim, Emile. *The Division of Labor in Society.* Translated by George Simpson. New York: Free, 1964.

Edmond, Mary. *Rare Sir William Davenant.* Manchester: Manchester UP, 1987.

Edwards, George W. *London.* Philadelphia: Penn, 1922.

Eisenstein, Elizabeth L. *The Printing Press as an Agent of Change.* 2 vols. Cambridge: Cambridge UP, 1979.

Ellis, Kate Ferguson. *The Contested Castle: Gothic Novels and the Subversion of Domestic Ideology.* Urbana: U of Illinois P, 1989.

Emberton, Wilfred. *Skippon's Brave Boys.* Birmingham: Barracuda, 1984.

Epstein, Julia. *The Iron Pen: Frances Burney and the Politics of Women's Writing.* Madison: U of Wisconsin P, 1989.

Erlanger, Philippe. *Louis XIV.* Translated by Stephen Cox. New York: Praeger, 1970.

Esslin, Martin. *An Anatomy of Drama.* London: Smith, 1976.

Evans, Bertrand. *Gothic Drama from Walpole to Shelley.* Berkeley: U of California P, 1947.

Ezell, Margaret. *The Patriarch's Wife: Literary Evidence and the History of the Family.* Chapel Hill: U of North Carolina P, 1987.

Faderman, Lillian. *Surpassing the Love of Men: Romantic Friendship and Love between Women from the Renaissance to the Present.* New York: Morrow, 1981.

Fairholt, Frederick W. *Lord Mayors' Pageants.* 30 vols. London: Percy Society, 1843–1965.

Faller, Lincoln. *Turned to Account.* Cambridge: Cambridge UP, 1987.

Fetterley, Judith. "Reading about Reading." In *Gender and Reading. See* Flynn and Schweickart.

Fiske, Roger. *English Theatre Music in the Eighteenth Century.* London: Oxford UP, 1973.

Flynn, Carol Houlihan. "Defoe's Idea of Conduct." In *The Ideology of Conduct. See* Armstrong and Tennenhouse 1987.

———. *Samuel Richardson: A Man of Letters.* Princeton: Princeton UP, 1982.

Flynn, Elizabeth A., and Patrocinio P. Schweickart, eds. *Gender and Reading: Essays on Readers, Texts, and Contexts.* Baltimore: Johns Hopkins UP, 1986.

Folena, Lucia. "Figures of Violence: Philologists, Witches, and Stalinistas." In *The Violence of Representation. See* Armstrong and Tennenhouse 1989.

Foucault, Michel. *Discipline and Punish: The Birth of the Prison*. Translated by Alan Sheridan. New York: Pantheon, 1977.

———. *The History of Sexuality*. Vol. 1, *An Introduction*. Translated by Robert Hurley. New York: Pantheon, 1978.

———. *Madness and Civilization*. Translated by Richard Howard. New York: Pantheon, 1965.

———. *The Order of Things*. 1970; New York: Vintage, 1973.

———. *Power/Knowledge*. Edited by Colin Gordon. 1972; New York: Pantheon, 1980.

———. "The Subject and Power." *Critical Inquiry* 8 (1982): 777–95.

———. "What Is an Author?" In *Language, Counter-Memory, Practice*, edited and translated by Donald F. Bouchard and Sherry Simon. Ithaca: Cornell UP, 1977.

Fraser, Antonia. *Cromwell: The Lord Protector*. New York: Knopf, 1973.

Freehafer, John. "The Formation of the London Patent Companies." *Theatre Notebook* 20 (1965): 6–30.

Freud, Sigmund. "Insights and Their Vicissitudes." In vol. 14, *The Standard Edition of the Complete Psychological Works of Sigmund Freud*, edited by James Strachey. 24 vols. London: Hogarth P and Inst. of Psycho-Analysis, 1962–74.

Fullard, Joyce. *British Women Poets, 1660–1800: An Anthology*. Troy, N.Y.: Whitston, 1990.

Gallagher, Catherine. "Who Was That Masked Woman? The Prostitute and the Playwright in the Comedies of Aphra Behn." *Women's Studies* 15 (1988): 23–42.

Gallagher, Catherine, and Thomas Laqueur, eds. *The Making of the Modern Body*. Berkeley: U of California P, 1987.

Geertz, Clifford. "Centers, Kings, and Charisma: Reflections on the Symbolics of Power." In *Culture and Its Creators*, edited by Joseph Ben-David and Terry Nichols Clark. Chicago: U of Chicago P, 1977.

———. *The Interpretation of Cultures*. New York: Basic, 1973.

Genest, John. *Some Account of the English Stage*. 10 vols. Bath, 1832.

George, Margaret. *Women in the First Capitalist Society*. Urbana: U of Illinois P, 1988.

Gibson, Rebecca Gould. " 'My Want of Skill': Apologias of British Women Poets, 1660–1800." In *Eighteenth-Century Women and the Arts*, edited by Frederick Keener and Susan Lorsch. New York: Greenwood, 1988.

Gilbert, Sandra, and Susan Gubar. *The Madwoman in the Attic*. New Haven: Yale UP, 1979.

Gill, James E. "The Fragmented Self in Three of Rochester's Poems." *Modern Language Quarterly* 49 (1988): 19–37.

Gilligan, Carol, Nona Lyons, and Trudy Hanmer, eds. *Making Connections.* Cambridge: Harvard UP, 1990.

Gilman, Richard. *The Confusion of Realms.* New York: Random, 1969.

Goffman, Erving. "The Arrangement between the Sexes." *Theory and Society* 4 (1977): 301–32.

Gombrich, E. H. "Renaissance and Golden Age." *Journal of the Warburg and Courtauld Institutes* 24 (1961): 306–9.

Goreau, Angeline. *Reconstructing Aphra.* New York: Dial, 1980.

Gramsci, Antonio. *Selections from the Prison Notebooks of Antonio Gramsci.* Translated by Quintin Hoare and Geoffrey Smith. 1971; New York: International, 1978.

Greenblatt, Stephen. "Invisible Bullets: Renaissance Authority and Its Subversion." *Glyph* 8 (1981): 40–60.

Greer, Germaine, Susan Hastings, Jeslyn Medoff, and Melinda Sansone, eds. *Kissing the Rod.* New York: Farrar, 1988.

Greer, Margaret Rich. "Art and Power in the Spectacle Plays of Calderon de la Barca." *PMLA* 104 (1989): 329–39.

Grixti, Joseph. *The Terrors of Uncertainty: The Cultural Contexts of Horror Fiction.* London: Routledge, 1989.

Grundy, Isobel, and Sue Wiseman, eds. *Women/Writing/History.* London: Batsford, 1992.

Guffey, George. "Aphra Behn's *Oroonoko.*" In *Two English Novelists.* Los Angeles: Clark, 1975.

Guillaumin, Collette. "The Question of Difference." *Feminist Issues* 2 (1982): 23–102.

Gunn, J.A.W. *Beyond Liberty and Property: The Process of Self-Recognition in Eighteeth-Century Thought.* Kingston: McGill–Queen's University P, 1983.

Habermas, Jürgen. *The Structural Transformation of the Public Sphere: An Inquiry into a Category of Bourgeois Society.* Translated by Thomas Burger with Frederick Lawrence. 1962; Cambridge: MIT P, 1989.

Hagstrum, Jean. "Pictures to the Heart: The Psychological Picturesque in Ann Radcliffe's *The Mysteries of Udolpho.*" In *Greene Centennial Studies,* edited by Paul J. Korshin and Robert R. Allen. Charlottesville: UP of Virginia, 1984.

Halfpenny, Eric. "The Citie's Loyalty Display'd." Guildhall Fo. Pam. 1173.

Hanley, Sarah. *The Lit de Justice of the Kings of France.* Princeton: Princeton UP, 1983.

Harbage, Alfred. *Cavalier Drama.* London: Oxford UP, 1936.

Harris, Mark, ed. *The Heart of Boswell: Highlights from the Journals.* New York: McGraw, 1981.

Harris, Tim. *London Crowds in the Reign of Charles II.* Cambridge: Cambridge UP, 1987.

Haviland, Thomas. "The *Roman de Longue Haleine* on English Soil." Ph.D. diss., U of Pennsylvania, 1931.

Hazlitt, Willam. *Hazlitt on the Theatre.* Edited by William Archer and Robert Lowe. New York: Hill, 1957.

———. "What is the People?" In *Political Essays, with Sketches of Public Characters.* London, 1819.

Heilbrun, Carolyn. *Hamlet's Mother.* New York: Columbia UP, 1990.

Heilman, Robert. "Tragedy and Melodrama: Speculations on Generic Form." In *Tragedy: Vision and Form,* edited by Robert Corrigan. San Francisco: Chandler, 1965.

Herrman, Claudine. *The Tongue Snatchers.* Translated by Nancy Kline. Lincoln: U of Nebraska P, 1989.

Hibbert, Christopher. *King Mob: The Story of Lord George Gordon and the Riots of 1780.* London: Longmans, 1958.

Highfill, Phillip, et al. *A Biographical Dictionary of Actors, Actresses, Musicians, Dancers, Managers, and Other Stage Personnel in London, 1660–1800.* 14 vols. Carbondale: Southern Illinois UP, 1973–.

Hill, Christopher. *The Intellectual Origins of the English Revolution.* Oxford: Clarendon, 1980.

———. *Puritanism and Revolution.* New York: Schocken, 1964.

Hobby, Elaine. *Virtue of Necessity: English Women's Writing, 1649–1688.* Ann Arbor: U of Michigan P, 1988.

Holland, Peter. *The Ornament of Action.* Cambridge: Cambridge UP, 1979.

Holmes, Clive. "The County Community in Stuart Historiography." *Journal of British Studies* 19 (1980): 54–73.

———. "Drainers and Fenmen: The Problem of Popular Political Consciousness in the Seventeenth Century." In *Order and Disorder in Early Modern England,* edited by Anthony Fletcher and John Stevenson. Cambridge: Cambridge UP, 1985.

Homans, Margaret. *Bearing the Word: Language and Female Experience.* Chicago: U of Chicago P, 1986.

Houlbrooke, Ralph A. "Women's Social Life and Common Action in England." *Continuity and Change* 1 (1986): 171–89.

Howe, Irving. *Politics and the Novel.* New York: Horizon, 1957.

Hume, Robert. *The Development of English Drama in the Late Seventeenth Century.* Oxford: Clarendon, 1977.

———. "Marital Discord in English Comedy from Dryden to Fielding." *Modern Philology* 74 (1977): 248–72.

Hunter, J. Paul. *Before Novels.* New York: Norton, 1990.

Hutton, Ronald. *Charles the Second.* Oxford: Clarendon, 1989.

Hyslop, Gabrielle. "Deviant and Dangerous Behavior: Women in Melodrama." *Journal of Popular Culture* 19 (1985): 65–77.

Inverso, MaryBeth. *The Gothic Impulse in Contemporary Drama.* Ann Arbor: UMI Res., 1990.

Irigaray, Luce. *This Sex Which Is Not One.* Translated by Catherine Porter. Ithaca: Cornell UP, 1985.

Iser, Wolfgang. "Interaction between Text and Reader." In *The Reader in the Text. See* Suleiman and Crosman.

———. "The Reading Process." In *Reader-Response Criticism: From Formalism to Post-Structuralism. See* Tompkins 1980.

Jameson, Fredric. "Metacommentary." *PMLA* 86 (1971): 9–18.

———. *The Political Unconscious: Narrative as Socially Symbolic Act.* Ithaca: Cornell UP, 1981.

———. "Reification and Utopia in Mass Culture." *Social Text* 1 (1979): 130–48.

Jauss, Hans R. *Toward an Aesthetic of Reception.* Minneapolis: U of Minnesota P, 1989.

Johnson, Claudia. *Jane Austen.* Chicago: U of Chicago P, 1988.

Jones, J. R. *Country and Court.* Cambridge: Harvard UP, 1979.

Jones, Vivien. *Women in the Eighteenth Century: Constructions of Femininity.* London: Routledge, 1990.

Kaplan, Cora. "Wild Nights: Pleasure/Sexuality/Feminism." In *The Ideology of Conduct. See* Armstrong and Tennenhouse 1987.

Katz, Candace Brook. "The Deserted Mistress Motif in Mrs. Manley's *Lost Lover,* 1696." *RECTR* 15 (1976): 27–39.

Kauffmann, Linda. *Discourses of Desire.* Ithaca: Cornell UP, 1986.

Kavenik, Frances. "Aphra Behn: The Playwright as 'Breeches Part.'" In *Curtain Calls. See* Schofield and Macheski.

Keeble, N. H. *The Literary Culture of Nonconformity in Later Seventeenth-Century England.* Athens: U of Georgia P, 1987.

Keech, James M. "The Survival of the Gothic Response." *Studies in the Novel* 6 (1974): 130–44.

Kelly, Gary. *English Fiction of the Romantic Period, 1789–1830.* London: Longmans, 1989.

―――. " 'Intrigue' and 'Gallantry': The Seventeenth-Century French *Nouvelle* and the 'Novels' of Aphra Behn." *Revue de Littérature Comparée* 55 (1981): 184–94.

―――. "Revolutionary and Romantic Feminism." In *Revolution and English Romanticism,* edited by Keith Hanley and Raman Selden. Hertfordshire, England: Harvester, 1990.

Kelly, Linda. *The Kemble Era.* New York: Random, 1980.

Kendall. "Finding the Good Parts." In *Curtain Calls. See* Schofield and Macheski.

―――. "From Lesbian Heroine to Devoted Wife: Or, What the Stage Would Allow." *Journal of Homosexuality* 12 (1986): 9–22.

Kennard, Jean E. "Convention Coverage, or How to Read Your Own Life." *New Literary History* 13 (1981): 69–88.

Keyssar, Helene. *Feminist Theatre: An Introduction to Plays and Contemporary British and American Women.* London: Macmillan, 1984.

Knowles, Ronald. "Introduction" to John Ogilby, *The Entertainment of His Most . . . Excellent Majestie Charles II in his passage through the City of London to his Coronation.* Binghamton, N.Y.: Med. and Ren. Texts and Stud., 1988.

Kolodny, Annette. "Dancing through the Minefield." In *The New Feminist Criticism. See* Showalter.

―――. "A Map for Rereading." In *The New Feminist Criticism. See* Showalter.

Kristeva, Julia. "Oscillation between Power and Denial." In *New French Feminisms. See* Marks and de Courtivron.

Laclau, Ernesto. *Politics and Ideology in Marxist Theory.* London: NLB, 1977.

Lamont, William, and Sybil Oldfield, eds. *Politics, Religion, and Literature in the Seventeenth Century.* London: Dent, 1975.

Landwehr, John. *Splendid Ceremonies: State Entries and Royal Funerals in the Low Countries.* Leiden: Sijthoff, 1971.

Laqueur, Thomas. *Making Sex: Body and Gender from the Greeks to Freud.* Cambridge: Harvard UP, 1990.

―――. "Orgasm, Generation, and the Politics of Reproductive Biology." In *The Making of the Modern Body. See* Gallagher and Laqueur.

Lesage, Julia. "Women and Film: A Discussion of Feminist Aesthetics." *New German Critique* 13 (1978): 83–107.

Le Tellier, Robert. *An Intensifying Vision of Evil.* Salzburg, Austria: Institut für Anglistik und Amerikanistik Universitat Salzburg, 1980.

Levy, F. J. "How Information Spread among the Gentry, 1550–1640." *Journal of British Studies* 21 (1982): 11–34.

Lock, F. P. "Astrea's 'Vacant Throne': The Successors of Aphra Behn." In *Women in the Eighteenth Century and Other Essays,* edited by Paul Fritz and Richard Morton. Toronto: Hakkert, 1976.

Lockhart, John Gibson. *Memoirs of the Life of Sir Walter Scott.* 5 vols. Boston: Houghton, 1902.

London Stage, The. Vol. 3, pt. 5, *1776–1800.* Edited by Charles Beecher Hogan. 3 vols. Carbondale: Southern Illinois UP, 1968.

Long, J. C. *George III: The Story of a Complex Man.* Boston: Little, 1960.

Longman, Derek, ed. *Gender, Genre, and Narrative Pleasure.* London: Unwin, 1989.

Love, Harold. "State Affairs on the Restoration Stage, 1660–1675." *RECTR* 14 (1975): 1–9.

Lukács, Georg. *The Theory of the Novel.* Translated by Anna Bostock. Cambridge: MIT P, 1971.

Lund, Roger. *"Bibliotecha* and 'the British Dames': An Early Critique of the Female Wits of the Restoration." *Restoration* 12 (1988): 96–105.

Lynch, Kathleen. "Conventions of Platonic Drama in the Heroic Plays of Orrery and Dryden." *PMLA* 44 (1929): 456–71.

Macalpine, Ida, and Richard Hunter. *George III and the Mad-Business.* New York: Pantheon, 1969.

McBurney, William, ed. *Four before Richardson.* Lincoln: U of Nebraska P, 1963.

MacCannell, Dean, and Juliet Flower MacCannell. "The Beauty System." In *The Ideology of Conduct. See* Armstrong and Tennenhouse 1987.

MacCoby, S. *The English Radical Tradition, 1763–1914.* New York: New York UP, 1957.

McConachie, Bruce A. "Using the Concept of Cultural Hegemony to Write Theatre History." In *Interpreting the Theatrical Past. See* Postlewait and McConachie.

Macherey, Pierre. *A Theory of Literary Production.* Translated by Geoffrey Wall. London: Routledge, 1978.

Mack, Phyllis. "The History of Women in Early Modern Britain: A Review Article." *Comparative Studies in Society and History* 28 (1986): 715–22.

Mackay, Janet. *Catherine of Braganza.* London: Long, 1937.

McKendrick, Neil. "Home Demand and Economic Growth: A New View of the Role of Women and Children in the Industrial Revolution." In *Historical Perspectives: Studies in English Thought and Society,* edited by Neil McKendrick. London: Europa, 1974.

McKeon, Michael. *The Origins of the English Novel, 1600–1740.* Baltimore: Johns Hopkins UP, 1987.

MacLean, Gerald. "The King on Trial: Judicial Poetics and the Restoration Settlement." *Michigan Academician* 17 (1985): 375–88.

———. "What Is a Restoration Poem? Editing a Discourse, Not an Author." In *Text: Transactions of the Society for Textual Scholarship,* edited by D. C. Greetham and W. Speed Hill. New York: AMS, 1987.

McLeod, Enid. *Héloise.* London: Chatto, 1971.

Maguire, Nancy K. "The Theatrical Mask/Masque of Politics: The Case of Charles I." *Journal of British Studies* 28 (1989): 1–22.

Malcolmson, Robert. *Life and Labour in England, 1700–1780.* New York: St. Martin's, 1981.

Mambretti, Catherine Cole. "Orinda on the Restoration Stage." *Comparative Literature* 37 (1985): 233–51.

Manvell, Roger. *Sarah Siddons: Portrait of an Actress.* New York: Putnam [1971].

Marinis, Marco de. "Dramaturgy of the Spectator." *Drama Review* 31 (1987): 100–114.

Marks, Elaine, and Isabelle de Courtivron, eds. *New French Feminisms.* New York: Schocken, 1981.

Marsden, Jean. "Pathos and Passivity." *Restoration* 14 (1990): 71–81.

Marshall, Madeleine Forell. *The Poetry of Elizabeth Singer Rowe (1674–1737).* Lewiston, N.Y.: Mellen, 1987.

Martin, John R. *The Decorations for the Pompa Introitus Ferdinandi.* London: Phaidon, 1972.

Mayne, Judith. "Marlene Dietrich, *The Blue Angel,* and Female Performance." In *Seduction and Theory: Readings of Gender, Representation, and Rhetoric,* edited by Dianne Hunter. Urbana: U of Illinois P, 1989.

Mayo, Robert D. *The English Novel in the Magazines, 1740–1815.* Evanston, Ill.: Northwestern UP, 1962.

Medoff, Jeslyn. "The Daughters of Behn and the Problem of Reputation." In *Women/ Writing/ History. See* Grundy and Wiseman.

Meisel, Martin. *Realizations: Narrative, Pictorial, and Theatrical Arts in Nineteenth-Century England.* Princeton: Princeton UP, 1983.

Michaelson, Patricia. "Women in the Reading Circle." *ECL* 13 (1989): 59–69.

Middleton, Robin, and David Watkin. *Neoclassical and Nineteenth-Century Architecture.* New York: Abrams, 1977.

Milhous, Judith. *Thomas Betterton and the Management of Lincoln's Inn Fields, 1695–1708.* Carbondale: Southern Illinois UP, 1979.

Milhous, Judith, and Robert Hume. "Dating Play Premieres from Publication Data, 1660–1700." *Harvard Library Bulletin* 22 (1974): 374–405.
———. *A Register of English Theatrical Documents, 1660–1737.* 2 vols. Carbondale: Southern Illinois UP, 1991.
———. "Two Plays by Elizabeth Polwhele." *PBSA* 71 (1977): 1–9.
Miller, Jane. *Women Writing about Men.* London: Virago, 1986.
Miller, Nancy K. "Rereading as a Woman: The Body in Practice." In *The Female Body in Western Culture: Contemporary Perspectives,* edited by Susan R. Suleiman. 1985; Cambridge: Harvard UP, 1986.
———. *Subject to Change.* New York: Columbia UP, 1988.
Mish, Charles, ed. *Restoration Prose Fiction, 1666–1700: An Anthology of Representative Restoration Prose Fiction.* Lincoln: U of Nebraska P, 1970.
Mitchell, W.J.T. *Iconology, Image, Text, Ideology.* Chicago: U of Chicago P, 1986.
Montrose, Louis. "Renaissance Literary Studies and the Subject of History." *English Literary Renaissance* 16 (1986): 5–12.
Moody, Ellen. "Orinda, Rosania, Lucasia *et aliae:* Towards a New Edition of the Works of Katherine Philips." *Philological Quarterly* 66 (1987): 325–54.
Morgan, Charlotte. *The Rise of the Novel of Manners.* New York: Columbia UP, 1911.
Morgan, Fidelis. *The Female Wits.* London: Virago, 1981.
———. *A Woman of No Character: An Autobiography of Mrs. Manley.* London: Faber, 1986.
Morrah, Patrick. *1660: The Year of the Restoration.* Boston: Beacon, 1960.
Morris, David B. "Gothic Sublimity." *New Literary History* 16 (1985): 299–319.
Morrissey, L. J. "English Pageant-Wagons." *ECS* 9 (1976): 353–74.
———. "Theatrical Records of the London Guilds, 1655–1708." *Theatre Notebook* 29 (1975): 99–113.
Morsley, Clifford. *News from the English Countryside, 1750–1850.* London: Harrap, 1979.
Mullan, John. *Sentiment and Sociability: The Language of Feeling in the Eighteenth Century.* Oxford: Clarendon, 1988.
Mullaney, Steven. *The Place of the Stage.* Chicago: U of Chicago P, 1988.
Mulvihill, Maureen. "A Feminist Link in the Old Boys' Network: The Cosseting of Katherine Philips." In *Curtain Calls. See* Schofield and Macheski.

Munn, Jessica. "Barton and Behn's *Rover;* or, the Text Transpos'd." *Restoration,* ser. 2.3 (1988): 11–22.

———. "I by a Double Right Thy Bounties Claim." In *Curtain Calls. See* Schofield and Macheski.

Myers, William. *Dryden.* London: Hutchinson, 1973.

Nell, Victor. *Lost in a Book: The Psychology of Reading for Pleasure.* New Haven: Yale UP, 1988.

Newton, Judith L. *Women, Power, and Subversion: Social Strategies in British Fiction, 1778–1860.* Athens: U of Georgia P, 1981.

Niklaus, Thelma. *Harlequin.* New York: Braziller, 1956.

North, Douglas, and Robert Thomas. *The Rise of the Western World: A New Economic History.* Cambridge: Cambridge UP, 1973.

Novak, Maximillian E. "The Closing of Lincoln's Inn Fields Theatre in 1695." *RECTR* 14 (1975): 51–60.

Nussbaum, Felicity. *The Autobiographical Subject.* Baltimore: Johns Hopkins UP, 1989.

Nussbaum, Felicity, and Laura Brown, eds. *The New Eighteenth Century.* New York: Methuen, 1987.

O'Donnell, Mary Ann. *Aphra Behn: An Annotated Bibliography of Primary and Secondary Sources.* New York: Garland, 1986.

Oliver, H. J. *Sir Robert Howard.* Durham, N.C.: Duke UP, 1963.

Opie, Iona, and Peter Opie. *The Lore and Language of Schoolchildren.* 1959; London: Oxford UP, 1976.

Orgel, Stephen. *The Illusion of Power: Political Theater in the English Renaissance.* Berkeley: U of California P, 1975.

Ousby, Ian. *The Englishman's England: Taste, Travel, and the Rise of Tourism.* Cambridge: Cambridge UP, 1990.

Parker, Rozsika. "Images of Men." In *No Turning Back,* edited by The Feminist Anthology Collective. London: Women's P, 1981.

Paulson, Ronald. *Popular and Polite Art in the Age of Hogarth and Fielding.* Notre Dame, Ind.: U of Notre Dame P, 1979.

———. *Representations of Revolution.* New Haven: Yale UP, 1983.

Payne, Deborah C. " 'And Poets Shall by Patron-Princes Live.' " In *Curtain Calls. See* Schofield and Macheski.

———. "The Restoration Dramatic Dedication as Symbolic Capital." *SECC* 20 (1990): 27–42.

Pearson, Jacqueline. *The Prostituted Muse: Images of Women and Women Dramatists, 1642–1737.* New York: St. Martin's, 1988.

Perry, Ruth. "The Veil of Chastity: Mary Astell's Feminism." In *Sexuality in*

Eighteenth-Century Britain, edited by Paul-Gabriel Boucé. Totowa, N.J.: Manchester UP–Barnes, 1982.

Petrides, Anne. *State Barges on the Thames.* London: Evelyn, 1959.

Plumb, J. H. *The First Four Georges.* New York: Macmillan, 1957.

Pocock, J.G.A. Review of John Brewer's *The Sinews of Power. ECS* 24 (1990–91): 270–72.

Poems on Affairs of State. Edited by George deForest Lord. 7 vols. New Haven: Yale UP, 1963–75.

Poovey, Mary. "Ideology and 'The Mysteries of Udolpho.'" *Criticism* 21 (1979): 307–30.

Postlewait, Thomas, and Bruce McConachie, eds. *Interpreting the Theatrical Past.* Iowa City: U of Iowa P, 1989.

Potter, Lois. *Secret Rites and Secret Writing.* Cambridge: Cambridge UP, 1989.

Price, Cecil. *Cold Caleb: The Scandalous Life of Ford Grey.* London: Melrose, 1956.

Punter, David. *The Literature of Terror.* London: Longmans, 1980.

———. "Narrative and Psychology in Gothic Fiction." In *Gothic Fictions: Prohibition/Transgression,* edited by Kenneth W. Graham. New York: AMS, 1989.

Ranger, Paul. *"Terror and Pity reign in every Breast": Gothic Drama in the London Patent Theatres, 1750–1820.* London: Soc. for Theatre Res., 1991.

Ray, William. *Story and History: Narrative Authority and Social Identity.* Cambridge: Blackwell, 1990.

Reed, John C. "Humphrey Moseley, Publisher." *Oxford Bibliographical Society, Proceedings and Papers* 2 (1927–30): 57–142.

Reedy, Gerard. "Mystical Politics: The Imagery of Charles II's Coronation." In *Studies in Change and Revolution,* edited by Paul Korshin. Menston: Scolar, 1972.

Reno, Robert P. "James Boaden's *Fontainville Forest* and Matthew G. Lewis' *The Castle Spectre:* Challenges of the Supernatural Ghost on the Late Eighteenth-Century Stage." *Eighteenth-Century Life,* n.s. 9 (1984): 94–106.

The Revels History of Drama in English. Edited by Clifford Leech and T. W. Craik. 7 vols. London: Methuen, 1975–78.

Richards, Kenneth. "The Restoration Pageants of John Tatham." In *Western Popular Theatre,* edited by David Mayer and Kenneth Richards. London: Methuen, 1977.

Richetti, John. *Defoe's Narratives: Situations and Structures.* Oxford: Clarendon, 1975.

———. *Popular Fiction before Richardson.* London: Oxford UP, 1969.

Roach, Joseph R. "Power's Body: The Inscription of Morality as Style." In *Interpreting the Theatrical Past. See* Postlewait and McConachie.

Roberts, David. *The Ladies: Female Patronage of Restoration Drama, 1660–1700.* Oxford: Clarendon, 1989.

Robinson, John M. *The Wyatts: An Architectural Dynasty.* Oxford: Oxford UP, 1979.

Rogers, Nicholas. *Whigs and Cities.* Oxford: Clarendon, 1989.

Rosenblum, Robert. "British Art and the Continent, 1760–1860." In *Romantic Art in Britain: Paintings and Drawings, 1760–1860,* edited by Frederick J. Cummings. Philadelphia Museum of Art, 1968.

Rosenfeld, Sybil. "Landscape in English Scenery in the Eighteenth Century." In *Essays on the Eighteenth-Century English Stage,* edited by Kenneth Richards and Peter Thomson. London: Methuen, 1972.

———. *A Short History of Scene Design in Great Britain.* Totowa, N.J.: Rowman, 1973.

Rudé, George. *The Crowd in History, 1730–1848.* New York: Wiley, 1964.

Russo, Mary. "Female Grotesques: Carnival and Theory." In *Feminist Studies/Critical Studies. See* De Lauretis 1986.

Sackville-West, Vita. *Nursery Rhymes.* London: Dropmore, 1947.

Said, Edward. "Travelling Theory." *Raritan* 1 (1982): 41–67.

Saintsbury, George. *Minor Poets of the Caroline Period.* 3 vols. Oxford: Clarendon, 1905–21.

Salzman, Paul. *"Absalom and Achitophel* and *The Fugitive Statesman." Restoration* 4 (1980): 11–13.

———. *English Prose Fiction, 1558–1700.* Oxford: Clarendon, 1985.

Schiebinger, Londa. *The Mind Has No Sex?* Cambridge: Harvard UP, 1989.

———. "Skeletons in the Closet: The First Illustrations of the Female Skeleton in Eighteenth-Century Anatomy." In *The Making of the Modern Body. See* Gallagher and Laqueur.

Schofield, Mary Anne, and Cecilia Macheski. *Curtain Calls: British and American Women and the Theater, 1660–1820.* Athens: Ohio UP, 1991.

Schweickart, Patrocinio. "Reading Ourselves: Toward a Feminist Theory of Reading." In *Gender and Reading. See* Flynn and Schweickart.

Schwoerer, Lois. "Propaganda in the Revolution of 1688–89." *American Historical Review* 82 (1977): 843–74.

———. "Women and the Glorious Revolution." *Albion* 18 (1986): 195–218.

Scull, Andrew. *Social Order/Mental Disorder: Anglo-American Psychiatry in Historical Perspective.* Berkeley: U of California P, 1989.

Sennett, Richard. *The Fall of Public Man.* New York: Knopf, 1977.

Sharpe, Reginald. *London and the Kingdom.* 3 vols. London: Longmans, 1894.

Shesgreen, Sean, ed. *The Criers and Hawkers of London.* Stanford: Stanford UP, 1990.

Shiach, Morag. *Discourse on Popular Culture: Class, Gender, and History in Cultural Analysis, 1730 to the Present.* Stanford: Stanford UP, 1989.

Shoemaker, Robert. "The London 'Mob' in the Early Eighteenth Century." *Journal of British Studies* 26 (1987): 273–304.

Showalter, Elaine. *The New Feminist Criticism.* New York: Pantheon, 1985.

Simon, Roger. *Gramsci's Political Thought.* London: Lawrence, 1982.

Smith, Hilda. *Reason's Disciples.* Urbana: U of Illinois P, 1982.

Smuts, R. Malcolm. "Public Ceremony and Royal Charisma: The English Royal Entry in London, 1485–1642." In *The First Modern Society,* edited by A. L. Beier, David Cannadine, and James M. Rosenheim. Cambridge: Cambridge UP, 1989.

Snitow, Ann Barr. "Mass Market Romance: Pornography for Women Is Different." In *Powers of Desire: The Politics of Sexuality,* edited by Ann Snitow, Christine Stansell, and Sharon Thompson. New York: Monthly Review, 1983.

Sorelius, Gunnar. "The Early History of the Restoration Theatre: Some Problems Reconsidered." *Theatre Notebook* 33 (1979): 52–61.

Souers, Philip W. *The Matchless Orinda.* Cambridge: Harvard UP, 1931.

Spacks, Patricia Meyer. *Desire and Truth: Functions of Plot in Eighteenth-Century English Novels.* Chicago: U of Chicago P, 1990.

———. "Energies of Mind: Plot's Possibilities in the 1790s." *ECF* 1 (1988): 37–51.

———. *Imagining a Self.* Cambridge: Harvard UP, 1976.

Spencer, Jane. "Creating the Woman Writer." *Tulsa Studies in Women's Literature* 2 (1983): 165–81.

———. *The Rise of the Woman Novelist.* Oxford: Blackwell, 1986.

Sprague, Arthur Colby. *Shakespearean Players and Performances.* Cambridge: Harvard UP, 1953.

Spufford, Margaret. *Small Books and Pleasant Histories.* Cambridge: Cambridge UP, 1982.

Stanton, Judith. "Statistical Profile of Women Writing in English from 1660–1800." In *Eighteenth-Century Women and the Arts,* edited by Frederick Keener and Susan Lorsch. New York: Greenwood, 1988.

Staves, Susan. *Players' Scepters: Fictions of Authority in the Restoration.* Lincoln: U of Nebraska P, 1979.

———. "Where Is History But in Texts?" In *The Golden and the Brazen World,* edited by John M. Wallace. Berkeley: U of California P, 1985.

Steiner-Adair, Catherine. "The Body Politic." In *Making Connections. See* Gilligan et al.

Stratton, Jon. *The Virgin Text: Fiction, Sexuality, and Ideology.* Brighton: Harvester, 1987.

Straub, Kristina. *Divided Fictions: Fanny Burney and Feminine Strategy.* Lexington: UP of Kentucky, 1987.

Strong, Roy. *Art and Power: Renaissance Festivals, 1450–1650.* Woodbridge, Suffolk: Boydell, 1984.

———. *Splendor at Court: Renaissance Spectacle and the Theater of Power.* Boston: Houghton, 1973.

Suleiman, Susan R., and Inge Crosman, eds. *The Reader in the Text.* Princeton: Princeton UP, 1980.

Sutcliffe, Barry. *Plays by George Colman the Younger and Thomas Morton.* Cambridge: Cambridge UP, 1983.

Sypher, Wylie. "Aesthetic of Revolution: The Marxist Melodrama." In *Tragedy: Vision and Form,* edited by Robert Corrigan. San Francisco: Chandler, 1965.

Tanner, Tony. *Adultery in the Novel.* Baltimore: Johns Hopkins UP, 1979.

Taylor, Aline M. *Next to Shakespeare: Otway's "Venice Preserv'd" and "The Orphan" and Their History on the London Stage.* Durham, N.C.: Duke UP, 1950.

Thomas, David, ed. *Restoration and Georgian England, 1660–1788.* Cambridge: Cambridge UP, 1989.

Thomas, Keith. *Religion and the Decline of Magic.* New York: Scribner's, 1971.

Thomas, Patrick. *Katherine Philips (Orinda).* Cardiff: U of Wales P, 1988.

Thomas, Russell. "Contemporary Taste in the Stage Decorations of London Theaters, 1770–1800." *Modern Philology* 42 (1944): 65–78.

Thompson, E. P. "Eighteenth-Century Crime, Popular Movements, and Social Control." *Bulletin of the Society for the Study of Labour History* 25 (1972): 9–11.

———. "The Moral Economy of the English Crowd in the Eighteenth Century." *Past and Present* 50 (1971): 76–136.

Thornbury, George Walter. *Old and New London: A Narrative of Its History, Its People, and Its Places.* 6 vols. [Vols. 1, 2 by Thornbury; vols. 3–6 by Edward Walford.] London: Cassell, 1879–85.

Thurber, Carryl N. *Sir Robert Howard's Comedy, "The Committee."* Urbana: U of Illinois P, 1921.

Todd, Janet. *The Sign of Angellica: Women, Writing, and Fiction, 1660–1800.* New York: Columbia UP, 1989.

Todorov, Tzvetan. *The Fantastic: A Structural Approach to a Literary Genre.* Translated by Richard Howard. Cleveland: Case, 1973.

Tompkins, Jane P. "Sentimental Power: *Uncle Tom's Cabin* and the Politics of Literary History." In *The New Feminist Criticism. See* Showalter.

———, ed. *Reader-Response Criticism: From Formalism to Post-Structuralism.* Baltimore: Johns Hopkins UP, 1980.

Tricomi, Albert. *Anticourt Drama in England, 1603–1642.* Charlottesville: UP of Virginia, 1989.

Trumbach, Randolph. *The Rise of the Egalitarian Family.* New York: Academic, 1978.

Twitchell, James B. *Dreadful Pleasures: An Anatomy of Modern Horror.* New York: Oxford UP, 1985.

Two Centuries of Testimony in Favour of Mrs. Aphra Behn. London: Pearson, 1872.

Upham, Alfred. *The French Influence in English Literature.* New York: Columbia UP, 1911.

Valenze, Deborah M. "Prophecy and Popular Literature in Eighteenth-Century England." *Journal of Ecclesiastical History* 29 (1978): 75–92.

Viala, Alain. "La Genèse des formes épistolaires en français et leurs sources latines et européennes." *Revue de Littérature Comparée* 55 (1981): 168–83.

The Victoria History of the Counties of England: Berkshire. Edited by P. H. Ditchfield and William Page. 4 vols. 1924–27; Folkestone: Dawsons, 1972.

Vieth, David M. *Attribution in Restoration Poetry: A Study of Rochester's Poems of 1680.* New Haven: Yale UP, 1963.

Visser, Colin. "Scenery and Technical Design." In *The London Theatre World, 1660–1800,* edited by Robert Hume. Carbondale: Southern Illinois UP, 1980.

Wagner, Peter. "The Pornographer in the Courtroom." In *Sexuality in Eighteenth-Century Britain,* edited by Paul-Gabriel Boucé. Totawa, N.J.: Manchester UP–Barnes, 1982.

Walford, Edward. *Old and New London: A Narrative of Its History, Its People, and Its Places.* 6 vols. [Vols. 1, 2 by George Walter Thornbury; vols. 3–6 by Walford.] London: Cassell, 1879–85.

————. *Westminster and the Western Suburbs.* Vols. 3, 4 of *Old and New London.* London: Cassell, 1881.

Wallace, John M., ed. *The Golden and the Brazen World.* Berkeley: U of California P, 1985.

Watt, Ian. *The Rise of the Novel.* Berkeley: U of California P, 1967.

Weimann, Robert. "Text, Author-Function, and Appropriation in Modern Narrative: Toward a Sociology of Representation." *Critical Inquiry* 14 (1988): 431–47.

Weinbrot, Howard. "The New Eighteenth Century and the New Mythology." *Age of Johnson* 3 (1990): 353–407.

Weinreb, Ben, and Christopher Hibbert. *The London Encyclopedia.* 1983; London: Macmillan, 1984.

White, R. J. *The Age of George III.* New York: Walker, 1968.

Wiener, Philip B. *Dictionary of the History of Ideas.* 5 vols. New York: Scribner's, 1973.

Wiles, Roy M. *Serial Publication in England before 1750.* Cambridge: Cambridge UP, 1957.

Williams, J. B. [pseud.]. *A History of English Journalism.* London: Longmans, 1908.

Williams, Raymond. *Culture and Society, 1780–1950.* Harmondsworth, England: Penguin, 1968.

————. *Keywords.* New York: Oxford UP, 1983.

————. *Marxism and Literature.* 1977; Oxford: Oxford UP, 1988.

Williamson, Marilyn L. *Raising Their Voices: British Women Writers, 1650–1750.* Detroit: Wayne State UP, 1990.

Wilson, Michael. "Columbine's Picturesque Passage: The Demise of Dramatic Action in the Evolution of Sublime Spectacle on the London Stage." *Eighteenth Century: Theory and Interpretation* 31 (1990): 191–210.

Wilt, Judith. *Ghosts of the Gothic.* Princeton: Princeton UP, 1980.

Winn, James A. *John Dryden and His World.* New Haven: Yale UP, 1987.

————. *"When Beauty Fires the Blood": Love and the Arts in the Age of Dryden.* Ann Arbor: U of Michigan P, 1992.

Withington, Robert. *English Pageantry.* 2 vols. Cambridge: Harvard UP, 1918.

Wittig, Monique. "The Category of Sex." *Feminist Issues* 2 (1982): 63–68.

————. "The Straight Mind." *Feminist Issues* 1 (1980): 103–10.

Woodcock, George. *Aphra Behn: The English Sappho.* Cheektowaga, N.Y.: Black Rose, 1989.

————. "Founding Mother of the English Novel: Aphra Behn." *Room of One's Own* 2–3 (1976): 31–44.

Woolf, Virginia. *A Room of One's Own.* 1929; New York: Harcourt, 1958.

Wright, Louis B. *Middle Class Culture in Elizabethan England.* 1935; Ithaca: Cornell UP, 1958.

Würzbach, Natascha. *The Novel in Letters.* Coral Gables, Fla.: U of Miami P, 1969.

Zimbardo, Rose. "Aphra Behn: A Dramatist in Search of the Novel." In *Curtain Calls. See* Schofield and Macheski.

Zucker, Paul. *Fascination of Decay.* Ridgewood, N.J.: Gregg, 1968.

INDEX